D0612131

EXPERIENCES IN MANAGEMENT AND ORGANIZATIONAL BEHAVIOR

ST. CLAIR SERIES IN MANAGEMENT AND ORGANIZATIONAL BEHAVIOR

EXPERIENCES IN MANAGEMENT AND ORGANIZATIONAL BEHAVIOR

SECOND EDITION

Douglas T. Hall
Boston University

Donald D. Bowen
University of Tulsa

Roy J. Lewicki
Duke University

Francine S. Hall
University of New Hampshire

1807 1982

JOHN WILEY & SONS
New York   Chichester   Brisbane   Toronto   Singapore

Copyright © 1982, by John Wiley & Sons, Inc.

All rights reserved. Published simultaneously in Canada.

Reproduction or translation of any part of
this work beyond that permitted by Sections
107 and 108 of the 1976 United States Copyright
Act without the permission of the copyright
owner is unlawful. Request for permission
or further information should be addressed to
the Permissions Department, John Wiley & Sons

Library of Congress Cataloging in Publication Data:

Experiences in management and organizational behavior.

(St. Clair series in management and organizational behavior)
Includes index.
1. Management—Problems, exercises, etc.
2. Organizational behavior—Problems, exercises,
etc.   I. Hall, Douglas T., 1940–   II. Series.

HD30.413.E95   1982   658.4   81-16463
ISBN 0-471-08210-4   AACR2

Printed in the United States of America

10 9 8 7 6 5 4 3 2 1

PREFACE

A funny thing happened on the way to the typewriter. This was supposed to be a fairly light revision, but by the time we had finished it, 32 exercises or folio pieces had either been added or substantially revised. Two entirely new sections had been added, "Organizational Realities" and "Organizational Structure and Design," in response to feedback that indicated the need for more "macro" organizational material. As requested by users, we also added more cases, teaching aids, and more practical, management-oriented material, such as time management and management by objectives. To make the book usable in a personnel course, we included an in-basket exercise and an assessment center design. (Colleagues such as Professor Ray Hill of the University of Michigan suggested that the book worked well for a behaviorally oriented personnel course, but that it needed these two additions.)

In this edition as in the previous one, our purpose is to provide exercises and readings (the number available is increased by almost one third) that can be used in a variety of ways and at a low cost to the student. This book should be easier and less expensive for the student to obtain than a specially packaged set of exercises and cases put together by the instructor.

As in the first edition, the Instructor's Manual is an integral part of the book. It contains extensive details on how to use the exercises, what to expect, hints on how to prepare, and the like. The manual has been extensively revised for the present edition. NOTE: *Instructors using this book can obtain copies of the manual from Wiley.*

We have been extremely pleased at the response to the book and to the concept of experiential learning over the last six years. Whereas many of the exercises in the book had seemed a bit unorthodox when the first edition appeared, they are now considered much more in the "mainstream" of teaching methods. (We have to admit to some mixed emotions about this, since we have always enjoyed being somewhat unconventional!)

We have been very pleased to work with our new publisher, John Wiley & Sons. The competence and professionalism of the Wiley staff are much appreciated. In particular, we thank our editors, Rick Leyh and Serje Seminoff.

Extremely helpful reviews were provided by Professors David Boje (University of California, Los Angeles), Ray Hill (University of Michigan), and Sam Rabinowitz (New York University).

As we worked on this edition, we were much aware of the absence of a person whom we consider to be a member of our group: Bob St. Clair. Bob was the head of St. Clair Press, the original publisher of the book, and a person with whom we worked very closely. More important, he is someone we love very much. Through his close relationships with individual professors and his publishing of high-quality management books, he has made a lasting contribution to our field. This edition is dedicated to the fifth member of our group, Robert G. St. Clair.

Douglas T. Hall
Donald D. Bowen
Roy J. Lewicki
Francine S. Hall

PREFACE TO THE FIRST EDITION

We are really writing this book for our own use. That is, over the years we have seen that classes in which participants actively experience course concepts seem to generate more involvement, continuing interest, and useful skills than the straight lecture or discussion format. However, running such experiences usually involves considerable planning, preparation time, and money. Therefore, we felt the need for a collection of popular, multiple-use exercises in one volume that could be sold at a low price. The exercises would be all together in one place, eliminating advance planning, reproduction, and getting-lost hassles. The volume would contain only exercises (including simulations, role plays, cases, and problems) and brief concept modules to be used with the exercises. The volume would be a *supplement* to a wide range of texts and books of readings. It would provide a large number of exercises—a choice of activities from which could be selected those that best fit each instructor's own course outline and teaching style. Finally, the cost would be low enough so that, assuming 10 or 15 activities are used, the cost per activity used would still be cheaper than overburdening the department Xerox machine.

In putting together our materials, we realized that each of us had a somewhat different orientation toward experiential activities—one of us might prefer simulations and role plays; another, emotion-arousing interpersonal activities; another, concrete management problems, and so forth. In our own classes, a combination of these approaches, as well as lectures, films, guest speakers, and field trips, has seemed most useful. Variety seems to be a key factor in creating excitement and involvement in a classroom. We have tried to provide variety and flexibility in this volume; any combination of activities can be used, in any order.

The book is written to be useful for both the instructor who may have used few or no experiential teaching activities before and for those who have used them previously. The Instructor's Manual communicates our experiences with these activities, giving an idea of what to expect and how to get the most learning out of each activity.

Now comes a most satisfying part of the book for us—giving recognition and thanks to the people who have contributed to it, either directly or indirectly. W. Clay Hamner and Jim Sitlington first raised the idea of preparing such a volume. Robert E. and Anne T. Hall provided an idyllic setting on a New Hampshire pond where the book was conceived. Robert B. Duncan and Clay Hamner provided feedback and helpful ideas as the manuscript progressed through its various stages of development.

Several colleagues generously contributed their exercises to this volume and provided corrective feedback to our writeups of them: Chris Argyris, Warren Bennis, Patrick Eady, Robert J. House, David A. Kolb, Edward E. Lawler, Norman R. F. Maier, Henry Mintzberg, Lyman Porter, William Reid, Benjamin Schneider, and Victor Vroom. Other colleagues who provided inputs and comments are Lawrence Foster, Rodney Plimpton, John Sherwood, and Ralph Kilmann.

In addition to these people who contributed directly to the book, there are others who strongly influenced our thinking in graduate school and later about teaching and learning, as reflected in this book: Chris Argyris and the organizational behavior group at Yale, Morton Deutsch, Matthew Miles, and Harvey Hornstein at Columbia, Robert Tannenbaum at UCLA, Warren Bennis, David Berlew, Douglas McGregor, and Edgar H. Schein at MIT, Robert J. House and Don Graham at the University of Toronto, and Raghu Nath and Dennis P. Slevin at Pittsburgh.

Three secretaries became very involved in the production of this book, a more difficult task than that for more conventional books: Eunice Bellam, Doris Singer, and Marlaine Moore.

Prefaces always contain a quick nod in the direction of the authors' families. In the case of this book, which was produced in a very short, intense time period, the burdens on family and home life were especially heavy, and the support (in terms of ideas and emotions) of our spouses was especially critical: Debbie, Fran, Polly, and Tim. Without them, this book would not be as close to what we hoped for as it is.

The dedication is with love to our children. We hope that by the time they are in college these teaching methods will be the norm, and that they will wonder why we ever got so excited about this book.

Douglas T. Hall
Donald D. Bowen
Roy J. Lewicki
Francine S. Hall

CONTENTS

PART IV CHANGE   277

SECTION TWELVE PLANNED CHANGE   278

SECTION THIRTEEN LIFE, WORK, AND CAREER ROLES   291

FOLIO OF RESOURCES READINGS AND ASSESSMENT TECHNIQUES   357

Exercises, Assignments, Instruments, Readings

Column key (items 1–27):

1. Concerns, Expectations, Resources
2. Learning and Problem Solving Styles: You're Never Too Jung!
3. Sherlock Holmes
4. Assessing Motivation Satisfaction and Congruent Jobs
5. Expectancy Theory: A Personal Application
6. Money Motivation Debate
7. What Do We Value in Work?
8. Assignment: The Meaning of Work
9. Job Redesign
10. Developing Effective Managers: Performance Appraisal
11. Performance Appraisal in Class: The Shoe is on the Other Foot
12. Redesigning Assembly Line Jobs: The Hovey and Beard Company
13. Motivation Through Compensation
14. Applied Motivation: Two Problems
15. Interviewing Trios: Interpersonal Problem Diagnosis and Resolution
16. Feedback
17. Assertiveness: Authentic Interpersonal Communication
18. Group Process Observation Analysis
19. Group Ranking Task: Lost at Sea
20. Values and Group Decision Making: The City Council
21. Two-Person Bargaining: The Ugli Orange Case
22. Competitive Escalation: The Dollar Auction
23. Competitive Advertising Strategy: A Matrix Game
24. Collective Bargaining and Labor Management Relations
25. The Storm Windows: A Role Play
26. Choosing a Leadership Style: Applying the Vroom and Yetton Model
27. Assignment: What Do Managers Do?

Topics	1	2	3	4	5	6	7	8	9	10	11	12	13	14	15	16	17	18	19	20	21	22	23	24	25	26	27
Icebreakers	X	X	X												O												
Motivation - Basic Concepts				X	X	X	X	X	O		O		O	O											O		
Applied Motivation and Job Design	O			O					O	X	X	X	X	X											O	O	
Interpersonal Communication	O	O	O			O		O	O						X	X	X	O	O	O					O		O
Group Decision Making and Problem Solving				O	O		O	O			O			O		O	O	X	X	X	O	O		O	O	O	
Negotiation and Conflict	O					O	O								O		O	O			X	X	X	X	O		
Managers as Leaders	O			O					O	O					O	O	O		O	O	O				X	X	X
Organizational Realities	O								O	O												O	O				O
Power							O									O	O				O	O	O	O	O O	O	O
Organizational Communication				O					O				O	O				O	O				O	O		O O	O
Organizational Structure and Design									O	O																	O
Planned Change	O					O	O		O		O	O		O											O		O
Life, Work, and Career Roles	O	O		O	O				O						O			O	O								O

X = Exercise as indexed in this text
O = Related topics touched upon in the exercise

Column key (items 28–58):

28. Larry Ross: A Case for Discussion
29. Career Orientation Inventory: An Assessment Exercise
30. Vanatin: Group Decision Making and Ethics Exercise
31. Situational Power: Circles, Squares and Triangles
32. Analysis of Personal Power
33. Coalition Bargaining
34. One-way Versus Two-way Communication
35. Upward Communication: Young Manufacturing Company
36. Words-In-Sentences Co.
37. Organizational Diagnosis: Hamburger Technology
38. Management By Objectives
39. Planning and Production Task: The Real Estate Company
40. People's National Bank-University Branch
41. Experiencing Organizational Climates
42. Square, Inc.
43. Change-of-Work Procedures
44. The Sanitary Company
45. The Hollow Square Planning Problem
46. Introduction: Life, Work, and Career Roles
47. Career Planning: Strengths and Weaknesses
48. Lifelines
49. The Awful Interview
50. Men, Women, and Work
51. Managing Role Conflict
52. Time Management/In-basket

Items Located in Folio of Resources:

53. The Learning Contract
54. Nondirective Interviewing
55. Feedback
56. Roles Nomination Form
57. Sociogram
58. Supervisory Behavior Questionnaire

Topics	28	29	30	31	32	33	34	35	36	37	38	39	40	41	42	43	44	45	46	47	48	49	50	51	52	53	54	55	56	57	58
Icebreakers																			O	O	O					X		X			
Motivation - Basic Concepts	O	O		O		O		O											O	O	O										O
Applied Motivation and Job Design								O		O	O	O		O	O	O	O										O				
Interpersonal Communication	O	O		O			O					O			O					O	O	O	O	O	O	X	X	O		O	
Group Decision Making and Problem Solving	O	O		O	O	O	O		O				O	O				O	O	O						O		X	X		
Negotiation and Conflict	O		O	O		O			O						O									O				O			
Managers as Leaders	O	O		O	O				O	O	O	O		O	O		O	O	O							O			O	O	X
Organizational Realities	X	X	X	O		O																				O			O		O
Power	O	O		X	X	X								O									O			O		O		O	O
Organizational Communication	O						O			O	X	X		O	O		O		O	O											
Organizational Structure and Design										O	O		X	X		X	X		X	X	X										
Planned Change																X	X	X		O	O			O		O			O	O	
Life, Work, and Career Roles	O	O			O														X		X	X	X	X	X	O	O	O			

X = Exercise as indexed in this text
O = Related topics touched upon in the exercise

Items Located in Folio of Resources

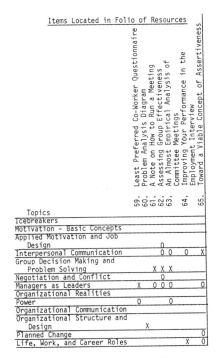

Topics	59. Least Preferred Co-Worker Questionnaire	60. Problem Analysis Diagram	61. A Note on How to Run a Meeting	62. Assessing Group Effectiveness	63. An Almost Empirical Analysis of Committee Meetings	64. Improving Your Performance in the Employment Interview	65. Toward a Viable Concept of Assertiveness
Icebreakers							
Motivation - Basic Concepts							
Applied Motivation and Job Design				0			
Interpersonal Communication				0	0	0	X
Group Decision Making and Problem Solving				X	X	X	
Negotiation and Conflict				0			
Managers as Leaders	X		0	0	0		0
Organizational Realities							
Power	0		0				
Organizational Communication							
Organizational Structure and Design			X				
Planned Change							0
Life, Work, and Career Roles						X	0

X = Exercise as indexed in this text
0 = Related topics touched upon in the exercise

NOTE TO USERS OF INDIVIDUAL EXERCISES

We would like to call your attention to the permissions statement on the copyright page of this book. We appeal to you as fellow instructors (perhaps also as fellow authors) to honor our rights and those of the other contributors to this book.

INTRODUCTION

Universities have trouble preparing their students for the job demands and problems they will encounter in the "real" world. Students report that the first full-time
job after graduation gives them a strong dose of reality shock. Their expectations
are often unrealistic and are usually not met. They may feel *technically* prepared
for their work, but not *socially*. They may have trouble adjusting to the "human
side" of the organization, the informal, interpersonal relationships that keep the
formal system running smoothly.

One reason for the problems students have making the transition from school
to work is that they do not have opportunities to integrate work-related experiences with their formal course learning. Students may have part-time jobs, but
these are seen as providing money, not learning. There is a need for learning to
include both active, personal *experiences* and general *concepts*, both *theory and
action*. Theory gives a person some general principles to guide action, but if there
is no opportunity to test theories in action, the theory remains just theory and
does not become part of the person.

THE FOCUS OF THIS BOOK

The assumption behind this book is that most academic courses do a better job of
providing theory than action. To provide a better balance, there is a need for
personal experiences and action exercises in which participants can test out their
newly learned theories and concepts. In this book we have tried to provide a
number of experiences that apply behavioral science concepts to the practice of
management. Although this book does not contain many cognitive inputs (i.e.,
readings or text matter), we do attempt to show how each exercise relates to
concepts and theories that you may be reading about in your text for this course.

This book, then, may be viewed as an *experience-based supplement* to a text or a book of readings in organizational behavior, personnel, or management.

As we selected exercises for this volume, we began to see that they seemed to vary according to two major dimensions. One dimension was the *focus* of the exercise. In many cases, the focus is a management problem, such as how to deal with resistance to change. In others, the focus is on the participant's own experiences, as in the analysis of one's own career or group processes. The second dimension is the *learning unit* in which the exercise is carried out. In the majority of exercises, the action takes place in a group setting, as in a role-play or group problem-solving task. In other exercises, you will work individually, as in some of the case analyses or a personal value inventory.

When we put the two dimensions together, we had four different types of activities, as shown below, with some examples of each type of exercise.

		Focus	
		Self	*Management Problem*
Learning Unit	*Group*	Group process analysis Career planning	Role play Group decision-making task
	Individual	Self-analysis Personal-motivation diagnosis	Case Problem task

We have attempted to provide a mix of the four types of exercises, since each provides benefits the others do not.

In selecting exercises, we employed several criteria. Not every exercise chosen met all the criteria, but—all other things being equal—we preferred exercises with the following characteristics:

1. original (versus previously used).
2. short (versus long).
3. management-relevant (versus not management-relevant).
4. clear and simple (versus complex).
5. personal experience (versus vicarious experience).
6. minimal logistical preparation (versus much advance preparation).

Our hope is that these selection criteria have been translated into exercises that make a clear, important point about management and organizational behavior, in a short time, with little or no advance preparation required. In other words, each

Copyright © 1982, John Wiley and Sons, Inc.

exercise should be like a supporting actor; it should do its work efficiently, unobtrusively, and without upstaging the leading characters (i.e., the conceptual material communicated by lectures, text, and discussion.) Many experiential exercises get people highly involved and excited, even to the point of tears, fighting, or ecstasy, but if the participants cannot verbalize the "point" afterwards, the exercise is a failure as a learning experience. It is our hope that in this volume the medium will not interfere with the message.

ASSUMPTIONS ABOUT EXPERIENTIAL LEARNING

As you will see more clearly in the readings and exercises that follow, a book of experiential exercises such as this is based upon a number of assumptions about learning. We'll try to be as explicit about these as we can.

1. *Learning is more effective when it is an active rather than a passive process.* When a student can take a theory, concept, or practice and "try it on for size," he or she will be much better able to get a good fit—that is, an integration of the new idea with past learnings. (Incidentally, that is the last time we will use the construction "he or she" in this book. It is an awkward construction. Hereafter, whatever the gender of the pronoun used, either sex may substitute the opposite pronoun at will.)

2. *Problem-centered learning is more enduring than theory-based learning.* If a person learns a new concept or theory only because it's "important" (i.e., it may be on the exam), there is no motivation to learn. On the other hand, when a person has a problem to solve and then scans for and applies knowledge that will help solve that problem, she has been internally motivated to master that knowledge. For example, one of the authors took two statistics courses in college, covered analysis of variance in each, and got good grades, yet he never really *learned* analysis of variance until he had to *use it.*

3. *Two-way communication produces better learning than one-way communication.* This is more a principle of communication than just an assumption, as you will see if you participate in the exercise on one-way versus two-way communication (Exercise 34). When the participant can interact with the group leader and other participants, information is communicated more accurately, and the participant's satisfaction with the process is greater.

4. *Participants will learn more when they share control over and responsibility for the learning process than when this responsibility lies solely with the group leader.* When the instructor is solely in charge, the participant feels little motivation to make a success out of the learning process—if the exercise bombs, it's the professor's fault! When the participant shares responsibility, more of her energy is directed toward creating a success.

5. *Learning is most effective when thought and action are integrated.* This key assumption has already been mentioned. If the course you are using this book with is designed to train people for action (such as jobs in management, personnel, labor relations, etc.), to get maximum transfer of learning to those future jobs, the training should contain action.

The foregoing assumptions have important implications for the role of the participant and the role of the group leader. The key words in describing the two roles are:

Participant	Group Leader
Shares responsibility	Shares responsibility
Examines own experiences	Expert resource for content and for process
Autonomous	Guide, coach
Active involvement	Collaborative
	Flexible

We have already said something about the role of the participant in experiential learning. The participant shares responsibility with the group leader for the learning process. He is expected to be open to the experiences that occur in the course of the learning exercises and to use these experiences as learning inputs on a par with readings, lectures, and class discussion. The participant has more autonomy in class than the usual lecture or discussion would provide, however. This is necessary if the person is to be able to explore the meaning and relevance of various ideas and techniques for his work interests and needs.

The role of the instructor or group leader is to act as a guide for participants through the experiences and ideas they will discover in the course, coaching them on how to use the ideas to better understand themselves and management situations. At times this may mean choosing exercises on the basis of where the class group is "at," where their needs or interests are right now, rather than on the basis of the course outline. This means being sensitive to the class and acting flexibly in providing experiences that are most appropriate at a particular time. In many ways the group leader acts as sort of a class "quarterback" in identifying useful ways to help the group get from here to there, but the whole team shares the effort, the responsibility—and the successes.

HOW TO USE EXPERIENTIAL EXERCISES

Using experiential exercises may be a new experience for you. And since we've made such a point about your responsibility for the process, you may be wondering just exactly what you're supposed to do. As you'll see after participating in an exercise or two, this really isn't much of a problem. Here are a few suggestions, however, about how you can make these learning experiences more effective for yourself.

1. *Get involved in the exercises.* Let yourself be free to do what the exercise asks you to do. If it's role playing, really try to get into the role. If it's analysis of what's happening in your group, take a good look. This class will give you a chance to *experiment* with some new behaviors; the stakes aren't very high, certainly nothing like the risks involved with experimenting with new behaviors in a full-time job. The more you get into an exercise the more you'll get out of it.

Copyright © 1982, John Wiley and Sons, Inc.

2. *As you go through an exercise, consciously think about the relevant course readings.* The whole purpose of experiential exercises is to integrate theory and action. Each exercise is based upon some theory or concepts in the field of organizational behavior. As you work in each exercise, think:

"What concepts or theory can help me here?"
"What does this theory or concept tell me to do in this situation?"
"What do my experiences with this exercise tell me about this theory or concept?"

3. *At the end of each exercise, write down your own conclusions and reactions.* Think about what happened in the exercise and about how you can generalize from it. Ask yourself "When might something like this happen again?" and "How and when can I use this learning again?" At first it may feel a little strange writing down your reactions. As you get in the habit of doing it, however, several things may happen. First, you may realize you have drawn more conclusions than you realized. Second, you may have observed more than you were aware of. Third, your observations and conclusions may give you more of a sense of "closure" at the end of each session. And fourth, at the end of the course, you will have your own log of the experiences and learnings you developed—which can be impressive when you see them all together.

Writing down your reactions and conclusions can help close the learning cycle. The learning cycle (Kolb, Rubin, and McIntyre, 1974) works like this: An exercise gives you a chance to test out some ideas and concepts in new situations (active experimentation). In the exercise, you have some new experiences (concrete experience). Later in the exercise, you examine what happened (reflective observation). Putting your learnings and conclusions down on paper helps you form new concepts and generalizations (abstract conceptualization), which completes the learning loop. Then you're ready to go on to try more active experimentation, based on your new concepts. At the end of each exercise is a section called "Participant's Reactions" for you to record your own learnings and conclusions.

WHAT'S GOING TO HAPPEN?

We think you will find that these exercises are fun to do. They put you into a management situation and challenge you to solve problems. You may be engaged in friendly competition with other groups or with established norms. You may learn a few new things about how you relate to other people. You will probably have more interaction with other class members than you would in more traditional classes.

One problem that has come up occasionally in the use of exercises such as those in this book is that participants enjoy the class sessions greatly, become highly involved, develop strong conclusions regarding the concepts studied, and then say, "But I'm not sure what I learned from it." It becomes clear upon closer inspection, however, that what has actually happened is that the participant simply may not *define* his own conclusions as "learning," since he may initially think that

"Learning is what the professor says or what the book contains, not what I conclude from a class exercise."

Another process at work here can be an unconscious attitude of "If this is fun, I can't be learning from it." Fun and learning may be seen as mutually exclusive. How do *you* define learning? It's our hope that through these experiences you will come to see how and how much you learn from your own experiences. And that you begin to label as "learning" thoughts that you let slip by unnoticed before. You may even begin to think that learning can occur outside the classroom!

You may also have a tendency to become so interested in the experiences themselves that you overlook the way they tie in with the readings and discussions in your course. In other classes we have observed a tendency toward "flight into process," a focus upon the class experiences to the exclusion of cognitive inputs. Two published evaluations of experiential courses have both shown that students report very high learning in terms of new attitudes, communication skills, and self-awareness, but relatively less in terms of cognitive outcomes, such as knowledge of business (Kolb, Rubin, and McIntyre, 1974; Hall and Steele, 1971). Although this, too, may be partly a matter of what is labeled as cognitive learning, it may also show that the "exciting" areas of examining one's own attitudes and communication skills may overshadow the new concepts and theories that are covered in the course. Although it's true that most traditional courses tilt the balance too far toward cognitive material, we would hope that these exercises, being action-grounded in theory, will provide a good mix of personal and cognitive learning.

THE ORGANIZATION OF THIS BOOK

The main sections of this book were selected to represent the areas covered in most courses in organizational behavior, management, and personnel. Our aim was to provide a *choice* of exercises in each area. In most sections there are at least three quite different activities from which to choose, sometimes four. The units have been grouped into 14 sections: 13 topical areas, and a Folio of Resources. The first 13 sections group the activities under subject headings based on the *primary* topical focus of the exercise—for examples, "Motivation: Basic Concepts," and "Applied Motivation and Job Design." Each unit has also been cross referenced to other, related areas, and a Content Matrix is provided as well. The first 13 sections have been grouped in four parts often used to organize courses: Individuals; Interpersonal and Group Relationships; Organizations; and Change.

This book was not designed to be used in its entirety. Our intention was to provide flexibility and a wide range of choice so that exercises that best suit the approach of a particular course could be selected. In a given term or semester, perhaps one-third of the exercises (about one per section) might be used. Nor are the sections and exercises in this book intended to be used in any particular order. Rather, they can be used to suit whatever order your course is structured to. The sections were selected to cover a broad range of concepts—basic motivation; applied motivation and job design; interpersonal communication; group decision making and problem solving; negotiation and conflict; managers as leaders; power;

Copyright © 1982, John Wiley and Sons, Inc.

organizational communication; organizational structure and design; planned change; and life, work, and career roles—and the exercises (and assignments) within each section provide appreciations of many current and widely covered theories and concepts in organizational behavior courses—Skinner, Maslow, Herzberg, Vroom, Lawler, and so on—in the area of motivation. Although we do not go deeply into cognitive (i.e., text) material, the exercises (role plays, problems, process analyses, etc.) require you to apply theory and concepts that you will be getting from your text or book of readings, as well as from class lectures and discussion.

The Folio of Resources at the end of this book contains two types of materials: (1) readings relevant to several exercises in the book, and (2) techniques for assessing various characteristics of people, groups, and organizations. The assessment techniques can be used either as class exercises on their own, as an adjunct to other class activities, or outside of class (e.g., for projects or assignments).

FEEDBACK

This book will be revised in future years. To do this well, it would help greatly to receive feedback from you on these exercises. We would be interested in such issues as:

Which exercise worked well or not so well?
Was there anything unclear or confusing in the write-up of any of the exercises?
What modifications did you make that improved the exercises?
Do you see important topic areas that are not covered (or are overcovered) in this book? If so, what would you add or delete?
What do you like and what do you dislike about the book?

Any feedback you might care to pass along should be sent to Douglas T. Hall, School of Management, Boston University, Boston, Mass. 02215. We'd really like to hear from you. Here's hoping you have as much learning and fun from these exercises as we've had!

REFERENCES

Hall, D. T., and Steele, F. I., "Self-directed, Self-relevant Learning," *School Review*, Nov. 1971.
Kolb, D. A., Rubin, I. M., and McIntyre, J. M., (Eds.), *Organizational Psychology: A Book of Readings* (2nd ed.), (Englewood Cliffs, N.J.: Prentice-Hall, 1974).

Copyright © 1982, John Wiley and Sons, Inc.

PART I

INDIVIDUALS

SECTION ONE
ICEBREAKERS

1
CONCERNS, EXPECTATIONS, AND RESOURCES

PURPOSE:
(1) To help a group of strangers get acquainted quickly.
(2) To assess the initial concerns, expectations, and resources of the group.

ADVANCE PREPARATION:
None.

GROUP SIZE: Up to 60; 35 or fewer is probably optimal.
TIME REQUIRED: Varies, depending on the size of the group. The following are estimates: 18 to 25 participants: 55 minutes; 26 to 40 participants: 60 minutes; 41 to 65 participants: 70 minutes.
SPECIAL MATERIALS: Felt-tip pens, masking tape, sheets of newsprint.
SPECIAL PHYSICAL REQUIREMENTS: Movable furniture so that small groups can converse comfortably.

PROCEDURE

Step 1: 5 Minutes
Form groups of six to eight persons. Choose people you know *least well*.

Step 2: 20 Minutes
Obtain a felt-tip pen and newsprint. Meet and prepare a set of three lists as a group:

Expectations. What are your expectations for this course or program? What do you hope to get from it?

This version of a widely used icebreaker was developed for this volume by Donald D. Bowen.

Copyright © 1982, John Wiley and Sons, Inc.

Concerns. Do you have any concerns or worries about this course or program?

Resources. What talents, skills, background, or experiences do the members of your group have that could be used to enrich the learning of the people in this class or program?

It is not necessary that a concern or expectation be shared by everyone in the group. Put it on your list if it sounds important. Do *not* put names on the lists!

Appoint one person spokesperson for your group and tape your list to the wall of the room.

Step 3: 3 Minutes per Group

Each spokesperson presents her group's lists. Questions are permitted *for clarification, only* at this point.

Step 4: 20 Minutes

Group leader responds to the issues raised on the lists. Participants and leader discuss.

DISCUSSION QUESTIONS

1. Are your expectations for this course or program different now than they were before the exercise? How?
2. In what ways might participant expectations become "self-fulfilling prophecies"? (A "self-fulfilling prophecy" is when expectations that something will happen actually make it happen. For example, a person who is always looking for a fight can usually succeed in starting one.)
3. What must *you* do to ensure that your expectations are met?
4. What did you learn about yourself or others during the group meeting?
   a. Were people relatively open or closed? Why?
   b. Did some people dominate the conversation? How did the others feel about this (and how do you know that was what they were feeling)?
   c. Whose ideas got included or excluded from the list? Why did this happen?
   d. Do you feel that the list your group produced really represents the concerns and expectations of your group? Why?

Participant's Reactions

2
LEARNING AND PROBLEM SOLVING: YOU'RE NEVER TOO JUNG!

PURPOSE:
(1) To focus your attention on your own learning and problem-solving style.
(2) *Option one:* To explore the compatibility between your preferred learning style and the types of learning experience you will encounter in this course.
(3) *Option two:* To explore some implications of learning and problem-solving styles for organizational behavior.

ADVANCE PREPARATION:
(1) Read "Cognitive Style in Learning and Problem Solving" in the Folio of Resources in the back of this book.
(2) Read the Introduction to this book.
(3) Complete Step 1 in the procedure, below.

GROUP SIZE: *Option one:* Single, large discussion group. *Option two:* break the larger group into four learning/problem-solving "type" subgroups. If groups exceed eight or nine people, subdivide the groups to make more than one group for each type.
TIME REQUIRED: *Option one:* 30 minutes. *Option two:* 2 hours.
SPECIAL MATERIALS: None.
SPECIAL PHYSICAL REQUIREMENTS: Large room for entire group to meet. For Option two, subgroups need to meet for private discussions—small group meeting rooms or movable furniture and space enough to separate subgroups for private discussions will be helpful.
RELATED TOPICS: Planned change, Negotiation and conflict, Applied motivation and job design, Interpersonal communication, Managers as leaders.

PROCEDURE
BOTH OPTIONS

Step 1: 5 Minutes
When you have completed the readings assigned under Advance Preparation, make the following ratings on the "Learning and Problem-Solving Type Locator" in Figure 1. As you make these ratings, put your marks *inside the cells* of the locator, *not on the lines.*

Developed by Donald D. Bowen.

Copyright © 1982, John Wiley and Sons, Inc.

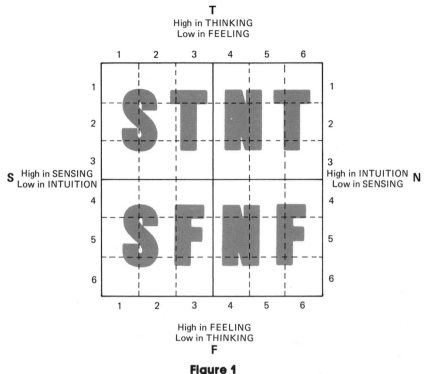

Figure 1

Learning and Problem Solving Type Locator

1. Rate *yourself* by putting an "X" on the Locator indicating how you see your own learning/problem-solving style.

    a. If you see yourself as very high in "thinking" (and therefore low in "feeling") on the *information-processing* dimension, you will probably wish to put your "X" in 5 or 6. If you see yourself as predominantly a "feeling" type, you will probably want to put your "X" in either row 1 or 2. If you see yourself as using both modes about equally, you probably fall in row 3 or 4.

    b. Similarly, on the *information-gathering* dimension, you may see yourself as primarily a "sensor" (columns 1 or 2, perhaps), primarily an "intuitor" (columns 5 or 6), or using a lot of both (columns 3 or 4).

    c. When you have located yourself by row and column, make your "X" in one of the cells. (You may find this is tough to do. "I'm a little of both poles," you might say. Jung foresaw this problem—he said that each of us has a "shadow self," a "weaker" style composed of the opposites to our predominant modes, that may take over in times of stress, conflict, and the like. Rate yourself according to what you see your predominant style to be).

d. If necessary, refer again to the characteristics of the different styles discussed in the reading, "Cognitive Style in Learning and Problem Solving" in the Folio.

2. Now think of the person you would *like to be*. Put a "B" in one of the cells of the Locator to indicate where your *ideal* self would be.

3. Now think of the *most effective manager* you have ever seen. Put an "M" on the Locator where you think this manager would fall. When you have finished your ratings, the group leader will instruct you to follow Option one or Option two.

OPTION ONE

25 minutes: Discuss the learning and problem-solving types in terms of the following questions:

1. Where would you guess most of the people in this program or class placed their "X" on the Locator? Their "B" (for the person they would like to become)? Why?

2. Survey the members of the class. How many are of each type? How many SFs? STs? and so on. Do students with different majors (e.g., accounting, engineering, liberal arts, marketing, etc.) tend to be similar to people with the same major? Different from those with different majors? Do the people with a particular major seem to be the "right" type for that major? Why?

3. Where do you think most people placed the "effective manager"? Why? Is an effective manager more likely to be of one type rather than another?

4. Do you think there would be any significant differences in how males and females would rate their present styles, their ideal styles, or their perceptions of an effective manager? Why?

5. What kind of person learns best from exercises such as those in this book? Why?

6. What can you do to learn to use your less preferred style of data gathering and information processing more effectively?

OPTION TWO

Step 2: 5 Minutes

Form learning/problem-solving "type" groups as directed by the group leader. This should create at least one group each of the following types:

STs	NTs
SFs	NFs

Which group you belong to depends on your self-perception—where your "X" was placed on the locator.

Step 3: 40 Minutes

Each group now meets to perform one of two tasks (the group leader will indicate 1 or 2):

Copyright © 1982, John Wiley and Sons, Inc.

1. Design a management development program for the people in the "opposite" group, that is:

    STs design for NFs, and vice versa.
    SFs design for NTs, and vice versa.

2. Develop a statement about the leadership style that should be used with people in the group "opposite" to you to maximize their effectiveness. What kind of a leader would be most successful with them, given their problem-solving style?

Appoint one member of the group to act as a *spokesperson* for the group. Prepare a presentation covering the following major points:

   a. What is the *objective* of the suggested measures your group is proposing?
   b. What *specific action* should be taken? (List four actions).
   c. What is the *rationale,* the reasoning behind the proposed actions your group is suggesting?

Step 4: 20 Minutes
Meet with your "opposite" group. Take turns presenting your proposal (your management development program or proposed leadership approach) to the other group (5 minutes for your proposal and 5 minutes for answering questions—have someone keep time).

Step 5: 5 Minutes
Meet again with just the group of your own type (the people you met with in Step 3). Quickly decide whether you would recommend the proposal that has been made to you for adoption by management (*and* why).

Step 6: 3 Minutes per Group
When called upon by the group leader, the group spokesperson very briefly reports the group's proposal (objective, actions, and rationales). When the spokesperson has finished, the spokesperson for the "opposite" group reports the outcome of the group's decision to accept or reject the proposal and why.

Step 7: 20 Minutes
Discuss the results of the exercise and their implications for organizational behavior in terms of the Discussion Questions.

DISCUSSION QUESTIONS
Discussion questions for Option one appear within the exercise. The following apply to Option two:
1. What did the different groups do when they designed for their "opposite" types? How did the opposite types feel about this?
2. Was there any evidence, in either the content or the style of the presentation, that people were properly classified?

3. How many people think they would *benefit* from the management development program or leadership style proposed by their opposite group? How many would *enjoy* the experience? Why?

GENERALIZATIONS AND CONCLUSIONS

Concluding Points

1. Is there a best learning/problem-solving style? Why?

2. How might the learning/problem-solving styles relate to problems that may arise in communication between people from different parts of the organization?

Participant's Reactions

READINGS AND REFERENCES

Kolb, D. A., "Four Styles of Managerial Learning." In D. A. Kolb, I. M. Rubin, and J. M. McIntyre (Eds.), *Organizational Psychology: A Book of Readings*, 2nd ed. (Englewood Cliffs, N.J.: Prentice-Hall, 1974), pp. 27–34.

Mann, H., Siegler, M., and Osmond, H. "Four Types of Personalities and Four Ways of Perceiving Time," *Psychology Today*, December (1972), 76–77, 79–80, 82, 84.

Mitroff, I. I., and Kilmann, R. H., "Stories Managers Tell: A New Tool for Organizational Problem Solving," *Management Review*, July (1975), 18–28.

Copyright © 1982, John Wiley and Sons, Inc.

3
SHERLOCK HOLMES

PURPOSE:
(1) To test your powers of reasoning and observation.
(2) To get to know one another and the instructor.

ADVANCE PREPARATION:
Read the "Introduction" to this exercise below.

GROUP SIZE: Not crucial, but probably works best in classes of 40 or fewer. A minimum class size of 18 is necessary for the procedure suggested here (see Instructor's Manual for alternatives to use with smaller groups).
TIME REQUIRED: 80 minutes.
SPECIAL MATERIALS: Questions to be answered about the instructor (to be prepared as a handout by the instructor).
SPECIAL PHYSICAL REQUIREMENTS: Optimally, a room with movable chairs or a large open space so that participants can walk around, form small groups, and hold group discussions.
RELATED TOPICS: Interpersonal communication.

INTRODUCTION

SHERLOCK HOLMES ON OBSERVATION AND DEDUCTION

Sir Arthur Conan Doyle's fictional detective, Sherlock Holmes, was a master at the art of careful observation and canny deduction. His close associate and friend, Dr. Watson, was initially annoyed by Holmes' smug self-confidence, and, in the passage here, attempts to outwit the cocksure detective by presenting him with a seemingly impossible task.

"But you spoke just now of observation and deduction. Surely the one to some extent implies the other."

"Why, hardly," he answered, leaning back luxuriously in his armchair and sending up thick blue wreaths from his pipe. "For example, observation shows me that you have been to the Wigmore Street Post-Office this morning, but deduction lets me know that when there you dispatched a telegram."

Reprinted with consent of the copyright owner.

"Right!" said I. "Right on both points!" But I confess that I don't see how you arrived at it. It was a sudden impulse upon my part, and I have mentioned it to no one."

"It is simplicity itself," he remarked, chuckling at my surprise—"so absurdly simple that an explanation is superfluous; and yet it may serve to define the limits of observation and of deduction. Observation tells me that you have a little reddish mould adhering to your instep. Just opposite the Wigmore Street Office they have taken up the pavement and thrown up some earth, which lies in such a way that it is difficult to avoid treading in it in entering. The earth is of this peculiar reddish tint which is found, as far as I know, nowhere else in the neighbourhood. So much is observation. The rest is deduction."

"How, then, did you deduce the telegram?"

"Why, of course I knew that you had not written a letter, since I sat opposite to you all morning. I see also in your open desk there that you have a sheet of stamps and a thick bundle of postcards. What could you go into the post-office for, then, but to send a wire? Eliminate all other factors, and the one which remains must be the truth."

"In this case it certainly is so," I replied after a little thought. "The thing however, is, as you say, of the simplest. Would you think me impertinent if I were to put your theories to a more severe test?"

"On the contrary," he answered, "it would prevent me from taking a second dose of cocaine. I should be delighted to look into any problem which you might submit to me."

"I have heard you say it is difficult for a man to have any object in daily use without leaving the impress of his individuality upon it in such a way that a trained observer might read it. Now, I have here a watch which has recently come into my possession. Would you have the kindness to let me have an opinion upon the character or habits of the late owner?"

I handed him over the watch with some slight feeling of amusement in my heart, for the test was, as I thought, an impossible one, and I intended it as a lesson against the somewhat dogmatic tone which he occasionally assumed. He balanced the watch in his hand, gazed hard at the dial, opened the back, and examined the works, first with his naked eyes and then with a powerful convex lens. I could hardly keep from smiling at his crestfallen face when he finally snapped the case to and handed it back.

"There are hardly any data," he remarked. "The watch has been recently cleaned, which robs me of my most suggestive facts."

"You are right," I answered. "It was cleaned before being sent to me."

In my heart I accused my companion of putting forward a most lame and impotent excuse to cover his failure. What data could he expect from an uncleaned watch?

"Though unsatisfactory, my research has not been entirely barren," he observed, staring up at the ceiling with dreamy, lack-lustre eyes. "Subject to your

Copyright © 1982, John Wiley and Sons, Inc.

correction, I should judge that the watch belonged to your elder brother, who inherited it from your father."

"That you gather, no doubt, from the H. W. upon the back?"

"Quite so. The W. suggests your own name. The date of the watch is nearly fifty years back, and the initials are as old as the watch: so it was made for the last generation. Jewellery usually descends to the eldest son, and he is most likely to have the same name as the father. Your father has, if I remember right, been dead many years. It has, therefore, been in the hands of your eldest brother."

"Right, so far," said I. "Anything else?"

"He was a man of untidy habits—very untidy and careless. He was left with good prospects, but he threw away his chances, lived for some time in poverty with occasional short intervals of prosperity, and finally, taking to drink, he died. That is all I can gather."

I sprang from my chair and limped impatiently about the room with considerable bitterness in my heart.

"This is unworthy of you, Holmes," I said. "I could not have believed that you would have descended to this. You have made inquiries into the history of my unhappy brother, and you now pretend to deduce this knowledge in some fanciful way. You cannot expect me to believe that you have read all this from his old watch! It is unkind and, to speak plainly, has a touch of charlatanism in it."

"My dear doctor," said he kindly, "pray accept my apologies. Viewing the matter as an abstract problem, I had forgotten how personal and painful a thing it might be to you. I assure you, however, that I never even knew that you had a brother until you handed me the watch."

"Then how in the name of all that is wonderful did you get these facts? They are absolutely correct in every particular."

"Ah, that is good luck. I could only say what was the balance of probability. I did not at all expect to be so accurate."

"But it was not mere guesswork?"

"No, no: I never guess. It is a shocking habit—destructive to the logical faculty. What seems strange to you is only so because you do not follow my train of thought or observe the small facts upon which large inferences may depend. For example, I began by stating that your brother was careless. When you observe the lower part of that watch-case you notice that it is not only dented in two places but it is cut and marked all over from the habit of keeping other hard objects, such as coins or keys, in the same pocket. Surely it is no great feat to assume that a man who treats a fifty-guinea watch so cavalierly must be a careless man. Neither is it a very far-fetched inference that a man who inherits one article of such value is pretty well provided for in other respects."

I nodded to show that I followed his reasoning.

"It is very customary for pawnbrokers in England, when they take a watch, to scratch the numbers of the ticket with a pin-point upon the inside of the case. It is more handy than a label as there is no risk of the number being lost or *transposed. There are no less than four such numbers visible to my lens on the inside of this case. Inference—that your brother was often at low water. Secondary inference—that he had occasional bursts of prosperity, or he could not have redeemed the pledge. Finally, I ask you to look at the inner plate, which contains the keyhole. Look at the thousands of scratches all round the hole—marks where the key has slipped. What sober man's key could have scored those grooves? But you will never see a drunkard's watch without them. He winds it at night, and he leaves these traces of his unsteady hand. Where is the mystery in all this?"*

"It is as clear as daylight," I answered. "I regret the injustice which I did you. I should have had more faith in your marvellous faculty. May I ask whether you have any professional inquiry on foot at present?"

"None. Hence the cocaine. I cannot live without brainwork. What else is there to live for?"[1]

Managers and students of organizations can benefit from development of their abilities to observe and infer meaning from the minutiae of daily life in the organization. Managers often point out that the most successful leaders are those who "understand their people." But why do some individuals seem to have a knack for understanding others, while others lack it? Perhaps the answer lies largely in the ability of some individuals to tune in and attend to subtle clues in the behavior of others. In the activity that follows, you will have an opportunity to test your ability to draw correct inferences from the behavior of another person, your instructor.

PROCEDURE

Step 1: 5 Minutes
The instructor will provide each participant with a short questionnaire. The questions you are to answer are questions about the instructor. Answer the questions as quickly and accurately as you can, based upon any observations you have been able to make about this person.

Step 2: 5 Minutes
In Step 3, you will be asked to pair with another student to compare answers, and revise them to reach some agreement. In talking with another student you might feel awkward, interested, nervous, bored, self-conscious, or some other way. Stop now and ask yourself how you think you will feel and, in the space provided, write down as many adjectives you can think of that describe how you think you will feel and behave when talking to one other person.

---

[1] Excerpted from Sir Arthur Conan Doyle, "The Sign of Four." In *A Study in Scarlet and The Sign of Four* (New York: Berkley Publishing, 1975), pp. 139–142. Used with permission of the publisher.

Copyright © 1982, John Wiley and Sons, Inc.

Adjectives: How I Will Act and Feel

Step 3: 10 Minutes

When the instructor gives the word, get up out of your chair and walk around the room until you have found another student who is *one of the people you know least well* in the room. As a pair, discuss your answers to the questions, why you answered them as you did (did you have any observations to draw on?), and try to reach a consensus about your answers.

Step 4: 5 Minutes

Working alone, reflect for a minute on your discussion with the other person in Step 3. Did you feel and behave as you had predicted in Step 2? Did anything of interest occur in the discussion? Write your thoughts down here.

Step 5: 5 Minutes

When you have finished this step, you and your partner will be asked to join up with two other pairs to form a group of six. The groups of six will compare answers and attempt to reach a consensus. How do you think you will feel? Behave? Write as many adjectives you can think of to describe how you think you will act and feel.

Adjectives: How I Will Act and Feel

Step 6: 20 Minutes

When the instructor signals, rejoin your partner, walk around the room and join up with two other pairs to form a group of six (if any smaller groups are to be used, your instructor will so indicate). Try to select people you do not know very well. Compare your answers to the questionnaire on the instructor and revise them until you reach a consensus (but be sure to finish in the time allotted).

Step 7: 5 Minutes

Think about your experience in the group of six. What was it like? Did you behave and feel as you had predicted in Step 5? Did anything of interest occur? What did you observe about the group as a unit? Write your thoughts for future reference.

Step 8: 10 Minutes

The instructor will assist the class in compiling data on the accuracy of the answers to the questions asked on the handout. The procedure to be followed is as follows:

1. The instructor will provide the correct answer to a question. By a show of hands, indicate how many *individuals* got the answer correct when they responded to the questionnaire. These data will be posted on the blackboard or on newsprint for each question.
2. Meet in the groups of six and appoint one person to be the spokesperson for the group. Quickly make the following tallies for each question:
   a. How many of the pairs got the answer correct (as opposed to incorrect or could not reach agreement)?
   b. Did the group of six arrive at a correct answer?
3. Reconvene with the rest of the class, and provide the requested data when called upon by the instructor.

Copyright © 1982, John Wiley and Sons, Inc.

DISCUSSION QUESTIONS

1. Were individuals more accurate? Pairs? Groups of six? Why?
2. What questions did people answer most accurately? Least accurately? Why? Do people tend to pick up certain types of cues rather than others? Are certain types of people more sensitive to certain types of cues than others?
3. What ideas did you develop from this exercise about how the instructor and the course will be different from other courses you have taken? What are your expectations for this course, now?

GENERALIZATIONS AND CONCLUSIONS

Concluding Points

1. Do groups or individuals make better decisions?

2. What are the implications of concluding point 1 for this class?

Participant's Reactions

READINGS AND REFERENCES

Athos, A.G., and Gabarro, J.J., *Interpersonal Behavior: Communication and Understanding in Relationships* (Englewood Cliffs, N.J.: Prentice-Hall, 1978). See especially Chapters 1 ("Communication: The Use of Time, Space, and Things") and 2 ("Communication: The Use of Body Languages") and M.B. McCaskey's paper, "Place, Imagery, and Nonverbal Clues" (pp. 63-73).

SECTION TWO
MOTIVATION: BASIC CONCEPTS

4
ASSESSING MOTIVATION, SATISFACTION, AND CONGRUENT JOBS

PURPOSE:
(1) To diagnose your own need strength and need satisfaction.
(2) To explore jobs and types of supervisors that would best fit your needs.
(3) To help others explore their own needs.

ADVANCE PREPARATION:
None required. However, it saves class time if participants fill out the questionnaire in this exercise and score it before class.

GROUP SIZE: Groups of three, total of 100 participants.
TIME REQUIRED: Assessment exercise: 50 minutes; Career-planning option: 55 minutes; Leadership-style option: 55 minutes.
SPECIAL MATERIALS: None.
SPECIAL PHYSICAL REQUIREMENTS: None.
RELATED TOPICS: Managers as leaders, Life, work, and career roles, Applied motivation and job design.

Questionnaire reprinted by permission of the author and the publisher from *Organizational Patterns of Job Attitudes* by Lyman W. Porter, © 1964 by American Foundation for Management Research, p. 14. All rights reserved. (Published by American Management Association, Inc.)

Copyright © 1982, John Wiley and Sons, Inc.

INTRODUCTION

If you ask managers what is the most important problem or process in the management of people at work, chances are they will mention motivation. (Leadership and communication are other frequent responses to this question.) Motivation activates human energy; it is a force that leads people to attempt to satisfy their important needs. Furthermore, as many students of the subject have said, *all* human behavior is motivated. The critical factor is the *direction* of that motivation—is it to work hard, to do high-quality work, to spend time with one's family, or to sleep as much as possible on the job without being caught by the foreman?

In this exercise we will focus not on assembly-line workers or clerks or executives, but on you and your own motivation. To do this, we will use a questionnaire developed by Lyman W. Porter originally to measure managerial motivation in national and worldwide samples. Since then, it has been widely used to measure needs and satisfactions in all types of people. Porter sees the assessment of a person's motivation as a means of determining his or her psychological "fit" with various types of jobs.

The Porter questionnaire measures all of the Maslow need levels, with the exception of the physiological needs, which we will assume to be relatively well satisfied for most participants. However, this assumption would not be valid for people who are ill (especially those with chronic illness); extremely poor people; people living in unsafe, high-crime areas; old people; and other groups whose physical well-being is unsatisfactory.

In this exercise you will be asked to assess your own motivation and satisfaction, either in your present job or in the kind of job you think you will be in when you finish this phase of your education. Then you may be asked to think about how these different levels of motivation might be linked to particular jobs or types of supervision.

PROCEDURE

Step 1: 10 Minutes

Complete the following questionnaire. *If you are currently employed,* either part-time or full-time, respond in terms of your present job. *If you are not currently employed,* describe your *last job*. If you have never worked, respond in terms of the kind of job you *realistically think you will have when you start working*.

Copyright © 1982, John Wiley and Sons, Inc.

QUESTIONNAIRE

Given below are several characteristics or qualities connected with your job. For each such characteristic, you will be asked to give three ratings:

a. *How much* of the characteristic *is there now* connected with your job?
b. *How much* of the characteristic do you think *should be* connected with your job?
c. *How important* is this characteristic *to you?*

Each rating will be on a seven-point scale, which will look like this:

(minimum) 1 2 3 4 5 6 7 (maximum)

You are to *circle the number* on the scale that represents the amount of the characteristic being rated. Low numbers represent low or minimum amounts, and high numbers represent high or maximum amounts. If you think there is "very little" or "none" of the characteristic presently associated with your job, you would circle numeral 1. If you think there is "just a little," you would circle numeral 2, and so on. If you think there is a "great deal but not a maximum amount," you would circle numeral 6. For each scale, circle only one number. *Please do not omit any scales.*

1. The *feeling of self-esteem* a person gets from being in my job position:
   a. How much is there now?   (min) 1   2   3   4   5   6   7 (max)
   b. How much should there be?   1   2   3   4   5   6   7
   c. How important is this to me?   1   2   3   4   5   6   7

2. The *opportunity for personal growth and development* in my job position:
   a. How much is there now?   (min) 1   2   3   4   5   6   7 (max)
   b. How much should there be?   1   2   3   4   5   6   7
   c. How important is this to me?   1   2   3   4   5   6   7

3. The *prestige* of my job *inside* the company (i.e. the regard received from others in the company):
   a. How much is there now?   (min) 1   2   3   4   5   6   7 (max)
   b. How much should there be?   1   2   3   4   5   6   7
   c. How important is this to me?   1   2   3   4   5   6   7

4. The *opportunity for independent thought and action* in my position:
   a. How much is there now?   (min) 1   2   3   4   5   6   7 (max)
   b. How much should there be?   1   2   3   4   5   6   7
   c. How important is this to me?   1   2   3   4   5   6   7

5. The *feeling of security* in my job position:
   a. How much is there now?   (min) 1   2   3   4   5   6   7 (max)
   b. How much should there be?   1   2   3   4   5   6   7
   c. How important is this to me?   1   2   3   4   5   6   7

6. The *feeling of self-fullfillment* a person gets from being in my job position, that is, the feeling of being able to use one's own unique capabilities, realizing one's potentialities:
   a. How much is there now?   (min) 1   2   3   4   5   6   7 (max)
   b. How much should there be?   1   2   3   4   5   6   7
   c. How important is this to me?   1   2   3   4   5   6   7

7. The *prestige* of my job position *outside* the company (i.e. the regard received from others not in the company):
   a. How much is there now?   (min)   1   2   3   4   5   6   7   (max)
   b. How much should there be?   1   2   3   4   5   6   7
   c. How important is this to me?   1   2   3   4   5   6   7

8. The *feeling of worthwhile accomplishment* in my job:
   a. How much is there now?   (min)   1   2   3   4   5   6   7   (max)
   b. How much should there be?   1   2   3   4   5   6   7
   c. How important is this to me?   1   2   3   4   5   6   7

9. The *opportunity, in my job, to give help to other people:*
   a. How much is there now?   (min)   1   2   3   4   5   6   7   (max)
   b. How much should there be?   1   2   3   4   5   6   7
   c. How important is this to me?   1   2   3   4   5   6   7

10. The *opportunity, in my job, for participation in the setting of goals:*
    a. How much is there now?   (min)   1   2   3   4   5   6   7   (max)
    b. How much should there be?   1   2   3   4   5   6   7
    c. How important is this to me?   1   2   3   4   5   6   7

11. The *opportunity, in my job, for participation in the determination of methods and procedures:*
    a. How much is there now?   (min)   1   2   3   4   5   6   7   (max)
    b. How much should there be?   1   2   3   4   5   6   7
    c. How important is this to me?   1   2   3   4   5   6   7

12. The *authority* connected with my job:
    a. How much is there now?   (min)   1   2   3   4   5   6   7   (max)
    b. How much should there be?   1   2   3   4   5   6   7
    c. How important is this to me?   1   2   3   4   5   6   7

13. The *opportunity to develop close friendships* in my job:
    a. How much is there now?   (min)   1   2   3   4   5   6   7   (max)
    b. How much should there be?   1   2   3   4   5   6   7
    c. How important is this to me?   1   2   3   4   5   6   7

Copyright © 1982, John Wiley and Sons, Inc.

Step 2: 10 Minutes

Compute your need scores for each of the need categories, using the following scoring form. Remember that under each job characteristic, you were asked to give three ratings, the third of which was *"How important* is this characteristic *to you?"* This question above measures the importance you attach to the various needs to be scored here.

1. Enter the number you circled in part (c) for each question in the space next to that number.
2. Next, add up the numbers in each column to obtain your total score for each need.
3. Then divide by the number of questions used to measure that need, to obtain your score.

	Security	Social	Esteem	Autonomy	Self-realization
	5c =	9c =	1c =	4c =	2c =
		13c =	3c =	10c =	6c =
			7c =	11c =	8c =
				12c =	
Total	___	___	___	___	___
Divided by	1	2	3	4	3
Equals Score	___	___	___	___	___
National Mean[a]	5.33	5.36	5.28	5.92	6.35

[a]National means from Porter's sample of 1,916 managers. These numbers are "grand means" for all levels of management combined.

For comparative purposes, Table 1 gives Porter's means for managers at all levels.

TABLE 1
Dissatisfaction and importance of needs (by level of management)

MEAN DISSATISFACTION[a]

	NEEDS				
Level	Security	Social	Esteem	Autonomy	Self-realization
President	0.26	0.34	0.28	0.18	0.63
Vice-president	0.45	0.29	0.45	0.55	0.90
Upper middle	0.41	0.33	0.66	0.87	1.12
Lower middle	0.38	0.32	0.71	0.96	1.17
Lower	0.82	0.56	1.15	1.40	1.52

Table 1 (continued).

MEAN IMPORTANCE[b]

			NEEDS		
Level	*Security*	*Social*	*Esteem*	*Autonomy*	*Self-realization*
President	5.69	5.38	5.27	6.11	6.50
Vice-president	5.44	5.46	5.33	6.10	6.40
Upper middle	5.20	5.31	5.27	5.89	6.34
Lower middle	5.29	5.33	5.26	5.74	6.25
Lower	5.30	5.27	5.18	5.58	6.32

Source: Lyman W. Porter, *Organizational Patterns of Managerial Job Attitudes* (New York: American Foundation for Management Research, 1964), p. 17.

[a]Dissatisfaction score based on difference between obtained and expected fulfillment. Therefore, a difference score of 0 = complete satisfaction; a difference score of 6 = complete dissatisfaction.

[b]1 = lowest degree of importance; 7 = highest degree of importance.

Step 3: 5 Minutes

In a similar manner, compute your raw scores and adjusted scores for dissatisfaction. The table is on the top of the next page.

Dissatisfaction with each job characteristic is scored as the score for (b) minus the score for (a); that is, "How much there should be" minus "How much there is now."

1. For each question, subtract part (a)'s score from part (b)'s score, that is, (b) − (a).
2. Enter the (b) − (a) score for each question in the space next to the number of that question in the columns below. If (a) is greater than (b) be sure to retain the minus sign for the difference.
3. Next, add up the numbers in each column to obtain a total for each need. Again, be sure to retain any minus signs.
4. Divide this total by the number of questions used to measure each need to obtain scores for each need.

Remember, this adjusted score is a measure of *dis*satisfaction. The lower it is, the more satisfied you are. The higher it is, the more dissatisfied you are.

Step 4: 15 Minutes

Meet in groups of three to discuss your need strength and satisfaction scores. If possible, meet with people who know you, rather than with strangers. Figure the *rank order* of your need importance scores (highest number = most important; lowest number = least important). Ask the other two group members to guess the rank order of your needs. Ask them *what behaviors* you show that lead them to perceive you as having that pattern of needs. Then read them the actual rank order of need importance that you have computed. Discuss why there was or was not a difference between your view and their view of your needs. Repeat this process for each member of the group.

Copyright © 1982, John Wiley and Sons, Inc.

	Security	Social	Esteem	Autonomy	Self-realization
	5b − 5a =	9b − 9a = 13b − 13a =	1b − 1a = 3b − 3a = 7b − 7a =	4b − 4a = 10b − 10a = 11b − 11a = 12b − 12a =	2b − 2a = 6b − 6a = 8b − 8a =
Total					
Divided by	1	2	3	4	3
Equals Raw Score					
National mean[a]	0.43	0.33	0.61	0.78	1.05

[a]National means from Porter's sample of 1,916 managers. The numbers are "grand means" for all levels of management combined.

Step 5: 10 Minutes

Next, discuss the rank order of each person's satisfaction scores. What *features of your job* were or are responsible for your areas of high and low satisfaction? How could the job be changed to remove the dissatisfaction? What different job would lead to greater satisfaction?

Note: If most of the participants have not had work experience, do not use Step 5.

CAREER PLANNING OPTION

Step 1: 5 Minutes

Form the group into four subgroups. One group will consist of people whose highest need score was self-realization. The second will be people whose highest need score was autonomy. The third group will be people who peaked on esteem, and the fourth will be people whose highest scores were in the social category. *Do not form a group of people who scored highest on security, as this is a less reliable, one-item scale. People whose highest need was security should be assigned to groups on the basis of their second-ranked need.*

Step 2: 20 Minutes

Each group designs an *ideal job (or a training program)* for one of the other groups. The group leader will specify which option you should work on here. The "autonomy" subgroup should design an ideal job or training program for the "social" subgroup, and vice versa. The "esteem" subgroup should design an ideal job or training program for the "self-realization" subgroup and vice versa.

Step 3: 30 Minutes

Meet again as a total group. Have each group identify the group it is counseling and make its presentation. Maximum time: 5 minutes per presentation. Take two or three minutes to discuss each presentation after it is finished. Be sure to get the reactions of the target or "counselee" group. Consider the following issues: (1) To what extent did each group impose their own needs on the other group? (2) How can we better deal with our own needs in working with or helping others?

LEADERSHIP-STYLE OPTION

Step 1: 5 Minutes

Form the group into four subgroups based upon each person's predominant need, as in Step 1 in the career-planning option above.

Step 2: 20 Minutes

Each subgroup meets separately. Your task as a subgroup is to describe how the *ideal supervisor* should behave to motivate you to perform at your best. (An alternative here is to describe the behavior of the ideal group leader or instructor for you.) Be as *specific* as you can, giving concrete examples of supervisor behaviors that would help bring out the best in you.

Step 3: 30 Minutes

Meet again as a total group. Have each subgroup present its description of its ideal supervisor to the rest of the group. Maximum time: 5 minutes per group. There should be no discussion until all four groups have made their presentations. Are all subgroups looking for pretty much the same type of supervision? Are there differences? Are they consistent with the different need patterns? Do you see any "blind spots" or gaps in the supervision any of the groups might receive from their ideal supervisors?

DISCUSSION QUESTIONS

See questions in the various steps under "Procedure."

GENERALIZATIONS AND CONCLUSIONS

Concluding Points

1. Other people often perceive our needs quite differently than we perceive them ourselves. Frequently, our greatest "blind spot" is in what area?

Copyright © 1982, John Wiley and Sons, Inc.

2. There is some indication that the strength of needs may do *what* as age increases, with security becoming (more or less?) important and self-realization becoming (more or less?) important with age?

Participant's Reactions

READINGS AND REFERENCES

Alderfer, C. P., *Existence, Relatedness, and Growth: Human Needs in Organizational Settings* (New York: Free Press, 1972).

Bowen, D. D., "Retrospective Comment on Maslow." In L. E. Boone and D. L. Bowen, (Eds.), *The Great Writings in Management and Organizational Behavior* (Tulsa, OK.: PPC Books, 1980), pp. 106–107.

Maslow, A. H., *Motivation and Personality* (New York: Harper & Row, 1954).

5
EXPECTANCY THEORY: A PERSONAL APPLICATION

PURPOSE:
To demonstrate the application of expectancy theory to one's own decisions.

ADVANCE PREPARATION:
Read text material or lecture notes on the expectancy theory of motivation.

GROUP SIZE: Any size.
TIME REQUIRED: 45 minutes.
SPECIAL MATERIALS: None.
SPECIAL PHYSICAL REQUIREMENTS: None.
RELATED TOPICS: Decision making, Life, work, and career roles.

INTRODUCTION

The expectancy theory of motivation is a theory of how people make choices between alternative courses of action. It is similar to rational economic theory in that it assumes that people, when faced with the need to make a decision about how to behave, will be influenced by the possible costs and benefits of each course of action. Individuals will select the course of action with the greatest perceived expected net (positive minus negative) outcomes.

However, the attractiveness (valence) of the outcomes is not the only factor that affects the person's behavior. The perceived probability (expectancy) that a given outcome will in fact occur is also important. For example, if I buy a ticket for the state lottery, one possible outcome would be winning $1 million. This outcome has rather high valence for me. On the other hand, the probability of winning this amount is extremely low, so low that my overall motivation to buy a lottery ticket is near zero. And there would be negative outcomes associated with buying a ticket, such as spending money on the ticket or walking to the store. This explains why I have never bought a lottery ticket.

The strength of a person's motivation to choose a given course of action, then, is a function of the sum of both the valence of the outcomes that might result from that course of action, multiplied by the expectancies of these outcomes' occurring.

Developed by Douglas T. Hall. The helpful comments of Lloyd Baird and Max Bazerman are greatly appreciated.

Copyright © 1982, John Wiley and Sons, Inc.

$$MF_i = f_i \sum_{j=1}^{n} (E_{ij}V_j)$$

where MF_i = motivational force to perform act i

Σ means summation

E_{ij} = the strength of the expectancy (a probability between 0 and 1) that act i will be followed by outcome j

V_j = the valence of outcome j

If you have taken a mathematics course, this equation may look familiar to you. Expectancy theory essentially says that people attempt to maximize subjective expected utility (which is the same as what mathematical decision theory tells us).

In this exercise you will be asked to apply expectancy theory to your own choices in a decision situation important to you.

PROCEDURE

Step 1: 15 Minutes

Think of a decision that you are in the process of making. You could be at any stage in the decision process. You could be just starting to think about it, as in the case of thinking about job choices when the recruiting season is still a couple of months away. You could be right in the middle of it; perhaps you have three job offers, and you have to decide by next week. Or, you could have just made a decision, but you're not totally comfortable that you have made the right choice, and you'd like to think it through a bit more. The decision could be about anything: what to major in, whether to get married, where to live, whether to change jobs, or what movie to see tonight.

The main thing is to think of a decision that is important and a "live issue" for you right now. However, don't pick one that is so personal that you would feel uncomfortable discussing it with someone else in this course.

1. List out all the possible courses of action that you are considering. Record them on Table 1. (Use additional paper if you need more space.)
2. For each alternative course of action, try to think of the important things that could happen as a result of choosing that action. List them in the second column from the left, "Possible Outcomes." (Don't forget to include negative outcomes, as well as positive ones.)
3. Think of how attractive or unattractive each of these outcomes would be to you. Use a scale from -10 to $+10$ to rate the valence of each outcome. List the valences in the third column from the left. (A valence of -10 would be

the most unpleasant, objectionable outcome you could think of; a valence of 0 would be for an outcome about which you are completely indifferent. A valence of + 10 would describe an outcome that would be one of the best things that could ever happen to you.)

4. Think of what the probabilities or expectancies are that each of these outcomes might occur if you chose that particular course of action. Rate these probabilities from 0 (a probability indicating you are certain it will not happen) to 1.0 (which would indicate you are certain it would happen); use tenths (e.g., .2, .5, .7) to indicate values between 0 and 1.0. Enter these probabilities or expectancies in the fourth column from the left.

5. Multiply each valence score by the expectancy score next to it. Enter these products in the column labeled, E × V.

6. For each course of action, add up all of the products of E × V. Enter each sum in the spaces in the far right-hand column of Table 1.

Step 2: Dyad Exercise, 20 Minutes

Get together with another person in the class whose opinion you respect. Spend 10 minutes discussing each person's expectancy table. When your partner's decision is being discussed, your objective is to be as helpful as possible to your partner as he or she describes the options being considered and the valences and expectancies involved. *How realistic* are the expectancies? What about the "*gut factor*" (what alternative does the person prefer in his or her "gut")?

At the end of your partner's 10 minutes, ask, "If you had to make a decision *right now*, what would it be?" This gives an idea of which way the person is "leaning." How does this choice compare with the alternative that has the highest expectancy analysis total? How does this choice compare with the "gut" preference? How does the "gut" preference compare with the expectancy total?

After spending 10 minutes on one partner's expectancy table, switch roles and discuss the other partner's table. Consider the same questions mentioned above.

Step 3: Class Discussion, 10 Minutes

Discuss the overall results of the various dyads' experiences. Use the Discussion Questions listed below.

DISCUSSION QUESTIONS

1. What kinds of decisions were people working on?
2. How difficult or easy was it to identify alternative courses of action, outcomes, valences, and expectancies? How rational do you think people are (or can be) in making personal decisions?
3. Based on your own experiences, how would you evaluate expectancy theory as a way of explaining motivation and decision making?

Copyright © 1982, John Wiley and Sons, Inc.

TABLE 1
Expectancy Analysis for Decisions

Course of Action	Possible Outcomes	Valences (−10 to +10)	Expectancies (0 to 1.0)	E × V	Sum of E × V

Note: Use additional paper if more space is needed.

Copyright © 1982, John Wiley and Sons, Inc.

GENERALIZATIONS AND CONCLUSIONS

Concluding Points

1. Upon what assumptions does expectancy theory rest?

2. What is the status of expectancy theory, as indicated by research?

Participant's Reactions

READINGS AND REFERENCES

Lawler III, E. E., *Motivation in Work Organizations* (Monterey, Calif.: Brooks/Cole, 1973).

Lawler III, E. E., Nadler, D. A., and Cammann, C., *Organizational Assessment: Perspectives on the Measurement of Organizational Behavior and the Quality of Working Life* (New York: Wiley-Interscience, 1979).

Vroom, V., *Work and Motivation* (New York: Wiley, 1964).

Wanous, J. P., "Organizational Entry: Newcomers Moving from Outside to Inside," *Psychological Bulletin*, 84 (1977), 601-618.

6
MONEY MOTIVATION DEBATE

PURPOSE:
(1) To examine the role of money in work motivation.
(2) To examine the importance of other factors in relation to money.
(3) To develop skills in using theory and research literature as a basis for
successfully communicating a point of view (i.e., selling an opinion).
(4) To experience the dynamics of intergroup competition.

ADVANCE PREPARATION:
Come to class prepared to discuss the role of money in motivation.

GROUP SIZE: Best for 10 to 30. Option for larger groups.
TIME REQUIRED: 55 minutes.
SPECIAL MATERIALS: None.
SPECIAL PHYSICAL REQUIREMENTS: None.
RELATED TOPICS: Organizational communication, Interpersonal commu-
nication, Intergroup issues and conflict, Group decision making and problem
solving.

INTRODUCTION

The role of money as a motivator of work behavior has been widely debated in
the literature on management and organizational behavior. Some theorists, such
as Herzberg (1968), see money as a "dissatisfier," a factor whose absence can cause
dissatisfaction but whose presence cannot cause high satisfaction or motivation.
Other theorists, such as Lawler (1971), argue that money can provide both direct
and symbolic gratification of human needs and can thus be a motivator if money
rewards are linked to good performance. In this exercise you will be asked to
think about motivation and to develop a convincing argument regarding the role
of money in human work motivation.

PROCEDURE

Step 1: 20 Minutes
The class breaks into two halves, with three or four students withdrawing to act as
judges. One-half of the class will prepare a debate, resolved that: *Money is a prime
motivator of people in the workplace.* The other half prepares to argue that: *Money
is not a prime motivator of people in the workplace.*

Each team appoints a discussion leader and spokesperson. They then prepare
their argument for *about 20 minutes.* During this time, the judging group decides
on the criteria it will use.

Originally developed by William H. Read. Adapted by Douglas T. Hall. Used with permission.

Copyright © 1982, John Wiley and Sons, Inc.

Step 2: 15 Minutes

The class reassembles, and the arguments (point form) are presented. Post them in "shorthand" style on the board. Each group is allowed 5 minutes to make its presentation. Then the groups will have 5 minutes to prepare their rebuttals. Each group is given 1 minute for rebuttal. The judges act as timekeepers.

Step 3: 5 Minutes

The judges then meet in front of the rest of the participants and decide on the winner. In announcing their decision, they should state clearly why they decided as they did.

Step 4: 10 Minutes

Discussion and conclusion—summary of major points—see below.

DISCUSSION QUESTIONS

1. Without renewing the debate now that it is over, how many people think money *is* a key motivator of work behavior? How many think it is not?
2. Can a given study or theory support either side of this debate? If so, how? If not, why not?
3. How can management affect the *degree* to which money is a motivator?
4. If money is *not* available as a possible motivator (e.g., because of union contracts or seniority traditions), what could you do to motivate effective performance?
5. How many of you changed your minds as a result of the debate?

GENERALIZATIONS AND CONCLUSIONS

Concluding Points

1. In surveys of what people look for in work, does pay usually rank fairly high or fairly low?

2. According to March and Simon, employees make two kinds of decisions about an organization: the "decision to participate" (i.e., to join or remain in the organization) and the "decision to produce" (i.e., to perform well). Which of these two decisions is probably more strongly affected by pay?

3. Money is most likely to act as a motivator of good performance under what conditions?

Participant's Reactions

READINGS AND REFERENCES

Hamner, W. C., "How to Ruin Motivation with Pay," *Compensation Review* (1975).

Herzberg, F., "One More Time: How Do You Motivate Employees?" *Harvard Business Review,* 46 (1968), 53-62.

Lawler III, E. E., *Pay and Organizational Effectiveness: A Psychological View* (New York: McGraw-Hill, 1971).

Copyright © 1982, John Wiley and Sons, Inc.

7
WHAT DO WE VALUE IN WORK?

PURPOSE:
(1) To assess the priorities of work values for participants.
(2) To compare the work values of men and women.

ADVANCE PREPARATION:
Fill out the questionnaire "What Do We Value in Work?" on page 45. You are not required to put your name on the questionnaire; the data for the entire group will be tabulated anonymously. (Keep p. 47 as your copy.)

GROUP SIZE: A single large group of up to 50 participants. Option two uses subgroups of 5 to 9 persons.
TIME REQUIRED: 45 minutes (add 5 minutes per group if Option two is followed).
SPECIAL MATERIALS: None.
SPECIAL PHYSICAL REQUIREMENTS: *Option One*: Single large room for all participants. *Option Two*: Separate meeting rooms for discussion groups or a single large room where groups can hold discussions separately to the extent necessary to minimize disturbance.
RELATED TOPICS: Life, work, and career roles, Negotiation and conflict.

INTRODUCTION

What do people want to get out of their work? What values do they want to fulfill through work? In this exercise you will have an opportunity to think about your own priorities for what you want from work. You will also have a chance to look at data on the priorities of other people.

In this exercise, you will have an opportunity to compare your own reasons for continuing to work with the answers given by a national sample of 2300 *Psychology Today* readers.

PROCEDURE

The group leader will designate Option one or Option two to be followed.

OPTION ONE

Step 1: 20 Minutes

The men in the group develop a consensual ranking of the items as they think the women in the sample ranked them. The women in the group *do not participate* in

Developed by Donald D. Bowen.

the ranking. (The women should take note of the primary issues raised while the men are making the rankings and comment on these in the discussion afterward.)

The instructor will lead the ranking process, tallying votes, suggestions, and so on, on a blackboard or easel. The ranking proceeds as follows:

1. The men nominate candidates from the list of seven work values for the value they believe women in general would rank first.
2. When all candidates have been identified, proponents of each candidate offer arguments as to why they think a particular value should be ranked first. When all arguments have been heard, a vote is taken by a show of hands. Items receiving the least votes are dropped from the list, and discussion is resumed. Votes are taken whenever the men indicate that they are ready. When one item finally receives a majority vote, it is ranked first.
3. Next, the group considers which item should be ranked *last*. The same procedure is followed until one of the remaining six values receives a majority vote for last place. The group then works on the item to be ranked second, then sixth, and so on, until all items have been ranked. When all items have been ranked, begin the discussion (see "Both Options," below).

OPTION TWO

Step 1: 20 Minutes

Form groups of five to nine persons. Each group should be composed entirely of men or women. Each group meets separately in a place designated by the instructor. Group meetings should last 15 minutes, and each group is to perform the following tasks:

1. Decide, as a group, which of the items was ranked number 1 by members of the opposite sex (from that of group members) in the *Psychology Today* study.
2. Identify the main reasons why your group feels that each one of the other six values was not the one ranked first.
3. Appoint a spokesperson to present the group's conclusions to the entire group. Rejoin the other members of the entire group at the end of the allotted 15 minutes for discussion.

Step 2: 5 Minutes per Group

Each group presents to the entire group its choice for number 1 and the reasons for rejecting the other values.

BOTH OPTIONS

20 Minutes

The instructor will provide the "correct" answers; that is, the answers found by *Psychology Today*. Discuss the issues raised by the exercise, using the discussion questions that follow.

Copyright © 1982, John Wiley and Sons, Inc.

WHAT DO WE VALUE IN WORK?

In September 1977, 2300 readers of *Psychology Today* magazine (about half female and half male) answered this question:

IF YOU WOULD CONTINUE TO WORK,
WHAT IS THE ONE MOST IMPORTANT
REASON?

The choices people were given were the seven reasons in the left-hand column below.

INSTRUCTIONS: Please *rank order* the seven items in terms of how important they would be for *you* as reasons to continue working. Indicate the most important reason by putting the number "1" by that item in *column A* ("Myself"). Put a "2" by the second most important, and so on until you have put a "7" by the least important (no ties, please). When you have finished ranking the items for yourself, rank them in *column B* as you think most *men* would rank them. (Think in terms of the "average person" rather than of individuals holding particular jobs.) Finally, rank order the items as you think most *women* would rank them in *column C*.

	A Myself	B Men	C Women
1. Work keeps me from being bored.	_____	_____	_____
2. I enjoy what I do on my job.	_____	_____	_____
3. I would feel guilty if I did not contribute to society.	_____	_____	_____
4. My work is important and valuable to others.	_____	_____	_____
5. I would continue out of habit.	_____	_____	_____
6. I enjoy the company of my co-workers.	_____	_____	_____
7. I derive a major part of my identity from my job.	_____	_____	_____

My sex: _____ Male

_____ Female

(To be torn out and handed in)

Reprinted from *Psychology Today Magazine*, copyright © 1978 Ziff Davis Publishing Company.

Copyright © 1982, John Wiley and Sons, Inc.

WHAT DO WE VALUE IN WORK?

In September 1977, 2300 readers of *Psychology Today* magazine (about half female and half male) answered this question:

IF YOU WOULD CONTINUE TO WORK,
WHAT IS THE ONE MOST IMPORTANT
REASON?

The choices people were given were the seven reasons in the left-hand column below.

INSTRUCTIONS: Please *rank order* the seven items in terms of how important they would be for *you* as reasons to continue working. Indicate the most important reason by putting the number "1" by that item in *column A* ("Myself"). Put a "2" by the second most important, and so on until you have put a "7" by the least important (no ties, please). When you have finished ranking the items for yourself, rank them in *column B* as you think most *men* would rank them. (Think in terms of the "average person" rather than of individuals holding particular jobs.) Finally, rank order the items as you think most *women* would rank them in *column C*.

	A Myself	B Men	C Women
1. Work keeps me from being bored.	_____	_____	_____
2. I enjoy what I do on my job.	_____	_____	_____
3. I would feel guilty if I did not contribute to society.	_____	_____	_____
4. My work is important and valuable to others.	_____	_____	_____
5. I would continue out of habit.	_____	_____	_____
6. I enjoy the company of my co-workers.	_____	_____	_____
7. I derive a major part of my identity from my job.	_____	_____	_____

My sex: _____Male

_____Female

(Keep as your reference copy.)

Reprinted from *Psychology Today Magazine*, copyright © 1978 Ziff Davis Publishing Company.

DISCUSSION QUESTIONS

1. What do people in the group rank first for themselves? For men in general? For women in general? (Tabulate, separately by sex, the items ranked number 1 by each person for themselves.)
2. Do both groups generally assume that other men and women want something different from work than they themselves want? Why? (Tabulate, separately, men's estimates of the value ranked number 1 by other men and by women. Similarly, tabulate the women's estimates for men and other women.)
3. Do the *Psychology Today* results seem consistent with theories of work motivation that you know about? Would any theories predict different results?
4. *For Option two, only*: Are women any more likely to rank the values accurately when they rank them for other women than men are? Did the men rank the values for other men more accurately than women? Why? What does this mean?
5. Compare the results obtained to those that have been reported for other groups.

GENERALIZATIONS AND CONCLUSIONS

Concluding Points

1. Most groups find it difficult to guess how the women in the *Psychology Today* sample ranked the items. And their rankings for men and women in general do not resemble the rankings for themselves. Why does this happen?

2. Many theories of work motivation would predict the outcomes of the *Psychology Today* study; "common sense" usually fails. What theories might be useful?

Copyright © 1982, John Wiley and Sons, Inc.

3. Are men and women similar or dissimilar in their statements of what they want from work? Why?

4. Why is it important for managers to know what people want from work?

Participant's Reactions

READINGS AND REFERENCES

Psychology Today, "How Do You Like Your Job? (Tell Us About It)," September (1977), 72-79.

Renwick, P. A., and Lawler III, E. E., "What You Really Want From Your Job," *Psychology Today*, May (1978), 53-58, 60, 62, 65, 118.

Terborg, J., "Women in Management: A Research Review," *Journal of Applied Psychology,* 62 (1977), 647-664.

8
ASSIGNMENT: THE MEANING OF WORK

PURPOSE:
To develop an understanding of the meaning of work to people in different occupational categories.

ADVANCE PREPARATION:
Read readings assigned by the instructor *before* starting the assignment.

GROUP SIZE: Groups of three to five.
TIME REQUIRED: Several days outside of class.
SPECIAL MATERIALS: None.
SPECIAL PHYSICAL REQUIREMENTS: None.
RELATED TOPICS: Applied motivation and job design, Life, work, and career roles.

INTRODUCTION

In this assignment, you will be asked to conduct interviews with a sample of people from different occupational walks of life. In a broad sense, you will be trying to find out what work means in their lives. Before you begin, be sure that you understand the instructions, especially those defining the job categories to be sampled.

PROCEDURE

1. Form teams of three to five persons if participants are not already working in groups.
2. The assignment: Each team is to interview six people and write a short paper (length to be announced by instructor) summarizing the interviews. Each paper is to describe:
   a. Each person interviewed—occupation, marital status, age (approximately).
   b. The person's responses to the questions asked.
   c. A brief summary of the major points or issues of interest you have identified in the process of collecting and analyzing your data.
   Turn the paper in on the date designated by the instructor.
3. The sample: Each group is to seek out six people and ask them if they will talk to you about *what their job means to them, personally.* Choose two people each from the following occupational categories:
   a. Blue collar (unskilled or semiskilled workers).

Developed by Donald D. Bowen.

Copyright © 1982, John Wiley and Sons, Inc.

b. White collar (clerical workers, retail or door-to-door sales).

c. Managerial or professional people.

People sometimes have difficulty in determining into which category a job fits. The following examples are intended to help you differentiate between categories. The list is not exhaustive; it is merely intended to give you a general idea of where jobs fit.

Blue-Collar Occupations	White-Collar Occcupations	Managerial or Professional Occupations
Service station attendant	File clerk	Lawyer
Steelworker	Secretary	Doctor
Custodian	Salesman (door-to-door	Engineer
Machine operator (but	or retail, but not	Foreman
not machinist or tool	industrial)	Manager
maker)	Receptionist	College professor
Bartender	Bank teller	Insurance broker
Security guard or	Insurance salesman	Accountant
policeman		

As a general rule, if you have difficulty classifying an occupation, include it with the highest possible category. Skilled tradesmen (machinists, tool makers, plumbers, etc.) will be difficult to categorize because, although we frequently think of them as blue-collar workers, their responses are more likely to sound like those of clerical or professional workers. Proprietors of small businesses are another group difficult to classify. Their attitudes toward work are likely to reflect their varied prior experience in working as employees before starting their own businesses. Don't interview part-time workers, such as college students, because their work is not a major component of their lives.

If you are female, find at least two women to talk to; if you are black, choose at least two blacks; and so on. In other words, try to find people you have something in common with.

4. Conducting the interview: *For each interview, try to have at least two members of the group present.* After the interview, you can check your impressions with the other person. Having at least two people present will also make it possible to take more comprehensive notes. During the interview, ask the following questions:

Required Questions

1. What are the major satisfactions you get in your work?
2. What are the major frustrations in your work?
3. If you had your life to live over again, would you go into the same line of work? Why?
4. What effect does your work have on your family life? How do you feel about this?

Optional Questions (follow group leader's directions on these)

5. How did you happen to get into this line of work?
6. Have you ever considered changing to another field or occupation?
7. Do you think most people are as satisfied (dissatisfied) with their work as you are? Why?
8. Do you have children? If you do, what advice do you give your children on preparing for a career? If you do not, what advice *should* people give to their children?

READINGS AND REFERENCES

Clark, J. V., "Motivation in Work Groups: A Tentative View," *Human Organization*, 19 (1960–61), 199-208.

Kanter, R. M., *Men and Women of the Corporation* (New York: Basic Books, 1977).

Maslow, A. H., "A Theory of Human Motivation," *Psychological Review*, 50 (1943), 370–71, 394-96.

McGregor, D. M., "The Human Side of Enterprise," *Management Review*, Nov. (1957), 22-28, 88-92.

Terkel, S., *Working* (New York: Pantheon, 1974).

Copyright © 1982, John Wiley and Sons, Inc.

SECTION THREE
APPLIED MOTIVATION AND JOB DESIGN

9
JOB REDESIGN

PURPOSE:
(1) To apply the theory of motivation to job design.
(2) To help participants learn to diagnose job characteristics.
(3) To provide practice in the techniques of brainstorming.

ADVANCE PREPARATION:
Read the "Introduction."

GROUP SIZE: Any size. Will be split into groups of three to seven persons each.
TIME REQUIRED: 50 minutes.
SPECIAL MATERIALS: None.
SPECIAL PHYSICAL REQUIREMENTS: None.
RELATED TOPICS: Motivation: Basic concepts, Planned change, Managers as leaders.

INTRODUCTION

The Job Characteristics Model of Work Motivation

A method of analyzing the motivating potential of a job, developed by Hackman and Oldham (1980), and called the job characteristics model of work design, is

Concepts and model developed by J. Richard Hackman and Greg R. Oldham. Exercise adapted and written by D. T. Hall. The cooperation of Richard Hackman is gratefully acknowledged. Introduction adapted from J. R. Hackman and G. R. Oldham, *Work Redesign,* © 1980, Addison-Wesley, Reading, Massachusetts, pp. 71–94, 107–127, and 135–141. Reprinted with permission.

summarized in Figure 1. The theory states that certain "core dimensions" of a job create critical psychological states in the person. Job outcomes then result from these psychological states. The concepts in the model are defined as follows:

Job dimensions. The instrument provides a measure of the five core dimensions, which are as follows:

Skill Variety. The degree to which a job requires a variety of different activities in carrying out the work, which involve the use of a number of different skills and talents of the employee.

Task Identify. The degree to which the job requires completion of a "whole" and identifiable piece of work—that is, doing a job from beginning to end with a visible outcome.

Task Significance. The degree to which the job has a substantial impact on the lives or work of other people—whether in the immediate organization or in the external environment.

Autonomy. The degree to which the job provides substantial freedom, independence, and discretion of the employee in scheduling the work and in determining the procedures to be used in carrying it out.

Feedback from the Job. The degree to which carrying out the work activities required by the job results in the employee obtaining direct and clear information about the effectiveness of his or her performance.

The overall "motivating potential" of a job can be assessed either by simply adding up respondent scores on the five core dimensions, or by computing the following Motivating Potential Score (MPS), which derives from the theory of work design summarized in Figure 1.

Critical psychological states. There are three psychological states that are shown in Figure 1 as mediating between the core job dimensions and the outcomes of the work. These are:

Experienced Meaningfulness of the Work. The degree to which the employee experiences the job as one that is generally meaningful, valuable, and worthwhile.

Experienced Responsibility for Work Outcomes. The degree to which the employee feels personally accountable and responsible for the results of the work he or she does.

Knowledge of Results. The degree to which the employee knows and understands, on a continuous basis, how effectively he or she is performing the job.

Affective outcomes. Three important personal, affective reactions or feelings a person obtains from performing the job are:

General Satisfaction. An overall measure of the degree to which the employee is satisfied and happy with the job.

Internal Work Motivation. The degree to which the employee is self-motivated to perform well on the job—that is, the employee experiences positive internal feelings when working effectively, and negative internal feelings when doing poorly.

Copyright © 1982, John Wiley and Sons, Inc.

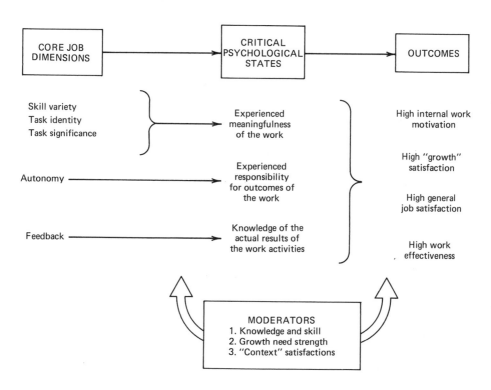

FIGURE 1

The Job Characteristics Model of Work Motivation (from Hackman and Oldham, 1980). Reprinted by Permission.

R. Hackman and G. Oldham, *Work Redesign*, Copyright © 1980, Addison-Wesley, Reading, Mass., Figure 4.6. Reprinted with permission.

Growth Satisfaction. The degree to which the employee is satisfied with opportunities for personal growth and development on the job.

Work Effectiveness. Obviously, from the organization's point of view, the critical test of any job redesign is the increase it produces in the quality and/or quantity of employee performance.

Planning, Installing, and Supporting Changes in Jobs

Implementing Concepts for Work Redesign

Five "implementing concepts" for enriching jobs are identified and discussed below. Each one is a specific action step aimed at improving both the quality of the work experience for the individual and his or her work productivity. They are:

1. Forming natural work units.
2. Combining tasks.
3. Establishing client relationships.

4. Vertical loading.
5. Opening feedback channels.

The links between the implementing concepts and the core job dimensions are shown in Figure 2. After completing a diagnosis of a job, a manager or change agent could turn to the implementing concepts to get ideas for how to improve the most problematic aspects of the job. How this might be done in practice is shown below, as each of the implementing concepts is discussed.

1. Forming Natural Work Units. The notion of distributing work in some logical way may seem to be an obvious part of the design of any job. In many cases, however, the logic is one imposed by just about any consideration except job-holder satisfaction and motivation. Such considerations include technological dictates; level of worker training or experience; "efficiency," as defined by industrial engineering; and current workload. In many cases the cluster of tasks a worker faces during a typical day or week is natural to anyone *but* the worker.

For example, suppose that a typing pool (consisting of one supervisor and ten typists) handles all work for one division of a company. Jobs are delivered in rough draft or dictated form to the supervisor, who distributes them as evenly as possible among the typists. In such circumstances the individual letters, reports, and other tasks performed by a given typist in one day or week are randomly assigned. There is no basis for identifying with the work or the person or department for whom it is performed, or for placing any personal value upon it.

The principle underlying natural units of work, by contrast, is "ownership"—a worker's sense of continuing responsibility for an identifiable body of work.

There are two steps involved in creating natural work units. The first is to identify the basic work items. In the typing pool, for example, the items might be "pages to be typed." The second step is to group the items in natural categories. For example, each typist might be assigned continuing responsibility for all jobs requested by one or several specific departments. The assignments should be made, of course, in such a way that workloads are about equal in the long run. (For example, one typist might end up with all the work from one busy department, while another handles jobs from several smaller "accounts.")

At this point we can begin to see specifically how the implementing concepts relate to the core dimensions (see Figure 2). The "ownership" fostered by natural units of work can make the difference between the feeling that work is meaningful and rewarding and the feeling that it is irrelevant and boring. As the diagram shows, natural units of work are directly related to two of the core dimensions: Task Identity and Task Significance.

A typist whose work is assigned naturally rather than randomly—say, by departments—has a much greater chance of performing a whole job to completion. Instead of typing one section of a large report, the individual is likely to type the whole thing, with knowledge of exactly what the product of the work is (Task Identity). Furthermore, over time the typist will develop a growing sense of how the work affects co-workers in the department services (Task Significance).

Copyright © 1982, John Wiley and Sons, Inc.

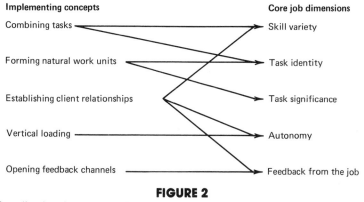

FIGURE 2
How the Implementing Concepts Relate to the Core Job Dimensions

2. Combining Tasks. The very existence of a pool made up entirely of persons whose sole function is typing reflects a fractionalization of jobs that has been a basic precept of "scientific management." Most obvious in assembly line work, fractionalization has been applied to nonmanufacturing jobs as well. It is typically justified by "efficiency," which is usually defined in terms of either low costs or some time-and-motion type of criteria.

It is hard to find fault with measuring efficiency ultimately in terms of cost effectiveness. In doing so, however, a manager should be sure to consider *all* the costs involved. It is possible, for example, for highly fractionalized jobs to meet all the time-and-motion criteria of "efficiency," but if the resulting job is so unrewarding that performing it day after day leads to high turnover, absenteeism, drugs, alcohol, and strikes, then productivity is really lower (and costs higher) than data on "efficiency" might indicate.

The principle of combining tasks, then, suggests that whenever possible existing and fractionalized tasks should be put together to form new and larger modules of work. At the Medfield, Massachusetts plant of Corning Glass Works, a laboratory hotplate now is assembled from start to finish by one operator, instead of going through several separate operations performed by different people.

Some tasks, if combined into a meaningfully large module of work, would be more than an individual could do alone. In such cases, it is often useful to consider assigning the new, larger task to a small *team* of workers—who are given great autonomy for its completion. At the Racine, Wisconsin plant of Emerson Electric, the assembly process for trash disposal appliances was restructured in this way. Instead of a sequence of moving the appliance from station to station, the assembly is now done from start to finish by one team. Such teams include both men and women to permit switching off the heavier and more delicate aspects of the work.

The team responsible is identified on the appliance. In case of customer complaints, the team often drafts the reply.

Task combination, like natural units of work, expands the Task Identity of the job. For example, the hotplate assembler can see and identify with a finished product ready for shipment, rather than a nearly invisible junction of solder. Moreover, the more tasks that are combined into a single worker's job, the greater the variety of skills he or she must call on in performing the job. So, task combination also leads directly to greater Skill Variety—the third core dimension that contributes to the overall experienced meaningfulness of the work (Figure 1).

3. Establishing Client Relationships. One consequence of fractionalization is that the typical worker has little or no contact with (or even awareness of) the ultimate user of his or her product or service. By encouraging and enabling employees to establish direct relationships with the "clients" of their work, improvements can often be realized simultaneously on three of the core dimensions. Feedback increases, because of additional opportunities for the individual to receive *direct* praise or criticism of his or her work outputs. Skill Variety often increases, because of the necessity to develop and exercise one's interpersonal skills in maintaining the client relationship. And Autonomy can increase because the individual often is given personal responsibility for deciding how to manage relationships with the "clients" of the work.

Creating client relationships is a three-step process: first, identification of who the client actually is; second, establishing the most direct possible contact betwen the worker and the client; third, setting up some criteria by which the client can judge the quality of the product or service that is received. And, whenever possible, the client should have a means of relaying those judgments directly back to the worker.

The contact between worker and the client should be as great as possible and as frequent as necessary. Face-to-face contact is highly desirable, at least occasionally. Where that is impossible or impractical, telephone and mail can suffice. In any case, it is important that the performance criteria by which the worker will be rated by the client must be mutually understood and agreed.

4. Vertical Loading. Typically the split between the "doing" of a job and the "planning" and "controlling" of the work has evolved along with horizontal fractionalization. Its rationale, once again, has been efficiency through specialization. And, once again, the excess of specialization that has emerged has resulted in unexpected but significant costs in motivation, morale, and work quality. In vertical loading, the intent is to partially close the gap between doing and the controlling parts of the job—and thereby reap some important motivational advantages.

Of all the implementing concepts, vertical loading may be the single most crucial one. In some cases, where it has been impossible to implement any other changes, vertical loading alone has had significant motivational effects.

When a job is vertically loaded, responsibilities and controls that were formerly reserved for higher levels of management are added to the job. There are numerous means of carrying this out:

Copyright © 1982, John Wiley and Sons, Inc.

Return to the job holder greater discretion in setting schedules, deciding on work methods, checking on quality, and advising or helping to train less experienced workers.

Grant additional authority. The objective should be to advance workers from a position of no authority or highly restricted authority to positions of reviewed, and eventually, near-total authority for their own work.

Time management. The job holder should have the greatest possible freedom to decide when to start and stop work, when to break, and how to assign priorities.

Troubleshooting and crisis decisions. Workers should be encouraged to seek problem solutions on their own, rather than calling immediately for the supervisor.

Financial controls. Some degree of knowledge and control over budgets and other financial aspects of a job can often be highly motivating. However, access to this information frequently tends to be restricted. Workers can benefit from knowing something about the costs of their jobs, the potential effect upon profit, and various financial and budgetary alternatives.

When a job is vertically loaded it will inevitably increase in Autonomy. And, as shown in Figure 1, this increase in objective personal control over the work should also lead to an increased feeling of personal responsibility for the work—and ultimately to higher internal work motivation.

5. Opening Feedback Channels. In virtually all jobs there are ways to open channels of feedback to individuals or teams to help them learn whether their performance is improving, deteriorating, or remaining at a constant level. Although there are numerous "channels" through which information about performance can be provided, it is generally better for a worker to learn about his or her performance *directly as the job is done*—rather than from management on an occasional basis.

Job-provided feedback usually is more immediate and private than supervisor-supplied feedback, and increases the worker's feelings of personal control over his or her work in the bargain. Moreover, it avoids many of the potentially disruptive interpersonal problems that can develop when the only way workers have to find out how they are doing is from direct messages or subtle cues from the boss.

Exactly what should be done to open channels for job-provided feedback varies from job to job and organization to organization. Yet often the changes involve simply removing existing blocks that isolate the individual from naturally occurring data about performance—rather than generating entirely new feedback mechanisms. For example:

Establishing direct client relationships (discussed above) often removes blocks between the worker and natural external sources of data about the work.

Quality control efforts in many organizations often eliminate a natural source of feedback The quality check on a product or service is done by people other than the individuals responsible for the work. Feedback to the workers—if there is any—is belated and diluted. It often fosters a tendency to think of quality as "someone else's concern."

By placing quality control close to the workers (perhaps even in their own hands), the quantity and quality of data about performance that is available to them can dramatically increase.

Tradition and established procedure in many organizations dictate that records about performance are kept by a supervisor and transmitted up (not down) the organizational hierarchy. Sometimes supervisors even check the work and correct any errors themselves. The worker who made the error never knows it occurred—and is denied the very information that can enhance both the internal work motivation and the technical adequacy of work performance. In many cases, it is possible to provide standard summaries of performance records directly to the worker (as well as to the supervisor), thereby giving workers personally and regularly the data they need to improve performance.

Computers and other automated operations sometimes can be used to provide individuals with data now blocked from them. Many clerical operations, for example, are now performed on computer consoles. These consoles often can be programmed to provide the clerk with immediate feedback in the form of a CRT display or a printout indicating that an error has been made. Some systems have even been programmed to provide the operator with a positive feedback message when a period of error-free performance has been sustained.

Many organizations simply have not recognized the importance of feedback as a motivator. Data on quality and other aspects of performance are viewed as being of interest only to management. Worse, the *standards* for acceptable performance often are kept from workers as well. As a result, workers who would be interested in following the daily or weekly ups and downs of their performance, and in trying accordingly to improve, are deprived of the very guidelines they need to do so.

PROCEDURE

Step 1: Five Minutes—Diagnosis of Need for Job Redesign—Identifying a Target Job

Ask for a member of the class to volunteer a job that they now hold or held at one time as a candidate for job redesign. (If several people volunteer, the class and/or the instructor can select the job that seems most interesting. Another possibility is to select a job with which someone in the class is very familiar, but it is more interesting if someone in the class has actually held the target job.) Everyone should be *thoroughly familiar* with the job selected.

To help identify a job that will be a good candidate for job redesign, be sure that it meets the following criteria.

A. *Assessing the Need for Work Redesign*
    1. *Is there a specific problem or exploitable opportunity?*

Copyright © 1982, John Wiley and Sons, Inc.

Sometimes work is redesigned for silly reasons. Unless a specific organizational problem can be identified for which work redesign *might* be helpful, the diagnosis should stop here.

2. *Does the problem or opportunity centrally involve employee motivation, satisfaction, or work effectiveness?*
If the issues are irrelevant to these matters, work redesign is unlikely to help. If JDS data are available, check scores for internal work motivation, growth satisfaction, and general satisfaction.

3. *Might the design of the work be responsible for observed problems?*
There are many possible reasons for suboptimal performance effectiveness, motivation, and satisfaction. Is there reason to believe that the design of the work might be casual in this instance? Check the MPS score for the job.

4. *What aspects of the job most need improvement?*
If the work is not motivationally well-structured, what specific aspects of the jobs are most troublesome, and therefore deserving of special attention in any job changes?

B. *Determining the Feasibility of Work Redesign*

5. *How ready are the employees for change?*
Check the level of employee knowledge and skill, growth need strength, and context satisfaction. If one or more of these factors is low, the decision might be to proceed with work redesign very cautiously—if at all.

6. *How hospitable are intact organizational systems to needed changes?*
Sometimes work redesign is called for, but simply cannot be done because of immutable organizational constraints. Give particular attention to the technological system, to the personnel system, and to the control system.

Careful attention to the six diagnostic questions summarized here often lead to a decision *not* to proceed with work redesign (or to delay changes until other features of the organization can be altered to create a more receptive climate for changes in the work itself). This conservatism is well-warranted, given the number of work-redesign "failures" that occur because the work system was not a realistic candidate for change in the first place.

Step 2: 10 Minutes

Allow the class to interview the person who holds (or held, or knows) the target job, so that everyone understands the job activities.

Before you proceed, make sure the group is in agreement on the activities performed by a person holding this job. *Check to see if anyone has any questions about the job.*

Step 3: 20 Minutes

Form groups of three to seven people. *Brainstorm* as many possible changes in the job as your group can think of.

RULES FOR BRAINSTORMING

1. Write down all ideas that are produced.
2. Praise one another's ideas, help one another develop ideas, and add to others' ideas wherever possible.
3. Do *not* evaluate or criticize anyone's ideas. We all have a strong tendency to do this, but fight it. The creative process is a fragile one; don't be critical!

After you have finished brainstorming, then you can be critical. Go back over your brainstormed list and remove changes that (a) will not affect the core job characteristics in the model, (b) are technologically impossible or obviously cost-ineffective, or (c) are very abstract and general. Then pick a spokesperson to report your recommended changes to the rest of the class.

Step 4: 10 Minutes

Each group's representative will read off that group's list of recommended changes. (To save time, each group's list could be written on the board or on sheets of newsprint, and the class could spend a few minutes walking around and looking at each group's ideas.)

Step 5: Job Incumbent's Reactions, 5 Minutes

Ask the person who holds (or held, or knows) this job to comment on these redesign ideas. How realistic are they? What impact would they have? Have they ever been tried?

DISCUSSION QUESTIONS

1. What areas of agreement are found in most of the group's recommendations? Areas of disagreement?
2. Which recommendations would have the *strongest* impact on employee satisfaction and performance? The most *immediate* impact? Which would be the *least costly* or *least difficult* to implement?
3. Would there be any resistance to these changes? If so, from whom? How would you deal with it?

GENERALIZATIONS AND CONCLUSIONS

Concluding Points

1. Which of the core job dimensions seem easiest to change?

Copyright © 1982, John Wiley and Sons, Inc.

2. What may be the initial reactions of employees and supervisors to job enrichment?

3. What type of employee would be most likely to perform better in an enriched job?

Participant's Reactions

READINGS AND REFERENCES

Fein, M., "Job Enrichment: A Reevaluation," *Sloan Management Review*, Winter (1974), 69-88.

Hackman, J. R., "The Design of Self-Managing Work Groups," In B. King, S. Streufert, and F. E. Fiedler (Eds.), *Managerial Control and Organizational Democracy* (Washington, D.C.: Winston, 1978).

Hackman, J. R., and Oldham, G. R., "Development of the Job Diagnostic Survey," *Journal of Applied Psychology*, 60 (1975), 159-170.

Hackman, J. R., and Oldham, G. R., *Work Redesign* (Reading, Mass.: Addison-Wesley, 1980).

Herzberg, F., "One More Time: How Do You Motivate Employees?" *Harvard Business Review*, January-February (1968), 53-62.

Herzberg, F., *The Managerial Choice* (Homewood, Ill.: Dow Jones-Irwin, 1976).

Walton, R.E., "The Diffusion of New Work Structures: Explaining Why Success Didn't Take," *Organizational Dynamics*, Winter (1975), 3-22.

10
DEVELOPING EFFECTIVE
MANAGERS: PERFORMANCE APPRAISAL

PURPOSE:
(1) To practice skills in performance appraisal and supervision of subordinates.
(2) To develop skills in communication and problem solving.

ADVANCE PREPARATION:
Read the "Introduction," below.

GROUP SIZE: Any size.
TIME REQUIRED: 40 to 60 minutes.
SPECIAL MATERIALS: None.
SPECIAL PHYSICAL REQUIREMENTS: None.
RELATED TOPICS: Managers as leaders, Group decision making and problem solving, Power, Interpersonal communication, Organizational communication, Life, work, and career roles.

INTRODUCTION

Any kind of system, whether it be a person, organization, or a spacecraft, needs feedback from its environment to tell how close it is to being "on target" in achieving its objectives. One of the most important and useful sources of feedback to an employee is his supervisor. However, in the day-to-day course of our work experiences, we usually obtain little direct feedback on our performance from our supervisors—and we give an equal amount to our own subordinates.

One of the most common mechanisms for feedback between supervisors and subordinates is the *performance appraisal* discussion. In many organizations this is a formal process in which the supervisor fills out a standard form describing the employee's work, they discuss it, and the employee signs it. Then it is sent to higher-level managers, and is finally placed in the employee's personnel file.

Senior managers in most organizations will describe their performance appraisal system in detail, stressing the requirements, such as the employee's signature, that ensure that the appraisal will, in fact, be conducted. However, when employees are asked about their performance appraisals, the response is often a blank stare. Many employees do not even know what a performance appraisal is. Others report that it is conducted in a cursory manner; many seem to be "conducted" in brief encounters in the hallway or by the coffee pot. Thus, there is a

Developed by Donald D. Bowen, inspired by a class demonstration used by Chris Argyris (who initially denied any memory of the exercise, whatsoever). This exercise is, therefore, dedicated to Chris Argyris, who has inspired all of us more than he knows (or at least more than he will admit). (Upon further reflection, however, his memory improved!) Adapted by Douglas T. Hall.

Copyright © 1982, John Wiley and Sons, Inc.

mysterious process whereby the performance appraisal is there when we talk to senior managers, but gone when we talk to employees. For this reason, the process has been dubbed the "vanishing performance appraisal" (Hall, 1976).

One of the reasons that performance appraisals disappear is that supervisors feel uncomfortable giving feedback in a one-to-one encounter. One reason they feel uncomfortable about it is that they have never developed the neccessary skills. The purpose of this exercise is for you to begin to develop performance appraisal skills.

First, let us consider two different approaches to performance appraisal. Let us say you agree with Douglas McGregor (1967) on the following seven propositions:

Human Growth Potential

1. People are capable of growing in a social climate that permits and encourages growth.
2. People tend to grow when they can achieve their own goals by achieving those of the organization.

The Role of Communication and Feedback

3. Feedback is necessary for the survival and growth of any system.
4. Effective problem solving requires open exchange of information.
5. Transactional management (where power is shared) facilitates communication.

Effective Versus Ineffective Communication

6. People tend to become defensive when threatened; that is, hostile, protective behavior, overt compliance, and selective or distorted perception result.
7. People will use information if they find it helpful in achieving their goals.

What then, are the implications of these propositions for performance appraisal and the supervision of subordinates?

One important implication is that a *problem-solving approach* to performance appraisal is probably going to get more results than the *tell-and-sell* method. These two approaches are identified by Maier (1958), who describes the objectives, assumptions, employee reactions, and supervisor skills associated with each method.

The tell- and-sell method, which is the more commonly applied of the two, has two objectives: (1) to communicate evaluation, and (2) to persuade the employee to improve. It is based upon four assumptions: (1) the employee desires to correct weaknesses if he or she knows them, (2) any person can improve if she or he so chooses, (3) a superior is qualified to evaluate a subordinate, and (4) people profit from criticism and appreciate help.

The skills required on the part of the supervisor are salesmanship and patience. The employee usually reacts in three ways: (1) suppressed defensive behavior, (2) attempts to cover hostility, and (3) little change in performance.

The objective of the problem-solving method is to stimulate growth and development in the employee. It is based upon three assumptions: (1) growth can occur without correcting faults, (2) discussing job problems leads to improved performance and (3) discussion develops new ideas and mutual interests.

The skills required of the supervisor are: (1) listening and reflecting feelings, (2) reflecting ideas, (3) using exploratory questions, and (4) summarizing. The reaction is often problem-solving behavior and employee commitment to the changes or objectives discussed (because they are *his* or *her* ideas).

PROCEDURE

Two sets of roles are available for this exercise. One set (J. J. Stein and T. T. Burns) is for a partner and an audit manager, respectively, in a public accounting firm. The other set (D. P. Jones and C. J. Marshall) is for the president and production manager, respectively, of a manufacturing company.

Both sets of roles and a set of instructions for observers are in the Appendix at the end of this volume. Appendix Table of Contents is on pages 418 and 419.

Step 1: 5 Minutes

The group leader will indicate which set of roles is to be used in this exercise. The class will be divided into groups of three people each. One person will play the role of the superior (D. P. Jones or J. J. Stein), one will be the subordinate (C. J. Marshall or T. T. Burns), and one will be an observer.

Read *only* the role description you have chosen or been assigned. Observers will read the "Instructions for Observers," as well as the role descriptions for both the superior and the subordinate.

Step 2: 20 Minutes

The superior conducts the appraisal interview with the subordinate. The observer is silent and takes notes on the process of the interviewer, using the "General Instructions" as a guide. At the conclusion of the interview, the observer gives feedback to the two participants. See page 427 of the Appendix.

Step 3: 15 Minutes

Discussion.

DISCUSSION QUESTIONS

1. *To observers*: Describe an interview that went very well. How did it start? Was there a "critical point" that turned things around? Describe an interview that did not work out well. What were the critical points here?
2. What evidence did you see of the tell-and-sell method? Of the problem-solving method?
3. How was the subordinate reacting to the method(s) that the boss used?
4. What could each person have done differently to help the discussion?

Copyright © 1982, John Wiley and Sons, Inc.

GENERALIZATIONS AND CONCLUSIONS

Concluding Points

1. Which method of performance appraisal is most likely to occur? Why?

2. What steps can the supervisor take to encourage a problem-solving discussion?

Participant's Reactions

READINGS AND REFERENCES

Hall, D. T. *Careers in Organizations* (Santa Monica, Calif.: Goodyear, 1976).

Levinson, H., "Management by Whose Objectives?" *Harvard Business Review*, July-Aug. (1970).

McGregor, D., *The Professional Manager* (New York: McGraw-Hill, 1967).

————, "An Uneasy Look at Performance Appraisal," *Harvard Business Review*, Sept.-Oct. (1972).

Maier, N. R. F., *The Appraisal Interview* (New York: Wiley, 1958).

Meyer, H. H., Kay, E., and French, J. R. P., Jr., "Split Roles in Performance Appraisal," *Harvard Business Review*, Jan.-Feb. (1965).

Oberg, W., "Make Performance Appraisal Relevant," *Harvard Business Review*, Jan-Feb. (1972).

11
PERFORMANCE APPRAISAL IN CLASS: THE SHOE IS ON THE OTHER FOOT

PURPOSE:
(1) To practice skills in performance appraisal.
(2) To observe critically an actual performance appraisal session.
(3) To collect data on students' likes and dislikes.
(4) To establish student-teacher goals or informal contracting.

ADVANCE PREPARATION:
None.

GROUP SIZE: Any size.
TIME REQUIRED: 1 hour (add an additional 30 minutes for Option two).
SPECIAL MATERIALS: Blackboard or newsprint.
SPECIAL PHYSICAL REQUIREMENTS: None.
RELATED TOPICS: Group decision making and problem solving, Interpersonal communication, Planned change.

INTRODUCTION

Performance appraisal is a dual-outcome process. It is an opportunity for subordinates to receive feedback on the quality of their performance, and an opportunity for organizations to receive feedback on their success. The latter is a result of reviewing and evaluating the performance of organizational members; this, in turn, generates information upon which many organizational decisions are made. Performance appraisal is a critical process—one that influences the efforts of subordinates, and one that helps organizations to assess the success of selection decisions, evaluate their training programs, and reward decisions.

Performance appraisal is also an activity required of most superiors, one that is critical to the quality of senior-subordinate relations. However, in spite of its importance, few people ever get the opportunity to observe or participate in an actual performance appraisal session before having to "go for record." This exercise will afford you with such an opportunity. As an additional benefit, this exercise may also lead to an expanded dialogue between students and instructors on how to improve on that which takes place in class.

Developed and written by Eugene S. Andrews, Ph. D. Used by permission of the author. An alternative approach to this exercise can be found in E. Owens, "Upward Appraisal: An Exercise in Subordinates' Critique of Superior's Performance," *Exchange, The Organizational Behavior Teaching Journal*, 3, No. 1 (1978).

Copyright © 1982, John Wiley and Sons, Inc.

OPTION ONE

PROCEDURE

Step 1: 10 Minutes
Review Maier's (1958) three approaches to performance appraisal (Tell and Sell, Tell and Listen, Problem Solving).

Step 2: 5 Minutes
Inform the class that they will be conducting an appraisal of their instructor's performance in terms of the following:

1. teaching style.
2. classroom environment.
3. homework assignments.
4. evaluation scheme.
5. student-teacher relations.

Instruct the students to select from among themselves one who will serve as the teacher's supervisor and conduct the performance appraisal interview. The designated "supervisor" then leads the group in a discussion of the five items cited above in order to generate the information needed to conduct the performance appraisal interview. The students are also told that they may rearrange the classroom facilities in order to properly conduct the interview.

In large classes, select a group of no more than five to eight to participate in the exercise while the others observe.

Step 3: 15 Minutes
The instructor leaves the classroom while the students work on Step 2.

Step 4: 10 Minutes
The instructor returns to the classroom, and the designated "supervisor" conducts the performance appraisal interview, while the rest of the group observes and records the behaviors both of the teacher and the designated supervisor.

Step 5: 20 Minutes
Process the interview in the following order:

1. The instructor shares with the group what he or she was feeling during the interview.
2. The designated supervisor reports what he or she was feeling during the interview and justifies the performance appraisal approach used.
3. The group reports on its observations.

Time permitting, repeat Steps 4 and 5 with a second designated supervisor.

OPTION TWO

Step 1: 1 hour
Complete Option one to its conclusion.

Step 2: 5 Minutes
Solicit and record students' expectations of the instructor on a blackboard or newsprint.

Step 3: 5 Minutes
The instructor presents and records his or her expectation of students.

Step 4: 20 Minutes
Negotiate an informal contract by discussing the reasonableness of both sets of expectations, determining which are mutually supportive, and agreeing to meet each other's expectations.

GENERALIZATIONS AND CONCLUSIONS

Concluding Points
1. Based upon this exercise, how do you think supervisors feel during a perform-ance appraisal discussion?

2. How do subordinates often feel?

Copyright © 1982, John Wiley and Sons, Inc.

3. What would you conclude are the most important things that a manager can do or say to conduct a successful performance appraisal?

Participant's Reactions

12
REDESIGNING ASSEMBLY-LINE JOBS: HOVEY AND BEARD COMPANY

PURPOSE:
(1) To evaluate a case of job redesign.
(2) To illustrate the systemwide, unanticipated consequences of planned change.

ADVANCE PREPARATION:
(1) For Option one: None.
(2) For Option two: Read Parts I and II of the Hovey and Beard Company case.
(3) For Option three: Read Parts I, II, and III of the Hovey and Beard Company case.

GROUP SIZE: Any size, split into subgroups of five to seven.
TIME REQUIRED: 50 to 105 minutes, depending upon option used. *Option one:* 105 minutes; *Option two:* 85 minutes; *Option three:* 50 minutes.
SPECIAL MATERIALS: None.
SPECIAL PHYSICAL REQUIREMENTS: Enough room for subgroup meetings.
RELATED TOPICS: Planned change, Power, Organizations, Motivation: Basic concepts.

INTRODUCTION

Much of the literature on planned change and job redesign describes the advantages of *participation* by employees in the change and job redesign process. Participation can increase the quality of the change, and the employees' acceptance of the change, although it can also increase the time required to plan and implement the change. On the other hand, there can be some unanticipated consequences of participation that are not always positive. Under what conditions is participation most effective?

PROCEDURE

OPTION ONE: START HERE

Step 1: 10 Minutes

Meet in groups of five to seven people. Read Part I of the Hovey and Beard Company case, below. Come to a group decision on the question at the end of Part I.

Adapted by D. T. Hall from "Group Dynamics and Intergroup Relations" by George Strauss and Alex Bavelas (under the title "The Hovey and Beard Case") from *Money and Motivation*, edited by William F. Whyte. Copyright © 1955 by Harper & Row, Publishers, Inc. Reprinted by permission of the publisher.

Copyright © 1982, John Wiley and Sons, Inc.

THE HOVEY AND BEARD COMPANY CASE[1]
PART I

The Hovey and Beard Company manufactured wooden toys of various kinds: wooden animals, pull toys, and the like. One part of the manufacturing process involved spraying paint on the partially assembled toys. This operation was staffed entirely by women.

The toys were cut, sanded, and partially assembled in the wood room. Then they were dipped into shellac, following which they were painted. The toys were predominantly two-colored; a few were made in more than two colors. Each color required an additional trip through the paint room.

For a number of years, production of these toys had been entirely handwork. However, to meet tremendously increased demand, the painting operation had recently been re-engineered so that the eight operators (all women) who did the painting sat in a line by an endless chain of hooks. These hooks were in continuous motion, past the line of operators and into a long horizontal oven. Each woman sat at her own painting booth so designed as to carry away fumes and to backstop excess paint. The operator would take a toy from the tray beside her, position it in a jig inside the painting cubicle, spray on the color according to a pattern, then release the toy and hang it on the hook passing by. The rate at which the hooks moved had been calculated by the engineers so that each woman, when fully trained, would be able to hang a painted toy on each hook before it passed beyond her reach.

The operators working in the paint room were on a group bonus plan. Since the operation was new to them, they were receiving a learning bonus that decreased by regular amounts each month. The learning bonus was scheduled to vanish in six months, by which time it was expected that they would be on their own—that is, able to meet the standard and to earn a group bonus when they exceeded it.

Discuss: What do you expect to happen over the next few months: Will production go up, down, or stay the same?

Step 2: 5 Minutes

Meet briefly as a total class group. Make a tally of how many groups think production will go up, how many think it will go down, and how many think it will stay the same.

Step 3: 5 Minutes

Now read Part II of the case. (Part II can be found in the Appendix at the end of this volume.)

OPTION TWO: START HERE

Make sure you have read Parts I and II of the case.

---

[1] From Chapter 10 of *Money and Motivation* (New York: Harper & Row, 1955). The chapter was written by two coauthors of the book, Alex Bavelas and George Strauss, and was based on Dr. Bavelas's experience as a consultant. Reproduced by permission.

Step 4: 15 Minutes

Meet in subgroups. Discuss the question at the end of Part II.

Step 5: 15 Minutes

Meet as a total class group. Each group then reports its recommendations. If there is time, briefly discuss the pros and cons of each recommendation.

Step 6: 5 Minutes

Now read part III of the case. (Part III can be found in the Appendix.)

OPTION THREE: START HERE

Make sure you have read Parts I, II, and III of the case.

Step 7: 15 Minutes

Meet again in subgroups. Discuss the question at the end of Part III.

Step 8: 5 Minutes

Meet briefly as a total class group. The group leader will count how many groups think production will go up, down, or stay the same. Make another tally for how many groups think satisfaction will go up, down, or stay the same.

Step 9: 10 Minutes

Meet in subgroups. Read Part IV (in the Appendix). Discuss the question at the end of Part IV.

Step 10: 10 Minutes

Meet as a total class group. In a general discussion, get brief predictions from each group on the question at the end of Part IV.

At this point, the group leader will read Part V to the group.

Step 11: 10 Minutes

Discuss the conclusions that can be drawn from this case.

DISCUSSION QUESTIONS

See discussion questions at the ends of Parts I through IV of the case.

GENERALIZATIONS AND CONCLUSIONS

Concluding Points

1. What often happens to motivation and satisfaction when employees participate in redesigning their own jobs?

Copyright © 1982, John Wiley and Sons, Inc.

2. What happens to production when employees participate in redesigning their own jobs?

3. What unintended consequences may occur when new procedures are introduced in one subsystem (e.g., work group or department) of a larger system (e.g., plant, organization)?

Participant's Reactions

READINGS AND REFERENCES

Bavelas, A., and Strauss, G., "Group Dynamics and Intergroup Relations." In Whyte, W.F., et al. (Eds.), *Money and Motivation* (New York: Harper & Row, 1955), pp. 90–96.

13
MOTIVATION THROUGH COMPENSATION

PURPOSE:
(1) To provide practice in making salary decisions.
(2) To evaluate and weigh different sources of information about employee performance.
(3) To develop skills in applying motivation theory to compensation decisions.

ADVANCE PREPARATION:
Do Step 1.

GROUP SIZE: Any size group.
TIME REQUIRED: 35 Minutes.
SPECIAL MATERIALS: None.
SPECIAL PHYSICAL REQUIREMENTS: None.
RELATED TOPICS: Managers as leaders, Organizational communication, Organizational Structure and Design, Life, work, and career roles.

INTRODUCTION

For most people, their annual pay raise may be the most concrete information they have on how the organization evaluates their performance. Therefore, whether you as a manager intend it or not, the pay raise will be seen by the employee as either a reward or a punishment for last year's work performance. In Skinnerian terms, with the pay raise, you are either positively or negatively reinforcing last year's performance. Therefore, the pay raise can be either motivating or demotivating, depending upon how the employee views the connection between good performance and financial rewards. Issues of equity, expectancy, psychological needs, and social comparison are also involved in people's reactions to pay decisions.

PROCEDURE

Step 1: 20 Minutes
Read the instructions on the "Employee Profile Sheet," below, and then decide on a percentage pay increase for each of the eight employees.

EMPLOYEE PROFILE SHEET

You have to make salary increase recommendations for eight managers that you supervise. They have just completed their first year with the company and are now to be considered for their first annual raise. Keep in mind that you may be setting

Originally developed by Edward E. Lawler III. Adapted by D. T. Hall. Used by permission.

Copyright © 1982, John Wiley and Sons, Inc.

precedents and that you need to keep salary costs down. However, there are no formal company restrictions on the kind of raises you can give. Indicate the size of the raise that you would like to give each manager by writing a dollar amount next to their names. You have a total of $17,000 available in your salary budget to use for pay raises.

$_____A. J. Adams. Adams is not, as far as you can tell, a good performer. You have checked your view with others, and they do not feel that Adams is effective either. However, you happen to know Adams has one of the toughest work groups to manage. Adams's subordinates have low skill levels, and the work is dirty and hard. If you lose Adams, you are not sure whom you could find as a replacement. *Salary: $20,000.*

$_____B. K. Berger. Berger is single and seems to live the life of a carefree swinger. In general, you feel that Berger's job performance is not up to par, and some of Berger's "goofs" are well known to the other employees. *Salary: $22,500.*

$_____C. C. Carter. You consider Carter to be one of your best subordinates. However, it is quite apparent that other people don't agree. Carter has married into wealth, and, as far as you know, doesn't need additional money. *Salary: $24,600.*

$_____D. Davis. You happen to know from your personal relationship that Davis badly needs more money because of certain personal problems. As far as you are concerned, Davis also happens to be one of the best of your subordinates. For some reason, your enthusiasm is not shared by your other subordinates, and you have heard them make joking remarks about Davis's performance. *Salary: $22,700.*

$_____E. J. Ellis. Ellis has been very successful so far. You are particularly impressed by this, since it is a hard job. Ellis needs money more than many of the other people and is respected for good performance. *Salary: $23,500.*

$_____F. M. Foster. Foster has turned out to be a very pleasant surprise to you, has done an excellent job, and is seen by peers as one of the best people in your group. This surprises you because Foster is generally frivolous and doesn't seem to care very much about money and promotion. *Salary: $21,800.*

$_____G. K. Gomez. Your opinion is that Gomez just isn't cutting the mustard. Surprisingly enough, however, when you check with others to see how they feel about Gomez, you discover that Gomez is very highly regarded. You also know that Gomez badly needs a raise. Gomez was just recently divorced and is finding it extremely difficult to support a house and a young family of four as a single parent. *Salary: $20,500.*

$_____H. A. Hunt. You know Hunt personally. This employee seems to squander money continually. Hunt has a fairly easy job assignment, and your own view is that Hunt doesn't do it particularly well. You are, therefore, quite surprised to find that several of the other new managers think that Hunt is the best of the new group. *Salary: $21,000.*

Step 2: 10 Minutes

When everyone has completed the task (or when almost everyone is finished), one person posts on the board the raises he or she has decided upon. Then this person will explain the criteria for these choices.

Step 3: 10 Minutes
Then someone who has a quite *different* pattern of raises posts them, and explains the criteria for his choices.

Step 4: 15 Minutes
Briefly discuss the differences between the two sets of pay raises. Identify particular employees for whom there was strong disagreement. See what the other class members think the raises should be for these employees.

DISCUSSION QUESTIONS
1. What were the factors that affected your pay raise decisions?
2. What are the *reasons* for basing pay raises on each of these factors?
3. What are the *behavioral effects* of basing pay on each of these factors?

GENERALIZATIONS AND CONCLUSIONS

Concluding Points
1. For a pay plan to be effective, you need clear links (as perceived by employees) between employee behavior (effort, achievement) and what?

2. In view of concluding point 1 above, good performance appraisal and feedback become essential to the success of a pay plan. What conditions does a good performance appraisal system require?

Copyright © 1982, John Wiley and Sons, Inc.

3. These points suggest that an organization can use pay as a motivator, but it may not be worth the cost. What are some of the problems associated with using pay as a motivator?

Participant's Reactions

READINGS AND REFERENCES

Hammer, W.C. "How to Ruin Motivation with Pay," *Compensation Review* (1975).
Lawler III, E.E., "The Mythology of Management Compensation," *California Management Review* (1966), 11-22.
————— *Pay and Organizational Effectiveness* (New York: McGraw-Hill, 1971).

14
APPLIED MOTIVATION: TWO PROBLEMS

PURPOSE:
(1) To apply motivation concepts to a real management problem.
(2) To compare the effectiveness and efficiency of different approaches to motivation.

ADVANCE PREPARATION:
None.

GROUP SIZE: Any size.
TIME REQUIRED: 45 Minutes
SPECIAL MATERIALS: None.
SPECIAL PHYSICAL REQUIREMENTS: None.
RELATED TOPICS: Planned change, Managers as leaders, Group decision making and problem solving, Organizational communication.

INTRODUCTION

Different motivation theorists stress different aspects of the work performance process. And they may all be right to a certain degree, just as were the three blind men who described an elephant, one feeling the trunk, one the side, and the last the ear. Each came up with a quite different description, and each was right for the part of the beast that he felt.

Some of the major motivation theorists and their foci are as follows.

Vroom (Expectancy Theory)

Motivation is a function of (a) the expectancy that good performance will lead to certain outcomes (rewards and punishments), multiplied by (b) the valence of these outcomes to the person; that is,

$$m = f (\Sigma E \times V)$$

Maslow (Need Theory)

People are motivated to satisfy needs in a hierarchical order, such that as the lower-order needs become satisfied, the higher-order needs become more important. In order, the needs are:

Self-actualization (highest).
Ego.
Affiliation.
Safety.
Physiological (lowest).

Copyright © 1982, John Wiley and Sons, Inc.

Adams (Equity Theory)

People are motivated to achieve an equitable balance between their inputs or contributions (effort, ideas, loyalty, etc.) and their outputs or rewards (pay, promotions, etc.), in comparison to the inputs and outputs of other people. If their rewards are too low in relation to their inputs, people might be motivated to attempt to obtain more rewards or to reduce their inputs (e.g., stop working so hard).

Skinner (Reinforcement Theory)

Behavior is a function of its consequences (i.e., the rewards and punishments that result). Performance is most likely to improve when:

1. The person gets positive feedback on his performance.
2. The person receives praise and other positive reinforcement for good performance, rather than punishment for poor work.
3. Reinforcement is given at variable intervals after good performance, not after every good performance.

Herzberg (Motivator/Hygiene Theory)

Motivators in the job can increase satisfaction and performance, but their absence will not necessarily cause dissatisfaction. Hygiene factors can cause dissatisfaction if they are missing, but they cannot cause satisfaction or motivation if they are present. *Motivators* are achievement, recognition, interest in the task itself, responsibility, and growth. *Hygienes* are company policies and administration, supervision, working conditions, interpersonal relations, salary, status, and security.

Classical Theory

People are rational-economic decision makers, primarily oriented toward financial rewards (pay). If a person sees a connection between working hard and making money, he will work hard.

PROCEDURE

Step 1: 5 Minutes

Review the approaches to motivation given above, or other theories that you have covered to date in your course or program.

Step 2: 25 Minutes

Split up into groups of five or six. Half the groups will work on Problem A below, and half on Problem B. Assume you are acting as management consultants to the plant manager. Consider first how you would *diagnose* the problem in terms of the motivation theory you have covered. In other words, what seems to be the cause of the problem? Take about 10 minutes to diagnose the problem.

Next, develop a *solution* to the problem based upon one or more motivation theories. State (1) what theory (theories) you are using, and (2) how you will apply this theory to solve this management problem.

PROBLEM A

You are (high-paid) consultants to the manager of the shipping plant of a large air-freight company. Your drivers pick up freight shipments from customers and deliver them to your facility, where the appropriate paperwork is processed, and the packages are sent on conveyers to cargo loading docks, where they are routed for the appropriate flights. Each dock handles shipments for a particular destination. Because of the ease of handling, small shipments intended for the same destination fly at lower rates when shipped together in large, standard-sized boxes, called "bulk cargo containers," rather than separately as many small packages. Thus, the air-freight company can reduce its freight costs considerably simply by making more use of bulk cargo containers on the loading docks.

Managers responsible for the shipping dock were under the impression that bulk containers already were being used most of the time. A study showed, however, that bulk containers are being used for only 45 percent of all possible such shipments.

The employees on the shipping dock seem indifferent about whether they use bulk containers or not. The amount of time and effort they have to expend is the same for either method. Relations between them and their supervisors are good.

Problem

How can the usage of bulk containers for small shipments be increased?

PROBLEM B

You are consultants to the district traffic manager of a telephone company. The traffic department is responsible for information service, long distance calls, and certain customer inquiries. Most of your employees are operators, both directory assistance (information) and long distance. About 85 percent are women, and most are in their late teens and early twenties.

Tardiness and absenteeism have been big problems in this district. As a result, the traffic manager has had to schedule 20 percent more operators than she needs for each shift, in order to have fully staffed boards. The personnel costs caused by this overstaffing are unbearable. Remedial action must be taken. If each operator would just show up for work each day, at the appointed time, personnel costs would drop back to their budgeted level.

Problem

Develop a plan that will motivate operators to come to work each day and to come on time.

Copyright © 1982, John Wiley and Sons, Inc.

Step 3: 15 Minutes

Return to the total class group. A spokesperson from each group will describe their problem solution to the rest of the class. Compare the effectiveness and efficiency of the different approaches.

These two problems were real problems faced by two large companies. The group leader will tell you how these companies actually solved the problems. Compare their solutions with yours.

DISCUSSION QUESTIONS

1. Which solution seems most likely to be successful?
2. Which solution seems easiest and least expensive to implement?
3. Which solution will generate the least employee resistance to change?
4. How do these solutions compare to yours in terms of effectiveness, ease and cost of implementation, and resistance to change? What other benefits and problems do you see in the actual solutions?

GENERALIZATIONS AND CONCLUSIONS

Concluding Points

1. There is a wide range of approaches that can be taken to solve a problem. The method used to solve a problem, and the success of your solution, depend greatly upon what?

2. In attempting to apply motivation theory, our solutions often get unnecessarily complex and manipulative. We often try to change attitudes, hoping that they will lead to changes in behavior. What are two problems with trying to improve performance by changing attitudes? (But see concluding point 3, below.)

3. Suppose you are faced with a situation where change is required and attitudes are very negative (alienation, mistrust, dissatisfaction, etc.). What might be the most helpful theoretical perspectives in the following cases?

  a. If boredom and monotony on the job are a problem, use what?

  b. If interpersonal relationships and conflict are a problem, use what?

  c. If people are experiencing role ambiguity, or if they are misperceiving the reward system, use what?

Copyright © 1982, John Wiley and Sons, Inc.

Participant's Reactions

READINGS AND REFERENCES

Herzberg, F., "One More Time: How Do You Motivate Employees?" *Harvard Business Review,* 46 (1968), 53-62.

Lawler III, E. E., *Motivation in Work Organizations* (Monterey, Calif.: Brooks/Cole, 1973).

Maslow, A. H., *Motivation and Personality* (New York: Harper, 1954).

In Tosi, H. L., and Hamner, W. C., *Organizational Behavior and Management: A Contingency Approach* (Chicago: St. Clair Press, 1977): Hamner, W. C., "Reinforcement Theory and Contingency Management in Organizational Setting," "At Emery Air Freight: Positive Reinforcement Boosts Performance," Nord, W. R., "Beyond the Teaching Machine: Operant Conditioning Management."

Vroom, V. H., *Work and Motivation* (New York: Wiley, 1964).

Copyright © 1982, John Wiley and Sons, Inc.

PART II

INTERPERSONAL AND GROUP RELATIONSHIPS

SECTION FOUR
INTERPERSONAL COMMUNICATION

15
INTERVIEWING TRIOS: INTERPERSONAL PROBLEM DIAGNOSIS AND RESOLUTION

PURPOSE:
(1) To provide practice in conducting an interview.
(2) To develop skills in observing interpersonal processes.
(3) To practice giving and receiving feedback.

ADVANCE PREPARATION:
(1) Read "Nondirective Interviewing" in the Folio of Resources at the back of this book.
(2) Read "Feedback: The Art of Giving and Receiving Help" in the Folio of Resources at the back of this book.

GROUP SIZE: Groups of three persons.

TIME REQUIRED: 1¼ hours plus discussion time (more if participants need lengthy introduction to concepts of feedback and nondirective interviewing).

SPECIAL MATERIALS: None.

SPECIAL PHYSICAL REQUIREMENTS: Several small rooms or a large area where each trio can conduct its interviews in reasonable privacy.

RELATED TOPICS: Icebreakers, Managers as leaders, Motivation, Basic concepts, Life, work and career roles, Negotiation and conflict.

Developed by Donald D. Bowen. Based on the "consulting trios" design.

Copyright © 1982, John Wiley and Sons, Inc.

INTRODUCTION

Managers frequently encounter situations where they need to help others solve problems—problems that cannot be solved simply by offering expert advice. Nondirective interviewing is a technique appropriate for these occasions. The nondirective interview is also extremely helpful in diagnosing organizational problems or conflicts (where each participant is likely to be operating from his own private perspective), and in interviewing prospective employees.

Nondirective interviewing is a difficult skill for most people to master, however. You should find that you get better at it as each member of your trio takes a turn and receives some feedback. A few tips may help you conduct the interview more effectively. For example:

You *must*

1. *Actively* listen.
2. Be receptive to the *feelings* the interviewee expresses.
3. *Reflect back* the feelings expressed (paraphrasing is particularly helpful here).

And you *must* not

4. Give *advice.*
5. *Probe* for information.
6. *Suggest* topics, ideas, or the like.
7. *Control* the interview (the interviewee should control it).

The interviewer's job is to create an atmosphere in which the interview*ee* can solve her own problem. Good interviewers probably do *less than 5 percent* of the talking!

This exercise will provide an opportunity for you to work on developing this difficult but useful skill.

PROCEDURE

Step 1: 5 Minutes

Participants choose two other persons with whom they can work comfortably. (If entire group does not divide evenly into groups of three, one or two groups of four can be formed; they will have two observers).

Step 2: 10 Minutes

Review the following instructions:

1. The instructor will indicate areas available to trios for their meetings.
2. Each trio is to meet by itself. Begin by having one member take the role of *interviewer,* one of the *interviewee,* and the third the role of *observer.* After the first interview, the interviewer becomes the interviewee, the observer the interviewer, and the interviewee the observer. Repeat the cycle until all persons have played each role.

Each interview is to take 15 minutes. The observer keeps time and ends the interview in exactly 15 minutes. Five minutes is then available for providing feedback to the interviewer on his interviewing technique.

The topic of the interview is to be chosen by the *interviewee*. The topic chosen should meet the following criteria:

1. It should be a problem that is very important to you right now. For example, you may decide you want to work on a problem related to your school work, your career, or a conflict that you have with someone. You may come up with an even better topic. That's okay, as long as it is an important issue for you. The interviewing approach being practiced here *only* works with important problems.
2. It should be an unresolved problem. Nondirective interviewing is not of much help if the problem is something you have pretty well worked out for yourself.

As the interviewer is interviewing the interviewee, *the observer is to take no part in the conversation.* The observer should sit to one side (but in a position with a good view of both parties) and take notes on the process of the interview. Observations may include observations of the interviewee's behavior, too, but the focus is to be on the interviewer's conduct of the interview.

Use the Interviewing Observation Form on page 91 to record your notes on the interview.

During the feedback session, the observer should check observations with both the interviewer and the interviewee to assess the accuracy of the feedback.

List behaviors that were particularly helpful or hindering to the process of the interview.

At the end of the exercise, reassemble at the location designated by the instructor.

Step 3: 60 Minutes
Conduct interviews.

DISCUSSION QUESTIONS
1. What differences in interviewing "style" did you observe within your trio?
2. Did you see any evidence during the interviews that the nondirective interviewing process helps the interviewee solve his or her problems? What occurred to lead you to this conclusion?
3. What behaviors helped or hindered the process of the interview?
4. What is your interpretation of the data collected for the questions asked? Do you see any evidence to indicate that the process of self-disclosure had a positive impact on the feelings of people for one another?
5. Did you find it hard or easy to maintain the nondirective stance as you conducted your interview? What parts were most difficult? Why are these difficult?

Copyright © 1982, John Wiley and Sons, Inc.

INTERVIEWING OBSERVATION FORM

Take notes on the interviewer's (*not* the interviewee's) behavior. The following suggestions may be helpful in deciding what to watch for.

Behaviors that facilitate the interview

Verbal behavior
1. Accepts feelings.
2. Reflects feelings.
3. Nonevaluative responses ("Uh-huh, I see," etc.).
4. Allows interviewee to end silent periods.

Non-verbal behavior
1. Eye contact (looks at interviewee without staring).
2. Posture (indicates interest, relaxation).
3. No distracting mannerisms.

Behaviors that inhibit the interview

Verbal behavior
1. Directs (gives advice, makes suggestions, etc.).
2. Cuts interviewee off.
3. Comments or questions that disrupt interviewee's train of thought.
4. Changes topic.
5. Speaks during a silence.

Nonverbal behavior
1. Eye contact (looks away from interviewee or stares at interviewee).
2. Posture (closed to or turned away from interviewee).
3. Nervous mannerisms or distracting behavior.

Copyright © 1982, John Wiley and Sons, Inc.

GENERALIZATIONS AND CONCLUSIONS

Concluding Points

1. Identify several situations in which a manager would want to use nondirective interviewing.

2. What is the most difficult problem in conducting an effective nondirective interview?

3. In what situations might a manager wish to use a more directive interviewing style?

Participant's Reactions

READINGS AND REFERENCES

Gibb, J. R., "Defensive Communication," *Journal of Communication* (1961), 141–48.

Maier, N. R. F., *Psychology in Industrial Organizations,* 4th ed. (Boston: Houghton-Mifflin, 1973), pp. 532–45.

Rogers, C.R., *Client Centered Therapy* (Boston: Houghton-Mifflin, 1951). See especially Chapter 2. "The Attitude and Orientation of the Counselor."

16
FEEDBACK

PURPOSE:
(1) To practice skills in providing and receiving feedback.
(2) To demonstrate the effect of feedback on working relationships in the group.
(3) To learn about one's own impact on other members of the group.

ADVANCE PREPARATION:
Read, and be thoroughly familiar with, Mill's article "Feedback: The Art of Giving and Receiving Help," in the Folio of Resources at the back of this book.

GROUP SIZE: For small, ongoing groups of seven or less.
TIME REQUIRED: Option one: 95 to 120 minutes; Option two: 85 to 110 minutes. Both options may be adapted to two or three shorter periods.
SPECIAL MATERIALS: None.
SPECIAL PHYSICAL REQUIREMENTS: A large room or area where small groups can spread out to hold conversations (movable chairs preferable if a classroom is used), or individual small group meeting rooms.
RELATED TOPICS: Life, work, and career roles, Group decision making and problem solving, Planned change.

INTRODUCTION

We often observe that people should be willing to accept "constructive criticism," and we usually claim that *we* are open to candid, helpful evaluation, even if *other people* are not. Secretly, however, we know that we sometimes have difficulty listening to criticism without becoming defensive. And, surprisingly, sometimes it is also difficult to accept praise and compliments without feeling uncomfortable.

If we are to become effective in working with other people, we must acquire the skills of giving and receiving *feedback*; we must know what impact we have on others, and we need to be able to tell them how we perceive them. Giving and receiving feedback without creating defensiveness and distortion is a skill that can be developed.

PROCEDURE

Step 1: 10 Minutes
Review the criteria for effective feedback described in Mill's article. Be sure that

Developed by Donald D. Bowen.

Copyright © 1982, John Wiley and Sons, Inc.

you understand the criteria. Review the "Procedure," below, and ask any questions you may have.

The instructor will indicate where each group is to meet and when the meetings are to end (at a particular time or after each member of the group has responded to a specified number of feedback questions).

OPTION ONE: FOR ONGOING GROUPS

Step 2: 60 Minutes (or More)

Sit in a circle and select one member of the group to be the first to receive feedback. Ask for volunteers, flip coins, or use any method you wish to select the first recipient of feedback. The person chosen is person A.

A asks any other person in the group to provide feedback on some aspect of A's behavior. A should ask for feedback on a specific point (see "Suggested Questions," below). The person to provide the feedback (B) is required to provide the feedback to A *as honestly and briefly as he can.*

When B has provided the feedback requested and A has asked whatever questions are necessary for clarification or verification, it becomes B's turn to ask a member of the group (A, C, or any other member) for feedback.

Continue the process for the remainder of the group meeting.

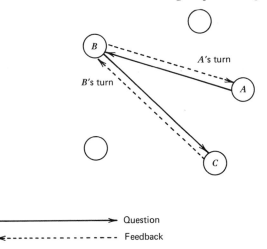

As you provide feedback to the others in your group, evaluate the feedback you, personally, provided on the set of scales, below. The first time you give some feedback, put the recipient's name and a "1" (e.g., "Joe 1") at the point on the scales that best reflects your assessment of the feedback you have just given. If you give feedback to another member next, put her name and a "1" on the scales. The second time you give feedback to a person, put the name and a "2" after it. As an example, at the end of the meeting, your first scale might look like this:

1	2	3	4	5

Descriptive
nonevaluative

Evaluative,
interpretive

SUGGESTED QUESTIONS

Sometimes it is difficult to identify a good question. If you need help, the following list may be useful. Don't restrict yourself to these questions, however.

1. What puzzles you about me?
2. Do you think I can help you learn anything in this group?
3. What changes have you seen in me since you met me?
4. What was your first impression of me?
5. What am I doing that you like most?
6. What part do you think I am playing in this group?
7. What is my greatest strength in this group?
8. How do you perceive me?
9. What kind of a relationship do you want with me?
10. What do you think I'm up to?
11. Are you angry with me about something?
12. What is my greatest weakness in the group?
13. How do you think I would assess you?
14. What am I doing that creates difficulty for you?

FEEDBACK ASSESSMENT SCALES

A.

1	2	3	4	5

Descriptive,
nonevaluative

Evaluative,
interpretive

B.

1	2	3	4	5

Specific,
concrete

General,
vague

Copyright © 1982, John Wiley and Sons, Inc.

C.

1	2	3	4	5

Expressed
my feelings

Did not express
my feelings

D.

1	2	3	4	5

Directed toward
controllable
behavior

Not directed
toward control-
lable behavior

E.

1	2	3	4	5

Verified
by others

Not verified
by others

Step 3: 10 Minutes

Share the data from your Feedback Assessment Scales with the others in the group. Do they have feedback on your feedback? Do they agree with your self-assessments? Did you get better at giving feedback as the meeting progressed? Were there particular individuals to whom you found it easier (or harder) to give feedback? Are there particular aspects of giving feedback that you need to work on?

Step 4: 10 Minutes (Optional)

Each member of the group should now write a brief "Participant's Paper" covering the following points.

1. What did I learn about myself that I did not know before from the feedback process? If the answer is "nothing," what does this imply about how the other group members feel about me or about my defenses?

2. How do I *feel* right now about what I have learned from receiving this feedback?
3. What did I learn about myself as a provider of feedback? What do I need to learn to do better?
4. What seems to have been the general impact on the group as a result of sharing the feedback? Were any problems found? Resolved? Do group members feel closer or more distant than they did before?

OPTION TWO: FOR AD HOC GROUPS

Step 2: 5 Minutes
Select two members of the group from whom you would like to receive feedback. The procedure for forming the sub-groups is simply for everyone to get up and walk around the room until they find the other two people they want to work with. In selecting your partners, you will probably want to think about who the individuals are that you feel most comfortable with and who may be able to give you the most informative feedback on your behavior.

Step 3: 55 to 65 Minutes
Proceed in Steps 2 through 4 of Option one, except that you should finish Step 2 in 45 minutes.

DISCUSSION QUESTIONS
1. Did you find giving and receiving feedback hard or easy to do? Why?
2. In what respects did your feedback seem most effective? Ineffective? How does this relate to the "criteria for useful feedback"?
3. What do you think will be the effect of this session on your group if you continue to work together in the future? Will you be more cohesive? Effective?

GENERALIZATIONS AND CONCLUSIONS

Concluding Points
1. Suggest how an exercise like "Feedback" might be used to improve organizational effectiveness.

Copyright © 1982, John Wiley and Sons, Inc.

2. Under what conditions might an exercise like "Feedback" be counterproductive in its effect on organizational effectiveness?

Participant's Reactions

READINGS AND REFERENCES

Athos, A. G., and Gabarro, J. J., *Interpersonal Behavior: Communication and Understanding in Relationships* (Englewood Cliffs, N.J.: Prentice-Hall, 1978).

Gibb, J. R., "Defensive Communication," *Journal of Communication,* 11 (1961), 141-48.

Luft, J., *Group Process: An Introduction to Group Dynamics,* 2nd ed. (Palo Alto, Calif: National Press, 1974).

McCaskey, M. B., "The Hidden Messages Managers Send," *Harvard Business Review,* Nov./Dec. (1979), 135-48.

17

ASSERTIVENESS: AUTHENTIC INTERPERSONAL COMMUNICATION

PURPOSE:

(1) To demonstrate the concept of assertive communication.

(2) To provide an assessment of participants' interpersonal styles.

(3) To guide practice of assertiveness skills.

ADVANCE PREPARATION:

Both options: Read "Toward a Viable Concept of Assertiveness," Unit 65 in the Folio of Resources. *Option one*: Complete Steps 1 through 3 before the class meeting. *Option two*: complete steps 1 through 3 of both options and Step 4 of Option two before the class meeting.

GROUP SIZE: Any size. Option two calls for subgroups of four to six participants.

TIME REQUIRED: *Both options*: 2 hours and 55 minutes; *Option one*: 50 minutes; *Option two*: 2 hours 10 minutes (or more) for option 2 (assuming subgroups of five persons each are used).

SPECIAL MATERIALS: None.

SPECIAL PHYSICAL REQUIREMENTS: Enough room for subgroup meetings in Option two.

RELATED TOPICS: Negotiation and conflict, Group decision making and problem solving, Managers as leaders, Power, Life, work and career roles.

PROCEDURE

ADVANCE PREPARATION FOR BOTH OPTIONS

Step 1: 5 Minutes

Complete the "Interpersonal Response Inventory" (IRI) page 101. (The group leader may ask you to turn in the questionnaire, but no names are required. You will be the only person who knows what your scores are, so feel free to be perfectly candid in your answers.)

Developed by Donald D. Bowen.

Copyright © 1982, John Wiley and Sons, Inc.

INTERPERSONAL RESPONSE INVENTORY

Please check one:

_____Male
_____Female

How true are the following statements as descriptions of your behavior? Enter the number that represents your answer in the space provided at the beginning of each statement.

4 = Always true   2 = Sometimes true

3 = Often true   1 = Never true

Please respond to *every* statement.

Your
response   Statement

_____ 1. I respond with more modesty than I really feel when my work is complimented.
_____ 2. If people are rude, I will be rude right back.
_____ 3. Other people find me interesting.
_____ 4. I find it difficult to speak up in a group of strangers.
_____ 5. I don't mind using sarcasm if it helps me make a point.
_____ 6. I ask for a raise when I feel I really deserve it.
_____ 7. If others interrupt me when I am talking, I suffer in silence.
_____ 8. If people criticize my work, I find a way to make them back down.
_____ 9. I can express pride in my accomplishments without being boastful.
_____10. People take advantage of me.
_____11. I tell people what they want to hear if it helps me get what I want.
_____12. I find it easy to ask for help.
_____13. I lend things to others even when I don't really want to.
_____14. I win arguments by dominating the discussion.
_____15. I can express my true feelings to someone I really care for.
_____16. When I feel angry with other people, I bottle it up rather than express it.
_____17. When I criticize someone else's work, they get mad.
_____18. I feel confident in my ability to stand up for my rights.

Step 2: 5 Minutes

When you have finished answering the IRI, score it as follows:

Pa: Sum your answers to items 1, 4, 7, 10, 13, 16, 19.

     Enter your *Pa* score here: _____

                                                  Pa (Passive)

Copyright © 1982, John Wiley and Sons, Inc.

Ag: Sum your answers to items 2, 5, 8, 11, 14, 17, 20.

Enter your *Ag* score here: _____

Ag (Aggressive)

As: Sum your answers to items 3, 6, 9, 12, 15, 18, 21.

Enter your *As* score here: _____

As (Assertive)

For each scale, you should have a score between 7 and 28.

Step 3: 10 minutes
Read "Toward a Viable Concept of Assertiveness," Unit 65 in the Folio of Resources.

OPTION ONE

Step 4: 30 Minutes
The group leader will lead a group discussion to complete Figure 1. The group is to invent passive, aggressive, and assertive responses to each situation. Since this is an exercise in distinguishing between assertive and nonassertive behaviors, be sure to understand *why* a response is either assertive or nonassertive.

Step 5: 5 Minutes
Review your answers to the IRI. Do you see why the items are scored as they are? Do they make sense to you? If you have any questions, raise them in the next step for class discussion.

Step 6: 10 Minutes
Discuss the IRI items. Are there any clues in the IRI as to what behaviors you need to work on to be more effectively assertive? (If the group leader instructs you to do both options of the exercise, go to Step 5 of Option two when this step is finished.)

Step 7: 5 Minutes
Discuss this exercise in terms of the discussion questions and concluding points, below.

OPTION TWO

Step 4: Advance Preparation for Option Two, 20 minutes
Using the format shown in Figure 2, develop two dialogues that portray situations in which you have particular difficulty being assertive.

Step 5: 5 Minutes
If you are not already working in a group, the group leader will instruct you on formation of subgroups.

FIGURE 1
Some Common Assertiveness Situations

Instructions: Develop a passive, an aggressive, and an assertive response to each of the following situations.

Situation	Passive Response	Aggressive Response	Assertive Response
1. You have just completed a task you are very proud of. Your boss compliments you on it. You say...			
2. You have just completed a task where you felt you had done a very good job. Your boss says it is totally unacceptable. You say...			
3. Your subordinate worked overtime all week to get an important report ready for you. Having read it, you realize there are serious flaws in it. You say...			
4. A colleague who constantly borrows office supplies from your department (but never pays you back), asks to borrow some supplies your own people need. You say...			
5. Your boss takes you out to lunch and makes an unmistakable "pass" at you. You like your job and would like to keep it. You say...			
6. You ask your boss for a raise you believe you deserve. You say...			

Copyright © 1982, John Wiley and Sons, Inc.

FIGURE 2

Format for Describing Difficult Assertiveness Situations[a]

Situation 1

State here what your goals are in the situation you describe. What is it you want to accomplish?

What Is Said	*What You Are Thinking But Not Saying*
(In play script form, duplicate the approximate dialogue as closely and in as much detail as you can. Indicate both what you say and what the other person(s) involved say.)	Indicate your thoughts here at various points during the dialogue.
Example:	
Me: Hello, Sue, this is Ed....	I hope she doesn't hang up.
Sue: (Impatiently) What do you want?	Oh, oh.
Me: ...	...

At the end, indicate how you feel about the interaction after it is *over*.

Prepare a second sheet in similar fashion for Situation 2.

Step 6: 10 Minutes per Person per Role Play (1 Hour and 40 Minutes for Five-Person Groups).

1. Person one shares one of her difficult assertiveness situations with the group.
2. Person two volunteers to role-play person one in a reenactment of the situation. Person two should play person one *behaving assertively* in one's situation. (If additional role players are needed, other members of the group should volunteer to play these parts.)
3. Person one role-plays *her antagonist*, or the person who represents the greatest problem for her in this situation.

Working from one's description of the situation, briefly role-play how it should go if person one were handling the situation assertively.

4. After each role play, provide feedback to each other on how you saw each other behaving.
5. Replay the scene until you feel that the group has developed an assertive solution. *NOTE:* If you are not sure whether a solution is assertive or not, compare it to the principles of assertiveness on pp. 415 to 416 of the Folio of Resources.

---

[a] The original idea for this format comes from C. Argyris and D. A. Schon, *Theory in Practice: Increasing Professional Effectiveness* (San Francisco: Jossey-Bass, 1974).

1. Person #1 shares one of her difficult assertiveness situations with the group.
2. Person #2 volunteers to role-play person #1 in a reenactment of the situation. Person #2 should play person #1 *behaving assertively* in one's situation. (If additional role players are needed, other members of the group should volunteer to play these parts.)
3. Person #1 role-plays *her antagonist*, or the person who represents the greatest problem for her in this situation.

Working from one's description of the situation, briefly role-play how it should go if person #1 were handling the situation assertively.

4. After each role play, provide feedback to each other on how you saw each other behaving.
5. Replay the scene until you feel that the group has developed an assertive solution. *NOTE*: If you are not sure whether a solution is assertive or not, compare it to the principles of assertiveness on pp. 415 to 416 of the Folio of Resources.

If person #2 is unable to discover an assertive solution, another group member should assume the role of person #1.

Work Quickly! You will need to move along very quickly to stay on schedule.

When the group has finished with one's situation, person #2 then presents one of his difficult assertiveness situations. Continue until all situations have been role-played and resolved.

Step 7: 15 Minutes

Working alone, review what you have learned in the role plays and look at your IRI scores. Did the IRI identify the types of problems you depicted in the difficult assertiveness situations? If not, does it suggest other areas where you may have problems with asssertiveness?

Write a brief "contract" for yourself covering the following.

What are the most difficult assertiveness situations for you?
What would you like to accomplish in these situations? What are your objectives?
What things can you begin to do to build your ability to be assertive in these situations? (You may need to start with some elementary behaviors and gradually build up to the tough stuff.)
Set a target date for completing your plan.

Step 8: 10 Minutes or More

Discuss this exercise in terms of the discussion questions and concluding points, below.

Copyright © 1982, John Wiley and Sons, Inc.

DISCUSSION QUESTIONS

1. Can assertiveness help you with problems like being effective in managing your time, taking off weight, or acquiring new friends? How?
2. If assertiveness means expressing yourself in such a way as to make it easier for others to do the same, what are some examples of how you might do this?
3. What happens to people who are not assertive at work? Passive people? Aggressive people? Why?

GENERALIZATIONS AND CONCLUSIONS

Concluding Points

1. Many people report that they become very anxious in situations where they know they should be assertive. What should a person do if her anxiety keeps her from being assertive in a certain type of situation?

2. Popular assertiveness training books prescribe a number of "techniques" for dealing with certain situations. Do you regard the following (from Smith, 1975) as assertive? Why?
   a. "Broken record." (When someone tries to talk you out of something, you simply repeat your position over and over again in a calm, controlled voice. For example, "I do not wish to buy any magazines today.")

b. "Fogging." (When someone criticizes you, you respond by agreeing, rather than becoming defensive or argumentative. You agree with the general principle of what they have to say, or you agree with any factual parts of their criticism. But you *don't* change your behavior. For example, *Boss*: "You'd better take it a little easy; no one can work and go to school at the same time." *Subordinate*: (Fogging) "It sure is a lot of work.")

Participant's Reactions

READINGS AND REFERENCES

See the readings listed at the end of "Toward a Viable Concept of Assertiveness" in the Folio of Resources.

Smith, M. J., *When I Say No I Feel Guilty* (New York: Dial Press, 1975).

Copyright © 1982, John Wiley and Sons, Inc.

SECTION FIVE
GROUP DECISION MAKING AND PROBLEM SOLVING

18
GROUP PROCESS OBSERVATION ANALYSIS

PURPOSE:
(1.) To provide a framework for evaluating group effectiveness.
(2.) To stimulate discussion among group members on ways to change or improve group dynamics.

ADVANCE PREPARATION:
None.

GROUP SIZE: This activity is usually done individually, either by group members or observers, in any size group.

TIME REQUIRED: 15 minutes to complete the evaluation; 30 minutes or more to share and discuss the ratings.

SPECIAL MATERIALS: None.

SPECIAL PHYSICAL REQUIREMENTS: None.

RELATED TOPICS: Interpersonal communication, Managers as leaders, Power, Organizational communication.

INTRODUCTION

The purpose of this activity is to provide a framework for evaluating the effectiveness of a group. The scales listed below have been developed to reflect a number of different dimensions of group effectiveness. They may be used to evaluate a group that you are a member of, or a group that you have been asked to observe. Once you have completed your ratings, the group leader will inform you how this information will be shared with others.

Prepared by Roy J. Lewicki.

OPTION ONE: OBSERVATION OF ANOTHER GROUP

Step 1: 15 Minutes

As you prepare to observe a group, first review the 11 different "Observational Categories" of group effectiveness in the questionnaire on page 111. Make sure you understand what *each* of these categories means. If you have questions, clarify the dimensions with the group leader or a classmate. Then actually observe the "target group" as it works on a task or problem. Make notes to yourself about each category. It is extremely important that you take as detailed notes as possible. Be *specific* about what people actually did or said to confirm your observation. *Avoid* trying to *interpret* why people might have done those things, and *avoid* evaluating whether you think those things are good or bad, healthy or unhealthy, and so on. Focus on making *descriptive, detailed observations,* rather than on making inferences or drawing conclusions.

Step 2: Actual Group Observation, Time to Be Assigned by Leader

Step 3: 5 Minutes

After you have observed the group, your group leader may also instruct you to *evaluate* the group on each of the criteria. Turn to the questionnaire on page 113. *Rate* the group on each criteria by evaluating its effectiveness on a scale of 1 to 7. Use your observations of the group as the basis for your overall rating.

Step 4: Time to Be Assigned

Your instructor will ask you to share your observations with the group that you observed. When discussing your Observational Categories, make sure that you report detailed, descriptive information for each of the categories. *Give specific examples* and *behaviors* to support the report. You may also report the *evaluations* of group effectiveness if your instructor requests this information. Again, give examples to support your evaluations.

OPTION TWO: EVALUATION OF OWN GROUP

Step 1: 10 Minutes

Turn to the questionnaire, "Rating Group Effectiveness," on page 113. Evaluate the group of which you have been a member, on each of the eleven categories. For each evaluation, you need to do two things:

1. Rate the group on the scale of 1 to 7, reflecting an evaluation between "poor" and "good" for that category.
2. Make note of specific incidents, examples, or behaviors of yourself or others that support (provide the reasons for) your evaluation.

Copyright © 1982, John Wiley and Sons, Inc.

OBSERVATIONAL CATEGORIES

Criteria	*Behaviors that I observed*

Goals
  Stated?
  Clarified?
  Shared by all?
  Interest?
  Shared commitment?

Problem Diagnosis
  Systematic diagnosis?
  Symptoms separated from causes?
  Jumping to solutions?

Decisions
  Decisions made?
  Made by one or two members or
    whole group?
  Level of commitment to solution?

Participation
  Who talks? How much?
  Participation by all or just a few?
  Who says least?

Listening
  People attentive?
  A lot of competition for "airtime"?
  People often interrupted, cut off?
  People ask for clarification or pursue
    ideas systematically?

Feelings
  Feelings expressed?
  Expression of feelings suported and
    encouraged?
  People considerate of others' feel-
    ings, empathy actively shown?

Influence
  Who influences others most? Least?
    Why?
  How many people have influence?
    When?
  Influence related to the task of the
    group?

OBSERVATIONAL CATEGORIES

Criteria	*Behaviors that I observed*

Leadership

Who is the "leader"? Appointed? Elected? "Self-chosen"?

What does leader do to control/manage the group?

Does leader overcontrol or undercontrol the group? How?

Conflict

Does conflict occur? When?

Is conflict avoided, minimized or left?Is conflict openly expressed and left unresolved?

Is conflict openly expressed and left unresolved?

How do people handle emotions (anger, difference of opinion, dislike)?

Trust

Do people trust each other?

Are people overly polite or "careful" about what they say?

Are people defensive?

Is criticism of other people or ideas avoided?

Creativity

Are people disinterested in the group and its work?

Are new ideas or approaches to problems encouraged and tried?

Is there a fixed routine or pattern of work that seems to be inhibiting the group?

Copyright © 1982, John Wiley and Sons, Inc.

RATING GROUP EFFECTIVENESS

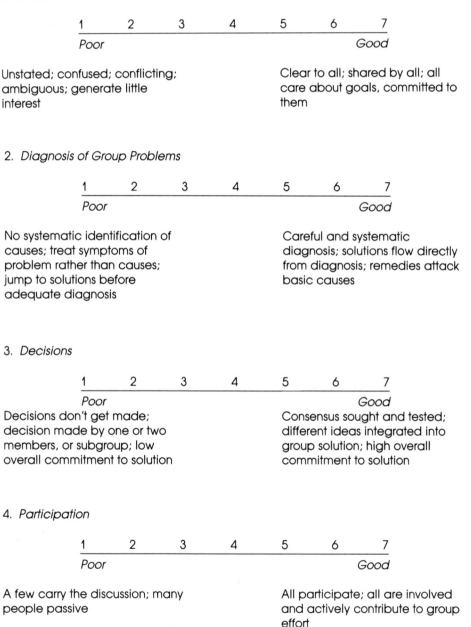

1. *Goals*

1	2	3	4	5	6	7
Poor						*Good*

Unstated; confused; conflicting; ambiguous; generate little interest

Clear to all; shared by all; all care about goals, committed to them

2. *Diagnosis of Group Problems*

1	2	3	4	5	6	7
Poor						*Good*

No systematic identification of causes; treat symptoms of problem rather than causes; jump to solutions before adequate diagnosis

Careful and systematic diagnosis; solutions flow directly from diagnosis; remedies attack basic causes

3. *Decisions*

1	2	3	4	5	6	7
Poor						*Good*

Decisions don't get made; decision made by one or two members, or subgroup; low overall commitment to solution

Consensus sought and tested; different ideas integrated into group solution; high overall commitment to solution

4. *Participation*

1	2	3	4	5	6	7
Poor						*Good*

A few carry the discussion; many people passive

All participate; all are involved and actively contribute to group effort

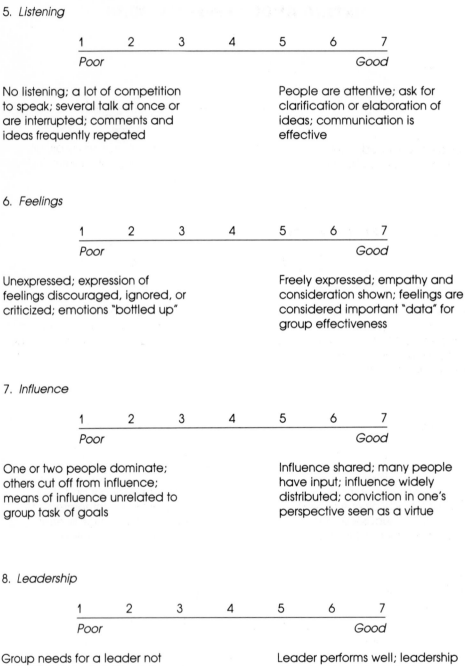

5. *Listening*

| 1 | 2 | 3 | 4 | 5 | 6 | 7 |

Poor   *Good*

No listening; a lot of competition to speak; several talk at once or are interrupted; comments and ideas frequently repeated

People are attentive; ask for clarification or elaboration of ideas; communication is effective

6. *Feelings*

| 1 | 2 | 3 | 4 | 5 | 6 | 7 |

Poor   *Good*

Unexpressed; expression of feelings discouraged, ignored, or criticized; emotions "bottled up"

Freely expressed; empathy and consideration shown; feelings are considered important "data" for group effectiveness

7. *Influence*

| 1 | 2 | 3 | 4 | 5 | 6 | 7 |

Poor   *Good*

One or two people dominate; others cut off from influence; means of influence unrelated to group task of goals

Influence shared; many people have input; influence widely distributed; conviction in one's perspective seen as a virtue

8. *Leadership*

| 1 | 2 | 3 | 4 | 5 | 6 | 7 |

Poor   *Good*

Group needs for a leader not met; either group depends too much on one or two people, or there is a leadership "vacuum"

Leader performs well; leadership role changes in group as different leadership needs become important

Copyright © 1982, John Wiley and Sons, Inc.

9. Conflict

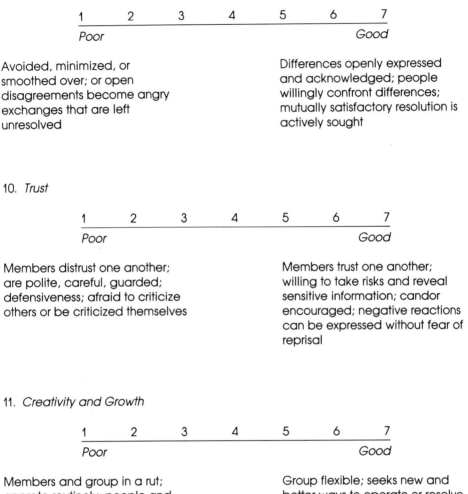

1	2	3	4	5	6	7

Poor   *Good*

Avoided, minimized, or smoothed over; or open disagreements become angry exchanges that are left unresolved

Differences openly expressed and acknowledged; people willingly confront differences; mutually satisfactory resolution is actively sought

10. Trust

1	2	3	4	5	6	7

Poor   *Good*

Members distrust one another; are polite, careful, guarded; defensiveness; afraid to criticize others or be criticized themselves

Members trust one another; willing to take risks and reveal sensitive information; candor encouraged; negative reactions can be expressed without fear of reprisal

11. Creativity and Growth

1	2	3	4	5	6	7

Poor   *Good*

Members and group in a rut; operate routinely; people and group are rigid in roles, stereotype one another; no progress, new ideas, or new approaches

Group flexible; seeks new and better ways to operate or resolve problems; innovation and experimentation encouraged; new ideas and approaches actively tried

Copyright © 1982, John Wiley and Sons, Inc.

Step 2: Time to Be Assigned

Share the evaluations with others in the group. Start with the first category (group goals) and proceed around the group, with each member sharing his or her rating. Contribute to the discussion specific incidents or examples to support your rating.

Pay attention to, but *do not criticize*, group members who have an evaluation different from yours or from the group's. Rather, make sure you know what evidence or data that member is using to support his or her evaluation.

DISCUSSION QUESTIONS

1. On what dimension was the group that you observed or rated most effective and least effective? How would you account for this?
2. Was there much variability among observers on any particular dimension? What does this tell you about group process?
3. How did the group that was evaluated react to the feedback? Was this reaction due to the evidence being presented, or the way that the information was presented by observers?
4. On what dimensions does the group need to improve the most?
5. What specific changes in behavior would lead to greater effectiveness on particular dimensions?

Participant's Reactions

READINGS AND REFERENCES

Cartwright, D., and Zander, A., *Group Dynamics*, 2nd ed. (New York: Harper and Row, 1968).

Davis, J. H., *Group Performance* (Reading, Mass.: Addison Wesley, 1969).

Dyer, W., *Team Building: Issues and Alternatives* (Reading, Mass.: Addison Wesley, 1977).

Luft, Joseph, *Group Process* (Palo Alto, Calif.: National Press, 1963).

McConnell, T., *Group Leadership for Self-Realization* (New York: Petrocelli Books, 1974).

Schein, E., *Process Consultation* (Reading, Mass.: Addison Wesley, 1969).

Smith, P. B., *Groups within Organizations* (New York: Harper and Row, 1973).

19
GROUP RANKING TASK: LOST AT SEA

PURPOSE:
(1) To develop an understanding of group problem solving.
(2) To compare individual versus group decision making.

ADVANCE PREPARATION
(1) Read the "Introduction" below.
(2) Complete Steps 1 and 2 before session. *Do not discuss this exercise with anyone.*

GROUP SIZE: Any number of five- to nine-person groups.
TIME REQUIRED: Approximately 1 1/2 hours. Allow more time for large groups.
SPECIAL MATERIALS: None.
SPECIAL PHYSICAL REQUIREMENTS: Movable chairs.
RELATED TOPICS: Interpersonal communication, Managers as leaders, Organizational communication.

INTRODUCTION

Research has shown that groups are frequently more effective than individuals in solving complex problems. This is especially true when the problem requires a quality decision. Groups may be more accurate and bring more knowledge to bear on the solution.

In this exercise you will have an opportunity to experiment and see whether this is true. In Steps 1 and 2, you will be asked to try to solve a problem by yourself. Do not discuss this problem with anyone, either in your group or outside it. Work on the problem by yourself. When you come to your next session you will have an opportunity to solve the problem with a group. What do you expect to happen? Do you think your solution will be better than your group's?

PROCEDURE

Step 1: Read "The Situation," below:
"The Situation"

You are adrift on a private yacht in the South Pacific. As a consequence of a fire of unknown origin, much of the yacht and its contents have been destroyed. The yacht is now slowly sinking. Your location is unclear because of the destruction of critical navigational equipment and because you and the crew were distracted

Adapted by Roy J. Lewicki from "Lost At Sea: A Consensus-Seeking Task" in *The 1975 Handbook for Group Facilitators.* Used with permission of University Associates, Inc.

Copyright © 1982, John Wiley and Sons, Inc.

trying to bring the fire under control. Your best estimate is that you are approximately one thousand miles south-southwest of the nearest land.

Step 2: The Problem (15 minutes)

On the next page is a list of fifteen items that are intact and undamaged after the fire. In addition to these articles, you have a serviceable, rubber life raft with oars large enough to carry yourself, the crew, and all the items listed. The total contents of all survivors' pockets are a package of cigarettes, several books of matches, and five one-dollar bills.

Your task is to rank these items in terms of their importance to you for survival. Place the number "1" by the most important item, "2" by the second most important item, and so on through the number "15", the least important. Enter your ranks in the column labeled "Individual Ranking".

You may assume that the number of people in your group are the number of people in the life raft, that you are the actual people in the situation, and that all items on the list are in good condition.

Step 3: 30 Minutes

As a team, rank the 15 items acccording to the *group's consensus* on order of importance to your survival. Do not vote; try to reach agreement on each item. Base your decision on knowledge, logic, or the experiences of group members. Try to avoid basing the decision on personal preference. Enter the group's rankings in the column on the "Scoring Sheet" labeled "Group Ranking."

Step 4: 5 Minutes

After all teams have finished, your group leader will read the ranking that the items were assigned by an expert. As these are read, please enter the "correct" rank in the "Survival Expert's" ranking column on the "Scoring Sheet."

SCORING SHEET

Items	Individual Ranking	Group Ranking	Survival Expert's Ranking	Influence	Individual Accuracy	Group Accuracy
Sextant						
Shaving Mirror						
Five-gallon can of water						
Mosquito netting						
One case of U.S. Army C rations						
Maps of the Pacific Ocean						
Seat cushion (flotation device approved by the Coast Guard)						
Two-gallon can of oil-gas mixture						
Small transistor radio						
Shark repellent						
Twenty square feet of opaque plastic						
One quart of 160-proof Puerto Rican rum						
Fifteen feet of nylon rope						
Two boxes of chocolate bars						
Fishing kit						

Your Accuracy Score: Group Accuracy Score:

Step 5: 10 Minutes

Compute the difference between your individual ranking and the group's ranking. Use the *absolute* difference—ignore plus and minus scores. Enter the difference for each item's ranking in the column on the "Scoring Sheet" labeled "Influence." Add these numbers to obtain a total of the differences.

This score might be called an "influence score." It may represent the extent that you influenced the group to "your way of thinking" about the correct way to rank the alternatives. Discuss for a few minutes in the group the people who you feel were most influential in group discussion. Then share your "influence scores," and see how they compare—the smaller the score, the more the group's score parallels the private ranking of certain individuals.

Copyright © 1982, John Wiley and Sons, Inc.

Step 6: 10 Minutes

Compute the absolute difference between your individual ranking and the expert's ranking. Again, ignore the plus or minus scores. Enter the difference for each item's ranking in the column labeled "Individual Accuracy." Again, obtain a total score. This score might best be called your "accuracy" score.

Share with your group your "accuracy" score, and compare these to the "influence" scores from Step 5. The difference between these two scores might be called the "appropriateness of influence." If you had a very *low* accuracy score and a *low* influence score, you were really "right" and the group listened to you. If your accuracy score is high but your influence is low, you might try to explore why you had so much influence in spite of not being accurate; similarly, if you were accurate but had very little influence, you might try to find out why you didn't have a bigger impact on the group.

Step 7: 5 Minutes

Compute the absolute difference between your group's rankings and the expert's rankings. Enter these in the column labeled "Group Accuracy," and compute the total.

Step 8: 5 Minutes

Compute the average of the individual accuracy scores of group members, by adding up all of the individual accuracy scores and dividing by the number of members in the group. Enter this in the space for your group's "Average Individual Score" on the "Composite Group Scoring Sheet."

COMPOSITE GROUP SCORING SHEET

			Team number			
	1	2	3	4	5	6
Average individual Score: Add up all the Individual accuracy scores in your group and divide by the number in the group						
Team Score						
Gain Score: The difference between the team score and the Average Individual Score. If the team score is lower than the Average individual Score, then gain is " + ." If team score is higher than Average Individual Score, then gain is " − ."						
Number of group members scoring better than Team Score						
Lowest Individual Score ("Best" Individual Score)						

Step 9: 2 Minutes

Compute your "gain score" on the Composite Scoring Sheet. This is the difference between the average individual accuracy score and the group accuracy score. If the score is positive (+), this means that the group's solution to the problem was better than what individuals could do by themselves without discussion. If the score is negative (−), this means that the group discussion did not make good use of the best resources among members, and that the group product was worse than what individuals, on the average, could do by themselves without discussion.

Step 10: 3 Minutes

Enter the lowest individual score in your group. This is the "best" score obtained by any individual alone. Compare this against the average individual score (Step 8) and the team accuracy score. If your group worked extremely well in sharing information and making decisions, it is likely that your team score was not only better than the average of individuals, but better than the best individual in the group. This shows that it is often possible for the group to excel even its best individual resource.

Step 11: 5 Minutes

When Steps 3 through 10 have been completed, the group leader will record the data from each group for the discussion. One member of your group should be prepared to provide these data.

Step 12: 15 Minutes

Discuss this experience as a total group with the group leader. Try to arrive at some conclusions about group problem solving and the relevance of the exercise to real-world problems in management.

DISCUSSION QUESTIONS

1. Based on the data generated in this exercise, does it appear that the groups solved the problem more accurately than individuals on the average? (Compare team scores with average individual scores for the groups.)
2. Did the groups do better than even the "best" individual?
3. Which people influenced your group the most? Was this influence based on perceived knowledge related to the solution or on other kinds of control?
4. Was the influence of various members reflected in your group's "accuracy" scores?
5. How was this task different from or similar to other tasks you have done as a group?
6. Do you think the nature of the task had any effect on how leadership needs were met in your group?
7. What were the characteristics of the decision-making process in the most accurate groups (those with the lowest team scores)?
8. What kinds of decision situations in organizations have elements in common with this exercise?

Copyright © 1982, John Wiley and Sons, Inc.

GENERALIZATIONS AND CONCLUSIONS

Concluding Points

1. Six factors to consider in managing decision making are:

   a.

   b.

   c.

   d.

   e.

   f.

2. Generally, group decision making or problem solving is more desirable and effective when:

   a.

   b.

   c.

   d.

   e.

3. Three advantages of group decision making are:
   a.

   b.

   c.

4. Four disadvantages of group decision making are:
   a.

   b.

   c.

   d.

5. The advantage of groups composed of people from different parts of the organization is what? The disadvantage is what?

Copyright © 1982, John Wiley and Sons, Inc.

Participant's Reactions

READINGS AND REFERENCES

Cartwright, D., and Zander, A., *Group Dynamics: Research and Theory* (New York: Harper & Row, 1968).

Hall, J., "Decisions, Decisions, Decisions," *Psychology Today,* 5 (1971), 55ff.

Hinton, B. L., and Reitz, H. J., *Groups and Organizations* (Belmont, Calif.: Wadsworth Publishing Co., 1971).

Janis, I. L., *Victims of Groupthink* (Boston: Houghton Mifflin, 1972).

Napier, R. W., and Gershenfeld, M. K., *Groups: Theory and Experience* (Boston: Houghton Mifflin, 1973).

20
VALUES AND GROUP DECISION MAKING: THE CITY COUNCIL

PURPOSE:
(1) To explore choices involving different value premises.
(2) To explore factors affecting group decision making.

ADVANCE PREPARATION:
None.

GROUP SIZE: Any number of small groups.
TIME: 1 hour.
SPECIAL MATERIALS: None.
SPECIAL PHYSICAL REQUIREMENTS: Movable chairs.
RELATED TOPICS: Power, Managers as leaders, Interpersonal communication, Organizational communication.

INTRODUCTION

In this exercise you will be given a decision to make that is not uncommon in public service. As a group, you will have to make a decision that will affect the entire community. Unfortunately, there is no single "right" answer. Only your group can decide what the members feel is right. As you will see, your decision will involve a question of values. In this exercise you may also discover some of the ways that conflicts arise in decision situations and how these can be minimized.

PROCEDURE

Step 1: 5 Minutes
Form small groups, situated far apart if possible.

Step 2: 5 Minutes
Read the "Problem Description," below.

PROBLEM DESCRIPTION

On March 13 the City Council of New Bristol received notification that Stanley and Sophie Kucinski had willed their property at 125 Ridge Road to the city. The letter stated that the Kucinskis had attached the following stipulation:

1. The Council must accept the donation within 3 months or forego any claim to it;
2. The Council must also decide on its use by this date;

Developed by Francine S. Hall.

Copyright © 1982, John Wiley and Sons, Inc.

3. If the Council chooses to lease, sell, or donate the property, it may do so to either a nonprofit or profit organization as long as the use "contributes to the quality of life of the community."

It is now June 12, and the Council members are meeting to make their decision. Prior to the meeting, they solicited requests and suggestions for use of the property, a 10-room brick structure located on approximately 1 acre of prime land.

The following "bids" were received:

1. The Friendship House, a United Fund agency that runs programs for minority and disadvantaged youth, has requested that the city arrange a lease/purchase agreement. New Bristol is primarily an industrial (steel) town with a growing black and Puerto Rican population. There is clearly a need for programs for the disadvantaged young people, but neighbors in the area have vocally come out against the Friendship House proposal, crying "We don't want 'them' over here."
2. Saint Stanislaus Church, whose property borders the Kucinskis' on the east, has offered to buy the property for $125,000. The Church would convert it to additional parking facilities to accommodate their growing crowds on Bingo nights. Many senior citizens support this use, since Bingo is one of few recreational outlets for them, and "safe" off-street parking is at a premium.
3. A local builder has offered to buy the property and develop it into a moderately priced retirement condominium building. This would require special building permits, but would help the tax base and also be attractive.
4. A local women's group has proposed a three-year lease to set up a Women's Center. It would provide workshops, birth control and abortion counseling (and possibly a clinic), and also serve as a refuge for battered women. According to police, wife beating has increased drastically as inflation and layoffs increase stress in this working class community. The Rector of Saint Stanislaus' Church is strongly opposed to letting the women's group have the property.
5. One of the major oil companies has submitted a bid of $300,000 for the property if the Council will grant a zoning change to allow a gas station. These funds could be used to buy sorely needed playground equipment, but the gas station would be an eyesore on Ridge Road.
6. John Lateck has offered to buy the property for $200,000 and convert it to a "private club." He has assured the Council that it would not be an "ordinary" bar. Rumors are that John is a homosexual. Parents of children at Saint Stanislaus School have besieged the Council with letters smearing John and alleging that the property would turn into a gay bar.
7. Nafco, a statewide drug addiction service, has asked to lease the property to set up a drug rehabilitation center with residential facilities.

Assume that as a group you form the City Council. What will you do with the Kucinski property? You must make a decision.

Step 3: 30 Minutes

After everyone is familiar with the problem, the group should discuss the alternatives until you reach consensus. You may not vote. All group members must agree to the final decision. Record the time it takes you to reach a decision.

The group leader may give special instructions to some groups. Proceed according to any special instructions you receive.

Step 4: 10 Minutes
Each group will report on its decision-making process and outcome. The instructor will record the data on the board.

Step 5: 10 Minutes
Discussion and conclusion.

GENERALIZATIONS AND CONCLUSIONS

Concluding Points
1. What frequently happens when group members make decisions solely on the basis of individual values?

2. What are some of the ways that groups can facilitate decision making when value issues arise?

3. What are some of the techniques that groups resort to in resolving value conflicts?

4. How can an organization reduce value conflicts in decision making?

Copyright © 1982, John Wiley and Sons, Inc.

5. How do decisions involving values differ from decisions where there is an objective "right" answer?

Participant's Reactions

READINGS AND REFERENCES

Robbins, Stephen P., *Managing Organizationsl Conflict* (Englewood Cliffs, N.J.: Prentice-Hall, 1974).

Guth, W. D., and Tagiuri, R., "Personal Values and Corporate Strategy," *Harvard Business Review*, Sept./Oct. (1965), 123-32.

SECTION SIX
NEGOTIATION AND CONFLICT

21
TWO-PERSON BARGAINING: THE UGLI ORANGE CASE

PURPOSE:
(1) To explore the dynamics of two-person bargaining.
(2) To experiment with creative problem solving.

ADVANCE PREPARATION:
None.

GROUP SIZE: Subgroups of two or three. Total group can be any size.
TIME REQUIRED: 30 minutes.
SPECIAL MATERIALS: None.
SPECIAL PHYSICAL REQUIREMENTS: None.
RELATED TOPICS: Group decision making and problem solving, Interpersonal communication.

INTRODUCTION

In many work settings it is not possible for people to work independently as they pursue their work goals. Often we find ourselves in situations where we must obtain the cooperation of other people, even though the other people's ultimate objectives may be different from our own. This will be your task in the present exercise.

Originally developed by Robert J. House. Adapted by D. T. Hall and R. J. Lewicki, with suggested modifications by H. Kolodny and T. Ruble. Used with permission.

Copyright © 1982, John Wiley and Sons, Inc.

PROCEDURE

OPTION ONE

Step 1: 5 Minutes

Count off the class in groups of three. In each group of three, one person will play the role of "Dr. Roland," one will play "Dr. Jones," and one will be an observer.

The person playing Dr. Jones should read the role description for Dr. Jones only, and the person playing the role of Dr. Roland should read the role description for Dr. Roland only. The observer should read both role descriptions. (Role descriptions can be found at the back of the volume in the Appendix.)

OPTION TWO

Step 1: 5 Minutes

Count off the class in groups of three. In each group of three, one person will play the role of "Dr. Roland," one will play "Dr. Jones," and one will be an observer.

The person playing Dr. Jones should read the role description for Dr. Jones only, and the person playing the role of Dr. Roland should read the role description for Dr. Roland only. The observer should read both role descriptions. (Role descriptions can be found at the back of this volume in the Appendix.)

BOTH OPTIONS

Step 2: 10 Minutes, Negotiation

At this point the group leader will read the following statement: "I am Mr. Cardoza, the owner of the remaining Ugli oranges. My fruit-exporting firm is based in South America. My country does not have diplomatic relations with your country, although we do have strong trade relations.

"After you have read about your roles, spend about 10 minutes meeting with the other firm's representative and decide on a course of action. Then pick a spokesperson who will tell me: (1) What do you plan to do? (2) If you want to buy the oranges, what price will you offer? (3) To whom and how will the oranges be delivered?

"After you have done this, you may negotiate with the other firm's representative."

Step 3: 15 Minutes

Following the negotiation, the spokesperson and the observer will report on the solution reached in each group and the process by which agreement was reached.

DISCUSSION QUESTIONS

1. Was there full disclosure by both sides in each group? How much information was shared?
2. Did the parties trust one another? Why or why not?
3. How creative and/or complex were the solutions? If solutions were very complex, why do you think this occurred?

Additional Question for Option 2

4. What was the impact of having an audience or constituency on the behavior of the negotiators? Did it make the problem harder or easier to solve?

GENERALIZATIONS AND CONCLUSIONS

Concluding Points

1. What is the relationship between trust and disclosure of information?

2. In a bargaining situation such as this, before competing or collaborating with the other person, what should you do first?

3. How does mistrust affect the creativity or complexity of bargaining agreements?

Copyright © 1982, John Wiley and Sons, Inc.

4. Do audiences to a negotiation increase competitiveness or cooperativeness? Why?

Participant's Reactions

READINGS AND REFERENCES

Filley, Alan, *Interpersonal Conflict Resolution*,. (Glenview, Ill.: Scott Foresman, 1975).
Thomas, Kenneth, "Conflict and Conflict Management," In M. Dunnette, *Handbook of Industrial and Organizational Psychology* (Chicago: Rand McNally, 1976).

22
COMPETITIVE ESCALATION: THE DOLLAR AUCTION

PURPOSE:
(1) To understand processes of escalation in competitive interaction.
(2) To understand individual differences in conflict styles in a competitive environment.

ADVANCED PREPARATION:
None.

GROUP SIZE: *Option One*: Groups of three. *Option two*: Entire class.
TIME REQUIRED: 25 minutes.
SPECIAL MATERIALS: Small change (nickels, dimes, and quarters), if specified by instructor.
SPECIAL PHYSICAL REQUIREMENTS: None.
RELATED TOPICS: Group decision making and problem solving, Organizational realities, Power, Organizational communication.

INTRODUCTION

In this activity, you will have the opportunity to explore the behavior of individuals in a competitive environment. The situation presented to you here is a simulation of a bidding exercise; the results demonstrate what usually occurs when individuals or groups are highly competitive with one another.

PROCEDURE

OPTION ONE

Step 1: 10 Minutes

Form teams of three members each. Extra class members may be observers. In each team, there will be three roles: an *auctioneer* and *two bidders*. There will be three rounds of the auction, and group members will alternate roles between each round. *During each round, there is no talking except for making bids.*

In each round, the auctioneer will auction off $1 to the highest bidder. A total of five separate dollars will be auctioned off by each auctioneer. Bids may be made in units of 5 cents. The opportunity for the first bid will go to Bidder A for the first $1, Bidder B for the second $1, and so on.

Bids and earnings should be recorded on a separate sheet of paper.

Adapted by Roy J. Lewicki from a research paradigm developed by Martin Shubik and Allan Teger.

Copyright © 1982, John Wiley and Sons, Inc.

Step 2: 15 Minutes

Proceed through three rounds of bidding, with each person taking the role of auctioneer once and bidder twice. Record the amount paid and your profit on a separate sheet of paper.

DISCUSSION QUESTIONS

(To be conducted among two or more trios grouped together.)
1. What differences, if any, did you notice between the first, second, and third rounds of the auction? Why did these differences occur?
2. When each member was a bidder, what was his or her goal?:
   a. to win the most money?
   b. to beat the other bidder?
   c. to lose as little as possible?
   d. to just be the winner?
3. When two bidders define their goals the same (or differently), what happens to the process and outcome of the bidding?
4. How does the individual's definition of a goal influence the type of behavior exhibited in the auction?
5. What happens when two individuals with different goals play in the auction? Which definition "wins out"?

OPTION TWO

(This option may be used in addition to, or instead of, Option one.)

Step 1: 5 Minutes

The instructor will play the role of auctioneer. In this auction, the instructor will auction off five $1 bills or coins to the highest bidder. This money is imaginary, unless otherwise specified by the instructor. All members of the class may participate in the auction at the same time.

The rules are slightly different from Option one. In this version, *both the highest bidder and the next highest bidder* will pay their last bids for the dollar. For example, if Bidder A bids 15 cents for the dollar and Bidder B bids 10 cents, and there is no further bidding, then A pays 15 cents for the dollar and receives the dollar, while B pays 10 cents and receives nothing. The auctioneer would lose 75 cents on the dollar just sold.

Bids must be made in multiples of 5 cents. The dollar will be sold when there is no further bidding. If two individuals bid the same amount at the same time, ties are resolved in favor of the bidder located physically closest to the auctioneer.

Step 2: 15 Minutes

The instructor (auctioneer) will auction off five individual dollars to the class. Any student may bid in an effort to win the dollar. A record sheet of the bidding and winners can be kept in the table below.

	Amount Paid by Winning Bidder	*Amount Paid by Second Bidder*	*Total Paid for This Dollar*
First dollar			
Second dollar			
Third dollar			
Fourth dollar			
Fifth dollar			

DISCUSSION QUESTIONS

1. Assume that the dollars actually belonged to the auctioneer, and that the auctioneer directly profited or lost depending on the selling price. Who made the most money in this exercise? Why?
2. As the auction proceeded, did the activity become more cooperative or competitive? Why?
3. Were there instances where two bidders together, or even one bidder, paid more than a dollar to win a dollar? Explain what happened in these situations.
4. Did you become involved in the bidding? Why or why not?
   a. If yes, what were your motivations and goals to become involved? Did you accomplish your objective?
   b. If no, why did you not become involved? What were your goals and objectives? What do you think are the goals and objectives of those who did actually participate?
5. During the auction, did people say things to one another to influence the course of the bidding? What was said, and how was it influential?

GENERALIZATIONS AND CONCLUSIONS

The exercise is presented in two variations. In the first variation, two individuals competed to purchase dollars, with the dollar going to the highest bidder. In the second variation, a number of individuals in the class could compete to purchase dollars, with somewhat different rules for how they would be paid for.

In the first variation, an individual could make as much as 95 cents on each dollar, or a total of $2.85 for one bidder and $1.90 for the other in the total auction. In order for this to happen, the first bidder would open with a 5-cent bid on the first dollar, and the other bidder would pass. On the next dollar, Bidder *B* opens with a 5-cent bid and Bidder *A* would pass. If the two bidders then pooled their money and split it evenly, they would each gain $2.42. Since each bidder plays the role of Bidder *A* and *B* in the auction, each would make $4.75 overall.

Does this ever happen? Yes—but not often. Some people believe that it is "unfair," calling it "collusion." But "collusion" is a pejorative term, implying some form of secrecy, conspiracy, or deception. Another way to view it would be to call the process "cooperation," in which one person (for example, Bidder *B*) is willing to trust the other by passing up the opportunity to escalate the bid, in exchange for Bidder *A* passing up the opportunity to escalate on the next. If this trust is betrayed—if one or both players do not pass up the opportunity to bid, in ex-

Copyright © 1982, John Wiley and Sons, Inc.

change for maximizing the overall winnings—then a more competitive cycle will occur.

More typically, in this game, bidders escalate their bids until one or both players have bid up to one dollar. Moreover, what occurs in the first or second round of bidding is likely to dictate what occurs later. Collaboration breeds more collaboration, competition breeds increased escalation. Frequently, bidders become so competitive that they are willing to bid more than one dollar to gain a dollar! In these situations, clearly, the motivation to "win" or "beat the opponent" totally dominates any motivation to win money.

The situation in Option two is a more complex version of the same process. The likelihood of cooperation is minimized by the large number of bidders. Many bidders will drop out because they don't like to compete, or don't think they understand the rules. Others will esclate the bidding quickly. Moreover, since the "second" bidder always has a major financial investment in the final bid—even though that bidder will not receive the dollar—there is more pressure for that bidder to escalate the bid in order to win the dollar. It is not uncommon in this version for the two top bidders to pay more than a dollar each in order to "recover their investment."

The psychology of the processes that occur in this exercise has been called "entrapment," and can occur when individuals invest more resources to justify or recover resources already spent. It can occur in severe conflict, when parties are so concerned about winning—or not losing—that they are willing to invest more resources than the victory itself is worth. Many critics of the Vietnam War would characterize American involvement there as a case of entrapment. Entrapment can also occur when individuals believe that further commitment of resources might "change their luck." Gamblers who have lost a great deal may continue to bet more, hoping that they will soon "hit it big." Similarly, banks and financial lending officers continue to lend money to poorly managed companies hoping that management will improve and the lenders will be able to recover their investment. Well-known examples of this process have occurred in recent years with the Penn-Central Railroad, Lockheed Corporation, and W. T. Grant Department Stores.

Competitive escalation and entrapment occur in a variety of settings—standing in a waiting line, being put on "hold" when telephoning for an airline reservation, deciding whether to repair an already dilapidated car, making a commitment of resources to a risky business venture, or the escalation of anger, threats, and destructive tactics that characterizes human conflict. Even when individuals are fully aware of the dynamics of entrapment, they nevertheless frequently become ensnared again. The following are several ways to avoid getting caught in this spiral.

1. *Set definite prior limits for how much of a commitment you will make.* A gambler who only takes $50 to the racetrack can only lose $50. If the gambler takes $100, even though he only intends to bet $50, he may be much more likely to bet the remainder.

2. *Get others to help you maintain these limits.* If you have to explain, justify, or defend the reasons why you exceeded your limits to someone else, you probably will expect to be embarrassed enough to want to avoid the situation. Inform others of your commitment or limits—make it public.

3. *Beware of your need to impress others.* Other people do not always help to prevent entrapment; there are times when the presence of others may encourage entrapment, particularly when we want to look good to these people. If people expect that maintaining or escalating a commitment will make them look good to others, even at cost to themselves, they are highly prone toward making entrapping commitments. While we all want to look good to others, we may be willing to make poor judgments as a consequence.

4. *Be pessimistic—keep costs in mind.* Evaluate your current situation in terms of *what you have already lost,* not what you are likely to gain if you win. Doing so will make current losses and future costs much more prominent in your decision to commit further resources, and make you more realistic about whether the risk of future gain is worth it.

Participant's Reactions

READINGS AND REFERENCES

Rubin, Jeffrey Z., "Psychological Traps," *Psychology Today,* 15, March (1981), 52–63.
Teger, Allan I., *Too Much Invested to Quit* (New York: Pergammon Press, 1980).

Copyright © 1982, John Wiley and Sons, Inc.

23
COMPETITIVE ADVERTISING STRATEGY: A MATRIX GAME

PURPOSE:
(1) To illustrate the dynamics of cooperation and competition.
(2) To explore trusting and suspicious behavior in a simulated business context.

ADVANCE PREPARATION:
None

GROUP SIZE: Three-person groups—two players (*A* and *B*) and an observer/scorekeeper.
TIME REQUIRED: 50 minutes, more if variations are used.
SPECIAL MATERIALS: Scenario instructions, matrix and decision forms; blackboard or newsprint.
SPECIAL PHYSICAL ARRANGEMENTS: Players *A* and *B* should sit sufficiently far away (back to back or across an aisle) so that they cannot see one another's decision forms. Observer should sit approximately halfway between the players.
RELATED TOPICS: Interpersonal communication, Organizational communication.

INTRODUCTION

The purpose of this exercise is to understand some of the factors that affect decision making in interpersonal relations. In the situation described below, you and your partner will be making decisions simultaneously. Each decision will affect your own profits, and the profits of the other. You cannot independently determine your own profits in this situation; your outcome will be jointly determined by the decision that both you and your partner make on each move. The nature of your choices, and how well you perform, will be determined by (1) your own goals and motivations, (2) the other person's goals and motivations, and (3) the communication between the two of you when this is permitted.

PROCEDURE

Step 1: 5 Minutes
The instructor will divide the class into three-person groups. One person will role-play the Vice President of Acme Rent-A-Car (see below), the second will role-play the Vice President of Bonanza Auto Rentals, and the third will be an observer/referee. The two decision makers should take seats so that they cannot see each

Developed by Roy J. Lewicki.

other's choices, but be close enough to communicate when necessary. The referee should sit approximately halfway between the two decision makers.

Step 2: 10 Minutes

Read the instructions for "Competitive Advertising Strategy," below. When you have finished reading, the group leader will answer questions and assign roles. You will then proceed to make decisions in the game.

COMPETITIVE ADVERTISING STRATEGY

You are the Vice President for Marketing of a large national automobile rental firm. Person A, you are the Vice President of the *Acme Rent-A-Car Company*. Person B, you are the Vice President of *Bonanza Automobile Rentals, Inc.* The two companies control most of the national automobile rental car market. Rental prices, number of locations, selection of automobiles, and so on, are all reasonably similar for both companies, and do not differ from year to year. What *does* vary is the *percentage* of the rental car market that your company captures each month; this largely depends on the size of your monthly advertising budget, and directly affects monthly profits. The amount of money that you spend on advertising allows you to finance more elaborate compaigns and reach more potential customers. However, recent studies have shown that the impact of advertising depends *not only* on the total dollars spent, but *also* on whether your competitor advertises as well.

Competition between you and the other rental car company has been hot and heavy recently. Advertising campaigns have become rather nasty, not only promoting your own product but trying to persuade the customer why he should *not* rent from the opposition. In an effort to develop the best advertising strategy, your marketing department has come up with two marketing programs. Program I costs $300,000 per month, and Program II costs $600,000 per month. The marketing department has also determined the effect of advertising decisions on your own and your competitor's profits. The profit to you as a company will be affected by the program you choose (I or II), and the program the other company chooses. The effect of each combination of choices on your company's monthly profit can be represented as follows:

	Bonanza's Choice of Programs	
	Program I ($300,000)	Program II ($600,000)
Program I ($300,000)	Acme: $500,000 profit Bonanza: $500,000 profit	Acme: ($200,000 loss) Bonanza: $1 million profit
Program II ($600,000)	Acme: $1 million profit Bonanza: ($200,000 loss)	Acme: $100,000 profit Bonanza: $100,000 profit

Acme's Choice of Programs

In other words, if both of you choose the Program I advertising strategy, you each make $500,000 profit for that month. If one of you chooses Program II while the other

Copyright © 1982, John Wiley and Sons, Inc.

chooses Program I, the company choosing Program II earns $1 million profit, while the other loses $200,000 for that month. If both of you choose Program II, you each earn only $100,000 for that month.

Forecasts of the rental car industry for the next year provide you with further information that you will want to take into consideration when formulating your overall marketing plan. First, the month of April is a big business month, because of travel during Spring vacations. Profits for companies during this month will be *doubled*. Second, the months of July and August, summer vacation months, are the peak months of the rental car season, and the impact of advertising on profits will be *tripled* during these two months. Finally, the Christmas season is also an active month, and profits will also be doubled during this month. These events are indicated and summarized on the "Profit Record Chart."

Profit Record Chart

Month		Acme's Choice (Program I or II)	Bonanza's Choice (Program I or II)	Acme's Profit	Bonanza's Profit
Prac-tice 1					
Prac-tice 2					
(5-minute planning period)					
1.	January				
2.	February				
3.	March				
(3-minute discussion)					
4.	April (double)				
5.	May				
6.	June				
7.	July (triple)				
8.	August (triple)				
9.	September				
(3-minute discussion)					
10.	October				
11.	November				
12.	December (double)				
			Total Profits	_____	_____

Normally, there is no communication between you and the Vice President of your competing firm. However, there are two major professional association meetings each year, in late March and late September, and you normally meet the other Vice President at that meeting. During the meeting, you may, if you choose, talk with the other Vice President about any aspect of your company's advertising strategy.

Your overall goal in this simulation is to *maximize your own company's profit*. Do not concern yourself with the other's profit; only be concerned with how well *your* company does.

Step 3: 10 Minutes

Review the scenario and make sure that you understand the choices you are to make, and the payoffs to each company. Ask the group leader if you need clarification on the scenario or the payoffs for each combination of choices.

The Vice Presidents should work by themselves for 5 minutes to plan a strategy for maximizing their overall profit during the simulation. The observers will meet briefly with the group leader to clarify the rules and the observer's role in conducting the simulation.

The observer is asked to enforce the rule that there is to be *no talking or other communication* between Acme and Bonanza, except during the two specified discussion periods after the March and September decisions. Before beginning the simulation, the observer will allow two *practice* decisions, in order to review the scoring. These decisions do not count toward the total profit for either Company.

Step 4: 20 Minutes

The observer will give each Vice President no longer than *one* minute to make a decision for each month. Each Vice President will announce his decision but *say nothing else*. The observer will announce the choices and profits for each company, and ask the Vice Presidents to record their own choice and profit and the other's choice and profit.

If you wish to have a discussion with the other Vice President during the two specified periods, you may say anything you wish or make any agreement that you wish to benefit your company. Any agreement made during discussions is not *necessarily* binding and the observer is is not *necessarily* bound to enforce agreements if he does not choose to. Remember that your objective is to maximize your own profit for your own company.

Step 5: 15 Minutes

The group leader will ask observers from each triad to record the profit of each company on a master chart. Comparisons will be made between subgroups to determine which Vice Presidents earned the most. While totals for the groups are being determined, the two players and the observer should discuss what happened during the simulation (see Discussion Questions, below, for additional ideas). Players and observers should share with the total group the most interesting events that occurred in each triad, and major factors that affected the winnings or losses of each company. The group leader will review the goals and objectives of the activity, and ask for general discussion.

Copyright © 1982, John Wiley and Sons, Inc.

DISCUSSION QUESTIONS

1. What were your basic objectives and strategy for this game before it began? How did you come to decide on those objectives and strategy?
2. Was your strategy affected ty the Practice Decisions? How?
3. Was your strategy affected by what the other player did in the first three moves? How?
4. What did you talk about in the first discussion period (after the March decision)? What did the other player talk about? Did you make any agreements? Were these agreements upheld?
5. What did you and your partner talk about in the second discussion (after the September decision)? Did you make any agreements? Were they upheld?
6. How did the "multiples" for the months of April, July, August, and December affect the decisions? Did you and/ or the other player become more cooperative? Competitive?
7. Overall, how well did you do compared to the other player? Compared to other pairs of players in the class?
8. How do you react to cooperation and competition? Why is cooperation and trust so difficult to achieve? What are the barriers that stand in the way of developing trust and a good cooperative relationship?

GENERALIZATIONS AND CONCLUSIONS

1. Write down what you learned about each of the following elements, based on your experience in this exercise:
   a. Trust and suspicion.

   b. Objectives and strategy in this type of a situation.

   c. Relations between people when they are potentially in competition or potentially cooperating.

d. Effects of greater incentives on cooperation and competition.

e. Types of agreements that need to be made to insure cooperative relations.

2. What are the parallels between this exercise and relations between individuals? Between individuals and groups in organizations?

Participant's Reactions

READINGS AND REFERENCES

Davis, M., *Game Theory: A Nontechnical Introduction*. (New York: Basic Books, 1970).
Deutsch, M., *The Resolution of Conflict* (New Haven, Conn.: Yale University Press, 1973).
Wrightsman, L. S., O'Connor, J., and Baker, N. J., *Cooperation and Competition: Readings on Mixed Motive Games* (Belmont, Calif.: Brooks Cole, 1972).

Copyright © 1982, John Wiley and Sons, Inc.

24
COLLECTIVE BARGAINING
AND LABOR MANAGEMENT RELATIONS

PURPOSE:

(1) To explore the dynamics of intergroup relations and negotiation in a labor-management context.

(2) To provide opportunities for experimenting with bargaining strategy and tactics in a simulated negotiation.

ADVANCE PREPARATION:

Instructor will specify whether Union and Management role positions are to be prepared before class or during class.

GROUP SIZE: Pairs of small groups, each group three to five members. Observers may be assigned to each pair if desirable.

TIME REQUIRED: 60 to 90 minutes, depending on Advance Preparation and time allowed for negotiation.

SPECIAL MATERIALS: None.

SPECIAL PHYSICAL ARRANGEMENTS: Moveable chairs to arrange in circles, or across tables; separate rooms for each negotiating dyad if available.

RELATED TOPICS: Group decision making and problem solving, Power, Organizational communication.

INTRODUCTION

In this exercise, you will experience some of the dynamics of collective bargaining. The class will be divided into a number of small teams, each representing either the union or the management position. After reviewing the background information, read the role position for your own team, and prepare for negotiations. Finally, you will be given the opportunity to actually negotiate a contract settlement with representatives of another team.

In this exercise, you will be able to observe several things. First, you will be able to understand how members of a negotiating team interact, and the problems that they might incur in working together or resolving disagreement among themselves. Second, you will experience the process of developing and executing a strategy in negotiation, in order to achieve your objectives. Third, you will be able to observe how individual differences in negotiation style can affect final outcomes. Finally, you will be able to comprehend the type of problems and difficulties frequently incurred by union and management groups, in their efforts to resolve disputes and establish mutually satisfactory working relationships.

Adapted by Roy J. Lewicki from an exercise developed by Richard J. Campbell and William A. Bigoness. Used with permission.

This negotiation will necessarily telescope the planning and negotiation periods in an abnormally short time frame. As a result, it cannot encompass an entire contract package, but must only include a few issues: wages, cost of living increase in wages, differential pay for night shift workers, vacation pay, and hospital/medical benefits package.

PROCEDURE

Step 1: 5 Minutes
The group leader will divide the class into one or more teams of Union and Management representatives. Observers may also be selected to take notes on each negotiating pair. Specific Labor and Management negotiating teams should be paired up, so that you will know who you are negotiating against.

Step 2: 15 Minutes
Once your team has been assigned and you have grouped together to begin planning strategy, read the Background Information sheet (below) on the Townsford Company. Also pay attention to the Issues for Bargaining, and the Data from the Independent Community Survey.

After you have read and studied this information, turn to the Appendix and read the assigned role position for either the "Company Negotiator" or the "Union Negotiator." Then meet with your team to review this material, and make sure that you understand all of the facts and information presented.

BACKGROUND INFORMATION

The Townsford Company is a small textile company located in a large southeastern city in the United States. Townsford is highly respected for its quality work in the dyeing and finishing of raw woven fabrics. It employs approximately 100 persons. Townsford's employees are among the most skilled to be found in the area.

The general business conditions of the country are good, and the financial conditions of Townsford are stable. Townsford is operating at full capacity and has a 6-month backlog of orders. Profits are not as high as at previous times, however, since the company has not raised the prices in several years in order to maintain a good competitive position with other sections of the country. The company has been able to maintain a 12 percent shareholders' dividend and has made recent purchases of more modern equipment.

The personnel policies at Townsford are not the most modern but are better than those of most plants the same size. The past President of the company, who retired three months ago, knew most of the workers personally and was well liked. He is largely responsible for the reputation of Townsford as a "good place to work." His successor is viewed with some suspicion by the workers, due mainly to his statements about changing some of the work procedures to achieve greater efficiency.

For the last 25 years, a majority of the employees have been members of the union. Relations of the union with the company, for the most part, have been quite good, with grievances promptly discussed and settled. The first strike occurred, however, 3

Copyright © 1982, John Wiley and Sons, Inc.

years ago and lasted 15 days. The workers lost the fight for a sliding-scale wage based on increases in the cost of living index, but did get the hospital and medical plan, a 5-cent-per-hour wage differential for night shift workers, and several other minor fringe benefits.

Although Townsford's wage scale, $3.94 per hour, compares favorably with most other textile firms in the area, it is 3 percent below those textile firms that employ workers of equivalent high skill and produce a similar high quality product. Wages in the industry have not increased in proportion to increases in the cost of living or increases in other industries.

Despite occasional small wage increases, over a period of years Townsford's workers have slipped from a relatively high pay scale to a position roughly equivalent to that of lowly skilled workers in other industries. This has caused some unrest among the workers, and there is some danger of the workers shifting into these other higher-paying industries. Unemployment is below normal in the area, and it has been difficult to obtain replacements who meet the skill requirements at Townsford.

Townsford gives seven paid holidays and 2 weeks of paid vacation to all workers with at least 1 year of service. The company also pays 1/4 of each employee's hospital and medical insurance and grants other minor fringe benefits. More detailed information on Townsford and other local firms may be found in the table that accompanies this background information.

The 3 year contract has now expired. Negotiations broke down in the final week, with both sides adamant in their positions. The only agreement reached was that each side would select a new bargaining agent to represent it, and scheduled a meeting for today (the first day of strike) in an attempt to reach a quick solution and avoid a long strike.

Issues for Bargaining

Hospital and Medical Plan
Past contract: Company paid 1/4 cost, employee paid remaining 3/4
UNION: demanded company pay full cost
COMPANY: refused to pay more than 1/4

Proportion of company payment

	1/4	2/4	3/4	4/4	
COMPANY					UNION
Total money value per 2 years	$0	$6,000	$12,000	$18,000	

Wages
Past Contract: $3.94 per hour
UNION: demanded an increase of 16 cents per hour
COMPANY: refused outright

Cents increase per hour (range 00–18)

COMPANY	00	02	04	06	08
Total money value per 2 years	$0	$8,000	$16,000	$24,000	$32,000

	10	12	14	16	18	UNION
	$40,000	$48,000	$56,000	$64,000	$72,000	

Sliding pay scale to conform to cost of living

Past contract: pay scale is fixed through the term of the contract
UNION: demanded pay increases in proportion to increases in the cost of living
COMPANY: rejected outright

COMPANY	NO	YES	UNION
Total money value per 2 years	$0	$20,000	

Vacation Pay

Past contract: 2 weeks paid vacation for all workers with 1 year service
UNION: wants 3 weeks paid vacation for workers with 10 years of service
COMPANY: rejected

COMPANY	2 wks for 1 yr service	3 wks for 20 yrs service	3 wks for 15 yrs service	3 wks for 10 yrs service	UNION
Total money value per 2 years	$0	$500	$2,000	$5,000	

Night Shift Differential

Past contract: $.05 per hour more paid to night shift workers
UNION: Demands $.15 per hour more for night shift workers
COMPANY: Refused to pay more than the current differential

Cents per hour differential

COMPANY	.05	.07	.09	.11	.13	.15	UNION
Total money value per 2 years	$0	$2,000	$4,000	$6,000	$8,000	$10,000	

Data from an Independent Community Survey

The following table gives information on Townsford, four other local textile plants and averages for nontextile industries in the community. The Moss Plant and the Rose Plant employ highly skilled workers.

	TOWNSFORD	MOSS	ROSE	BAXTER	KRAFT	AVERAGE FOR OTHER INDUSTRIES IN THE COMMUNITY
Number of Workers	100	300	90	150	300	60
Company Payment for Hosp. & Med. Insurance	¼	¾	¾	4/4	0	½

Copyright © 1982, John Wiley and Sons, Inc.

	TOWNSFORD	MOSS	ROSE	BAXTER	KRAFT	AVERAGE FOR OTHER INDUSTRIES IN THE COMMUNITY
Hourly Wage Rate	$3.94	$4.00	$4.00	$3.86	$3.88	$4.10
Cost of Living Increases	No	Yes	Yes	No	Yes	40%, yes
Night Shift Differential	$0.05	$0.09	$0.11	$0.08	$0.03	$0.10
Paid Vacation	2 wks for 1 yr	2 wks for 1 yr	2 wks for 1 yr	2 wks for 1 yr	2 wks for 1 yr, 3 wks for 20 yrs	2 wks for 1 yr, 3 wks for 15 yrs

Step 3: At Least 15 Minutes

Meet with other members of your union or management team. Plan to do the following things:

1. Make sure that you understand each of the issues that will be negotiated. If you have questions, ask the instructor.
2. Select one person to be the spokesman for the group. Other members of the team may be asked to be a recorder, or a spokesman on a specific issue, or play some other role in the strategy and tactics of the team.
3. Clarify your objectives on each issue. Define for your own team (a) the opening demand that you will make on each issue, (b) the point where you would like to settle on each issue, and (c) the point at which you will "go no further" (resistance point) on each issue.
4. Plan any other strategy or tactics you will use in the negotiation.

Step 4: 30 Minutes

Meet with the Management or Union team that you have been paired against. Decide who will make the first new set of offers or demands, and then attempt to arrive at a settlement by the end of the time available.

Use your time wisely. Remember that you are allowed to call a caucus at any point, and/or to control the negotiations in any way that you and your opposing team agree.

Step 5: 5 Minutes

At the end of the negotiation, please record the specific details of your contract in the following table:

Issue	Settlement	Cost to Company
Hospital and medical plan	_____	_____
Wages	_____	_____
Cost of living sliding scale	_____	_____
Vacation pay	_____	_____
Night shift differential	_____	_____
Total Cost of Settlement Package to Company	_____	_____

Be prepared to present this information to the instructor when it is asked for.

DISCUSSION QUESTIONS

1. How effectively did your Union or Management team work together? What kind of problems occurred, if any? How did these affect your negotiation with the other team?
2. Who was selected as negotiator? What criteria were used? Upon hindsight, were these good criteria to use?
3. What other roles were played by other team members? Were these assignments effective?
4. Was your strategy affected by knowing which individuals were on the opposing team? How?
5. How did you determine what you would set as an opening bid, and as a "settlement point?" Upon hindsight, were these good decisions?
6. How were the course of negotiations determined by the style, strategy, and tactics of the negotiators? Which tactics seemed most effective? Least effective? Why?
7. Did you reach a settlement within the time period? If not, what factors kept the two groups from agreeing on all five points?
8. How satisfied were you with your settlement after you had completed the negotiations?
9. How satisfied were you with your settlement after you saw how other groups settled? What is the impact of this kind of information on satisfaction with the settlement you achieved?

GENERALIZATIONS AND CONCLUSIONS

1. What strategy and tactics are likely to be most effective in this type of situation? Least effective?

Copyright © 1982, John Wiley and Sons, Inc.

2. What can negotiators do to increase the likelihood of achieving a satisfactory solution to a negotiated agreement?

Participant's Reactions

READINGS AND REFERENCES

Filley, A., *Interpersonal Conflict Resolution* (New York: Scott Foresman, 1976).
Mills, D. Q., *Labor Management Relations* (New York: McGraw-Hill, 1978).
Nierenberg, G. I., *Fundamentals of Negotiating* (New York: Hawthorne Books, 1973).

SECTION SEVEN
MANAGERS AS LEADERS

25
THE STORM WINDOWS: A ROLE PLAY

PURPOSE:
(1) To analyze a simulated case showing a difficult leadership problem.
(2) To experiment with and identify alternative ways of dealing with leadership problems.
(3) To give practice in diagnosing employee motivation and in responding flexibly.

ADVANCE PREPARATION:
None. Participants are asked *not* to read the case materials *before* participating in the exercise.

GROUP SIZE: Any size.
TIME REQUIRED: 50 minutes.
SPECIAL MATERIALS: None.
SPECIAL PHYSICAL REQUIREMENTS: Table and four chairs at front of room.
RELATED TOPICS: Motivation: Basic concepts, Interpersonal communication, Organizational communication, Group decision making and problem solving, Negotiation and conflict, Power.

INTRODUCTION
Textbooks in management and organizational behavior stress the need for managers to be sensitive to the needs of different employees, and to be flexible in

From Maier, N.R.F., Solem, A.R., and Maier, A. A. *Supervisory and Executive Development: A Manual for Role Playing* (New York: Wiley, 1957). Adapted by D.T. Hall. Used with permission.

Copyright © 1982, John Wiley and Sons, Inc.

dealing with people. Yet textbooks also stress the need to recognize problems quickly and to take decisive action. It is often harder to apply concepts of leadership than it is to learn them. Here's a chance for you to apply what you know about leadership and motivation.

PROCEDURE

Step 1: 5 Minutes

1. Arrange a table and four chairs around it at the front of the room so that all occupants face the group as well as each other.
2. The group leader picks two people to play the role of "Paul Brown," the foreman. (This person could also be "Paula Brown.") Both people playing the role of Brown are to leave the room and study "The Settling" and "Role Instructions." They are told that when they return they will be asked to read a script, after which they will be on their own. The people playing Brown should not return until instructed to do so.
3. The group leader selects four persons to occupy the seats at the table, each with a copy of the script. The other members of the class will act as observers.
4. Read "The Setting" and "Role Instructions," which follow.

THE SETTING

The National Telephone Company stationed a group of five telephone installers and repairmen, including the foreman-in-charge, in the community of Basking Ridge. The facility was a two-story frame structure, which housed the four small trucks used by the men. The second floor contained supplies, equipment, small tools, and the like, which the men required in their work. Of some significance to this case was the fact that the building had three windows on the first floor and three windows on the second floor on each of two sides of the building.

Because of the fact that the flow of work for the men was intermittent in character, depending upon the number of new telephones to be installed, weather conditions that might damage the lines, and similar variables, the men did all of the maintenance work required to keep the building in a clean and orderly condition. During those times when they were not otherwise occupied, they washed and greased their trucks, performed minor repairs on the building, and did a variety of "odd jobs."

The men got along well with the working foreman and with each other. The informality of the situation gave the men considerable freedom from "work rules" and other restraints that might be aggravating.

Many of their activities followed the lines of custom and practice that had developed through the years and were generally understood and accepted by all concerned. Among these was the practice of having the man with the least seniority in the group assigned the "odd job" of putting up storm windows in the fall of the year and replacing them with window screens in the spring.

The day on which the incident we are about to witness occurred was a balmy spring day. The foreman had gone to the local bank on his lunch hour to transact some personal business. The four telephone installers had been sitting around the lunch table, where they were accustomed to heating some soup and making coffee, if they so desired, to go along with their lunches that they brought to work with them. They had been talking about current topics of local interest.

Cast of Characters

Paul Brown ....Working foreman
Tom Jones ....Telephone installer—20 years' service
Dick Smith ....Telephone installer—18 years' service
Harry Oswald ....Telephone installer—14 years' service
Bill Bryan ....Telephone installer— 5 years' service

ROLE INSTRUCTIONS

The group is very close-knit and there is a great deal of respect for each member of the group by the other members. Because of this harmony within the group, members have a tendency to "kid" other members—sometimes to an excess. There is less "kidding " with Brown, the working foreman, than among the other members of the group. He is seen in a position of authority, even though this authority is seldom exercised. None of the members wants to put up the windows or see Bill fired.

Paul Brown

Brown is 50 years old and has a wife and two children, both of whom are through school. He gets along well with the men and has little difficulty in getting the work done that has been assigned to his group from General Headquarters. At the present time, he has to get the task of taking down the storm windows and putting up the screens done.

Tom Jones

Jones is 52 years old and has a wife and four children, the youngest two of whom are still in high school. Jones is a heavy-set man and shows his years. Jones is "cutting" with some of his remarks—to such a degree that he sometimes makes people defensive. He is proud of his long service record with the company.

Dick Smith

Smith is 46 years old and has a wife and four children, all of whom are still in school. Smith has never worked for anyone else but the National Telephone Company. He has the longest company-wide seniority but has been in Basking Ridge two years less than Jones.

Harry Oswald

Oswald is 34 years old and is a bachelor—the talk of all the girls in the town. He has a good work record and keeps his extracurricular activities confined to after hours. Oswald is usually the instigator of the kiddling that goes on at work and has been known to have started more than one good argument among other members of the group. He is a "needler." He is known for getting a person in a corner and then not letting him work his way out. He does get along with the other members of the group and would not want to see anyone get hurt. He feels most strongly about Bill not

Copyright © 1982, John Wiley and Sons, Inc.

putting up the windows, for he is next in line seniority-wise. He also knows if Bill is fired, there will be a new man before the windows have to go up in the fall, meaning he would do the job only once. He is a man of principles.

Bill Bryan
Bill is 28 and has a wife and five children, three preschool and two in grade school. His wife takes in laundry and does typing to help meet the family expenses. Bill is very defensive and hates to feel that he is being "taken advantage of." He is the slowest thinker in the group and is easily trapped by the kidding of the group, especially by Oswald. Bill finds it extremely difficult to back down and is vitally concerned with presenting an acceptable "face" and preserving the "face" once it is presented. He wants to feel that he is an equal member of the group.

Step 2: 25 Minutes
1. The group leader reads aloud to the class and the actors "The Setting." He then gives the signal for the reading of the script for scene 1, which can be found in the Appendix at the back of this book.
2. After scene 1 has been read, the two people playing the foreman, Paul Brown, are asked to return to the room. One is asked to observe, and one is asked to read the script for scene 2, below. After this, Paul and Bill make up their own lines, proceeding as they see fit.

SCRIPT FOR SCENE 2 OF "THE STORM WINDOWS"

(Enter Paul or Paula Brown)

Brown: Hi, fellows! Sure is a beautiful day. Say, Bill, I've got a nice light new aluminum ladder out there in the truck that I think ought to make your job of taking down the storm windows and putting up the screens quite a bit easier. Why don't you get started on it, if you're through with your lunch. Don't bother to wash the windows when you put them away, because they always get dirty during the summer while they're in storage.

(Telephone installers, except for Bill, all exit hastily)

3. Role playing should continue to a point where the decision reached by the role players terminates the interview or where something else happens that requires an interruption.
4. If subsequent interviews are implied in the decision, such as having a discussion with the other employees as a group, role-play such meetings.
5. After the first "Paul" or "Paula Brown" has finished his or her role play, stop for a brief discussion. The group leader will ask what Paul(a) and Bill were trying to accomplish, what needs they were feeling. The rest of the class may suggest what might be done differently.
6. With the second "Paul(a) Brown," repeat the role play (Step 2, parts 2 to 4 above).

Step 3: 20 Minutes
Discussion.

DISCUSSION QUESTIONS

1. Use discussion to evaluate the process observed. How do the observers feel about the decision(s)?
2. List all the things Bill did in the role playing that indicated he had a problem that was more than a dislike of working on storm windows. Distinctions should be made between (a) the status of the job; (b) the number of times Bill has done the job; (c) the influence of "kidding " on Bill; (d) Bill's statement to the other men about what he would do.
3. Analyze face-saving and insubordination as employee behaviors, and determine the extent of agreement in the class.
4. Evaluate face-saving problems of Foreman Brown and consider what can be done to avoid them.
5. Determine whether the group considers this a problem between the foreman and the crew or between the foreman and Bill.
6. See if the group can agree on some rule that will guide them as individuals in determining when a problem involves the group and when it does not.

GENERALIZATIONS AND CONCLUSIONS

Concluding Points
1. In handling a leadership problem, an extremely important first step is what?

2. To perform this activity (described in the answer to Question 1 above), what kind of skills must the manager develop?

Copyright © 1982, John Wiley and Sons, Inc.

3. Can the manager's needs affect the success of his leadership? If so, how?

Participant's Reactions

READINGS AND REFERENCES

Fiedler, F. E., *A Theory of Leadership Effectiveness* (New York: McGraw-Hill, 1967).

Filley, A., House, R., and Kerr, S., *Managerial Process and Organizational Behavior* (Glenview, Ill.; Scott, Foresman 1976). See Chapters 11 and 12.

Maier, N. R. F., *Psychology in Industrial Organizations,* 4th ed. (Boston: Houghton-Mifflin, 1973). See Chapter 13, "Basic Principles in Motivation."

26
CHOOSING A LEADERSHIP STYLE: APPLYING THE VROOM AND YETTON MODEL

PURPOSE:
(1) To learn a method of diagnosing leadership situations.
(2) To learn how to choose managerial decision-making processes more effectively.

ADVANCE PREPARATION:
Read "A New Look at Managerial Decision-Making" in the "Introduction" to this exercise, an article that describes the Vroom and Yetton model.

GROUP SIZE: Subgroups of three to five. Total group can be any size.
TIME REQUIRED: 50 Minutes.
SPECIAL MATERIALS: None.
SPECIAL PHYSICAL REQUIREMENTS: None.
RELATED TOPICS: Group decision making and problem solving, Applied motivation and job design, Organizational communication, Power, Planned Change.

OPTION ONE[1]

1. Before doing any of the following reading by Vroom, read Cases I to IV, which appear later in this exercise (pp. 166–168). For each case, decide which of the following decision styles would be most appropriate, assuming you were the leader in each situation:

   AI: You solve the problem or make the decision yourself, using information available to you at the time.

   AII: You obtain the necessary information from your subordinate(s), then decide on the solution to the problem yourself.

   CI: You share the problem with relevant subordinates individually, getting their ideas and suggestions without bringing them together as a group. Then *you* make the decision, which may or may not reflect your subordinates' influence.

   CII: You share the problem with your subordinates as a group, collectively obtaining their ideas and suggestions. Then *you* make the decision, which may or may not reflect your subordinates' influence.

   GII: You share a problem with your subordinates as a group. Together you generate and evaluate alternatives and attempt to reach agreement (consensus) on a solution, as a group.

---

[1]The authors are indebted to Professor David Boje for suggesting this option.

Copyright © 1982, John Wiley and Sons, Inc.

2. Now read the Vroom article. How do your recommendations compare with what Vroom might recommend?
3. Analyze each case with the decision tree in Figure 1. What decision style does the decision tree analysis lead to for each case?

OPTION TWO

INTRODUCTION: Read the following

A NEW LOOK AT MANAGERIAL DECISION-MAKING
Victor H. Vroom

While there are many differences in the roles that managers are called upon to play in organizations, all managers are decision-makers. Futhermore, there is little doubt that their effectiveness as managers is largely reflected in their "track record" in making the right decisions.

Several scholarly disciplines share an interest in the decision-making process. On one hand, we have the fields of operations research and management science, both concerned with how to improve the decisions which are made. Their models of decision-making, which are aimed at providing a rational basis for selecting among alternative courses of action, are termed normative or prescriptive models. On the other hand, we have, in the efforts of psychologists, sociologists, and political scientists, attempts to understand the decisions and choices that people do make. March and Simon were among the first to suggest that an understanding of the decision-making process could be central to an understanding of the behavior of organizations—a point of view that was later amplified by Cyert and March in their behavioral theory of the firm. In this tradition, the goal is understanding rather than improvement, and the models descriptive rather than normative.

Whether the models are normative or descriptive, the common ingredient is a conception of decision-making as an information-processing activity, frequently one which takes place within a single manager. Both sets of models focus on the set of alternative decisions or problem solutions from which the choice is, or should be, made. The normative models are based on the consequenses of choices among these alternatives; the descriptive models on the determinants of these choices. Alternatively, one could view the decision-making which occurs in organizations as a social or interpersonal process rather than a cognitive one. A major aspect of the manager's role in the decision-making process is to determine which person or persons should take part in the solution of the problem—or to put it more broadly—which social process should be engaged in the solution of the problem or the making of the decision.

...Underlying traditional approaches to leadership is the conviction that the manager is *the* problem-solver or decision-maker—that the task of translating problems into solutions is inevitably his task. In the alternative view of decision-making as a

*Reprinted by permission of the publisher, from *Organizational Dynamics* (Spring 1973), © 1973 by AMACOM, a division of American Management Associations. All rights reserved.

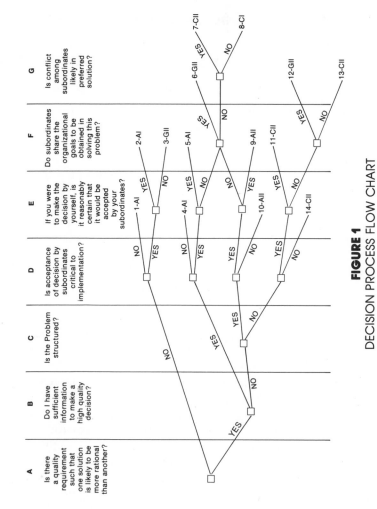

FIGURE 1
DECISION PROCESS FLOW CHART

Copyright © 1982, John Wiley and Sons, Inc.

social process, we see the manager's task as determining how the problem is to be solved, not the solution to be adopted....

Toward a Normative Model

[Let us begin] with [a] normative question. What would be a rational way of deciding on the form and amount of participation in decision-making that should be used in different situations? We [are] tired of debates over the relative merits of theory X and theory Y and of the truism that leadership depends upon the situation. We [feel] that it [is] time for the behavioral sciences to move beyond such generalities and to attempt to come to grips with the complexities of the phenomena with which they intended to deal.

TABLE 1:
Types of Management Decision Styles

AI:	You solve the problem or make the decision yourself, using information available to you at that time.
AII	You obtain the necessary information from your subordinate(s), then decide on the solution to the problem yourself. You may or may not tell your subordinates what the problem is in getting the information from them. The role played by your subordinates in making the decision is clearly one of providing the necessary informatiion to you, rather than generating or evaluating alternative solutions.
CI	You share the problem with relevant subordinates individually, getting their ideas and suggestions without bringing them together as a group. Then *you* make the decision which may or may not reflect your subordinates' influence.
CII	You share the problem with your subordinates as a group, collectively obtaining their ideas and suggestions. Then *you* make the decision which may or may not reflect your subordinates' influence.
GII	You share a problem with your subordinates as a group. Together you generate and evaluate alternatives and attempt to reach agreement (concensus) on a solution. Your role is much like that of chairman. You do not try to influence the group to adopt "your" solution and you are willing to accept and implement any solution which has the support of the entire group.

Table 1 shows a set of alternative decision processes which we have employed in our research. Each process is represented by a symbol (e.g., AI, CI, GII) which will be used as a convenient method of referring to each process. The first letter in this symbol signifies the basic properties of the processs (A stands for autocratic, C for consultative, and G for group). The roman numerals which follow the first letter constitute variants on that process. Thus AI represents the first variant on an autocratic process, and AII the second variant, etc.[2]

[2] The absence of GI from the code is attributable to the fact that the list of decision processes used in this paper is a part of a larger set of such processes used in broader and more comprehensive models. A complete explication of the entire set of prodesses and of the models which use them may be found in Vroom and Yetton (1973).

Conceptual and Empirical Basis of the Model

A model designed to regulate, in some rational way, choices among the decision processes shown in Table 1 should be based on sound empirical evidence concerning the likely consequences of the styles. The more complete the empirical base of knowledge, the greater the certainty with which one can develop the model and the greater will be its usefulness. To aid in understanding the conceptual basis of the model, it is important to distinguish three classes of outcomes which bear on the ultimate effectiveness of decisions. These are:

1. The quality or rationality of the decision.
2. The acceptance or commitment on the part of subordinates to execute the decision effectively.
3. The amount of time required to make the decision.

The evidence regarding the effects of participation on each of these outcomes of consequences has been reviewed in a chapter written by the author for *The Handbook of Social Psychology.* It was concluded that:

> *The results suggest that allocating problem solving and decision-making tasks to entire groups, requires a greater investment of man hours but produces higher acceptance of decisions and a higher probability that the decision will be executed efficiently. Differences between these two methods in quality of decisions and in elapsed time are inconclusive and probably highly variable ....It would be naive to think that group decision-making is always more "effective" than autocratic decision-making, or vice versa; the relative effectiveness of these two extreme methods depends both on the weights attached to quality, acceptance, and time variables, and on differences in amounts of these outcomes resulting from these methods, neither of which is invariant from one situation to another. The critics and proponents of participative management would do well to direct their efforts toward identifying the properties of situations in which different decision-making approaches are effective rather than wholesale condemnation or deification of one approach* (Vroom, 1970, pp. 239-40).

Stemming from this review, an attempt has been made to identify these properties of the situation or problem which will be the basic elements in the model. These problem attributes are of two types: (1) those which specify the importance for a particular problem of quality and acceptance, and (2) those which on the basis of available evidence have a high probability of moderating the effects of participation on each of these outcomes. Table 2 shows the problem attributes used in the present form of the model. For each attribute a question is provided which might be used by a leader in diagnosing a particular problem prior to choosing his leadership style.

In phrasing the questions, technical language has been held to a minimum. Furthermore, the questions have been phrased in Yes-No form, translating the continuous variables defined above into dichotomous variables. For example, instead of attempting to determine how important the decision quality is to the

Copyright © 1982, John Wiley and Sons, Inc.

effectiveness of the decision (attribute A), the leader is asked in the first question to judge whether there is any quality component to the problem. Similarly, the difficult task of specifying exactly how much information the leader possesses that is relevant to the decision (attribute B) is reduced to a simple judgment by the leader concerning whether he has sufficient information to make a high-quality decision.

It has been found that managers can diagnose a situation quite quickly and accurately by answering this set of seven questions concerning it. But how can such responses generate a prescription concerning the most effective leadership style or decision process? What kind of normative model of participation in decision-making can be built from this set of problem attributes?

TABLE 2
Problem Attributes Used in the Model

	Problem Attributes	*Diagnostic Questions*
A.	The importance of the quality of the decision.	Is there a quality requirement such that one solution is likely to be more rational than another?
B.	The extent to which the leader possesses sufficient information/expertise to make a high-quality decision by himself.	Do I have sufficient information to make a high-quality decision?
C.	The extent to which the problem is structured.	Is the problem structured?
D.	The extent to which acceptance or commitment on the part of subordinates is critical to the effective implementation of the decision.	Is acceptance of decision by subordinates critical to effective implementation?
E.	The prior probability that the leader's autocratic decision will receive acceptance by subordinates.	If you were to make the decision by yourself, is it reasonably certain that it would be accepted by your subordinates?
F.	The extent to which the subordinates are motivated to attain the organizational goals as represented in the objectives explicit in the statement of the problem.	Do subordinates share the organizational goals to be obtained in solving this problem?
G.	The extent to which subordinates are likely to be in conflict over preferred solutions.	Is conflict among subordinates likely in preferred solutions?

Figure 1 shows one such model expressed in the form of a decision tree. It is the seventh version of such a model which we have developed over the last three years.

The problem attributes, expressed in question form are arranged along the top of the figure. To use the model for a particular decision-making situation, one starts at the left-hand side and works toward the right, asking oneself the question immediately above any box that is encountered. When a terminal node is reached, a number will be found designating the problem type[3] and one of the decision-making processes appearing in Table 1. AI is prescribed for four problem types (1, 2, 4, and 5): AII is prescribed for two problem types (9 and 10); CI is prescribed for only one problem type (8); CII is prescribed for four problem types (7, 11, 13, and 14); and GII is prescribed for three problem types (3, 6, and 12). The relative frequency with which each of the five decision processes would be prescribed for any manager would, of course, be dependent on the distribution of problem types in his role.

Once all seven questions have been applied to a given problem a feasible set of decision processes is given. The feasible set for each of the 14 problem types is shown in Table 3. It can be seen that there are some problem types for which only one method remains in the feasible set, others for which two methods remain feasible, and still others for which five methods remain feasible.

When more than one method remains in the feasible set, there are a number of alternative decision rules which might dictate the choice among them. One, which underlies the prescriptions of the model shown in Figure 1, utilizes the number of manhours used in solving the problem as the basis for choice. Given a set of

TABLE 3
Problem Types and the Feasible Set of Decision Processes

Problem type	Acceptable methods
1	AI, AII, CI, CII, GII
2	AI, AII, CI, CII, GII
3	GII
4	AI, AII, CI, CII, GII[a]
5	AI, AII, CI, CII, GII[a]
6	GII
7	CII
8	CI, CII
9	AII, CI, CII, GII[a]
10	AII, CI, CII, GII[a]
11	CII, GII[a]
12	GII
13	CII
14	CII, GII[a]

[a]Within the feasible set only when the answer to question F is Yes.

[3]Problem type is a nominal variable designating classes of problems generated by the paths which lead to the terminal nodes.

Copyright © 1982, John Wiley and Sons, Inc.

methods with equal likelihood of meeting both quality and acceptance require-ments for the decision, it chooses that method which requires the least investment in manhours. On the basis of the empirical evidence summarized earlier, this is deemed to be the method furthest to the left within the feasible set. For example, since AI, AII, CI, CII, and GII are all feasible as in Problem Types 1 and 2, AI would be the method chosen. This decision rule acts to minimize manhours subject to quality and acceptance constraints.

Application of the Model

To illustrate how the model might be applied in actual administrative situations, a case will be presented and analyzed with the use of the model. Following the description of the case, the author's analysis will be given including a specification of problem type, feasible set, and solution indicated by the model. While an at-tempt has been made to describe (this) case as completely as is necessary to permit the reader to make the judgments required by the model, there may remain some room for subjectivity. The reader may wish after reading the case to analyze it himself using the model and then to compare his analysis with that of the authors.

...You are manufacturing manager in a large electronics plant. The company's management has always been searching for ways of increasing efficiency. They have recently installed new machines and put in a new simplified work system, but to the surprise of everyone, including yourself, the expected increase in produc-tivity was not realized. In fact, production has begun to drop, quality has fallen off, and the number of employee separations has risen.

You do not believe that there is anything wrong with the machines. You have had reports from other companies who are using them and they confirm this opinion. You have also had representatives from the firm that built the machines go over them and they report that they are operating at peak efficiency.

You suspect that some parts of the new work system may be responsible for the change, but this view is not widely shared among your immediate subordinates, who are four first-line supervisors, each in charge of a section, and your supply manager. The drop in production has been variously attributed to poor training of the operators, lack of an adequate system of financial incentives, and poor morale. Clearly, this is an issue about which there is considerable depth of feeling within individuals and potential disagreement between your subordinates.

This morning you received a phone call from your division manager. He had just received your production figures for the last six months and was calling to express his concern. He indicated that the problem was yours to solve in any way that you think best, but that he would like to know within a week what steps you plan to take.

You share your division manager's concern with the falling productivity and know that your men are also concerned. The problem is to decide what steps to take to rectify the situation.

Analysis

Questions A (Quality?) = Yes
         B (Manager's Information?) = No
         C (Structured?) = No
         D (Acceptance?) = Yes
         E (Prior Probability of Acceptance?) = No
         F (Goal Congruence?) = Yes
         [G (Conflict?) = Yes]
Problem Type: 12
Feasible Set: GII
Minimum Man-Hours Solution (from Figure 1): GII

Therefore, in the example, the appropriate decision process would be GII: you share the problem with your subordinates and arrive at a decision as a group.

PROCEDURE

Step 1: 10 Minutes
Review the "Decision Process Flow Chart" in Figure 1 of the Vroom article. Discuss any questions that you may have about it. Run through the illustrative case at the end of the reading, and discuss the analysis at the end of the case. Be sure that you understand the Vroom and Yetton model before proceeding to Step 2.

Step 2: 25 Minutes
In groups of three to five, analyze each of the four cases given below. Using the model in Figure 1 of the Vroom reading, decide upon the appropriate decision style to be used in each case. Try to achieve consensus, but if you reach an impasse, go on to the next case and return to the disputed one later. Pick a spokesperson to report your group's solutions to the rest of the class.

CASE I

You are general foreman in charge of a large gang laying an oil pipeline. It is now necessary to estimate your expected rate of progress in order to schedule material deliveries to the next field site.

You know the nature of the terrain you will be traveling and have the historical data needed to compute the mean and variance in the rate of speed over that type of terrain. Given these two variables, it is a simple matter to calculate the earliest and latest times at which materials and support facilities will be needed at the next site. It is important that your estimate be reasonably accurate. Underestimates result in idle foremen and workers, and an overestimate results in tying up materials for a period of time before they are to be used.

Progress has been good, and your five foremen and other members of the gang stand to receive substantial bonuses if the project is completed ahead of schedule.

Copyright © 1982, John Wiley and Sons, Inc.

CASE II

You are supervising the work of 12 engineers. Their formal training and work experience are very similar, permitting you to use them interchangeably on projects. Yesterday your manager informed you that a request had been received from an overseas affiliate for four engineers to go abroad on extended loan for a period of six to eight months. For a number of reasons, he argued and you agreed that this request should be met from your group.

All your engineers are capable of handling this assignment, and from the standpoint of present and future projects there is no particular reason why any one should be retained over any other. The problem is somewhat complicated by the fact that the overseas assignment is in what is generally regarded in the company as an undesirable location.

CASE III

You are the head of a staff unit reporting to the vice-president of finance. He has asked you to provide a report on the firm's current portfolio to include recommendations for changes in the selection criteria currently employed. Doubts have been raised about the efficiency of the existing system in the current market conditions, and there is considerable dissatisfaction with prevailing rates of return.

You plan to write the report, but at the moment you are quite perplexed about the approach to take. Your own specialty is the bond market, and it is clear to you that a detailed knowledge of the equity market, which you lack, would greatly enhance the value of the report. Fortunately, four members of your staff are specialists in different segments of the equity market. Together, they possess a vast amount of knowledge about the intricacies of investment. However, they seldom agree on the best way to achieve anything when it comes to the stock market. Although they are obviously conscientious as well as knowledgeable, they have major differences when it comes to investment philosophy and strategy.

You have six weeks before the report is due. You have already begun to familiarize yourself with the firm's current portfolio and have been provided by management with a specific set of constraints that any portfolio must satisfy. Your immediate problem is to come up with some alternatives to the firm's present practices and select the most promising for detailed analysis in your report.

CASE IV

You are on the division manager's staff and work on a wide variety of problems of both an administrative and technical nature. You have been given the assignment of developing a universal method to be used in each of the five plants in the division for manually reading equipment registers, recording the readings, and transmitting the scorings to a centralized information system. All plants are located in a relatively small geographical region.

Until now there has been a high error rate in the reading and/or transmittal of the data. Some locations have considerably higher error rates than others, and the methods used to record and transmit the data vary between plants. It is probable, therefore, that part of the error variance is a function of specific local conditions rather than anything else, and this will complicate the establishment of any system common to all plants. You have the information on error rates but no information on the local practices that generate these errors or on the local conditions that necessitate the different practices.

Everyone would benefit from an improvement in the quality of the data as they are used in a number of important decisions. Your contacts with the plants are through the quality-control supervisors who are responsible for collecting the data. They are a conscientious group committed to doing their jobs well, but are highly sensitive to interference on the part of higher management in their own operations. Any solution that does not receive the active support of the various plant supervisors is unlikely to reduce the error rate significantly.

Step 3: 15 Minutes

Meet again as a total class group. First, each group reports on the decision style it thought was appropriate for each case. (If there are more than three or four groups, take a vote to see how many groups chose which style for each case.) Next, the group leader will present Vroom's analysis of each case and the styles that are appropriate according to his analysis. Finally, discuss Vroom's and the class's analyses and the discrepancies (if any) between them.

DISCUSSION QUESTIONS

1. How much agreement was there within the class about the appropriate decision style for each case? Why?
2. How much agreement was there between the class's solutions and Vroom's analysis? Why? When in doubt between two styles, which one would you choose? Why?

GENERALIZATIONS AND CONCLUSIONS

Concluding Points

1. Before you choose the process that you will use to make a management decision, it is important first to do what?

Copyright © 1982, John Wiley and Sons, Inc.

2. Even though the Vroom and Yetton model seems clear-cut, people often differ on their answers to the diagnostic questions (A-G in Figure 1) about the situation. What factors may account for differences in the way people diagnose leadership situations?

3. To recapitulate, the appropriateness of a particular style of decision making depends upon the importance of what three factors?

Participant's Reactions

READINGS AND REFERENCES

Vroom, V., and Yetton, P., *Leadership and Decision-Making* (Pittsburgh: University of Pittsburgh Press, 1973).

27
ASSIGNMENT: WHAT DO MANAGERS DO?

PURPOSE:
To generate an analysis of the managerial job in terms of the roles performed by managers.

ADVANCE PREPARATION:
Read readings assigned by the group leader before starting assignment.

RELATED TOPICS: Managers as leaders; Life, work, and career roles; Organizational communication; Interpersonal communication; Organizational structure and design, Planned change, Organizational realities.

INTRODUCTION

Students of management have attempted to develop a comprehensive description of the managerial job for many years. Fayol (1916) was one of the first to propose looking at managerial work in terms of the functions performed by a manager. Other approaches have been suggested as well, but the result has been a "jungle" of theoretical frameworks and empirical findings (Koontz, 1961), rather than a convergence toward a shared view of the managerial job.

Most recently, the work of Henry Mintzberg (1971, 1973a, 1973b) has attracted considerable attention and acclaim. Based on observations of managers at work, Mintzberg has developed a role model of the managerial job. Ten roles, falling into three broad categories or "families" of roles, were identified by Mintzberg. These ten roles form the basis of the interview you will conduct in this exercise.

PROCEDURE

After you have read the assignment, interview a manager, using the "What Do Managers Do?—Interviewing Questionnaire," below. Follow the instructions for the questionnaire carefully; be sure that you have read them over and understand them before you begin the interview.

For purposes of this assignment, a manager is any person whose job primarily involves *supervising the work of other people*. The manager may work in a business, public or private agency, school, etc. The nature of the duties, not the type of organization, is the important criterion.

Developed by Donald D. Bowen. Based upon the theoretical framework proposed by Mintzberg (1971, 1973a, 1973b).

Copyright © 1982, John Wiley and Sons, Inc.

The Mintzberg roles are given—though not labeled—on the questionnaire in the following order:

Interpersonal roles	*Information roles*	*Decisional roles*
1. Figurehead	4. Monitor	7. Entrepreneur
2. Leader	("Nerve Center" in	8. Disturbance handler
3. Liaison	Mintzberg)	9. Resource allocator
	5. Disseminator	10. Negotiator
	6. Spokesman	

The role titles are left unlabeled on the questionnaire because managers tend to respond to the title rather than the content of the role. Bring the completed interview to the session specified by the group leader. The data will be summarized and discussed by the entire group.

Copyright © 1982, John Wiley and Sons, Inc.

WHAT DO MANAGERS DO?
—INTERVIEWING QUESTIONNAIRE

On the following pages, you will find a list of ten "roles"—that is, functions that have been found in studies of managerial work. Not every manager performs every role; not every role is equally important in each manager's job. And there may be things managers do that are not on the list. Note that there is an "Other" category for listing important things not already on the form.

The objective of this assignment is to provide an experience in which you can collect some information on what contributions managers make to achieving the organization's goals. Remember, for purposes of this study, *a manager is anyone whose job consists primarily of supervising other people.*

Instructions

1. Find a manager and conduct the interview, using the attached form as a guide. Obtain numerical answers, using the scale provided, for *all* of the questions in the first two columns:
   a. Which are the most important roles—*those which contribute to effective performance in the job?*
   b. Which are the most *time-consuming?*
   For the third column, ask the manager for an example of this role.
2. Discuss the results with the manager. Ask: Were there any roles that you had expected to be more (or less) important before the interview? Were there any roles where the time consumed seemed disproportionate to the importance of the role? Which are the most difficult roles? You may think of other questions you wish to ask, as well.
3. Take notes on the interview and bring them with you to refer to in the group discussion.
4. *You do not need to supply the name of the manager interviewed.* We are only interested in developing a sample of managerial views of their job. The responses will be *anonymous,* and you should treat the interview as a *confidential* communication.

Ten roles and the typical activities involved in them are listed below, together with a space for you to list items that may be important but not provided for. For each role, enter the appropriate numbers based upon the following scale. In column 1, enter a number reflecting *how important the role is to effective* job performance for the manager.

Scale values for column 1:

1 = Of no importance; 2 = Of minimal importance; 3 = Of some importance; 4 = Of considerable importance; 5 = Of very high importance

Next, in column 2, enter a number from the scale to describe *how time-consuming the role is for the manager.*

Scale values for column 2:

1 = No time consumed; 2 = Minimal time consumed; 3 = Some time consumed; 4 = Considerable time consumed; 5 = A very high amount of time consumed

Finally, in the last column, briefly note *an example* of the job duties performed in fulfilling this role.

Fill in columns 1 and 2 for *every* job role, even if you have difficulty identifying an example for column 3.

Role Activities and Examples

	1. Importance to effective performance on the job	2. Time-consuming parts of the job	3. A typical example
1. Acts as legal and symbolic head; performs obligatory social, ceremonial, or legal duties (retirement dinner, luncheon for employees, plant dedication, annual dinner dance, civic affairs, signs contract on behalf of firm)			
2. Motivates, develops, and guides subordinates; staffing, training, and associated duties (management by objectives, provides challenging assignments, develops people, selects personnel, encourages subordinates, trains new employees)			
3. Maintains a network of contacts and information sources outside own group to obtain information and assistance (attends staff meetings, takes customer to lunch, attends professional meetings, meets with manager of department X, keeps abreast of upcoming design changes)			

Copyright © 1982, John Wiley and Sons, Inc.

	1. Importance to effective performance on the job	2. Time-consuming parts of the job	3. A typical example
4. Seeks and obtains information to understand organization and environment. Acts as nerve center for organization (chart work flow, workplace meetings, audits expense control statements, reviews exception reports, reviews quotations, meets with production control)			
5. Transmits information to subordinates within own organizational area of responsibility (workplace meetings, disseminates results of meetings, transmits policy letters, briefs subordinates, sends out copies of information, posts schedules and forecasts)			
6. Transmits information to persons outside of organizational area of responsibility (works with product committee, prepares weekly status reports, participates in meetings, deals with customer's coordinator, field sales)			
7. Searches organization and its environment for "improvement projects" to change products, processes, procedures, and organization. Supervises design and implementation of change projects as well (cost reduction program, plant trip to X Division, changes forecasting system, brings in subcontract work to level work load, reorganizes department.			

	1. Importance to effective performance on the job	2. Time-consuming parts of the job	3. A typical example
8. Takes corrective action in time of disturbance or crisis (handles union grievances, negotiates sales problems, redistributes work during "crash programs," handles customer complaints, resolves personal conflicts, assigns engineers to problem jobs)			
9. Allocates organizational resources by making or approving decisions. Scheduling, budgeting, planning, programming of subordinate's work, etc. (budgeting, program scheduling, assigns personnel, strategic planning, plans manpower load, sets objectives)			
10. Represents organization in negotiating of sales, labor, or other agreements. Represents department or group negotiating with other functions within the organization (negotiates with suppliers, assists in quoting on new work, negotiates with union, hires, resolves jurisdictional dispute with department X, negotiates sales contract)			
Other:			

Copyright © 1982, John Wiley and Sons, Inc.

READINGS AND REFERENCES

Fayol, H., *Administration Industrielle et Generale* (Paris: Dunod, 1916). Available in English as *General and Industrial Management* (London: Pitman, 1949).

Koontz, H., "The Management Theory Jungle," *Journal of the Academy of Management,* 4 (1961), 174–88.

Koontz, H., "Retrospective Comment." In L. E. Boone and D. D. Bowen (Eds.) *The Great Writings in Management and Organizational Behavior* (Tulsa: PPC Books, 1980), pp. 271–276. Koontz's "The Management Theory Jungle" is also reprinted in this volume.

Mintzberg, H., "Managerial Work: Analysis from Observation," *Management Science,* Oct. (1971), B97–B110.

Mintzberg, H., *The Nature of Managerial Work* (New York: Harper & Row, 1973a).

Mintzberg, H., "A New Look at the Chief Executive's Job," *Organizational Dynamics,* 1 (1973b), 20–41.

Copyright © 1982, John Wiley and Sons, Inc.

PART III
ORGANIZATIONS

SECTION EIGHT
ORGANIZATIONAL REALITIES

28
LARRY ROSS: A CASE FOR DISCUSSION

PURPOSE:
To provide a basis for discussion of organizational power and politics and their relationships to our own careers.

ADVANCE PREPARATION:
Read "Larry Ross" and prepare your answers to the questions provided.

GROUP SIZE: Any size that permits case discussion. For large groups (over 50) see the Instructor's Manual for alternative procedures.
TIME REQUIRED: 50 minutes or more.
SPECIAL MATERIALS: None.
SPECIAL PHYSICAL REQUIREMENTS: None.
RELATED TOPICS: Managers as leaders; Motivation: basic concepts; Power; Organizational communication; Life, work, and career roles; Negotiation and conflict.

LARRY ROSS[1]

The corporation is a jungle. It's exciting. You're thrown in on your own and you're constantly battling to survive. When you learn to survive, the game is to become the conqueror, the leader.

Adapted by Donald D. Bowen. Originally used as a case in A. R. Cohen, S. L. Fink, H. Gadon, and R. D. Willits in *Effective Behavior in Organizations* (Homewood, Ill.: Irwin, 1976).

[1] "Larry Ross" is from S. Terkel, *Working: People Talk About What They Do All Day and How They Feel About What They Do*. Copyright © 1972, 1974 by Studs Terkel. Reprinted by permission of Pantheon Books, a division of Random House, Inc. Abridged by permission of the author and publisher.

Copyright © 1982, John Wiley and Sons, Inc.

"I've been called a business consultant. Some say I'm a business psychiatrist. You can describe me as an advisor to top management in a corporation." He's been at it since 1968.

I started in the corporate world, oh gosh—'42. After kicking around in the Depression, having all kinds of jobs and no formal education, I wasn't equipped to become an engineer, a lawyer, or a doctor. I gravitated to selling. Now they call it marketing. I grew up in various corporations. I became the executive vice president of a large corporation and then of an even larger one. Before I quit I became president and chief executive officer of another. All nationally known companies.

Sixty-eight, we sold out our corporation. There was enough money in the transaction where I didn't have to go back in business. I decided that I wasn't going to get involved in the corporate battle any more. It lost its excitement, its appeal. People often ask me, "Why weren't you in your own business? You'd probably have made a lot of money." I often ask it myself, I can't explain it, except....

Most corporations I've been in, they were on the New York Stock Exchange with thousands and thousands of stockholders. The last one—whereas, I was the president and chief executive, I was always subject to the board of directors, who had pressure from the stockholders. I owned a portion of the business, but I wasn't in control. I don't know of any situation in the corporate world where an executive is completely free and sure of his job from moment to moment.

Corporations always have to be right. That's their face to the public. When things go bad, they have to protect themselves and fire somebody. "We had nothing to do with it. We had an executive that just screwed everything up." He's never really ever been his own boss.

The danger starts as soon as you become a district manager. You have men working for you and you have a boss above. You're caught in a squeeze. The squeeze progresses from station to station. I'll tell you what a squeeze is. You have the guys working for you that are shooting for your job. The guy you're working for is scared stiff you're gonna shove him out of his job. Everybody goes around and says, "The test of the true executive is that you have men working for you that can replace you, so you can move up." That's a lot of boloney. The manager is afraid of the bright young guy coming up.

Fear is always prevalent in the corporate structure. Even if you're a top man, even if you're hard, even if you do your job—by the slight flick of a finger, your boss can fire you. There's always the insecurity. You bungle a job. You're fearful of losing a big customer. You're fearful so many things will appear on your record, stand against you. You're always fearful of the big mistake. You've got to be careful when you go to corporation parties. Your wife, your children have to behave properly. You've got to fit in the mold. You've got to be on guard.

When I was president of this big corporation, we lived in a small Ohio town, where the main plant was located. The corporation specified who you could socialize with, and on what level. (His wife interjects: "Who were the wives you could play bridge with.") The president's wife could do what she wants, as long as it's with dignity and grace. In a small town they didn't have to keep check on you. Everybody knew. There are certain sets of rules.

Not every corporation has that. The older the corporation, the longer it's been in a powerful position, the more rigid, the more conservative they are in their approach. Your swinging corporations are generally the new ones, the upstarts, the *nouveau riche*. But as they get older, like duPont, General Motors, General Electric, they became more rigid. I'd compare them to the old, old rich—the Rockefellers and the Mellons—that train their children how to handle money, how to conserve their money, and how to grow with their money. That's what happened to the older corporations. It's only when they get in trouble that they'll have a young upstart of a president come in and try to shake things up.

The executive is a lonely animal in the jungle who doesn't have a friend. Business is related to life. I think in our everyday living we're lonely. I have only a wife to talk to, but beyond that....When I talked business to her, I don't know whether she understood me. But that was unimportant. What's important is that I was able to talk out loud and hear myself—which is the function I serve as a consultant.

The executive who calls me usually knows the answer to his problem. He just has to have somebody to talk to and hear his decision out loud. If it sounds good when he speaks it out loud, then it's pretty good. As he's talking, he may suddenly realize his errors and he corrects them out loud. That's a great benefit wives provide for executives. She's listening and you know she's on your side. She's not gonna hurt you.

Gossip and rumor are always prevalent in a corporation. There's absolutely no secrets. I have always felt every office was wired. You come out of the board meeting and people in the office already know what's happened. I've tried many times to track down a rumor, but never could. I think people have been there so many years and have developed an ability to read reactions. From these reactions they make a good, educated guess. Gossip actually develops into fact.

It used to be a ploy for many minor executives to gain some information. "I heard that the district manager of California is being transferred to Seattle." He knows there's been talk going on about changing district managers. By using this ploy—"I know something"—he's making it clear to the person he's talking to that he's been in on it all along. So it's all right to tell him. Gossip is another way of building up importance within a person who starts the rumor. He's in, he's part of the inner circle. Again, we're back in the jungle. Every ploy, every trick is used to survive.

When you're gonna merge with a company or acquire another company, it's supposed to be top secret. You have to do something to stem the rumors because it might screw up the deal. Talk of the merger, the whole place is in a turmoil. It's like somebody saying there's a bomb in the building and we don't know where it is and when it's going to go off. There've been so many mergers where top executives are laid off, the accounting department is cut by sixty percent, the manufacturing is cut by twenty percent. I have yet to find anybody in a corporation who was so secure to honestly believe it couldn't happen to him.

Copyright © 1982, John Wiley and Sons, Inc.

They put on a front: "Oh, it can't happen to me. I'm too important." But deep down, they're scared stiff. The fear is there. You can smell it. You can see it on their faces. I'm not so sure you couldn't see it on my face many, many times during my climb up.

I always used to say—rough, tough Larry—I always said, "If you do a good job, I'll give you a great reward. You'll keep your job." I'll have a sales contest and the men who make their quota will win a prize—they'll keep their jobs. I'm not saying there aren't executives who instill fear in their people. He's no different than anybody walking down the street. We're all subject to the same damn insecurities and neuroses—at every level. Competitiveness, that's the basis of it.

Why didn't I stay in the corporate structure? As a kid, living through the Depression, you always heard about the tycoons, the men of power, the men of industry. And you kind of dream that. Gee, these are supermen. These are the guys that have no feeling, aren't subject to human emotions, the insecurities that everybody else has. You get in the corporate structure, you find they all button their pants the same way everybody else does. They all get the same fears.

The corporation is made up of many, many people. I call 'em the gray people and the black—or white—people. Blacks and whites are definite colors, solid. Gray isn't. The gray people come there from nine to five, do their job, aren't particularly ambitious. There's no fear there, sure. But they're not subject to great demands. They're only subject to dismissal when business goes bad and they cut off people. They go from corporation to corporation and get jobs. Then you have the black—or white—people. The ambitious people, the leaders, the ones who want to get ahead.

When the individual reaches the vice presidency or he's general manager, you know he's an ambitious, dedicated guy who wants to get to the top. He isn't one of the gray people. He's one of the black-and-white vicious people—the leaders, the ones who stick out in the crowd.

As he struggles in this jungle, every position he's in, he's terribly lonely. He can't confide and talk with the guy working under him. He can't confide and talk to the man he's working for. To give vent to his feeling, his fears, and his insecurities, he'd expose himself. This goes all the way up the line until he gets to be president. The president *really* doesn't have anybody to talk to, because the vicepresidents are waiting for him to die or make a mistake and get knocked off so they can get his job.

He can't talk to the board of directors, because to them he has to appear as a tower of strength, knowledge, and wisdom, and have the ability to walk on water. The board of directors, they're cold, they're hard. They don't have any direct-line responsibilities. They sit in a staff capacity and they really play God. They're interested in profits. They're interested in progress. They're interested in keeping a good face in the community—if it's profitable. You have the tremendous infighting of man against man for survival and clawing to the top. Progress.

We always saw signs of physical afflictions because of the stress and strain. Ulcers, violent headaches. I remember one of the giant corporations I was in, the chief executive officer ate Gelusil by the minute. That's for ulcers. Had a private dining room with his private chef. All he ever ate was well-done steak and well-done hamburgers.

There's one corporation chief I had who worked, conservatively, nineteen, twenty hours a day. His whole life was his business. And he demanded the same of his executives. There was nothing sacred in life except the business. Meetings might be called on Christmas Eve or New Year's Eve, Saturdays, Sundays. He was lonesome when he wasn't involved with his business. He was always creating situations where he could be surrounded by his flunkies, regardless of what level they were, presidential, vice presidential....It was his life.

In the corporate structure, the buck keeps passing up until it comes to the chief executive. Then there ain't nobody to pass the buck to. You sit there in your lonely office and finally you have to make a decision. It could involve a million dollars or hundreds of jobs or moving people from Los Angeles, which they love, to Detroit or Winnipeg. So you're sitting at the desk, playing God.

You say, "Money isn't important. You can make some bad decisions about money, that's not important. What is important is the decisions you make about people working for you, their livelihood, their lives." It isn't true.

To the board of directors, the dollars are as important as human lives. There's only yourself sitting there making the decision, and you hope it's right. You're always on guard. Did you ever see a jungle animal that wasn't on guard? You're always looking over your shoulder. You don't know who's following you.

The most stupid phrase anybody can use in business is loyalty. If a person is working for a corporation, he's supposed to be loyal. This corporation is paying him less than he could get somewhere else at a comparable job. It's stupid of him to hang around and say he's loyal. The only loyal people are the people who can't get a job anyplace else. Working in a corporation, in a business, isn't a game. It isn't a collegiate event. It's a question of living or dying. It's a question of eating or not eating. Who is he loyal to? It isn't his country. It isn't his religion. It isn't his political party. He's working for some company that's paying him a salary for what he's doing. The corporation is out to make money. The ambitious guy will say, "I'm doing my job. I'm not embarrassed taking my money. I've got to progress and when I won't progress, I won't be here." The schnook is the loyal guy, because he can't get a job anyplace else.

Many corporations will hang on to a guy or promote him to a place where he doesn't belong. Suddenly, after the man's been there twenty-five years, he's outlived his usefulness. And he's too old to start all over again. That's part of the cruelty. You can't only condemn the corporation for that. The man himself should be smart enough and intuitive enough to know he isn't getting anyplace, to get the hell out and start all over. It was much more difficult at first to lay off a guy. But if you live in a jungle, you become hard, unfortunately.

When a top executive is let go, the king is dead, long live the king. Suddenly he's a *persona non grata*. When it happens, the shock is tremendous. Overnight.

Copyright © 1982, John Wiley and Sons, Inc.

He doesn't know what hit him. Suddenly everybody in the organization walks away and shuns him because they don't want to be associated with him. In corporations, if you back the wrong guy, you're in his corner, and he's fired, you're guilty by association. So what a lot of corporations have done is when they call a guy in — sometimes they'll call him in on a Friday night and say, "Go home now and come in tomorrow morning and clean out your desk and leave. We don't want any farewells or anything. Just get up and get the hell out." It's done in nice language. We say, "Look, why cause any trouble? Why cause any unrest in the organization? It's best that you just fade away." Immediately his Cadillac is taken away from him. His phone extension on the WATS line is taken away from him.* All these things are done quietly and—bingo! he's dead. His phone at home stops ringing because the fear of association continues after the severance. The smell of death is there.

We hired a vice president. He came highly recommended. He was with us about six months and he was completely inadequate. A complete misfit. Called him in the office, told him he was gonna go, gave him a nice severance pay. He broke down and cried. "What did I do wrong? I've done a marvelous job. Please don't do this to me. My daughter's getting married next month. How am I going to face the people?" He cried and cried and cried. But we couldn't keep him around. We just had to let him go.

I was just involved with a gigantic corporation. They had a shake-up two Thursdays ago. It's now known as Black Thursday. Fifteen of twenty guys were let go overnight. The intelligent corporations say, "Clear, leave tonight, even if it's midweek. Come in Saturday morning and clean your desk. That's all. No good-bys or anything." They could be guys that have been there anywhere from a year to thirty years. If it's a successful operation, they're very generous. But then again, the human element creeps in. The boss might be vindictive and cut him off without anything. It may depend what the corporation wants to maintain as its image.

And what it does to the ego! A guy in a key position, everybody wants to talk to him. All his subordinates are trying to get an audience with him to build up their own positions. Customers are calling him, everybody is calling him. Now his phone's dead. He's sitting at home and nobody calls him. He goes out and starts visiting his friends, who are busy with their own business, who haven't got time for him. Suddenly he's a failure. Regardless what the reason was—regardless of the press release that said he resigned—he was fired.

The only time the guy isn't considered a failure is when he resigns and announces his new job. That's the tipoff. "John Smith resigned, future plans unknown" means he was fired. "John Smith resigned to accept the position of president of X Company"—then you know he resigned. This little nuance you recognize immediately when you're in corporate life.

---

*Wide area telecommunications service. A perrogative granted important executives by some corporations: unlimited use of the telephone to make a call anywhere in the world.

DISCUSSION QUESTIONS

1. Does Larry Ross provide an accurate and realistic picture of how organizations operate? If you think so, is it true of all, most, some or only a few organizations? Why did you answer as you did?
2. Is the organization better (or worse) off if managers behave like Larry Ross? Why?
3. Assuming that you would like to become an executive in a large organization, would you be willing to do the things Ross does to achieve your goal? Why?
4. Do you see Larry Ross as a person who has largely contributed to his own problems, or as a person who simply goes along with a world he did not create? Why?

GENERALIZATIONS AND CONCLUSIONS

Concluding Points

1. Are people like Larry Ross usually successful in getting themselves promoted into top executive positions? Once there, are they effective leaders?

2. Is there any reason to suspect that Ross contributes to his own problems?

Copyright © 1982, John Wiley and Sons, Inc.

Participant's Reactions

READINGS AND REFERENCES

Argyris, C. "Interpersonal Barriers to Decision Making," *Harvard Business Review*, March-April, 44 (1966), 84-97.

Frost, P. J., Mitchell, V. F., and Nord, W. R. (Eds.), *Organizational Reality: Reports From the Firing Line* (Santa Monica, Calif.: Goodyear, 1978).

Hamner, W. C. (Ed.), *Organizational Shock* (New York: Wiley, 1980).

Livingston, J. S., "Pygmalion in Management," *Harvard Business Review*, July-August, 47 (1969), 81-89.

Maccoby, M., *The Gamesman* (New York: Simon & Schuster, 1976).

Ritti, R. R., and Funkhouser, G. R., *The Ropes to Skip and the Ropes to Know: Studies in Organizational Behavior* (Columbus, Ohio: Grid Publishing, 1977).

Rotter, J. B., "Interpersonal Trust, Trustworthiness, and Gulllibility," *American Psychologist*, 35 (1980), 1-7.

29
CAREER STYLE INVENTORY: AN ASSESSMENT EXERCISE

PURPOSE:
(1) To engage in an assessment of the personal style that one currently expresses, or intends to express, in organizational life.
(2) To explore the dynamics of that style with others of similar disposition, and understand how individuals of different styles perceive one another in organizational environments.

ADVANCE PREPARATION:
The questionnaire may be completed as a homework assignment, if specified by the instructor.

GROUP SIZE: *Option one:* Break larger group into subgroups, based on responses to the questionnaire. If subgroup exceeds eight to nine members, subdivide into more than one group for each "style." *Option two:* Single large discussion group.

TIME REQUIRED: *Option one*: 2 hours. *Option two*: 30 minutes.

SPECIAL MATERIALS: None.

SPECIAL PHYSICAL REQUIREMENTS: For Option one, additional small meeting rooms for subgroup meetings, or movable chairs and space sufficient to separate subgroups for private discussion.

RELATED TOPICS: Larry Ross (Exercise 28); Motivation: basic concepts; Managers as leaders; Power; Life, work and career roles.

INTRODUCTION

There have been a number of efforts by behavioral scientists to describe, categorize, and classify different personal styles in organizations. Many of these efforts have concentrated on describing different styles of leaders (e.g., Blake and Mouton, 1964; Tannenbaum and Schmidt, 1958; Hersey and Blanchard, 1977), while other works have focused on the basic characteristics of those who work for organizations (e.g., Whyte, 1956; Jay, 1968, 1971).

The following questionnaire was developed to measure individual dispositions toward another set of personal styles in organizations, proposed by Michael Maccoby (1976). After completing the questionnaire below, you will have the opportunity to read about these styles, and to evaluate your own responses to the questionnaire.

Developed by Roy J. Lewicki.

Copyright © 1982, John Wiley and Sons, Inc.

BOTH OPTIONS

Step 1: 20 Minutes
Complete the questionnaire that begins on page 191.

Step 2: 10 Minutes
When you have evaluated each paragraph, turn to page 195 and "score" the questionnaire by entering your ratings for each paragraph. Then obtain a Total Score for each of the four orientations.

Step 3: 10 Minutes
Read the following description of the four styles.

THE CORPORATE CLIMBER HAS TO FIND HIS HEART[1]

A new type of man is taking over the leadership of the most technically advanced large companies in America. In contrast to the jungle-fighter industrialists commonly associated with the turn of the century, the new leader is driven not to build or preside over empires, but to organize winning teams. Unlike the security-seeking organization man who became the stereotype of the Fifties, he is excited by the chance to cut deals and to gamble.

The new industrial leader is not as hardhearted as the autocratic empire builder, nor is he as dependent on the company as the organization man. But he is more detached and emotionally inaccessible than either. And he is troubled by that fact: he recognizes that his work develops his head but not his heart.

As a practicing psychoanalyst, I reached these conclusions on the basis of interviews with 250 managers, ranging from chief executives down to lower-level professional employees in twelve well-known corporations. The study was sponsored by the Harvard Seminar on Science, Technology, and Public Policy and supported by the Andrew W. Mellon Foundation. With the help of Douglass Carmichael, Rolando Weissmann, Dennis M. Greene, Cynthia Elliott, and Katherine A. Terzi, I conducted the interviews over six years.

In some cases we returned to particular managers several times to talk about how their work was influencing the development of their characters. All together, we spent at least three hours with most, as long as twenty hours with some. In a few cases we also interviewed their wives and children, and seventy five executives took Rorschach tests.

In contrast to psychoanalysts who study the emotionally disturbed, we concentrated on healthy people in healthy companies. Most of the companies have sales exceeding $1 billion a year and all are highly technological, creators of some of the most advanced products of our age. They practice, and some invented, managerial techniques and business strategies that others admire and copy. Their top

(Continued on page 197.)

[1]Excerpt from article by Michael Maccoby in *Fortune* (December 1976). Reprinted by permission of Dr. Maccoby.

Copyright © 1982, John Wiley and Sons, Inc.

CAREER STYLE INVENTORY

Below are a number of descriptive paragraphs. They describe a set of beliefs or perceptions that may be held by different individuals that work for large organizations. The paragraphs are divided into four sections: Life Goals, Motivation, Self-Image, and Relations with Others. For each section, there are four paragraphs. Please evaluate these paragraphs as follows:

1. Read the paragraph. Treating the paragraph as an entity—that is, using *all* of the information in the paragraph, not just one or two sentences—*rate* the paragraph as it describes you. Indicate in a scale from "not at all characteristic of me" (1) to "highly characteristic of me" (7). Rate each paragraph in the section on this scale.
2. Rate each paragraph in terms of the way you would *like* to be. Regardless of how you are now, rate each description as it represents an "ideal" managerial style. Rate each on a scale from "not like to be like this at all" (1) to "very much like to be like this" (7).

Please be as honest, realistic and candid in your self-evaluations as possible. Try to accurately describe yourself, not represent what you think others might want you to say or believe.

Scales:

1	2	3	4	5	6	7
Not at all characteristic of me		Somewhat characteristic of me		Generally characteristic of me		Highly characteristic of me

1	2	3	4	5	6	7
I would not like to be like this at all		I would somewhat like to be like this		I would generally like to be like this		I would very strongly like to be like this

A. Life Goals

1. I equate my personal success in life with the long-term development and success of the organization that I work for. I enjoy a sense of belonging, responsibility, and loyalty to an organization. I believe that I will benefit most if my organization prospers. I would be satisfied with my career if I progressed no higher than a middle management level.
   How characteristic is this of you (1-7)_____?
   How much would you like to be like this (1-7)_____?
2. I have two major goals in life: to do my job well, and to be committed to my family. I believe strongly in the work ethic, and want to succeed by skillfully and creatively accomplishing goals and tasks. I also want to be a good parent and provider for my family. Work and family are equally important.
   How characteristic is this of you (1-7)_____?
   How much would you like to be like this (1-7)_____?

3. My goal in life is to acquire power; success for me means being involved in a number of successful, diverse enterprises. I generally experience life and work as a jungle; like it or not, it's a dog-eat-dog world, and there will always be winners and losers. I want to be one of the winners.
How characteristic is this of you (1-7)_____?
How much would you like to be like this (1-7)_____?

4. I tend to view life and work as a game. I see my work, my relations with others, and my career in terms of options and possibilities as if they were part of a strategic game that I was playing. My main goal in life is to be a winner at this game.
How characteristic is this of you (1-7)_____?
How much would you like to be like this (1-7)_____?

B. Motivation

1. My interest in work is in the process of building something. I am motivated by problems that need to be solved; the challenge of work itself or the creation of a quality product gets me excited. I would prefer to miss a deadline rather than do something halfway—quality is more important to me than quantity.
How characteristic is this of you (1-7)_____?
How much would you like to be like this (1-7)_____?

2. I like to take risks, and am fascinated by new methods, techniques, and approaches. I want to motivate myself and others by pushing everyone to their limits, beyond their normal pace. My interest is in challenge, or competitive activity, where I can prove myself to be a winner. The greatest sense of exhiliration for me comes from managing a team of people and gaining victories. When work is no longer challenging, I feel bored and slightly depressed.
How characteristic is this of you (1-7)_____?
How much would you like to be like this (1-7)_____?

3. I like to control other people and to acquire power. I want to succeed by climbing the corporate ladder, acquiring greater positions of power and resonsibility. I want to use this power to gain prestige, visibility, financial success, and to be able to make decisions that affect many other people. Being good at "politics" is essential to this success.
How characteristic is this of you (1-7)_____?
How much would you like to be like this (1-7)_____?

4. My interest in work is to derive a sense of security from organizational membership, and to have good relations with others. I am concerned with the feelings of people who I work with, and am committed to maintaining the integrity of my organization. As long as the organization rewards my efforts, I am willing to let my commitment to my organization take precedence over my own self-interest.
How characteristic is this of you (1-7)_____?
How much would you like to be like this (1-7)_____?

C. Self-Image

1. I am competitive and innovative. My speech and my thinking are dynamic, and come in quick flashes. I like to emphasize my strengths, and I like to be in control. I have a lot of trouble realizing and living within my limitations. I pride myself on

Copyright © 1982, John Wiley and Sons, Inc.

being fair with others; I have very few prejudices. I like to have limitless options to succeed; my biggest fears are being trapped, or being labeled as a loser.

How characteristic is this of you (1-7)_____?

How much would you like to be like this (1-7)_____?

2. My identity depends upon being part of a prestigious, protective organization. I see myself as trustworthy, responsible, a "nice guy" who can get along with almost everyone. I'm concerned with making a good impression on others, and representing the company well. I'm not sure that I have as much confidence, toughness, aggressiveness, and risk-taking as I would like. I am aware of these weaknesses, but I also think I should receive credit for the contributions I have made to my organization.

How characteristic is this of you (1-7)_____?

How much would you like to be like this (1-7)_____?

3. My sense of self-worth is based on my assessment of my skills, abilities, self-discipline, and self-reliance. I tend to be quiet, sincere, modest, and practical. I like to stay with a project from conception to completion.

How characteristic is this of you (1-7)_____?

How much would you like to be like this (1-7)_____?

4. I tend to be brighter, more courageous, and stronger than most of the people I work with. I see myself as bold, innovative, and an entrepreneur. I can be exceptionally creative at times, particularly in seeing entrepreneurial possibilities and opportunities. I am willing to take major risks in order to succeed, and willing to be secretive or manipulative with others if it will further my own goals.

How characteristic is this of you (1-7)_____?

How much would you like to be like this (1-7)_____?

D. Relations with Others

1. I tend to dominate other people because my ideas are better, and/or I am willing to take risks and withstand a lot of criticism. I generally don't like to work closely and cooperate with others. I would rather have other people working for me, following my directions. I don't think anyone has ever really freely helped me; either I controlled and directed them, or they were expecting me to do something for me in return.

How characteristic is this of you (1-7)_____?

How much would you like to be like this (1-7)_____?

2. My relations with others are generally good. I value highly other people who are trustworthy, committed to this organization, and act with integrity in the things that they do. In my workgroup, I attempt to sustain an atmosphere of cooperation, mild excitement, and mutuality. I get "turned off" by others in the organization who are out for themselves, who show no respect for others, or who get so involved with their own little problems that they lose sight of the "big picture."

How characteristic is this of you (1-7)_____?

How much would you like to be like this (1-7)_____?

3. I like to be in control; I am tough and dominating, but I don't think I am destructive. I tend to classify other people as winners and losers. I evaluate almost everyone in terms of what they can do for the team. I coax other people to share their knowledge with others, trying to get a work atmosphere that is both exciting and productive. I am impatient with others who are slower and more

cautious, and don't like to see weakness in others.

How characteristic is this of you (1-7)_____?

How much would you like to be like this (1-7)_____?

4. My relations with others are generally determined by the work that we do. I feel more comfortable working in a small group, or on a project with a defined and understandable structure. I tend to evaluate others (my co-workers and superiors) in terms of whether they can help or hinder me in doing a craftsmanlike job. I do not compete against other people as much as I do against my own standards of quality. On the other hand, I often find myself on the defensive, trying to preserve my integrity from the exploitative demands of the more aggressive managerial types around me.

How characteristic is this of you (1-7)_____?

How much would you like to be like this (1-7)_____?

Copyright © 1982, John Wiley and Sons, Inc.

CAREER STYLE INVENTORY
SCORING KEY

For *each* orientation, refer to the respective sections and paragraphs listed below. *Add* the rating scale values for the "characteristic of me" scales, and for the "would like to be" scales, in each grouping.

	Characteristic of me	Would like to be like this
Craftsman Orientation		
Life Goals—Paragraph 2		
Motivation—Paragraph 1		
Self-Image—Paragraph 3		
Relations with Others—Paragraph 4		
TOTAL score for Craftsman		
Company Orientation		
Life Goals—Paragraph 1		
Motivation—Paragraph 4		
Self-Image—Paragraph 2		
Relations with Others—Paragraph 2		
TOTAL score for Company Man		
Jungle Fighter Orientation		
Life Goals—Paragraph 3		
Motivation—Paragraph 3		
Self-Image—Paragraph 4		
Relations with Others—Paragraph 3		
TOTAL score for Jungle Fighter		
Gamesman Orientation		
Life Goals—Paragraph 4		
Motivation—Paragraph 2		
Self-Image—Paragraph 1		
Relations with Others—Paragraph 1		
TOTAL score for Gamesman		

Copyright © 1982, John Wiley and Sons, Inc.

managers tend to speak out on major public issues, and a few have held high government positions. No one has accused these companies of trying to overthrow governments, bribe officials, or beg Washington to bail them out of their mistakes.

Creatures in a Corporate Culture

I wanted to find out what motivates the managers of these corporations—what mix of ambition, greed, scientific interest, security seeking, or idealism. How are managers molded by their work? What is the quality of their lives? What type of person reaches the top (and which falls by the wayside)? Once we had studied the interviews and Rorschach tests, it became clear that the corporation is populated by four basically different character types. These are "ideal" types in the sense that few people fit any one of them exactly. Most executives are mixtures of two or more, but in practically every case, we were able to agree on which type best described a person. And the individual and his colleagues almost always agreed with our assessment.

The types:

The Craftsman, as the name implies, holds traditional values, including the work ethic, respect for people, concern for quality, and thrift. When he talks about his work, he shows an interest in the *process* of making something; he enjoys building. He sees others, co-workers as well as superiors, in terms of whether they help or hinder him in doing a craftsmanlike job.

Many of the managers in the great corporate laboratories, such as Du Pont and Bell Labs, are craftsmen by character. Their virtues are admired by almost everyone. Yet they are so absorbed in perfecting their own creations—even to the exclusion of broader corporate goals—that they are unable to lead complex and changing organizations.

The Jungle Fighter lusts for power. He experiences life and work as a jungle where it is eat or be eaten, and the winners destroy the losers. A major part of his psychic resources are budgeted for his internal department of defense. Jungle fighters tend to see their peers as either accomplices or enemies, and their subordinates as objects to be used.

There are two types of jungle fighters, lions and foxes. The lions are the conquerors who, when successful, may build an empire. In large industry, the day of the lions—the Carnegies and Fords—seems virtually ended. The foxes make their nests in the corporate hierarchy and more ahead by stealth and politicking. The most gifted foxes we encountered rose rapidly, by making use of their entrepreneurial skills. But in each case they were eventually destroyed by those they had used or betrayed.

The Company Man bases his sense of identity on being part of the protective organization. At his weakest, he is fearful and submissive, seeking security even more than success. At his strongest, he is concerned with the human side of the company, interested in the feelings of the people around him, and committed to maintaining corporate integrity. The most creative company men sustain an atmosphere of cooperation and stimulation, but they tend to lack the daring to lead highly competitive and innovative organizations.

The Gamesman sees business life in general, and his career in particular, in terms of options and possibilities, as if he were playing a game. He likes to take calculated risks and is fascinated by techniques and new methods. The contest hypes him up and he communicates his enthusiasm, energizing his peers and subordinates like the quarterback on a football team. Unlike the jungle fighter, the gamesman competes not to build an empire or to pile up riches, but to gain fame, glory, the exhilaration of victory. His main goal is to be known as a winner, his deepest fear to be labeled a loser.

Molded by the Psychostructure

The higher our interviews took us in the corporation, the more frequently we encountered the gamesman—he is the new corporate leader. Again, it must be emphasized that the top-level executive is not a pure type, but rather a mixture. He most often combines many of the traits of the gamesman with some attributes of the company man. He is a team player who identifies closely with the corporation.

The gamesman reaches the top in a process of social (in contrast to natural) selection. The companies that excel tend to be run by people who are well adapted to fulfill the requirements of the market and the technology, and who create an atmosphere that encourages productive work. These executives in turn stimulate traits in their subordinates that are useful to the work, while discouraging those that are unnecessary or impede it. As an executive moves to the top, therefore, his character is refined.

Any organization of work—industrial, service, blue or white collar—can be described as a "psychostructure" that selects and molds character. One difference between the psychostructure of the modern corporate hierarchy and that of the factory is the fineness of fit required between work and character. Managers must have characters closely attuned to the "brain work" they perform. Only a minimal fit is required to perform simplified, repetitive tasks in a factory.

The gamesman's character, which might seem a collection of near paradoxes, can best be understood in terms of its adaptation to the requirements of the organization. The gamesman is cooperative but competitive, detached and playful but compulsively driven to succeed, a team player but a would-be superstar, a team leader but often a rebel against bureaucratic hierarchy, fair and unprejudiced but contemptuous of weakness, tough and dominating but not destructive. Competition and innovation in modern business require these gamelike attitudes, and of all the character types, only the gamesman is emotionally attuned to the environment.

OPTION ONE

Step 4: 5 Minutes

Form "career style" groups as directed by the group leader. This should create at least one group in each of the following types:

Copyright © 1982, John Wiley and Sons, Inc.

Craftsmen	Jungle Fighters
Company Men	Gamesmen

Which group you belong to depends on your self perception, and/or "would like to be like" score on the questionnaire.

Step 5: 40 Minutes

Each group now meets to perform one or more of the following tasks (the group leader will indicate which):

1. Evaluate whether you think the description of the people in your group is generally valid, based on (a) the questionnaire paragraphs that describe this style, and (b) the overall description in the reading. That is, do you think that the description of you is generally accurate or inaccurate? If inaccurate, what modifications or changes would you make?
2. Evaluate the advantages and disadvantages of this style. Think about this style in an organization. What would be the strong points, and the weak points of having this style? What kind of problems would a person with your type of style encounter in his/her first job?
3. Evaluate the kind of organization that your style would function well in. What kind of organization would your style function poorly in?
4. What would you expect the career path of people with your style to look like? What types of things would you have to do in your career in order to maximize success, and feelings of personal satisfaction? What things would you do well? What kind of problems would you create for yourself?
5. Examine each of the groups with styles *different* from yours. What kind of leadership or supervisory style should be used with people from each of these groups, in order to maximize their effectiveness?

Appoint one member of the group to act as a spokesperson for the group. Prepare a presentation to be made back to the class, covering the topics of your discussion.

Step 6: 20 Minutes

After the groups reconvene, each group makes a presentation of the discussion topics covered in your small group. Take careful note of the comments made about your group by the other groups. Evaluate whether you agree or disagree with these views.

OPTION TWO

Step 4: Discussion Questions

Discuss the different career styles in terms of the following questions:

1. In this program or class, what would be your guess as to the style that most people use to describe themselves? What is the least frequently used style? Why?

2. In this program or class, what would be your guess as to the style that most people would like to be? What is the style that they would least like to be? Why?

3. Survey the members of the class. How many are there of each type? How many are there of each "desired" (would like to be) type? Do you think these numbers would be characteristic of other student groups completing this questionnaire?

4. How many people wanted to be styles different from the ones that they are now? What were their reasons for wanting to be different?

5. Do you think there are any significant differences in how males and females would rate their present styles or their ideal styles? Why?

6. What would be the best type of job, managerial role, or organization for each style? Why?

7. What would be the advantages, or assests, for individuals possessing each style, in an organizational setting? What would be the disadvantages, or weaknesses, of each style?

8. What can people in each style learn to do, in order to function more effectively in a variety of organizational roles and responsibilities?

DISCUSSION QUESTIONS

Discussion questions for Option two appear in the exercise. The following apply to Option one:

1. How effective were the members of each style group at identifying their strong points and weak points? What kind of problems would each have on the first job, or progressing in a management career?

2. What did the different groups do when they evaluated styles different from their own? Do you agree with their analysis?

3. Was there any evidence, in either the content or the style of the presentation, that people were properly classified? How or Why?

GENERALIZATIONS AND CONCLUSIONS

1. How easy or difficult is it to classify individuals according to corporate styles? Is this a useful classification to make, and to know about oneself?

2. Is there a "best" corporate style, in terms of what people are, or what they would like to be? Why?

Copyright © 1982, John Wiley and Sons, Inc.

3. How might the differences in corporate style reflect differences in the kinds of jobs people like to do, the career paths they follow, and the ways that they are rewarded by their organizations?

Participant's Reactions

READINGS AND REFERENCES

Blake, R. R., and Mouton, J. S., *The Managerial Grid* (Houston, Tx.: Gulf Publishing Co., 1964).

Hersey, P., and Blanchard, K., *Management of Organizational Behavior: Utilizing Human Resources* (Englewood Cliffs, N.J.: Prentice Hall, 1977).

Jay, A., *Management and Machiavelli* (New York: Holt, Rinehart and Winston, 1968).

Jay, A., *Corporation Man* (New York: Random House, 1971).

Maccoby, M., *The Gamesman* (New York: Simon and Schuster, 1976).

Maccoby, M., "The Corporate Climber Has to Find His Heart," *Fortune,* December (1976), 98-108.

Tannenbaum, R., and Schmidt, W., "How to Choose a Leadership Pattern," *Harvard Business Review,* March-April (1958), 95-102.

Whyte, W. F., *The Organization Man* (New York: Simon and Schuster, 1956).

30
VANATIN:
GROUP DECISION MAKING AND ETHICS

PURPOSE:
(1) To understand the factors that contribute to decision making about ethical practices.
(2) To explore the aspects of group dynamics that affect ethical decisions.

ADVANCE PREPARATION:
None. Roles may be prepared in advance if time is a problem, but this is not encouraged.

GROUP SIZE: Seven-person groups. If there are less than seven members in a group, individuals may be assigned as observers, or roles may be deleted (see Instructor's Manual).

TIME REQUIRED: 1½ hours. Exercise may be divided into two class periods—see Instructor's Manual.

SPECIAL MATERIALS: Scenario Instructions, role-play forms for each class member, decision recording form. File cards or self-stick labels that can be used as nametags for role players to identify their roles.

SPECIAL REQUIREMENTS: Movable furniture arranged in a circle of seven chairs, and/or extra space for groups to spread out.

RELATED TOPICS: Negotiation and conflict; Group decision making and conflict.

INTRODUCTION

The Vanatin case provides an opportunity for group members to struggle with questions of social responsibility and ethics in decision making. The case is constructed around a medical product, considered by experts to be injurious to the health of consumers—even to the point of possibly causing death. These consequences must be evaluated against the potential economic losses to the company, which would be substantial if sale of the drug were discontinued. The decision is not an easy one, but nevertheless the problem is common to many corporate and governmental groups that must consider both their own interest and the overall interests of society and public welfare.

Step 1: 10 Minutes

The instructor will divide the class into groups and assign you one of the seven roles (see the Appendix). Read the scenario below. Then read *only* your own role. Make notes on the points you want to emphasize in the group discussion.

Adapted by Roy J. Lewicki from an exercise developed by J. Scott Armstrong, University of Pennsylvania. Used by permission.

Copyright © 1982, John Wiley and Sons, Inc.

BACKGROUND INFORMATION FOR THE VANATIN CASE

Assume that it is August 1969 and that you are a member of the Booth Pharmaceutical Corporation Board of Directors. You have been called to a Special Board Meeting to discuss what should be done with the product known as "Vanatin."

Vanatin is a "fixed-ratio" antibiotic sold by prescription. That is, it contains a combination of drugs. It has been on the market for more than 13 years and has been highly successful. It now accounts for about 18 million dollars per year, which is 12 percent of Booth Company's gross income in the United States (and a greater percentage of net profits). Profits from foreign markets, where Booth is marketed under a different name, is roughly comparable to that in the United States.

Over the past 20 years there have been numerous medical scientists (e.g., the AMA's Council on Drugs) objecting to the sale of most fixed-ratio drugs. The argument has been that (1) there is no evidence that these fixed-ratio drugs have improved benefits over single-drugs, and (2) the possibility of detrimental side effects, including death, *at least* doubled. For example, these scientists have estimated that Vanatin is causing about 30 to 40 unnecessary deaths per year (i.e., deaths that could be prevented if the patients had used a substitute made by a competitor of Booth). Despite these recommendations to remove fixed-ratio drugs from the market, doctors have continued to use them. They offer a shotgun approach for the doctor who is unsure of his diagnosis.

Recently a National Academy of Science–National Research Council panel, a group of impartial scientists, carried out extensive research studies and recommended unanimously that the Food and Drug Administration (FDA) ban the sale of Vanatin. One of the members of the panel, Dr. Peterson of the University of Texas, was quoted by the press as saying, "There are few instances in medicine when so many experts have agreed unanimously and without reservation [about banning Vanatin]." This view was typical of comments made by other members of the panel. In fact, it was typical of comments that had been made about fixed-ratio drugs over the past 20 years. These impartial experts, then, believe that, while all drugs have some possibility of side effects, the costs associated with Vanatin far exceed the possible effects.

The special Board Meeting has arisen out of an emergency situation. The FDA has told you that it plans to ban Vanatin in the United States and wants to give Booth time for a final appeal to them. Should the ban become effective, Booth would have to stop all sales of Vanatin and attempt to remove inventories from the market. Booth has no close substitutes to Vanatin, so that consumers will be switched to close substitutes currently marketed by rival firms. (Some of these substitutes apparently have no serious side effects.) It is extremely unlikely that bad publicity from this case would have any significant effect upon the long-term profits of other products made by Booth.

The Board is meeting to review and make decisions on two issues:

1. What should be done with Vanatin in the U.S. market (the immediate problem)?
2. Assuming that Vanatin is banned from the U.S. market, what should Booth do in the foreign markets? (No government action is anticipated in any of the foreign markets.)

Decisions on each of these issues must be reached at today's meeting. The Chairman of the Board has sent out this background information, and he also wanted you to give some thought as to which of the following alternatives you would prefer for the domestic market:

a. Recall Vanatin immediately and destroy.
b. Stop production of Vanatin immediately, but allow what's been made to be sold.
c. Stop all advertising and promotion of Vanatin, but provide it for those doctors that request it.
d. Continue efforts to most effectively market Vanatin until sale is actually banned.
e. Continue efforts to most effectively market Vanatin and take legal, political, and other necessary actions to prevent the authorities from banning Vanatin.

A similar decision must also be made for the foreign market *under the assumption that the sale was banned in the United States.*

Step 2: 45 Minutes

The Chairman of the Board will conduct the discussion of the Vanatin problem. By the end of 45 minutes, the group should reach a decision on what to do about *both* the domestic and international distribution of Vanatin.

At the end of the 45 minutes, each Chairman should record the decisions of the group, tear out the recording form on page 205 and hand it to the instructor.

Step 3: 20 to 35 minutes, Discussion

The instructor will review the decision forms and tabulate the type of decisions made by each group for the U.S. and foreign markets. You may record the decisions on the table below.

1. *Record* in columns 1 and 2 the actual decisions made by the discussion groups.
2. *Privately* note to yourself what you think Booth actually did in this case. The instructor will tally the predictions, and you may record these predictions in Columns 3 and 4.
3. *Record* in columns 5 and 6 what Booth actually did.

Decision	Decisions Made by Groups[a]		What Do You Think Happened?		What Actually Happened	
	U.S.	Foreign	U.S.	Foreign[b]	U.S.	Foreign
a. Recall Immediately						
b. Stop Production						
c. Stop Advertising and Promotion						
d. Continue to Market						
e. Block FDA						
	(1)	*(2)*	*(3)*	*(4)*	*(5)*	*(6)*

[a] Record the letter designation of the group in the proper place.

[b] You can skip this column temporarily until you discuss what actually happened in the U.S. market (see next column).

Copyright © 1982, John Wiley and Sons, Inc.

RECORDING FORM

Group Decision on Vanatin

1. Check the category that most closely approximates your position with regard to the U.S. market (circle one letter only):
   a. Recall Vanatin immediately and destroy.
   b. Stop production of Vanatin immediately, but allow what's been made to be sold.
   c. Stop all advertising and promotion of Vanatin, but provide it for those doctors that request it.
   d. Continue efforts to most effectively market Vanatin until sale is actually banned by the FDA.
   e. Continue efforts to most effectively market Vanatin and take legal, political, and other necessary action to prevent the FDA from banning Vanatin.

2. Assume that the FDA did succeed in banning Vanatin but that it was still legal to sell Vanatin in foreign countries. What category most closely approximates your position with regard to foreign markets (circle one letter only)?
   a. Recall Vanatin immediately and destroy.
   b. Stop production of Vanatin immediately, but allow what's been made to be sold.
   c. Stop all advertising and promotion of Vanatin, but provide it for those doctors that request it.
   d. Continue efforts to most effectively market Vanatin until sale is banned in each particular country.
   e. Continue efforts to most effectively market Vanatin and take legal, political, and other necessary actions to prevent the FDA from banning Vanatin.

Copyright © 1982, John Wiley and Sons, Inc.

DISCUSSION QUESTIONS

1. What factors in your own group's discussion affected the way the decision was arrived at? For example,
    a. How much control did the Chairman of the Board exercise over the *type* of decisions arrived at?
    b. Which group members had the most influence, in terms of the *persuasiveness* of their arguments on the group's final decision?
    c. Which group members had the most influence, in terms of *persuasion techniques* that they used to get other people to agree with them?
    d. How were group members viewed and treated when they made strongly *ethical* arguments for banning Vanatin?
    e. How were group members viewed and treated when they made strongly *pragmatic* arguments for the effects of the ban on corporate profits and sales?
2. How similar or different is this decision from other decisions you have made as a group?
3. What kinds of decision situations in organizations have elements in common with this exercise?

GENERALIZATIONS AND CONCLUSIONS

The basic model for this case is this: what would happen if one constructed an extreme case where there were obvious and direct tradeoffs between profits and the quality of life? Under what conditions would people continue to make decisions to maximize profits in such a case?

There have been a number of variations in the construction of this case. Each variation seems to result in the same conclusion. While these conclusions are not pleasant, they reflect the dynamics of groups and the behavior of individuals who may not have to "live with" or directly experience the pain and suffering that particular policies or practices may be causing.

Participant's Reactions

READINGS AND REFERENCES

Heilbroner, Robert, *In the Name of Profit* (Garden City, N.Y.: Doubleday, 1972).

Janis, I., *Victims of Groupthink* (Boston: Houghton-Mifflin, 1972).

Latane, B., and Darley, J., *The Unresponsive Bystander* (New York: Appleton Century Crofts, 1970).

Milgram, Stanley, *Obedience to Authority* (New York: Harper and Row, 1974).

Mintz, Morton, "FDA and Panalba: A Conflict of Commercial and Therapeutic Goals," *Science,* 165, (August 1969), 875–881.

Copyright © 1982, John Wiley and Sons, Inc.

SECTION NINE
POWER

31
SITUATIONAL POWER: CIRCLES, SQUARES, AND TRIANGLES

PURPOSE:
(1) To examine the nature of bargaining and negotiation between groups.
(2) To explore the impact of within-group dynamics on between-group relations.
(3) To understand the nature of relationships between individuals and groups when power is important.

ADVANCE PREPARATION:
None.

GROUP SIZE: Approximately 24 to 40, divided into three equal teams. Larger groups should be divided further.

TIME REQUIRED: 2 hours for the activity, plus 45 minutes for discussion.

SPECIAL MATERIALS: Assortment of colored papers or chips, prepared by the group leader. Identification tags for each person, prepared by the group leader.

SPECIAL PHYSICAL REQUIREMENTS: A large room with chairs that can be arranged in three circles (each as far away from the other as possible), and lots of space for people to walk around.

RELATED TOPICS: Negotiation and conflict, Motivation: basic concepts, Group decision making and problem solving, Interpersonal communication, Organizational communication.

Adapted by Roy J. Lewicki from an exercise developed by James Shultz. Originally adapted from *Starpower*, Simile II, P.O. Box 1023, La Jolla, California 92037.

INTRODUCTION

This activity concerns your relations with other individuals and groups when bargaining, negotiation, and power are important variables. As you participate in this activity, be aware of the ways that you are relating to others and others are relating to you. Your group leader will provide you with the necessary materials; the basic instructions are printed in the "Participant's Rule Sheet," below.

PARTICIPANT'S RULE SHEET: CIRCLES, SQUARES, AND TRIANGLES

"Circles, Squares, and Triangles" is a game of bargaining and negotiation. There are three teams—Circles, Squares, and Triangles. All players on each team must wear their identifying group tag at all times during the game. Your tag must be plainly visible.

The object of the game is to improve your *individual* score by bargaining advantageously. At the end of each round the three individual highest scorers are declared the winners for that round.

Each player will begin and *must* end with five chips. Here are the values of each type of chip:

A black chip is worth 50 points.
A gold chip is worth 25 points.
A red chip is worth 15 points.
A white chip is worth 10 points.
A blue chip is worth 5 points.

As a bonus:

5 chips of the same color are worth an additional 20 points.
4 chips of the same color are worth an additional 10 points.
3 chips of the same color are worth an additional 5 points.

Bonus chips, during the Bonus Round, are worth 20 points each.

Rules for the Bargaining Round
1. Each bargaining round will last for only ten minutes.
2. When the round begins, get up and walk around the room. If you wish to trade with someone, nonverbally ask them if they want to. If the answer is yes, then you must clasp hands. *There can be no talking for any reason unless your hands are clasped.*
3. Participants must be holding hands to make a trade. You can hold only one other person's hand at a time.
4. You may not break hands until you have agreed on a trade, or until the round is complete. If you cannot agree, you must hold hands until the end of the round.
5. If you do not wish to trade, fold your arms.
6. Only one-for-one trades are legal. Persons having more or less than 5 chips at any time during the game are automatically disqualified.
7. Only trades of different colors are legal.

Copyright © 1982, John Wiley and Sons, Inc.

8. Hide your chips from all other participants or they might prevent you from getting the combination of chips you are after.
9. Violence is prohibited in this exercise.

Do not *proceed until* you are told to do so.

PROCEDURE

15 minutes	Set up, read and understand the instructions. Distribute chips to each individual
10 minutes	First Bargaining Round
5 minutes	Scoring of first Bargaining Round
5 minutes	First Bonus Round
5 minutes	Point adjustments
10 minutes	Second Bargaining Round
5 minutes	Scoring of second Bargaining Round
5 minutes	Second Bonus Round
5 minutes	Point adjustments
10 minutes	Special Bonus Round
10 minutes	Third Bargaining Round
10 minutes	Scoring of the third Bargaining Round
20 minutes	Each additional Bargaining Round and scoring
45 minutes	Discussion

DISCUSSION QUESTIONS

1. How did it feel to be a Square? A Circle? A Triangle?
2. Depending on which group you were in, how would you describe the behavior of the other two groups?
3. What kind of experiences did you have in the individual bargaining? Did you find it easy or hard to strike a bargain? What about holding hands?
4. How were the bonus points distributed in each group on the first round? How were they distributed on subsequent rounds?
5. How did the people behave who changed groups after the Bonus Rounds? How do you feel about that?
6. How did the Squares behave after the Special Bonus Round? How did the Circles behave? How did the Triangles behave?
7. What were the things that were discussed in the Squares group during the Special Bonus Round?
8. What were the things that were discussed in the Circles group, or the Triangles group, during the Special Bonus Round?
9. How did the Squares behave after the Special Bonus Round? How did the Circles behave? The Triangles?
10. How well did the three groups work together in making decisions? What were the factors that helped or hindered this working relationship?

GENERALIZATIONS AND CONCLUSIONS

Concluding Points

1. What generalizations can you make about power, based on the behavior of people in this exercise?

2. What, specifically, do you feel you learned about power, based on the behavior of the Squares? The behavior of the Circles and Triangles? The behavior of people who changed groups?

3. What parallels do you see between this exercise and certain real-world problems—for example, race relations? Status of minority groups? Educational systems? Life in organizations?

Copyright © 1982, John Wiley and Sons, Inc.

Participant's Reactions

READINGS AND REFERENCES

Alinsky, S., *Rules for Radicals* (New York: Random House, 1971).

Fogelson, R., *Violence as Protest* (New York: Doubleday, 1971).

Gamson, W., *Power and Discontent* (Homewood, Ill.: The Dorsey Press, 1968).

Report of the National Advisory Commission on Civil Disorders (New York: Bantam Books, 1968).

32
ANALYSIS OF PERSONAL POWER

PURPOSE:
(1) To help you explore the typical ways that you interact with people.
(2) To help you think about the meaning of power to you, in terms of your relations with other people.
(3) To identify those individuals in the learning environment who have more or less power, and to understand how this power is derived.

ADVANCE PREPARATION:
At discretion of group leader.

GROUP SIZE: Unlimited group size; three-to four-person groups may be used to discuss the results.
TIME REQUIRED: Part I, 1 hour; Part II, 1 hour.
SPECIAL MATERIALS: None.
SPECIAL PHYSICAL REQUIREMENTS: None.
RELATED TOPICS: Motivation: basic concepts, Managers as leaders.

INTRODUCTION

The first part of this exercise is designed to help you explore some aspects of your relations with other people. You will do this by responding to a questionnaire. That questionnaire will be scored in class, and the group leader will explain the concepts needed to help you interpret your scores. The second part of this exercise will help you to explore the different ways that power can be used, and the impact of that approach on behavior.

PROCEDURE

Step 1: 15 Minutes
Complete the "FIRO-B" questionnaire given below. Be sure to read the instructions at the top. Remember that there are no *right* answers; you should attempt to describe how you *actually behave*, not what you think someone else wants you to say.

Adapted by Roy J. Lewicki from *The Interpersonal Underworld* by W. C. Schutz (Palo Alto, Calif.: Science and Behavior Books, 1966), and from *FIRO: A Three Dimensional Theory of Interpersonal Behavior* by William C. Schutz (New York: Rinehart & Co., 1958); the FIRO-B scale is used with permission. Part II is adapted from "An Exercise in Social Power" by Gib Akin, *Exchange*, Vol. 3, No. 4 (1979).

Copyright © 1982, John Wiley and Sons, Inc.

FIRO-B

This questionnaire is designed to help you explore the typical ways you interact with people. There are, of course, no right or wrong answers. Each person has his own ways of behaving. Sometimes people are tempted to answer questions like these in terms of what they think a person *should* do. This is *not* what is desired here. This questionnaire is an attempt to help you learn more about yourself and how you actually behave. Some of the questions which follow may seem similar to others. However, each is different so please answer each one without regard to the others.

Please place the number of the answer that best applies to you in the box at the left of the statement. Be honest with *yourself.*

For each statement below, decide which of the following answers best applies to you. Place the number of the answer at the left of the statement.

1. *usually*   2. *often*   3. *sometimes*   4. *occasionally*   5. *rarely*   6. *never*

_____ 1. I try to be with people.
_____ 2. I let other people decide what to do.
_____ 3. I join social groups.
_____ 4. I try to have close relationships with people.
_____ 5. I tend to join social organizations when I have an opportunity.
_____ 6. I let other people strongly influence my actions.
_____ 7. I try to be included in informal social activities.
_____ 8. I try to have close, personal relationships with people.

_____ 9. I try to include other people in my plans.
_____ 10. I let other people control my actions.
_____ 11. I try to have people around me.
_____ 12. I try to get close and personal with people.
_____ 13. When people are doing things together I tend to join them.
_____ 14. I am easily led by people.
_____ 15. I try to avoid being alone.
_____ 16. I try to participate in group activities.

For each of the next group of statements, choose one of the following answers:

1. *most people*   2. *many people*   3. *some people*   4. *a few people*   5. *one or two people*   6. *nobody*

_____ 17. I try to be friendly to people.
_____ 18. I let other people decide what to do.
_____ 19. My personal relationships with people are cool and distant.
_____ 20. I let other people take charge of things.
_____ 21. I try to have close relationships with people.
_____ 22. I let other people strongly influence my actions.

_____ 23. I try to get close and personal with people.
_____ 24. I let other people control my actions.
_____ 25. I act cool and distant with people.
_____ 26. I am easily led by people.
_____ 27. I try to have close, personal relationships with people.

For each of the next group of statements, choose one of the following answers:

| 1. *most people* | 2. *many people* | 3. *some people* | 4. *a few people* | 5. *one or two people* | 6. *nobody* |

_____ 28. I like people to invite me to things.

_____ 29. I like people to act close and personal with me.

_____ 30. I try to influence strongly other people's actions.

_____ 31. I like people to invite me to join in their activities.

_____ 32. I like people to act close toward me.

_____ 33. I try to take charge of things when I am with people.

_____ 34. I like people to include me in their activities.

_____ 35. I like people to act cool and distant toward me.

_____ 36. I try to have other people do things the way I want them done.

_____ 37. I like people to ask me to participate in their discussions.

_____ 38. I like people to act friendly toward me.

_____ 39. I like people to invite me to participate in their activities.

_____ 40. I like people to act distant toward me.

For each of the next group of statements, choose one of the following answers:

| 1. *usually* | 2. *often* | 3. *sometimes* | 4. *occasionally* | 5. *rarely* | 6. *never* |

_____ 41. I try to be the dominant person when I am with people.

_____ 42. I like people to invite me to things.

_____ 43. I like people to act close toward me.

_____ 44. I try to have other people do things I want done.

_____ 45. I like people to invite me to join their activities.

_____ 46. I like people to act cool and distant toward me.

_____ 47. I try to influence strongly other people's actions.

_____ 48. I like people to include me in their activities.

_____ 49. I like people to act close and personal with me.

_____ 50. I try to take charge of things when I'm with people.

_____ 51. I like people to invite me to participate in their activities.

_____ 52. I like people to act distant toward me.

_____ 53. I try to have other people do things the way I want them done.

_____ 54. I take charge of things when I'm with people.

Step 2: 15 Minutes

Your group leader will now tell you how to score your responses to the questionnaire. The scoring key may be found on page 425 of this book.

Copyright © 1982, John Wiley and Sons, Inc.

The group leader may help you score the entire questionnaire, or only parts of it. As you obtain a score (from 0 to 9), enter it in the appropriate space below:

	Inclusion	Control	Affection
You give (express to others)	e^i =	e^c =	e^a =
You get (want from others)	w^i =	w^c =	w^a =

Each of these scores, individually and together with the others, can tell you something about yourself and your relations with others. As you read the brief description below, and think about your scores, compare that against your own feelings and beliefs about yourself. When you have read the description you may want to share your scores with others who know you well, to verify their accuracy.

Remember that each individual, if he answers the questions honestly, will probably have a different profile of scores. There is no "right" answer to this questionnaire, except that it is "right" for your impressions about yourself.

Step 3: 10 Minutes

The FIRO-B questionnaire's full name is "Fundamental Interpersonal Response Orientation, Form B." It was developed by Dr. William Schutz as a measure of an individual's orientation to other individuals in three major ways: inclusion, control, and affection. For each dimension, there are two major subscales: *expressed* and *wanted*.

The *inclusion* scales are designed to measure your needs to establish and maintain contact with other people. The first column of the chart measures two dimensions of this need: *expressed* inclusion (scale e^i), indicating the strength of your need to include others in your group activities, and *wanted* inclusion (scale w^i), indicating your desire to have others include you in their group activities.

How might some people behave, based on their scores? A person who has a score of 9 on *expressed* inclusion, and 0 on *wanted* inclusion, will be very outgoing toward others. He will be continually making gestures toward others to include them in group activities—sports, parties, work activities, going out to lunch, and so on. However, he probably has no strong needs for others to include him in their groupings. On the other hand, a person who has a score of 0 on *expressed* inclusion and 9 on *wanted* inclusion will seldom make invitation gestures toward others, but desperately wants others to include him. People who have strong scores in both categories will both want and express a lot of inclusion, and a person with two low scores on inclusion will be more of a "private" person, who neither wants to include a lot of people in his activities or be included in theirs.

More interesting problems occur when you explore the needs of two people and their "compatibility" based on inclusion scores. Two people who are strong on both *expressed* and *wanted* inclusion will probably see a lot of one another, since each wants to involve the other and get satisfaction from being involved. Similarly, people with "complementary needs" may also find their relationship satisfactory, since one is always initiating inclusion and the other wants to receive it. (The 9,0 says, "Hey, let's go to the movies," and the 0,9 says, "I thought you'd never ask.") Difficulties arise where both people are high in *expressed* inclusion, but low in *wanted* inclusion ("Hey, let's go to the movies." "No I really don't want to, but would you like to go to the ball game tomorrow?") or when both are high in *wanted* but low in *expressed*. (Each thinks, "I wish he would invite me to go to the movies.") People low on both inclusion scales will probably be very comfortable spending a lot of time by themselves, rather than in group situations.

The *control* scales are designed to measure your needs to control or be controlled by other people. The second column of the chart measures two dimensions of this need: *expressed* control (scale e^c), indicating the strength of your need to control other people and have power over them, and *wanted* control (scale w^c), indicating the strength of your need to have other people control you or tell you how to behave.

A person with a high *expressed* power score (9,0) will like to be in charge. When he encounters another 9,0 person, there is likely to be a strong battle for leadership in the group. The 0,9 person likes to be controlled, and will make an excellent subordinate for any 9,0. (In addition, he probably will not understand the conflict between the two 9,0s—"How could anyone get that concerned about wanting to run things?") However, when the 0,9 person meets another 0,9 person, there is a "power gap" in which each waits for the other to take over and run things—there is usually no action, and no productivity. The 0,0 person withdraws from power, having no strong needs either to be controlled or to control others.

The 9,9 individual may seem "enigmatic"—how can a person both like to be controlled and control others at the same time? However, when we explore the role of middle management in most organizations, we find that the 9,9 thrives on his dual responsibilities of (1) taking orders and direction from above, and (2) at the same time managing and controlling those below him. The 9,9 is really the "perfect second lieutenant" in the military, completely willing and able to be a good subordinate to his superiors and a good superior to his subordinates.

Comparing inclusion to control, we can say that individuals with strong inclusion needs want to be on the team, regardless of what it is doing and how it is performing. The person with strong control needs wants to be a winner, regardless of what team he is on or who the people on it are.

The *affection* scales are designed to measure your needs to express love and affection to others, or have it expressed to you. The third column of the chart measures two dimensions of affection: *expressed* affection (scale e^a), indicating the strength of your desire to be affectionate and loving toward others, and *wanted* affection (scale w^a), indicating the magnitude of your need to have other people be loving and affectionate toward you.

A person with a high *expressed* affection score (9,0) will be likely to show others how much he cares for them. He has strong needs for (and will be very comfortable) being warm, caring, and demonstrating his liking. The person with the high

Copyright © 1982, John Wiley and Sons, Inc.

wanted affection score (0,9) will be drawn to this expression, and so we can expect that a 9,0 and an 0,9 could form a very strong relationship, but in which the affection is all one way. Similarly, two 9,9 individuals, high on both *expressed* and *wanted* affection, will constantly be preoccupied with showing their liking for one another, and receiving those gestures. Obviously, two 0,0 people will neither show much affection for the other, nor really need it for themselves.

Again, problems may occur when two individuals have mutually strong *expressed* scores without want (9,0s), or mutually strong *wanted* scores without expression (0,9). In the first case, the two individuals probably offer the other individual a lot of liking and attraction, yet they are uncomfortable about receiving it. Each may come to see the other as "gushy" and overly affectionate because they can't manage the receiving end of the affection. Similarly, two 0,9s will be attracted to one another but very seldom express it, and draw away from one another *not* because of their feelings but because of their low need to or ability to express their feelings for the other person.

Overall Pattern of Scores

We may look at the six overall scores, and also make the following inferences:

1. Obtain the *total* for each column (inclusion, control and affection); this should indicate how much inclusion, power or affection are important to you and the ways that you spend your time.
2. Obtain the *discrepancy* for the scores in each column (inclusion, control and affection); this should indicate how much more you express things toward others rather than like them to express them toward you (or the reverse).
3. Obtain the *total* of all six scores. This will be a number from 0 to 54, and should give you some strong indication of the relative importance of people in your life. The higher the total score, the more important your relations with people are.

Step 4: Discussion, 15 to 30 Minutes

The previous steps asked you to rate yourself on the "magnitude" of your concern for personal power in relation to interpersonal needs for inclusion in social groupings and affection with others. As you review these scores, consider the following:

1. Look at each of your scores on FIRO-B, and the "pairs" of scores in each area (inclusion, control and affection):
   a. Does each score seem to represent the way you feel about yourself? That is, if you were to ask yourself a single question about each category, rated on a scale from 0 to 9, would your evaluation be the same?
   b. If your scores do not seem "right" for you, which ones seem to be the most accurate? Which ones seem to be the least accurate? Why? Is this related to what you were thinking about when you completed the questionnaire?
2. Think about examples or situations from your experience that reflect your scores—for example, instances where you wanted to be included or wanted

to include others, wanted to be in charge, and so on. Which examples confirm your scores, and which ones disconfirm them?

3. Think about a situation in which you had a problem relating to other people in a group—deciding who was a "member" of the group, who was in "charge" or making decisions for the group, or who belonged to subgroups that were very close to one another. Do the ideas of "compatibility" between two or more people's styles help you to understand how people behaved?

4. Try completing this questionnaire several times, each time with respect to a particular social group. That is, try responding to the questionnaire in terms of your family, work group, student friends, fraternity or sorority, and so on. Do the responses differ? What does this say about how your needs vary from group to group?

PART II

Step 1: 5 Minutes

The instructor will divide the class into three equal-size groups. These groups may be subdivided if there are more than six people per group.

Step 2: 5 Minutes

Read the following scenario:

You are the manager of a group of research scientists and laboratory technicians in a chemical research laboratory. The scientists and technicians receive a monthly salary, and are expected to work from 8:30 to 4:30, 5 days a week. In fact, many of the scientists work late or come into the laboratory on weekends in order to complete their experiments.

Recently, you have become aware that one of your best laboratory technicians is repeatedly late for work, and sometimes goes out for too long a coffee break soon after getting to work. The technician seems to be satisfied with his salary and his overall performance is good, but you would like to see him come in on time, work harder in the morning, and thus do even better in his job performance. You even feel that the technician might get turned on to starting research experiments of his own, and perhaps be promoted to a project leader position.

As a manager, you are respected and liked by the others in the lab, and it irritates you that this person treats your dedicated management with such a cavalier attitude. You want to influence the technician to start work on time.

Step 3: 15 Minutes

Each group has the task of preparing an *actual influence strategy* to be used by the manager in correcting the technician's behavior. This strategy will be role-played in class; therefore, you must:

1. Specify exactly what the manager will do with the technician.
2. Select one member of your group to role-play the manager.
3. Select one member of your group to role-play the technician with a manager from another group.

Copyright © 1982, John Wiley and Sons, Inc.

4. Decide on the "environment" in which the role play will take place (the manager's office, coffee shop, chemistry laboratory, etc.).

Step 4: 15 to 20 Minutes
The instructor will select several groups. Each group will role-play the strategy developed.

Step 5: Discussion
1. As each group role-plays each influence attempt, think of yourself on the receiving end of the influence (i.e., as the technician). Record your own reaction:

	Group 1	Group 2	Group 3	Group 4
a. As a result of the influence attempt, I will ... 1 2 3 4 5 definitely comply / definitely not comply	_____	_____	_____	_____
b. Any change that does come about will be ... 1 2 3 4 5 temporary / permanent	_____	_____	_____	_____
c. My own personal reaction is ... 1 2 3 4 5 resistant / acceptant	_____	_____	_____	_____
d. As a result of this influence attempt, my relationship with the manager of the laboratory will probably be... 1 2 3 4 5 worse / better	_____	_____	_____	_____

2. Look at your reactions to these questions for each influence attempt. Compare them to the reactions of others when the instructor asks for the information.
   a. Which group designed the influence attempt that would most likely result in *immediate* change of the technician's behavior.
   b. Which group's strategy will have the most long-lasting effects?
   c. Which strategy do people find the most acceptable?

3. By now, your instructor will have told you how the groups were composed at the beginning of the activity. What difference did you observe in the ways that the groups worked together to plan their role play? What implications does this have for considering individual member "styles" in the formation of the task groups?

GENERALIZATIONS AND CONCLUSIONS

Concluding points:

1. FIRO-B is an instrument with three scales (inclusion, control and affection) and two subscales for each scale (expressed and wanted). Describe the behavior patterns of a person scoring high on each of the six scales.

2. Which scales on the FIRO-B would be most related to the ability to:
   a. Work with others on a team project?

   b. Follow the direction of a leader?

   c. Reorganize a department in a company?

   d. Develop good relationships in a marriage?

Copyright © 1982, John Wiley and Sons, Inc.

3. (For Part II) Identify the types of influence strategies that are developed when people of a similar style work together, as well as the problems that may occur in these groups as a result of all members having similar styles.

Participant's Reactions

READINGS AND REFERENCES

Jacobsen, W., *Power and Interpersonal Relations* (Belmont, Calif.: Wadsworth Publishing Co., 1972).

French, J. R. P., and Raven, B. H., "The Bases of Social Power," in D. Cartwright (Ed.), *Studies in Social Power* (Ann Arbor, Michigan: Institute for Social Research, 1959).

Schutz, W., *The Interpersonal Underworld* (Palo Alto, Calif.: Science and Behavior Books, 1966).

Winter, D., *The Power Motive* (New York: The Free Press, 1973).

33
COALITION BARGAINING

PURPOSE:

(1) To understand the different sources of power, or "leverage," that groups have in multiparty decision making.

(2) To observe the types of power and influence that are actually used, and their impact on others.

(3) To explore the dynamics of trust and cooperation in a strongly competitive situation.

ADVANCE PREPARATION:

None.

GROUP SIZE: Three teams of 3 to 10 members, approximately the same number of members on each team. Other class members may be used as observers.

TIME REQUIRED: 1½ hours; may be divided into two class periods if necessary (see Instructor's Manual).

SPECIAL MATERIALS: None, unless real money is used.

SPECIAL PHYSICAL REQUIREMENTS: One or two other rooms, near the classroom, are useful for a "caucus" room for the team not directly involved in negotiations. Hallways may be used if necessary.

RELATED TOPICS: Negotiation and conflict, Managers as leaders, Organizational communication, Group decision making and problem solving, Organizational realities.

INTRODUCTION

A coalition may be loosely defined as a group of individuals, or subgroups, that assembles together to exert influence on one another. In an environment where there are many individuals, there are often many different points of view. Each individual views things differently, and each individual would like to have the "system" represent his views. In a dictatorship, the system usually represents the views of the dictator, but in a democratic environment, the views that are represented are usually those of a subgroup who have agreed to "work together" and collectively support one another's views in exchange for having a stronger impact on the system than each individual could have by himself.

Many of us are familiar with the work of coalitions. The patterns of influence in national politics and government provide us with some excellent examples. Whether it be the "coalitions" that are formed along traditional party lines—Democrats or

Developed by Roy J. Lewicki.

Copyright © 1982, John Wiley and Sons, Inc.

Republicans—or along the concerns of special interest groups—Common Cause, Moral Majority, The Sierra Club, AFL-CIO, National Rifle Association, National Organization for Women, or hundreds of others—each group is attempting to influence the direction of the larger system by effectively pooling its resources, working together as a team, and persuading those who have control of the current system.

Coalitions are a common phenomenon in organizations as well. Most organizations are composed of a variety of different groups—Production, Sales, Research and Development, Accounting, and so on—who have different perspectives on the functioning of the organization, different views on the major problems and challenges to the organization, and hence different priorities on the policies and practices that the organization needs to adopt and follow. But these are not the only groups who exert pressure; other groups in the environment also make demands on organizations—employees, shareholders, customers, suppliers, and governmental agencies. Hence organizations are a complex web of pressures among various subgroups, each one striving to have its own priorities adopted as the primary goals of the total organization.

This activity will help you understand, by either participating or observing negotiations between groups, how coalitions form and how they can exert influence. You will also observe what type of rewards various coalitions feel they deserve if they are successful at influence attempts.

PROCEDURE

Step 1: 5 Minutes
Form three teams with approximately an equal number of members on each team. Your group leader may assign you to a team, or this may be done randomly. Designate teams *A, B,* and *C.*

Each member should contribute $1.00 to the "stake" or "prize" for the game. (You may want to use "points" rather than real money. The group leader will announce this.)

Step 2: 10 Minutes
Read the following rules:

RULES OF THE GAME

Objective
To form a coalition with another team, in order to divide the stake. The coalition must also decide on a way of dividing the stake so as to satisfy both parties.

The Stake
Each team has *unequal* resources. In spite of the fact that you each contributed $1.00, you will receive a different stake, depending on the coalition you form. The

following table should be filled in with information provided by the group leader (the individual payoffs are determined by the number of participants in the activity):

AB coalition will receive a stake of $_____
AC coalition will receive a stake of $_____
BC coalition will receive a stake of $_____

The Strategy

Each team will meet separately to develop a strategy before the negotiations. You should also select a negotiator.

Rules for Negotiation

1. All members on a team may be present for negotiations; however, *only* the negotiator may speak.
2. Notes may be passed to negotiators if desired.
3. A team may change its negotiator between conversations.
4. At the termination of the game, the stake will be allocated only if a coalition has been formed.
5. Only one formal coalition is permitted.
6. If no coalition is reached, no funds are allocated.
7. Negotiations will be conducted in the following *fixed* order, and for the following *fixed* periods of time:

Order of Negotiation	Time for First Round of Negotiation	Time for Second and Third Rounds of Negotiation
Team *A* and *B*	5 min.	3 min.
Team *A* and *C*	5 min.	3 min.
Team *B* and *C*	5 min.	3 min.

8. The team *not* in negotiations—that is, while the other two teams are negotiating—must leave the negotiation room.

Valid Coalitions

1. A coalition will be recognized by the group leader only if (a) no two teams are permitted to receive the same amount of money, and (b) neither team in the coalition is allowed to receive zero.
2. After negotiations, all three teams are given the opportunity to submit a written statement in the following form: "Team *X* has a coalition with Team *Y*, whereby Team *X* gets $9.00 and *Y* gets $3.00." When written statements meeting the above requirements from any two teams agree, a valid coalition has been formed.

Step 3: 10 Minutes

Meet in a separate area with your team to plan your strategy. During the strategy session, you will want to decide which team you might want to coalesce with, how you will want to decide which team you might want to coalesce with, how you might want to divide resources, what kind of offers the other team might make, and so on. You must also select a negotiator.

Copyright © 1982, John Wiley and Sons, Inc.

Step 4: 15 Minutes

Each pair of teams will report to the "negotiation area" for *five* minutes to conduct its discussions. Only the negotiators will speak,. but other team members can be present and pass notes. At the end of each 5-minute block, the group leader will stop the negotiations and move to the next pair. The team *not* in negotiations on a particular round *must leave the negotiating room*.

Step 5: 20 Minutes

Each pair of teams reports to the negotiating area for 3-minute discussions for the *second* and *third* rounds (in the same sequence as above).

Step 6: 5 Minutes

The group leader will ask each team to meet separately, and to submit a ballot stating the coalition that they believe was formed. The ballot should be in the following format: "Team_____has a coalition with Team_____, whereby Team _____receives_____ (dollars or points) and Team_____receives_____ (dollars or points)." Put your own team number on the ballot.

Each team brings its written statement to the negotiating room. The group leader will announce whether a valid coalition has been formed (two ballots agree); the money is then distributed as specified on the ballots. If a coalition has *not* been formed, or if the coalition that has formed does not use up all of the initial stake, a problem will arise as to what to do with the funds.

Step 7: 30 Minutes, Discussion

1. What was the initial strategy that each team decided on?
2. How were strategies influenced by the resources (dollars or points) that each team could contribute to a coalition?
3. How did the sequence of conversations between teams influence strategy?
4. How did the prior "reputation" of people on your own team, or the other team, affect your strategy?
5. Was your strategy modified after you had talked to the other teams? How?
6. How were strategic decisions made within your team?
7. How was the negotiator chosen? In looking back on the negotiations, did you make the right choice? Why or why not?
8. What did the negotiators do that encouraged or hurt the development of trust between teams?
9. Were negotiators ever changed? If so, for what reason?
10. What factors most influenced the ultimate settlement between teams? Do you think you could have predicted this earlier? Why?

GENERALIZATIONS AND CONCLUSIONS

In this activity, you observed how two important factors—the amount of "worth" to the final settlement, and the relative position in the order of negotiations—directly affected the view that each group took toward the division of the stake. In addition, you observed how the personal reputations, trustworthiness, and credibility of various group members affected the willingness of others to make deals with them. In organizations, the amount of power and influence that a particular subgroup or constituency may have on overall goals and policy will also be determined by these same three factors. First, the relative "resource power" that the group possesses (e.g., how much the group contributes to the organization's final product) will affect its amount of influence. Second, the "strategic position" that a group occupies (e.g., whether it has final veto power or whether it can disrupt others from accomplishing goals) will determine whether a group uses its power to enhance its own goals, or to impede others from achieving their goals. Finally, individuals within an organization clearly differ in their personal reputations and in their ability to influence others toward their point of view; the better the reputation and the skills, the more likely it will be that these individuals will be successful in achieving their objectives.

Participant's Reactions

READINGS AND REFERENCES

Caplow, T., *Two Against One* (Englewood Cliffs, N.J.: Prentice Hall, 1968).

Cyert, R. M., and J. G. March, *A Behavioral Theory of the Firm* (Englewood Cliffs, N.J.: Prentice Hall, 1963).

Pfeffer, Jeffrey, and Salancik, G. E., "Organization Design: The Case for a Coalitional Model of Organizations," *Organizational Dynamics,* Autumn (1977), 15-29.

Weick, K., "Educational Organizations as Loosely Coupled Systems," *Administrative Science Quarterly,* March (1976), 1-19.

Copyright © 1982, John Wiley and Sons, Inc.

SECTION TEN
ORGANIZATIONAL COMMUNICATION

34
ONE-WAY VERSUS TWO-WAY COMMUNICATION

PURPOSE:
To demonstrate the differences between one-way and two-way communication.

ADVANCE PREPARATION:
None.

GROUP SIZE: Six or more.
TIME REQUIRED: 40 minutes (including discussion).
SPECIAL MATERIALS: None.
SPECIAL PHYSICAL REQUIREMENTS: None.
RELATED TOPICS: Applied motivation and job design, Managers as leaders, Organizational Structure and Design, Group decision making and problem solving.

INTRODUCTION

Most communication in organizations can be described as either *one-way* or *two-way*. In two-way communication, information can flow back and forth between the original communicator of a message and the receiver. The receiver can ask questions, receive clarifications, and in other ways give the communicator *feedback* on what has been heard. Through this feedback, mutual understanding is increased. In one-way communication there is no feedback from the receiver back to the original communicator; the sender tells the receiver something, and this message ends the communication.

The following are examples of one-way communication: memos, lectures, written instructions on a test, and mass media (television, radio, newspapers, and

This exercise is based upon H. Leavitt and R. Mueller, "Some Effects of Feedback on Communication." *Human Relations,* 4 (1951), 401-10. The exercise has been used in numerous publications in various forms. The present version was written by D. T. Hall and D. D. Bowen.

magazines). Examples of two-way communication are telephone conversations, question-and-answer sessions, and discussions. (Of course, if one party monopolizes conversations or discussions, they can possibly become in effect more one-way than two-way.)

In this exercise we will examine both one-way and two-way communication and see which takes more time, which is more accurate, and which is more sastisfying. Before we start, which do you think is more accurate? Takes more time? Is more satisfying?

PROCEDURE

Step 1: 5 Minutes
The group leader will ask class members to select one person who is an especially good communicator, capable of giving directions clearly. This person will be the communicator in this exercise. The remainder of the group will be the receivers. You should be ready with paper and pencil to follow the communicator's instructions.

On one sheet of paper, you are to reproduce the geometric figure described to you by the communicator. The communicator will attempt to explain it so well that each participant will be able to make one exactly like it. The communicator will have her back turned to you while describing the figure to be copied. During this time *you may not speak to the communicator,* and *the communicator will not answer any questions.* Do not look at anyone else's drawing—base your drawing entirely upon the instructions provided by the communicator. At this point, the group leader will answer any questions you may have.

Step 2: 5 Minutes—One-Way Communication
When questions have been answered, the communicator will stand, *back* to audience, and direct you in drawing Figure 1.

Step 3: 10 Minutes—Two-Way Communication
After everyone has completed the first drawing, the communicator will face you and give instructions for drawing Figure 2. You may ask questions at any time to clarify the instructions, but the communicator may not use gestures in giving her answers.

Step 4: 10 Minutes—Scoring
When both figures have been drawn, the group leader will ask you to estimate how many objects in the first figure you think you have drawn correctly under the one-way condition (five, four, three, two, or one), and will record your estimates on the board. Then the group leader will ask for the same estimates for the second figure, under two-way communication.

To examine *attitudes* under both conditions, the group leader will ask the communicator how she felt under the one-way condition. Under the two-way condi-

Copyright © 1982, John Wiley and Sons, Inc.

tion? Then the group leader will ask how the rest of the participants felt under one-way communication, and under two-way communication.

Next, the group leader will draw the correct figures on the board. Count the number of figures you had correct under one-way communication. Then count how many you had correct under two-way communication. (*To be correct,* an object must be the *right shape* and *in proper relation to the other objects.*)

Next, the group leader will ask how many people had all five figures correct for the *one*-way communication. How many? Four? Three? Two? One? He will record these answers on the board, and then ask how many people had five figures correct for the *two*-way communication. How many? Four? Three? Two? One? He will record these responses on the board.

DISCUSSION QUESTIONS

1. What do the accuracy scores tell us about the relative efficiency of the two communication tactics?
2. What do the elapsed time scores suggest in regard to the relative efficiency of the two communication tactics?
3. Would you say that time or accuracy is the more important consideration in most organizational situations?
4. Which of the two conditions was most satisfying to the communicator? To the receivers?
5. How do these communication styles relate to the leadership style of a manager?
6. Give an example of one-way organizational communication. Give an example of two-way organizational communication.

GENERALIZATIONS AND CONCLUSIONS

Concluding Points

1. Two-way communication, compared to one-way, usually takes much (more/less) time.

2. Two-way communication, compared to one-way, results in (greater/less) accuracy.

3. In one-way communication, the communicator usually feels what? The receiver feels what?

4. In two-way communication, the communicator usually feels what? The receiver usually feels what?

Participant's Reactions

READINGS AND REFERENCES

Leavitt, H., *Managerial Psychology,* 3rd ed. (Chicago: University of Chicago Press, 1972), esp. pp. 114-24.
Leavitt, H., and Mueller, R., "Some Effects of Feedback on Communication," *Human Relations,* 4 (1951), 401-10.

Copyright © 1982, John Wiley and Sons, Inc.

35
UPWARD COMMUNICATION: YOUNG MANUFACTURING COMPANY

PURPOSE:
To explore organizational communication and decision-making processes.

ADVANCE PREPARATION:
Read the "Introduction," below.

GROUP SIZE: *Option one* (multiple role play): Requires groups of five. Ten or more groups can do the exercise simultaneously. *Option two* (demonstration role play): unlimited group size.

TIME REQUIRED: Both options: 1 hour.

SPECIAL MATERIALS: None.

SPECIAL PHYSICAL REQUIREMENTS: *Option one:* Small group meeting rooms or large room with movable chairs to accomodate each group. *Option two:* Table and five chairs at front of or in middle of room.

RELATED TOPICS: Managers as leaders, Power, Organizational structure and design, Motivation: basic concepts, Group decision making and problem solving, Interpersonal communication, Organizational realities.

INTRODUCTION

The Young Manufacturing Company is a role-play exercise of a meeting between the President of a small company and four of his subordinates. Each character's role is designed to re-create the reality of a business meeting. Each character comes to the meeting with a unique perspective on a major problem facing the company as well as some personal impressions of the other characters, developed over several years of business and social associations.

THE CAST OF CHARACTERS

Bob Young, the President, is the principal owner of Young Manufacturing, a small fabricator of automotive replacement parts. The firm employs 500 people, and during its nine years of operations has enjoyed better profits than its competitors because of a reputation for high-quality products at a modest cost. Recently, however, competitors have begun to overtake Young Manufacturing, resulting in declining profits for it. Bob Young is expending every possible effort to keep his company comfortably at the top.

Roy Conti, Manager of Quality Control, reports directly to Young. He has held this position since he helped Young establish the company nine years ago.

Developed by Donald D. Bowen. Helpful suggestions for this version were supplied by David Bradford.

Donna Kelly, Production Manager, also reports to Young. She has been with the firm seven years, having worked before that for one of the "big three" auto firms in production management.

Mike Cohen, Supervisor of Final Assembly, reports to Donna Kelly. He came to Young Manufacturing at Kelly's request, having worked with Kelly previously at the same large auto firm.

Fran Kurowski, Supervisor of Subassembly, also works for Donna Kelly. Kurowski was promoted to this postion two years ago. Prior to that time, Fran had gone through a year's management training program after receiving an MBA from a large urban university.

The company organization chart is shown in Figure 1.

Today's Meeting
Bob Young has called a meeting with these four managers, the Operations Committee, in order to attempt to solve some problems that have developed in meeting production schedules. Young must catch a plane to Detroit in half an hour; he has an appointment to negotiate a key contract that means a great deal to the future of Young Manufacturing. He has only 20 minutes to meet with his managers and still catch the plane. Young feels that swinging the Detroit deal is absolutely crucial to the future of the company. The meeting will begin when you receive instructions from your instructor. It will last for *exactly 20 minutes.*

PROCEDURE

BOTH OPTIONS

Step 1: 10 Minutes
The group leader will divide the total group into five equal-sized groups. The members of each of these first groups will all prepare to play the same character later in the roleplay. That is, the members of one of these preliminary groups will all be preparing for the part of Bob Young; another group will concentrate on Donna Kelly, a third on Roy Conti, and so on—one group for each character.

Go to the meeting place designated by the group leader to meet with the other persons who will also be playing the role you have been assigned. When you have all assembled, the group leader will tell you where to find the role instructions for the role you are to play.

From this point on, until you receive instructions from the group leader to the contrary, you are not to share any details of your role with people playing other characters. Stay *in role* until you are explicitly instructed to stop role-playing. Do not let the other managers hear your planning or see your role instructions. Share your thoughts about how your character will feel or behave only with people who have been assigned the same role.

Step 2: 15 Minutes
Prepare, with the assistance of others assigned the same role, to play the part of your character. Ask yourselves questions such as the following: What does it feel like to be this person? What does it feel like to be in the situation of this character?

Copyright © 1982, John Wiley and Sons, Inc.

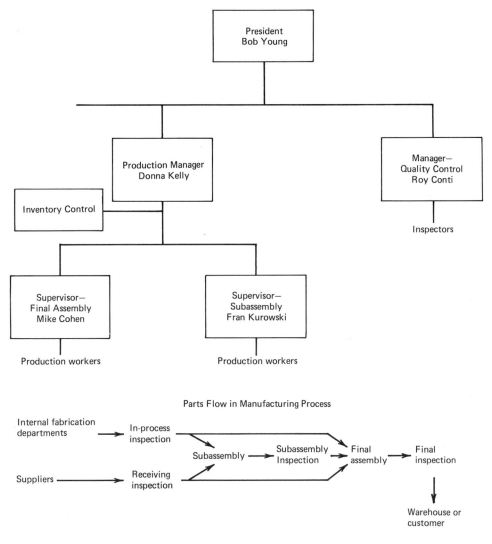

FIGURE 1

Organization Chart and Parts Flow: Young Manufacturing Company

How would your character react to the other characters in the role play? What are the implications of your position in the organization for your behavior? What will you try to get out of the meeting? What outcomes will you try to avoid?

Talk about these questions, and develop perspectives on the role with others assigned to the same role.

It is not necessary that everyone should play the role in exactly the same way. The point is, given the role, how would *you* play it? What do others assigned to this role think of your approach?

OPTION ONE

20 minutes: Following the instructor's directions, meet in a five-person group with the four others assigned to play the roles of the other managers. Start the meeting only when told to proceed by the instructor. Remember: *Stay in role,* even if you should happen to finish before 20 minutes have elapsed. At the end of the meeting, go to Step 3, "Both Options," below.

OPTION TWO

20 minutes: During the preliminary meeting, members of the group select one person to play the role. The role players meet in an "office" set up in the front or middle of the room. Remember: *Stay in the role,* even if you are not chosen to play the part. Remain in the role even after the end of the role play. The designated role players hold the meeting, ending in exactly 20 minutes.

BOTH OPTIONS

Step 3: 15 Minutes

Discuss the exercise, following the Discussion Questions suggested below. Stay in role until after Bob Young has responded to Question 1.

DISCUSSION QUESTIONS

1. Bob Young, how did you see the situation at the end of the meeting? In particular:
   a. How would you define the problem?
   b. Is there any evidence that any of your subordinates have made any serious mistakes or goofs?
   c. Did you find any of your subordinates particularly *helpful* in solving the problem? Who? Were any of them a hindrance? Who?
   d. Did you feel that it was relatively easy or relatively difficult to get the information you wanted from the group?
   What do these data mean? (Discuss.)
2. What factors operated to create the kind of communication you saw in the Young Manufacturing Company? Can anything be done to improve these communications?

GENERALIZATIONS AND CONCLUSIONS

Concluding Points

1. What are the central variables operating to affect communications at Young Manufacturing Company, and what effect do they have?

Copyright © 1982, John Wiley and Sons, Inc.

2. What might Bob Young do, by way of a long-term solution, if he begins to experience the typical difficulties so often found in the Young Manufacturing Company?

Participant's Reactions

READINGS AND REFERENCES

Argyris, C., *Interpersonal Competence and Organizational Effectiveness* (Homewood, Ill.: Irwin-Dorsey, 1962).

Gibb, Jack R., "Defensive Communication," *Journal of Communication,* 11 (1961), 141–148.

Read, W. H., "Upward Communication in Industrial Hierarchies," *Human Relations,* 15 (1963), 3–15.

Roethlisberger, F., "The Foreman: Master and Victim of Double-Talk," *Harvard Business Review,* 45 (1965), 23ff.

SECTION ELEVEN
ORGANIZATIONAL STRUCTURE AND DESIGN

36
WORDS-IN-SENTENCES COMPANY

PURPOSE:
(1) To experiment with designing and operating an organization.
(2) To compare production and quality outputs under different organization structures and/or leadership styles.

ADVANCE PREPARATION:
None.

GROUP SIZE: Any number of 5 to 15-person groups.
TIME REQUIRED: 1½ hours.
SPECIAL MATERIALS: None.
SPECIAL PHYSICAL REQUIREMENTS: Movable chairs, or separate rooms if groups are large; table helpful but not essential.
RELATED TOPICS: Applied motivation and job design, Group decision making and problem solving, Negotiation and conflict, Managers as leaders, Organizational communication.

INTRODUCTION
In this exercise you will form a "miniorganization" with several other people. You will be competing with other companies in your industry. The success of your

Adapted by Francine S. Hall. After contacting several persons thought to have developed this task, the editors were unable to identify its originator. We regret we cannot acknowledge the source of this contribution to experiential learning.

Copyright © 1982, John Wiley and Sons, Inc.

company will depend on your (1) objectives, (2) planning, (3) organization structure, and (4) quality control. It may also depend on leadership style. It is important, therefore, that you spend some time thinking about the best design for your organization.

PROCEDURE

Step 1: 5 Minutes
Form companies and assign workplaces. The total group should be subdivided into small groups of comparable size. Since the success of any one group will not be dependent on size alone, do not be concerned if some groups are larger than others. *Each group should consider itself a company.* Your instructor may designate a manager and give him/her special directions.

Step 2: 10 Minutes
Read the "Directions" below and ask the group leader about any points that need clarification. Everyone should be familiar with the task before beginning Step 3.

DIRECTIONS

You are a small company that manufactures words and then packages them in meaningful (English language) sentences. Market research has established that sentences of at least three words but not more than six words each are in demand. Therefore, packaging, distribution, and sales should be set up for three-to-six-word sentences.

The "words-in-sentences" (WIS) industry is highly competitive; several new firms have recently entered what appears to be an expanding market. Since raw materials, technology, and pricing are all standard for the industry, your ability to compete depends on two factors: (1) volume and (2) quality.

Group Task
Your group must design and participate in running a WIS company. You should design your organization to be as efficient as possible during each 10-minute production run. After the first production run, you will have an opportunity to reorganize your company if you want to.

Raw Materials
For each production run you will be given a "raw material word or phrase." The letters found in the word or phrase serve as the raw materials available to produce new words in sentences. For example, if the raw material word is "organization," you could produce the words and sentence: "Nat ran to a zoo."

Production Standards

There are several rules that have to be followed in producing "words-in-sentences." If these rules are not followed, your output will not meet production specifications and will not pass quality-control inspection.

1. The same letter may appear only as often in a manufactured word as it appears in the raw material word or phrase; for example, "organization" has two *o*'s. Thus "zoo" is legitimate, but "zoonosis" is not. It has too many *o*'s and *s*'s.
2. Raw material letters can be used again in different manufactured words.
3. A manufactured word may be used only once in a sentence and in only one sentence during a production run; if a word—for example, *a*—is used once in a sentence, it is out of stock.
4. A new word may not be made by adding *s* to form the plural of an already used manufactured word.
5. A word is defined by its spelling, not its meaning.
6. Nonsense words or nonsense sentences are unacceptable.
7. All words must be in the English language.
8. Names and places are acceptable.
9. Slang is not acceptable.

Measuring Performance

The output of your WIS company is measured by the *total number of acceptable words* that are packaged in sentences. The sentences must be legible, listed on no more than two sheets of paper, and handed to the Quality Control Review Board at the completion of each production run.

Delivery

Delivery must be made to the Quality Control Review Board 30 seconds after the end of each production run.

Quality Control

If any word in a sentence does not meet the standards set forth above, *all* the words in the sentence will be rejected. The Quality Control Review Board (composed of one member from each company) is the final arbiter of acceptability. In the event of a tie vote on the Review Board, a coin toss will determine the outcome.

Step 3: 15 Minutes

Design your organization using as many group members as you see fit to produce your "words-in-sentences." There are many potential ways of organizing. Since some are more efficient than others, you may want to consider the following:

1. What is your company's objective?
2. How will you achieve your objective? How should you plan your work, given the time allowed?
3. What division of labor, authority, and responsibility is most appropriate, given your objective, your task, and the technology?

Copyright © 1982, John Wiley and Sons, Inc.

4. Which group members are most qualified to perform certain tasks?

Assign one member of your group to serve on the Quality Review Board. This person may also participate in production runs.

Step 4: 10 Minutes—Production Run 1
1. The group leader will hand each WIS company a sheet with a raw material word or phrase.
2. When the Instructor announces "Begin production," you are to manufacture as many words as possible and package them in sentences for delivery to the Quality Control Review Board. You will have 10 minutes.
3. When the group leader announces "Stop production," you will have 30 seconds to deliver your output to the Quality Control Review Board. Output received after 30 seconds does not meet the delivery schedule and will not be counted.

Step 5: 10 Minutes
1. The designated members from the companies of the Quality Control Review Board review output from each company. The total output should be recorded (after quality control approval) on the board or easel.
2. While the Board is completing its task, each WIS company should discuss what happened during Production Run 1.

Step 6: 10 Minutes
Each company should evaluate its performance and organization. Companies may reorganize for Run 2.

Step 7: 10 Minutes—Production Run 2
1. The group leader will hand each WIS company a sheet with a raw material word or phrase.
2. Proceed as in Step 4 (Production Run 1). You will have 10 minutes for production.

Step 8: 10 Minutes
1. The Quality Control Review Board will review each company's output and record it on the board or easel. The total for Runs 1 and 2 should be tallied.
2. While the Board is completing its task, each WIS company should prepare an organization chart depicting its structure for both production runs. If the group had a "manager," what effect did the manager's leadership style have on the group's motivation and production?

Step 9: 10 Minutes
Discuss this exercise as a total group. The group leader will provide discussion questions. Each company should share the organization charts it prepared in Step 8.

GENERALIZATIONS AND CONCLUSIONS

Concluding Points

1. How do classical and contemporary theories of organization differ in their treatment of organization structure and design?

2. How would you classify the technology of a WIS company? Why?

3. What would theory predict to be the best or most appropriate structure for a WIS company? Why?

Copyright © 1982, John Wiley and Sons, Inc.

4. How did leadership style affect the groups? Were all styles equally effective?

Participant's Reactions

READINGS AND REFERENCES

Brown, W. B. and Moberg, D. J., *Organization and Management: A Macro Approach* (New York, Wiley, 1980).

Galbraith, J., *Designing Complex Organizations* (Reading, Mass.: Addison-Wesley, 1973).

Hall, R., *Organizations: Structure and Process* (Englewood Cliffs, N.J.: Prentice-Hall, 1972).

Perrow, C., *Organizational Analysis: A Sociological View* (Belmont, Calif.: Wadsworth Publishing Co., 1970).

Thompson, J. D., *Organizations in Action* (New York: McGraw-Hill, 1967).

Miles, R. H., *Macro Organization Behavior* (Santa Monica, Calif.: Goodyear Publishing Co., 1980).

37
ORGANIZATIONAL DIAGNOSIS: HAMBURGER TECHNOLOGY

PURPOSE:
(1) To diagnose an organization in terms of goals, policies, procedures, structure, climate, technology, environment, job design, communication, and leadership.
(2) To compare and contrast two organizations on these variables.

ADVANCE PREPARATION:
Form groups and do Steps 1 and 2 in advance. Be prepared to report your diagnosis and recommendations to management to the rest of the group on the assigned day.

GROUP SIZE: Subgroups of four or six.
TIME REQUIRED: Several days out of class for preparation; 50 minutes or 1 hour in class, depending on size of total group.
SPECIAL MATERIALS: None.
SPECIAL PHYSICAL REQUIREMENTS: None.
RELATED TOPICS: Applied motivation and job design, Managers as leaders, Organizational communication, Planned change.

INTRODUCTION

A critical first step in improving or changing any organization is *diagnosing* or analyzing its present functioning. Many change and organization development efforts fall short of their objectives because this important step was not taken, or was taken superficially. To illustrate this, imagine how you would feel if you went to your doctor complaining of stomach pains, and he recommended surgery without conducting any tests, without obtaining any further information, and without a careful physical examination. You would probably switch doctors! Yet, managers often attempt major changes with correspondingly little diagnostic work in advance. (It could be said that they undertake vast projects with half-vast ideas.)

In this exercise you will be asked to conduct a group diagnosis of two different organizations in the same business. The exercise will provide an opportunity to integrate much of the knowledge you have gained in other exercises and in studying other topics. Your task will be to describe the organizations as carefully as you can in terms of several key organizational concepts. Although the organizations are probably very familiar to you, try to step back and look at them as though you were seeing them for the first time.

Developed by D. T. Hall and F. S. Hall.

Copyright © 1982, John Wiley and Sons, Inc.

PROCEDURE

Step 1: 10 Minutes

The group will be formed into subgroups of four or six people. Your assignment is described below.

YOUR ASSIGNMENT

One experience most people in this country have shared is that of dining in the hamburger establishment known as McDonald's. In fact, someone has claimed that 25th-century archeologists may dig into the ruins of our present civilization and conclude that 20-century religion was devoted to the worship of golden arches.

Your group, Fastalk Consultants, is known as the shrewdest, most insightful, and most overpaid management consulting firm in the country. You have been hired by the president of McDonald's to make recommendations for improving the motivation and performance of personnel in their franchise operations. Let us assume that the key job activities in franchise operations are food preparation, order-taking and dealing with customers, and routine clean-up operations.

Recently the president of McDonald's has come to suspect that his company's competitors such as Burger King, Wendy's, Jack in the Box, and others are making heavy inroads into McDonald's market. He has also hired a market research firm to investigate and compare the relative merits of the sandwiches, french fries, and drinks served in McDonald's and the competitor, and has asked the market research firm to assess the advertising campaigns of the two organizations. Hence, you will not need to be concerned with marketing issues, except as they may have an impact on employee behavior. The president wants *you* to look into the *organization* of the franchises to determine the strengths and weaknesses of each. Select a competitor who gives McDonald's a good "run for its money" in your area.

The president has established an unusual contract with you. *He wants you to make your recommendations based upon your observations as a customer.* He does not want you to do a complete diagnosis with interviews, surveys, or behind-the-scenes observations. He wants your report in two parts.

1. Given his organization's goals of profitability, sales volume, fast and courteous service, and cleanliness, he wants an analysis that will *compare and contrast McDonald's and the competitor* in terms of the following concepts:

   Organizational goals
   Organizational structure
   Technology
   Environment
   Employee motivation
   Communication
   Leadership style
   Policies/procedures/rules/standards
   Job design
   Organizational climate

2. Given the corporate goals listed under point 1 above, what specific actions might McDonald's management and franchise owners take in the following areas to achieve these goals (profitability, sales volume, fast and courteous service, and cleanliness)?

Job design and workflow
Organization structure (at the individual restaurant level)
Employee incentives
Leadership
Employee selection

How do McDonald's and the competitor differ in these aspects? Which company has the best approach?

Some guidelines

Substantiate your recommendations by reference to one or more theories of motivation, leadership, small groups, or job design.

The president wants concrete, specific, and practical recommendations. Avoid vague generalizations such as "Improve communications" or "Increase trust." Say very clearly *how* management can improve organizational performance.

As you make your group presentation, the rest of the group will play the role of the top management executive committee. They may be a bit skeptical. They will ask tough questions. They will have to be sold on your ideas.

You will have *10 minutes* in which to present your ideas to the executive committee and to respond to their questions.

Step 2: Approximately 3 Hours outside of Class

Complete the assignment by going as a group to one McDonald's and one competitor's restaurant. If possible, have a meal in each place. To get a more valid comparison, visit a McDonald's and a competitor located in the same area. After observing each restaurant, meet with your group and prepare your 10-minute report to the executive committee.

Step 3: 50 Minutes

In class, each subgroup will present its report to the rest of the group, who will act as the executive committee. The group leader will appoint a timekeeper to be sure that each subgroup sticks to its 10-minute time limit.

DISCUSSION QUESTIONS

1. What similarities are there between the two organizations?
2. What differences are there between the organizations?
3. Do you have any "hunches" about the reasons for the particular organizational characteristics you found? For example, can you try to explain why one organization might have a particular type of structure? Incentive system? Climate?
4. Can you try to explain one set of characteristics in terms of some other characteristics you found? For example, do the goals account for structure? Does the environment explain the structure? Is leadership or communication in the or-

Copyright © 1982, John Wiley and Sons, Inc.

ganization a function of the tasks to be performed or the people working in the organization?

5. To what extent do you think the structures of the organizations "fit" with the technology in the organization?

6. To what extent do the organizations' structures "fit" with their environment?

7. What are the major strengths of each organization? What are the major weaknesses? What changes would you recommend to improve the effectiveness of the organization?

GENERALIZATIONS AND CONCLUSIONS

Concluding Points

1. The factors that had the strongest direct influence on employee behavior were:

2. The technology employed in cooking the food in both places was what? Which calls for what kind of supervision, according to Woodward?

3. Overall, the structure of the two organizations, in Burns and Stalker's terms, is what? This type of structure fits best with what kind of environment?

Participant's Reactions

READINGS AND REFERENCES

Filley, A. C., *The Compleat Manager: What Works When* (Champaign, IL,: Research Press, 1978).

Hall, R., *Organizations: Structure and Process* (Englewood Cliffs, N.J.: Prentice-Hall, 1972).

Levinson, H., *Organizational Diagnosis* (Cambridge: Harvard University Press, 1972).

Perrow, C., *Organizational Analysis: A Sociological View* (Belmont, Calif.: Wadsworth Publishing Co., 1970).

Pfeffer, J., *Organizational Design* (Arlington Heights, Ill.: AHM Publishing, 1978).

Thompson, J. D., *Organizations in Action* (New York: McGraw-Hill, 1967).

Copyright © 1982, John Wiley and Sons, Inc.

38
MANAGEMENT BY OBJECTIVES

PURPOSE:
(1) To understand what "management by objectives" is and how it works in an organization.
(2) To learn to write objectives that are: (a) clear, (b) acceptable to you and to your superior, and (c) useful in a performance appraisal.

ADVANCE PREPARATION:
Read "Introduction to Management by Objectives," below. Your instructor will have assigned you a role. After you have read the introduction complete Steps 1 and 2. Step 2 will require you to assume your role (boss/subordinate) as assigned.

GROUP SIZE: Any number of two-person groups.
TIME REQUIRED: 50 to 60 minutes in class, approximately 1 hour preparation.
SPECIAL MATERIALS: Chalk board or newsprint helpful.
SPECIAL PHYSICAL REQUIREMENTS: Movable chairs.
RELATED TOPICS: Managers as leaders, Applied motivation and job design, Life, work, and career roles, Motivation: basic concepts, Interpersonal communication.

INTRODUCTION TO MANAGEMENT BY OBJECTIVES

Management by Objectives (MBO) is both a management "technique" and process that has become increasingly popular in organizations. The reasons for its popularity are: (1) it is "results"-oriented—designed to produce tangible outcomes; (2) it follows a natural cycle, beginning with planning and following through production and performance evaluation; (3) it can be used at any or all levels in the organization and with all categories of employees; (4) it is relatively simple and inexpensive, depending only on the resources of managers and their employees (once trained).

What is MBO? Very simply, MBO is the use of stated, written performance objectives, developed by involving subordinates to achieve goals of the organization. In theory, MBO helps an organization in at least four ways. First, it *develops commitment* to the goals and objectives of the organization. Second, it helps to *motivate* people to achieve these. Third, it helps to keep people focused on producing results. In this sense it *guides activities* and program development. Finally, MBO *ensures a measure of performance*. Results are evaluated against the outcomes stated in the objective.

Developed and written by Francine S. Hall, who is grateful to colleagues at Western Michigan University and the U.S. Military Academy, West Point, for materials shared.

How does MBO actually work? It works both from the "top down" and the "bottom up." To be effective, both the superior and the subordinate at each level at which MBO is used must be involved. Typically, the superior will have a set of objectives for the unit under his domain. If the entire organization or several levels are using MBO, then he/she will have set these objectives in accordance with prior negotiation with a superior at the next higher level. Next, the objectives for the unit are shared with subordinates. Each subordinate then drafts a set of objectives for his/her own area of responsibility. Typically, the superior will have certain expectations for each subordinate. At a convenient time, the two meet and discuss the subordinate's objectives until both agree that they are acceptable and can establish a method for measuring performance.

Usually, the superior and subordinate will meet periodically to review progress in achieving objectives. This is essential since conditions may change and objectives may need to be revised or simply rejected as currently inappropriate. At the end of the performance cycle (the deadline for accomplishing the objective), the superior and subordinate will again meet to review performance against the standards established in the objectives. At this point, a new MBO cycle may begin.

Up to this point we have discussed MBO mainly in terms of performance objectives. In fact, MBO may include a range of objectives and usually does. These may include: (1) innovative objectives—new things you will do; (2) problem solving objectives—problems you will reduce or eliminate; (3) routine objectives—ongoing responsibilities; and (4) personal growth objectives—career and development outcomes you wish to achieve.

Regardless of the type of objectives to which you and your boss agree (given the context of your job description and organization's goals), you should also consider the priorities assigned to objectives. Typically, they will fall into one of three categories. *Essential* objectives are those upon which success or failure of an assignment or responsibility rests. They are critical to meeting higher-level objectives in the organization. *Beneficial* objectives are necessary for improved performance in meeting the organization's or unit's goals. Finally, *nice to do* objectives are desirable, but if necessary could be postponed.

Guidelines

Regardless of the types of objectives you may find yourself developing (and their priority), it is important to learn to write meaningful objectives. The following guidelines will help you formulate objectives in your own position. Although every objective may not necessarily conform to all of these criteria, it is recommended that objectives be checked against each criterion. Only when a conscious decision had been made that a specific guideline does not apply should it be bypassed as a factor in validating a particular objective. Guidelines for writing objectives are:

1. *It should start with the word "to" followed by an action verb*. The achievement of a particular objective should come as a result of some sort of action.

Copyright © 1982, John Wiley and Sons, Inc.

Consequently, the commitment to action is basic to the formulation of an objective.

2. *It should specify a single key result to be accomplished.* In order for a particular objective to be effectively measured, each ratee and rater should have a clear picture of when it has or has not been accomplished. Therefore, a single key result should be identified in each performance objective.

3. *It should specify a target date for its accomplishment.* If the objective is the result of normal work output, then the objective would likely be continuing in nature. In this case the target date could be assumed to be the end of the evaluation period. On the other hand, if the objective is a result of improvement analysis, it should generally have a specific target date identified.

4. *It should be as specific and quantitative (and hence measurable and verifiable) as possible.* Probably no area of performance objectives generates a greater degree of skepticism than this criterion. Managers frequently wonder how they can place objective criteria on inherently subjective areas. There is no doubt that this is an extremely difficult challenge, but it can be done. Some progress can be made in resolving this potential dilemma by identifying *specific measurable* activities that, if accomplished, should logically enable achievement of the desired improvement.

5. *It should relate directly to the rated person's roles and to the superior's mission and objectives.* Although this guideline is relatively obvious, it is an important criterion to evaluate when testing the validity of a particular performance objective.

6. *It should be understandable by those who will be contributing to its attainment.* Performance objectives need only to be understood by the rated and rating person, not to someone who may not be part of the work group. A performance objective that is clearly understood is easier to implement.

7. *It should be realistic and attainable but still represent a significant challenge.* A well-formulated performance objective can and should serve as a motivational tool for the individual. Therefore, it should be one that is within reach, yet not too easy to accomplish.

8. *It should be consistent with the available organizational resources.* A potentially outstanding objective could result in an inefficient use of time and energy if, realistically, the organization is unable or unwilling to devote the required resources necessary to accomplish the objective.

9. *It should be willingly agreed to by the rated person and rater without undue pressure or coercion.* Discussion between the rated person and rater is essential to the success of the program. This guideline does suggest that the actual content of an objective should be the subject of discussion and possibly negotiation between the ratee and rater. Such discussion should result in a mutually understood and agreed-upon objective that reflects the best thinking of each. Generally the motivation of the ratee to effectively achieve the objective will be greater as a result of having reached such an agreement.

In summary, the following key questions can be asked as a final check of each performance objective:

1. Is the performance objective constructed properly? To (*action verb*) (*single key result*) by (*target date*) requiring (*what organizational resources*).
2. Is it measurable and verifiable?
3. Does it relate directly to the unit's objectives and to higher-level mission and objectives?
4. Can it be readily understood by those who must implement it?
5. Is the objective a realistic and attainable one that still represents a significant challenge?
6. Will the result, when achieved, justify the expenditure of time and resources to achieve it?
7. Is the objective consistent with the basic department and organizational policies and practices?

PROCEDURE

Step 1: 10 to 30 Minutes (In Advance)

Below is a worksheet with a list of seven objectives. Critique each objective using the Guidelines (1 to 4) found in the "Introduction to Management by Objectives." If any of the objectives do not meet these criteria, rewrite the objective to conform to the guidelines. Bring your worksheet to class, as assigned.

SETTING OBJECTIVES WORKSHEET

	Action Verb?	Result?	Target Date?	Measurable?
1. To improve the communications and working relations among key employees so that high quality work can be produced.				
2. To develop an improved method to maintain all material-handling equipment. Have in operation by December of this year.				
3. To reduce rejects in electronic component K-234G to 2 percent by August of this year.				

Copyright © 1982, John Wiley and Sons, Inc.

SETTING OBJECTIVES WORKSHEET

	Action Verb?	Result?	Target Date?	Measurable?
4. To continue cost-saving study and implement its recommendations upon completion.				
5. Within 3 months have all grievances processed, recorded, and answered within 48 hours of receipt.				
6. To increase production per man-hour this year by 2 percent over the last year's average.				
7. To begin a procedure for proper distribution of job description sheets.				

Step 2: 30 Minutes or More (in Advance)

Read the following, then assume the role assigned (Newman or Petricelli) and complete Step 2 as directed.

GENERAL OFFICE: BACKGROUND INFORMATION

General Office serves a faculty of 30 officers in an academic department at one of the nation's service academies. All employees hold temporary or permanent civil service appointments. The office is currently managed by Newman, who is very efficient, outgoing, and interested in encouraging employee development and career advancement.

Four persons report to Newman. Together they are responsible for answering phones, filing, ordering supplies, typing for the faculty, processing of forms and orders, photocopying and duplicating. A separate secretary works for the department administrators.

Typically, three staff members rotate between phones, filing, and typing. The fourth handles all supplies, copying, and duplicating.

Upon assuming the position, Newman found several problems: (1) friction between certain staff members; (2) complaints from officers regarding the turnaround time on class handouts and tests; (3) requests for collating being ignored because of "backlogs and time pressure."

Because of the civil service system and affirmative action policies, Newman cannot fire any of the staff members. Newman has decided that the best chance for eliminating the problems listed above is to use an MBO system with the staff. Newman has shared objectives with the staff and is now preparing to meet with staff members to discuss their objectives.

The first person scheduled for a meeting is Petricelli, a 45-year-old man who has 15 years in the civil service system. Because he doesn't type he has been assigned to be in charge of the supplies, copying, and duplicating functions. Over the years he has come to see this as his "domain," even to the extent of decorating the duplicating room to suit his taste. This has given him a great deal of autonomy in his job compared to the others, who all work in the large outer office. At times he flaunts his role, acting as if his job is higher status. Actually his GS rating is lower than others in the office. Because of this, Petricelli has occasionally had run-ins with the others who *feel* that he is uncooperative and receiving preferential treatment. He routinely complains of being overworked but is all too often found in the halls "shooting the breeze." Since the duplicating and copying frequently tie in to typing orders, Petricelli and the others are interdependent when there is a deadline.

Role Assignment: Newman
Develop four objectives you would like to see Petricelli accomplish in the next three months. Write these in the space below. Bring these to class and be prepared to discuss them with him.

1. Innovative objective:

2. Problem solving objective:

3. Routine objective:

4. Personal growth objective:

Role Assignment: Petricelli
Develop four objectives of the type shown below that you would like to accomplish over the next three months. Write these in the space provided and bring to class. Be prepared to discuss these with Newman.

1. Innovative objective:

2. Problem solving objective:

Copyright © 1982, John Wiley and Sons, Inc.

3. Routine objective:

4. Personal growth objective:

Step 3: 10 to 15 Minutes

As a total group, discuss your critiques of the objectives completed in Step 1.

Step 4: 20 to 30 Minutes

Meet in pairs, assuming your role as Newman or Petricelli. The purpose of your meeting is to come to an agreement regarding Petricelli's objectives for the next 3 months. Since these may differ somewhat from what each of you originally wrote (in Step 2), be prepared to present your *final* written objectives to the class. In addition, be prepared to indicate how each objective will be measured in the next quarterly performance evaluation review.

Step 5: 10 Minutes

Your instructor will ask selected pairs to state their objectives. The rest of the class will discuss and critique according to the guidelines presented earlier.

GENERALIZATIONS AND CONCLUSIONS

1. What is the most difficult part of using MBO in an organization?
   Initially?

   Ongoing?

2. What is the most difficult step in formulating objectives?

3. What is most likely to cause a "breakdown" in an MBO system?

4. What are the major benefits of MBO?

Participant's Reactions (Personal Learning Outcomes)

1. Did you find yourself having difficulty either in evaluating, writing objectives, or negotiating objectives?

Copyright © 1982, John Wiley and Sons, Inc.

2. If so, what was the major area of difficulty?

3. What will you do to improve your skills in working with MBO? (State an objective.)

READINGS AND REFERENCES

Carroll, Steven, and Tosi, Henry, *Management By Objectives*, 2nd ed. (New York: MacMillan, 1980).

French, W. L., and Hollman, R. W., "Management by Objectives: The Team Approach," *California Management Review*, 17, 3 (1975), 13-22.

Jamieson, B., "Behavioral Problems with Management by Objectives," *Academy of Management Journal*, 16 (1973), 496-505.

Morrissey, George L., *Appraisal and Development Through Objectives and Results.* (Reading, Mass.: Addison-Wesley, 1972.)

Odiorne, George, *Management Decisions By Objectives.* (Englewood Cliffs, N.J.: Prentice-Hall, 1968.)

39
PLANNING AND PRODUCTION TASK: REAL ESTATE PROBLEM

PURPOSE:
(1) To explore the effects of objectives, planning, and organizing on group productivity and output.
(2) To examine different factors that may affect profitability in a production company.

ADVANCE PREPARATION:
(1) Read "introduction" below. (2) Form teams. (3) Complete steps 1 and 2 of the exercise.

GROUP SIZE: Any number of five- to ten-person groups.
TIME REQUIRED: 1 hour in class.
SPECIAL MATERIALS: Computer cards, staplers and staples, tape, scissors, rulers, 3 × 5 cards.
SPECIAL PHYSICAL REQUIREMENTS: Tables or movable desks, easel, separate rooms if large number of groups.
RELATED TOPICS: Managers as leaders, Organizational communication, Organizational structure and design.

INTRODUCTION

Most textbooks describe the management process as one that involves four functions: planning, organizing, directing, and controlling. How each of these functions is performed will determine to a great extent whether a company is successful or not in meeting its objectives.

Like larger systems, small groups must also consider these functions if they are to be successful. Frequently, group task accomplishment involves interdependencies among members and requires a high degree of coordination.

In both cases, tasks to be accomplished must be analyzed and objectives established in advance. Once these objectives are clear, the company or group can plan how it will organize its members and utilize resources to achieve these objectives. In many companies, one of the objectives will involve profitability. Just as companies must plan and organize for production, they also need to plan and organize to ensure that profit objectives are met.

In this exercise you will have an opportunity to compete with other groups in constructing a building. The success of your group will be measured by the profit you make in your project. Profit is determined by subtracting costs from the total appraised value of the finished structure. As you will see, several factors are involved in determining the appraised value. Therefore, it is essential that your

Copyright © 1982, John Wiley and Sons, Inc.

group analyze this task carefully, set some objectives, and plan the best possible organization that will allow you to meet them.

PROCEDURE

Step 1

Each team should allow itself sufficient time to become familiar with the "Task Directions" given below. Discuss these until everyone understands them, then proceed to Step 2.

TASK DIRECTIONS

Each group will be required to construct a building out of computer (e.g., IBM) cards and to "sell" it at the end of the exercise. The sale price will be the total appraised value as determined by the real estate board valuation standards outlined below. The winning group will be the group with the greatest profit, regardless of the appraised value of the building.

Materials and Tools

Every group will have the same raw materials and tools available. These are: computer cards, one ruler, one scissors, one stapler, and one roll of tape. Extra staples and tape will be available, upon request, without extra charge. The cost of computer cards (raw materials) is decribed below.

Cost of Cards

Cards cost $70 each. At the beginning of the exercise each group will receive a package of 100 cards and be charged $7,000, as an initial, startup investment. Additional cards may be purchased from the supplier at the regular price. At the end of the exercise, you may redeem any unused cards for $50 each. If you need to purchase or redeem cards, one person and only one person from your group must go to the supply depot to carry out the transaction. The group leader will designate the supply depot at the beginning of the exercise.

Construction and Delivery Time

At the beginning of the exercise, the group leader will announce the amount of time you will be allotted to construct your building. No team is allowed to build until the group leader announces "Begin production." When the time is up, the group leader will announce "Stop production." No construction is allowed after this point. You will have *30 seconds* in which to deliver your completed structure to the real estate board for appraisal. Buildings received after 30 seconds will not be appraised. No team members are allowed to remain with the building after it is delivered, except for the board members.

Real Estate Board

Each group should designate one member to serve on the board. The board is responsible for appraising each building and assuring that building codes are met. The board will convene during the construction period to decide on criteria for the "drop-shock" test and quality and aesthetic values. The board must appraise one building before going on to the next. Once a building is appraised, it cannot be reappraised later.

Building Code
All buildings must be fully enclosed (floors and roofs). They must also have ceilings that are 3 inches from the floor, and be capable of withstanding a "drop-shock" test. The "drop-shock" test may consist of dropping the building or dropping an object (e.g., heavy book) on the building. It will be the real estate board's responsibility to decide on the test.

Appraisal Values
Buildings are appraised on the basis of quality and aesthetics. The *total* of the quality and aesthetic values is then multiplied by the total square inches of floor space in the building to obtain the total appraised value.

Quality Valuation
Quality is determined by subjecting the building to the "drop-shock" test. Various qualities are assigned values as follows:

Minimal quality:	$12.00 per square inch of floor space
Good quality:	$14.00 per square inch of floor space
Better quality:	$16.00 per square inch of floor space
Top quality:	$18.00 per square inch of floor space

Aesthetic Valuation
The real estate board can set this anywhere from zero to $3.00 per square inch, depending on their appraisal of aesthetic value.

Other Instructions
Once construction begins (Step 4), you will not be allowed to ask the group leader to clarify any game rules or resolve any group difficulties. You are on your own. Five minutes before construction is to stop, the group leader will notify you of the time remaining. While the real estate board is appraising buildings, each group will be expected to clean up left-over raw materials and return them to the supply depot. All unused cards should be redeemed.

Step 2
Your group should discuss the task and then establish the following:

1. What are your objectives in this project?
2. What plan will you use to achieve your objectives?
3. How will group members be organized and coordinated to accomplish the group's tasks?
4. How will you utilize resources?
5. Who will serve on the real estate board?
6. How will you deal with the uncertainties, that is, unknown time allocation and "drop-shock" test?

Copyright © 1982, John Wiley and Sons, Inc.

One member of the group should be designated to report on your objectives, plan, and organization structure during the discussion at the end of the exercise.

Step 3 (Beginning of Session)
Each group should assemble together at one work place (table or cluster of desks). The group leader will designate the following: (1) supply depot and supply person(s); (2) delivery station for real estate board; and (3) construction time. In addition, the group leader will distribute all materials and tools to groups. Finally, the people designated to serve on the real estate board will be asked to convene. No one is to use any materials or tools at this point.

Step 4
When the group leader announces "Begin production," you may build. When group leader announces "Stop production," you must deliver your building to the real estate board.

Step 5: 10 Minutes
The real estate board appraises the buildings. The groups clean up and return the raw materials. The group leader and supply person(s) compute total cost and enter figures on board or easel. The real estate board enters total value of buildings on board or easel.

Step 6
Compute the profit for each group. The total costs are subtracted from the total appraised value for each building. Determine the winning group (most profitable).

Step 7
The total group and the group leader should discuss the results in terms of the objectives, plan, and organization of each group to determine how these factors affected output and profits. Group members should respond to discussion questions for their own groups.

DISCUSSION QUESTIONS
1. What was the primary objective in this task?
2. Given this objective, what other objectives did your group set? Did you try to minimize/maximize floor space? Quality? Resources used? Aesthetic value? Costs?
3. Did your group's plan allow for the uncertainty associated with construction time? Did you establish any contingency plans or alternatives for long or short construction periods? Different shock tests?
4. Did your group members attempt to influence the real estate board either before or during the appraisal?
5. What factors in your group's efforts do you think account for its success or failure in this task?

6. How did your group's division of labor and coordination of efforts affect your performance?

GENERALIZATIONS AND CONCLUSIONS

Concluding Points

1. What does this exercise demonstrate about the role of group objectives?

2. What is the value of planning as demonstrated in this exercise?

Participant's Reactions

READINGS AND REFERENCES

Carroll, S. J., and Tosi, H. L., *Management by Objectives* (New York: Macmillan, 1980).

Donnelly, J. H., Gibson, J. L., and Ivancevich, J. M., *Fundamentals of Management: Functions, Behavior, Models* (Austin, Texas: Business Publications, 1971).

Hellreigel, D., and Slocum, J.W., *Management: A Contingency Approach* (Reading, Mass.: Addison-Wesley, 1974).

Copyright © 1982, John Wiley and Sons, Inc.

40
PEOPLE'S NATIONAL BANK, UNIVERSITY BRANCH

PURPOSE:
(1) To analyze the structure and design of an organization.
(2) To develop action steps to improve organizational effectiveness.

ADVANCE PREPARATION:
Read the case. Come to class prepared to discuss the two questions at the end of the case.

GROUP SIZE: Any Size. Can be discussed in small groups or in the total class.
TIME REQUIRED: 50 minutes to 2 hours, depending on number of issues covered.
SPECIAL MATERIALS: None.
SPECIAL PHYSICAL REQUIREMENTS: None.
RELATED TOPICS: Motivation: basic concepts, Applied motivation and job design, Managers as leaders, Group decision making and problem solving.

INTRODUCTION

The topic of organization design is often difficult for people to comprehend because of the size and complexity of many organizations. This is a case study of a branch bank, which has the twin benefits of being small enough to really study in detail, yet being large enough to have a fairly full set of organizational functions and problems. This case will put you in the role of a young, new branch manager, a recent graduate. You may find yourself in a similar situation in a few years!

PROCEDURE

Read the following case. Discuss the two questions at the end of the case.

PNB UNIVERSITY BRANCH

People's National Bank (PNB) is the lead bank of a moderate-sized bank holding company located in a large midwestern state. As the major bank in the company, located in the state's capital city, PNB accounts for $600 million of the company's $2 billion in assets. At the core of PNB is its branch banking system. Unlike many East Coast banks, branch banking accounts for a large percentage of PNB's income,

Case written by David Nadler. Adapted by D. T. Hall. Used by permission.

and many of the top managers of the bank have come up through the branch system.

The senior vice-president for branch operations, John B. Green, directly supervises the operations of 21 branch banks. Approximately 10 more branches are planned for the next three years. Each branch is headed up by a branch manager, who runs the branch with a relatively high degree of freedom. A typical branch includes a group of tellers, directed by a teller supervisor, and a "desk" staff of financial consultants, loan officers, and some clerical personnel. Some of the larger branches have assistant managers who may supervise either operations or the loan activity. Although the actual work technology is extremely standardized (i.e., procedures for opening accounts, processing loans, etc.), the branch manager is free to manage the branch as he desires, and different branches have greatly varying structures, procedures, and climates.

Each branch is a profit center within the larger bank. Branch revenue is figured by adding income from loan volume together with a figure representing income derived from the funds that the branch has brought in (based on deposit figures). From the revenue figure actual branch expenses, building expenses, and allocated overhead are subtracted to yield a branch profit figure, monthly. Each year, the branch manager and John B. Green develop a profit plan for the coming year, and managers are paid a sizable bonus depending upon the performance of their branch against the profit plan.

A Change at the University Branch

Two weeks ago, the branch manager of the University Branch of PNB informed John B. Green that he would be leaving the bank at the end of the following week to "join the ministry of God." Faced with an unanticipated managerial vacancy in a large and critical branch, Green met with his staff and decided to appoint Gary Herline, an up-and-coming young man in the commerical lending department, as manager of the University Branch. Herline was notified on Wednesday and was told to report to the University Branch on the following Monday to take up his duties as branch manager.

Herline's Background

Herline had been with the bank for a few years when he received the sudden notice of his appointment as branch manager. He received his MBA from a well-known business school four years ago and upon graduation was faced with several offers from financial institutions. He chose PNB, rather than one of the large New York banks, because he felt that there would be greater opportunities to move up in the organization quickly at PNB. He started out his first year in the bank's training program, and was rotated through a wide variety of assignments, including a brief assignment as a financial consultant at a branch. During this period, Gary learned that he had been identified by management as a "hot prospect" and that his performance was being watched closely. After the training rotation period, he spent two years in the trust department and had worked in the commercial lending department for a year when he heard about his move to the University Branch.

Copyright © 1982, John Wiley and Sons, Inc.

Information about University Branch

Having heard about his move late on Wednesday, Gary spent most of Thursday and Friday talking to some of his contacts within the bank about the University Branch, while he tried to conclude his work in commercial lending. The University Branch, one of the largest in the system, had been a problem branch for some time, with quite a bit of turnover among the employees and the managerial staff. Located adjacent to the state university campus, it faced a market area different from almost any other branch in the system. By Friday afternoon, Gary had listed the important things that he had learned about the branch (see Exhibit 1). As he prepared to start at University Branch on Monday morning, he asked himself the following questions:

1. "From what I know about the branch, what are the critical issues I am going to have to deal with during the next 6 months at University Branch?"
2. "When I get to the branch on Monday, what are the first things that I should do—what should my first day look like?"

Exhibit 1: PNB University Branch

Herline's summary of important information about University Branch:

It's a large branch. 8 desk people, 18 tellers, fairly good physical plant, high volume.

Loan volume has been very poor during the past three years, but there has been a recent increase over the past two or three months. Some people feel that this reflects an absence of any management and that the loans are not "good" ones (that delinquency will go up in the coming months).

Very young staff, particularly the tellers. All except two of the tellers are women and many have Bachelor of Arts degrees; some even have Masters degrees.

Branch has the highest number of accounts and highest volume of transactions of any branch in the system; however, many accounts are very small, and many transactions are for small amounts of money (i.e., checks for 50 cents to $5.00).

There is no official assistant manager, but one of the loan officers seems to function as an assistant manager. He is resented by the tellers, however, and seems to get into disagreements with the teller supervisor, who has been at the branch for 17 years.

Desk staff seem to be of uneven quality. Some real winners, but some dead wood also.

Turnover among tellers is very high. It has run at about 75 percent per year for the last five years. Recently the tellers submitted an informal group grievance to the manager complaining about working hours and low pay.

Competition for the university area business is keen. The other two major commercial banks in town have branches on the same block as PNB. Both branches are newer and better laid out than the PNB branch. Also, several S&Ls are close by.

Some of the key commercial accounts in the University Branch area have been taken by aggressive loan officers and branch managers of other nearby PNB branches as well as by competing banks.

For the last year, the branch has consistently failed to meet the profit plan, and has even shown losses in several months.

GENERALIZATIONS AND CONCLUSIONS

Concluding Points

1. In what ways are the financial performance of this organization affected strongly by employee motivation and behavior?

2. Why is it difficult for Herline to be too specific at this point about what immediate actions he will take?

Participant's Reactions

READINGS AND REFERENCES

Mirvis, P. H., and Lawler III, E. E., "Measuring the Financial Impact of Employee Attitudes," *Journal of Applied Psychology,* 62 (1977), 1-8.
Schneider, B., "The Perception of Organizational Climate: The Customer's View," *Journal of Applied Psychology,* 57 (1973), 248-256.

Copyright © 1982, John Wiley and Sons, Inc.

41
EXPERIENCING ORGANIZATIONAL CLIMATES

PURPOSE:
To assess the relationship between specific organizational experiences and the climate perceptions that they produce.

ADVANCE PREPARATION:
None.

GROUP SIZE: Any number of five-to-ten-person groups.
TIME REQUIRED: 30 to 50 minutes.
SPECIAL MATERIALS: None.
SPECIAL PHYSICAL REQUIREMENTS: None.
RELATED TOPICS: Managers as leaders, Motivation: basic concepts.

INTRODUCTION

Organization climate has become an increasingly popular concept for describing the generalized perceptions that people employ in thinking about and describing the organizations in which they work. Climate is an "umbrella concept" in that it is a way of summarizing numerous specific, detailed perceptions in a small number of general dimensions.

When new people enter a work setting, exactly how they should behave is one of the first things they need to figure out. Are people friendly with their bosses? Do people get along really well with each other? Do people really "put out" with effort? Is "shoddy" work tolerated? Are customers and clients all treated courteously? Is safety important? These are the kinds of impressions new employees pick up as they perceive what happens around them and to them.

New employees probably form an impression about *each* of the issues noted and many others. Each impression is based on the perception of numerous events, practices and procedures, that is, on the basis of the kinds of behaviors that new employees note are rewarded and supported by supervisors, co-workers, and organizational policy. The more *particular* kinds of events, practices, and procedures happen to, and around, employees the more they begin to sense that a particular atmosphere or climate exists.

New employees sense particular climates, then, as a function of the ebb and flow of everyday activities, events, practices, and procedures in a work place. Because no one can remember each and every little thing that happens to them and around them, people tend to group or "chunk" perceptions into meaningful clusters. These clusters are made up of the perceptions of activities, events, practices, and procedures that tend to connote a common theme.

Exercise developed by Benjamin Schneider. Adapted by D. T. Hall. Used by permission of Dr. Schneider.

How do we detect the climate of an organization? One of the best ways to determine climate is to identify *norms* in the environment—the (mostly) unwritten rules that people seem to follow about how to behave in an environment. One way to help people identify these factors is to identify the "dos and don'ts" or "OKs and no-nos" that characterize life in a particular culture. For example, "It's not OK to come to work without your hard hat" or "Although you're supposed to wear your hard hat all the time, it's OK to take it off when you're in the office."

This exercise will ask you to think about the climate of an organization in terms of these "dos and don'ts" that govern people's behavior in a particular environment.

OPTION ONE

Step 1: 15 Minutes

Meet in small groups. Think of yourselves as new employees in a work setting. The setting is a paint factory. Think about the climate for physical safety in the plant. When you report for work, you are told that "you should try to be careful, to follow the safety rules here; otherwise you're liable to get hurt."

What are the "dos and don'ts" around you that would create a *climate for safe behavior?* Brainstorm as many norms and characteristics of the work environment as you think of that would indicate a climate for safe behavior. Pick a spokesperson to present your list to the rest of the class.

Step 2: 15 to 35 Minutes

Report each group's list to the rest of the class. Examine the ways in which very specific experiences and features of the work organization combine to produce global perceptions of the climate of the organization.

GENERALIZATIONS AND CONCLUSIONS

Concluding Points

1. How are perceptions of organizational climate formed?

Copyright © 1982, John Wiley and Sons, Inc.

2. What effect do climate perceptions have on an employee's behavior? On a client or customer's behavior?

3. In this exercise we have focused on the climate for safety. What other aspects of climate can you think of, say, in a bank (a service organization)?

4. Based on what we have concluded about how climate perceptions are formed, what can you say about how climates are changed?

OPTION TWO

Consider an organization with which you are all familiar, such as the institution in which you are presently attending this class. (Another possibility would be to consider the organization in which you are currently employed, if you are now employed.)

Step 1: Completing and Scoring the Questionnaire

First complete the questionnaire below, describing first the ideal and then the actual state of the organization, as you see it. (The "organization" can be this class, a work group, your employer, or any other organization.) Then compute your ideal and actual scores on the six dimensions of climate given at the end of the questionnaire. Compute the gap between ideal and actual states on each dimension.

Step 2: Computing Group Averages and Discrepancies

If other members of your organization or group have also completed the Organization Climate Questionnaire, get together with them and compute group means for the ideal and actual organization climate. Then compute the gap between ideal and actual climate scores on each of these group means.

Discuss where the greatest gaps occurred and the reasons for this state of affairs. What could be done to reduce this gap?

Discuss where the smallest gaps occurred. What accounts for this state of affairs?

READINGS AND REFERENCES

Hall, D. T., and Schneider, B., *Organizational Climates and Careers: The Work Lives of Priests* (New York: Seminar Press, 1973).

Schneider, B., "Organizational Climate: Individual Preferences and Organizational Realities," *Journal of Applied Psychology,* 56 (1972), 211–17.

Schneider, B., "The Perception of Organizational Climate: The Customer's View," *Journal of Applied Psychology,* 57 (1973), 248–256.

Schneider, B., "Organizational Climates: An Essay," *Personnel Psychology,* 28 (1975), 447–479.

Schneider, B., Parkington, J. J., and Buxton, V. M., "Employee and Customer Perceptions of Service in Banks," *Administrative Science Quarterly* (1981), in press.

Zohar, D., "Safety Climate in Industrial Organizations: Theoretical and Applied Implications," *Journal of Applied Psychology,* 65 (1980), 96–102.

Copyright © 1982, John Wiley and Sons, Inc.

Organization Climate Questionnaire

Using the spaces in the left-hand column, first describe the *ideal* practices and procedures you would like to see in this organization. Next, using the spaces in the right-hand column, describe what you believe *actually happens now* in this organization. Put a number in the space beside each statement according to the following key: 1 = almost never; 2 = infrequently; 3 = sometimes; 4 = frequently; 5 = very frequently.

Ideal   *Actual*

_____ 1. This organization takes care of the people who work for it.   _____

_____ 2. Members enjoy keeping up with national and international current events.   _____

_____ 3. People in this organization ask each other how they are doing in reaching their goals.   _____

_____ 4. Management effectively balances people problems and production problems.   _____

_____ 5. There are definite "in" and "out" groups within the organization.   _____

_____ 6. This organization encourages employees to exercise their own initiative.   _____

_____ 7. This organization takes an active interest in the progress of its members.   _____

_____ 8. Members of this organization have a wide range of interests.   _____

_____ 9. More experienced members of this organization take time to help newer members.   _____

_____ 10. The management runs a people-oriented organization.   _____

_____ 11. Members of this organization always have grievances no matter what is done to correct them.   _____

_____ 12. This organization willingly accepts the ideas of its members for change.   _____

Developed by Benjamin Schneider and C. J. Bartlett. Used by permission. This version of the questionnaire is not presented for research purposes. Those interested in the total set of items should contact Benjamin Schneider, Department of Psychology, Michigan State University, East Lansing, MI 48824.

_____ 13. This organization recognizes that its life depends upon its _____ members.

_____ 14. Members keep themselves informed on many topics be- _____ sides their immediate job-related activities.

_____ 15. People in this organization speak openly about each oth- _____ ers' shortcomings.

_____ 16. There is a sense of purpose and direction in this organization. _____

_____ 17. Members are prone to overstate and exaggerate their _____ accomplishments.

_____ 18. Management does not exercise authoritarian control over _____ members' activities.

Scoring:

Scale	Add Items	Ideal Total	Actual Total	Gap (Ideal-Actual)
Organizational Support	1, 7, 13	_____	_____	_____
Member Quality	2, 8, 14	_____	_____	_____
Openness	3, 9, 15	_____	_____	_____
Supervisory Style	4, 10, 16	_____	_____	_____
Member Conflict	5, 11, 17	_____	_____	_____
Member Autonomy	6, 12, 18	_____	_____	_____

Copyright © 1982, John Wiley and Sons, Inc.

42
SQUARE, INC.

PURPOSE:
(1) To demonstrate the impacts of subunit interdependence and goal suboptimization on traditional hierarchical structures.
(2) To compare the information transfer mechanisms of strict traditional hierarchies and structures allowing direct contact between organizational members.

GROUP SIZE: Any size, divided into subgroups of six members each.
TIME REQUIRED: 1 to 1½ hours.
SPECIAL MATERIALS: Geometric pieces cut from cardstock. One set for each group of six.
SPECIAL PHYSICAL REQUIREMENTS: A separate room or area for each group, and another small room for the member of each group appointed as division manager. Flip chart or blackboard for each group, accessible to both the manager and the rest of the group members. If you are limited on room space, see "Procedure" below for suggestions on room set-up.
RELATED TOPICS: Organizational communication, Managers as leaders, Power.

INTRODUCTION

Square, Inc., is a traditional hierarchial organization engaged in the manufacture and sale of industrial equipment. The industry is intensely competitive. The corporation has several divisions, each comprised of five plants producing basically the same product, and headed by a division manager.

Your instructor will assign each plant manager to a separate area of the room and distribute job descriptions and raw materials to each plant. Read your instructions carefully, then begin your production process; that is, assemble your raw materials into a finished product (a square). Your division manager will be located somewhere outside the room.

PROCEDURE

Step 1: 5 Minutes
Form teams of six members each. If any persons are left over, they may be used as observers, to note the number and type of contacts made within a division of the Square corporation, or they may be used as memo runners.

Adapted and written by L. Delf Dodge and V. Jean Ramsey from an experiment designed by A. Bavelas, and reported in "Communication Patterns in Task-oriented Groups," *Journal of the Acoustical Soceity of America,* 22 (1950), 725–730. Published by permission of Dr. Dodge.

Step 2: 5 Minutes

Assign each team to a separate room or general geographic area of a large room. The instructor will announce how plant managers and division managers will be selected. Plant managers should seat themselves in such a way that they do not see or hear each other. Placing yourselves in separate areas of the room with your backs toward the center of the room works well. The division managers should place themselves in a separate room close by, or just outside the door of the room containing the plant managers. A chalkboard, flipchart, or tablet of paper should also be placed near the door to serve as a communication link between the division and plant managers.

Step 3: 5 Minutes

Distribute role descriptions and raw materials to division and plant managers.

Step 4: 20 to 30 Minutes

Allow organizations to operate until 5 squares have been produced.

Step 5: 30 to 40 Minutes

Reassemble as a class, debrief, and discuss.

DISCUSSION QUESTIONS

1. Did any suboptimization occur? How long did it last? How did it affect other plants?
2. How involved was the division manager in the parts allocation process? What appeared to affect his/her level of involvement?
3. What behaviors on the part of the plant managers facilitated solution of the problem? What did they do that was dysfunctional? What about the division managers?
4. What would have made the parts allocation process easier?
5. How would you characterize the morale of the organizations's employees? Why do you think they felt the way they did? Would a change in the organization's structure affect morale? How?
6. How effective do you feel your division was? Given the costs of travel and parts transferring, do you think you were efficient in your attempts to solve the parts allocation problem?

Copyright © 1982, John Wiley and Sons, Inc.

Participant's Reactions

READINGS AND REFERENCES

Galbraith, Jay, *Organization Design* (Reading, Mass.: Addison-Wesley, 1977).

Dodge, L. Delf, and Tosi, Henry L. "The Effects of Environment on Organization Systems," in H. L. Tosi and C. W. Hamner, eds., *Organizational Behavior: A Contingency Approach* (Chicago: St. Clair Press, 1977).

Miles, Robert H., *Macro Organizational Behavior* (Santa Monica, Calif.: Goodyear Publishing, 1980).

Copyright © 1982, John Wiley and Sons, Inc.

PART IV
CHANGE

SECTION TWELVE
PLANNED CHANGE

43
CHANGE OF WORK PROCEDURES

PURPOSE:
(1) To diagnose and practice overcoming resistance to change.
(2) To illustrate the distinction between the quality of a decision and its acceptability.
(3) To provide practice in participative decision making.

ADVANCE PREPARATION:
None.

GROUP SIZE: Subgroups of five. Total class can be any size. Works best with groups of from four to six.
TIME REQUIRED: 50 minutes.
SPECIAL MATERIALS: None.
SPECIAL PHYSICAL REQUIREMENTS: None.
RELATED TOPICS: Applied motivation and job design, Group decision making and problem solving, Managers as leaders, Power, Interpersonal communication.

INTRODUCTION

Most changes in organizations are seldom confined to the technical aspects of production; they may also require alterations in the *work* and *social* satisfactions of the employees. New methods must be not only of high *quality* (i.e., workable and efficient from an objective standpoint), but they must also be *acceptable* to the employees who will be using them.

Developed by N. R. F. Maier. Adapted for the present volume by D. T. Hall. Used by permission.

Copyright © 1982, John Wiley and Sons, Inc.

This added factor of acceptance makes the problem of introducing changes different from purely technical problems of evaluating new equipment or procedures. For one thing, the quality of a solution and its acceptability are different characteristics and do not necessarily go together. A second complication is that although management can control solution quality by reserving decision making to itself, acceptance is inherently voluntary with the employees and is not subject to the will of management. At the same time, failure to obtain employee acceptance of changes that affect them aggravates many of the problems of management. In some instances resistance is expressed directly in the form of grievances about rates and earnings, quits, work stoppages and open hostility toward management. In other instances, the resistance may be shown in such indirect ways as restriction of output, waste, low-quality workmanship, slow learning of the new methods, excessive absenteeism, and the like.

One might think of two general approaches to introducing change: *selling* and *mutual problem solving.* In selling, facts and arguments are presented to employees showing the advantages of change. In mutual problem solving, the manager and his subordinates discuss the need for change and arrive jointly at a plan for change. In between these two approaches is *consultation,* in which the manager discusses the need for change with subordinates, solicits their ideas, and then makes the decision alone.

In order to deal with problems of change, the first step is to learn the nature of the resistance to change. In the present case there are a variety of forces operating. Some of these are in the direction of change, some opposed or resisting. The supervisor in charge will want to identify the resistance forces and try to reduce them, while trying to constructively use the positive forces.

The kind of discussion the new supervisor stimulates may introduce new negative or new positive forces so that the outcome may, in part, be determined by the discussion he initiates.

PROCEDURE

Step 1: 5 Minutes

The group is divided into subgroups of five. If the total group size is not a multiple of five, some subgroups of four or six can be used. All groups are to select one of their members to act as the foreman, "Thompson." After the foremen have been chosen, they should raise their hands to indicate that the group has a leader.

The other members in each group will be crew members and observer(s). Beginning with the foreman and going in clockwise order, their names will be "Jackson," "Stevenson," and "Walters." The fifth members (and sixth, if present) will be observers.

Step 2: 5 Minutes

When all members have received their roles, the group leader will read aloud the section entitled "General Information," below.

GENERAL INFORMATION

This role play takes place in a company that manufactures small hand-held electronic calculators and components for computer systems. In this company, the assembly work is done by small groups of employees. Several of these employees are under the supervision of a foreman, Thompson. In one of these groups, Jackson, Stevenson, and Walters work together assembling components for hand-held calculators. Because of the constant change in model, style, and capability of hand-held calculators, and the popular demand for them, the men usually have a fairly constant backlog of 2 to 3 weeks in work orders.

This operation is divided into three jobs or positions, called position 1, position 2, and position 3. Supplies for each position are located next to the bench where the man works. The men work side by side and can help each other out if they wish. Since all the jobs are simple and fairly similar, these three employees exchange positions on the line every now and then. This trading of positions was developed by the men themselves. It creates no financial problem because the crew is paid by a group piece rate. In this way the three members share the production pay equally.

Presently each of you will be asked to be one of the following: Thompson, Jackson, Walters, or Stevenson. Today, Thompson, the foreman, has asked Jackson, Walters, and Stevenson to meet with him in his office. He said he wanted to talk about "something."

Next, the role players should study (only) their individual roles in preparation for the small group discussions. The roles for Thompson, Jackson, Stevenson, and Walters are found in the Appendix to this book, as are the instructions for observers.

The Thompsons should stand up beside their groups when they have finished studying their roles, thus giving the group leader a signal that they are ready to begin.

When all foremen are standing, the group leader will set the stage for the role-playing by commenting that the foreman has asked the crew members to meet with him to discuss a problem before starting work. He will explain that when the foreman is asked to sit down, this will be the signal that Thompson has entered his office. He hopes that the employees will speak to him as he enters.

Step 3: 25 Minutes

The leader will ask if anyone has any questions. When everyone understands his function, the leader will ask the foremen to sit down. All groups should role-play simultaneously. Approximately 25 minutes is needed by the average group to reach a decision.

Step 4: 15 Minutes

Collect results.

DISCUSSION QUESTIONS

1. What conclusions can be drawn from the table of results? Is there any relation-

Copyright © 1982, John Wiley and Sons, Inc.

ship between the method used and the degree of acceptance or resistance? What method was used most often?

2. Construct a problem analysis diagram of this situation. What were the *resistance* forces (i.e., the members' objections to the change)? What were the *change* forces (i.e., possible gains or advantages to the crew under the new method)?

3. Which of the forces in the diagram are based on emotions (fear, hostility, etc.)? Which are based on actual information about the changes?

GENERALIZATIONS AND CONCLUSIONS

Concluding Points

1. As a strategy for change, is it generally better to try to reduce the resistance forces or to increase the change forces?

2. What three factors primarily determine the effectiveness of change?

3. What generally happens to resistance to change when groups participate in planning for change? Why?

4. What are two major dimensions of change in organizations?

5. When resistance to change is caused by negative attitudes and emotions, how should the group leader deal with these findings?

Participant's Reactions

READINGS AND REFERENCES

Coch, L., and French, J. R. P., Jr., "Overcoming Resistance to Change," *Human Relations,* 1 (1948), 512-32.

Frost, C., Wakeley, J., and Ruh, R., *The Scanlon Plan for Organization Development: Identity, Participation, and Equity* (East Lansing: Michigan State University Press, 1974).

Marrow, A., Bowers D., and Seashore, S., *Management by Participation* (New York: Harper & Row, 1967).

Copyright © 1982, John Wiley and Sons, Inc.

44
THE SANITARY COMPANY

PURPOSE:
(1) To develop an understanding of how different theories and change strategies can be used to solve a problem of employee behavior.
(2) To develop an understanding of factors affecting efforts to implement change.
(3) To illustrate the effects of decision making and resistance on planned change programs.

ADVANCE PREPARATION:
Read the "Introduction," below, and complete Steps 1 to 3 (Part I) in advance.

GROUP SIZE: Any number of small groups. May be done individually.
TIME REQUIRED Part I: 1 hour. Part II: 45 minutes.
SPECIAL MATERIALS: None.
SPECIAL PHYSICAL REQUIREMENTS: Movable chairs or separate rooms.
RELATED TOPICS: Applied motivation and job design, Group decision making and problem solving, Managers as leaders.

INTRODUCTION

Changing worker behavior, like skinning cats, may be approached in a variety of ways. How it is approached will depend on the nature of the underlying problem, the theories about behavior we apply in developing a strategy for solving the problem, and how we go about introducing or implementing the strategy. In the first part of this exercise, you will have an opportunity to (1) analyze the problem of absenteeism and turnover in a small company, (2) develop a change strategy, and (3) select a method for implementing your strategy. There are no "right" answers, although some solutions may have more merit than others.

Later, you will be given information and data reported by the consultants who actually intervened in the Sanitary Company situation. At various points in the case you will be asked to predict what you think actually happened. As you will see, the consultants discovered several unforeseen consequences associated with their strategy and method of implementing it.

Developed by Francine S. Hall. Case material adapted from E. E. Lawler, III and J. R. Hackman, "Impact of Employee Participation in the Development of Pay Incentive Plans," *Journal of Applied Psychology* 53 (1969), 467-71; and K. Scheflen, E. E. Lawler, and J. R. Hackman, "Long Term Impact of Employee Participation in Development of Pay Incentive Plans," *Journal of Applied Psychology,* 55 (1971), 182-86.

PART I

PROCEDURE

Step 1

Read the following case description of Sanitary Company.

THE CASE OF THE SANITARY COMPANY

The Sanitary Company is a small company that provides building maintenance services on a contract basis. Employees work part time cleaning buildings and offices during the evening. Most employees work four hours a night, five nights a week. They are paid at an hourly rate.

Employees work in groups ranging in size from 2 to 25 persons. There are about 15 such "work groups" in the company. Each group is responsible for doing all the cleaning in one building. The actual cleaning work is similar for each group.

Employees are expected to report for work each night at the building to be cleaned. The company has managers who are responsible for supervising the cleaning crews, but they are not members of the actual work groups.

Employees tend to have low levels of education. Some of them are illiterate. About half of the employees are women. Many of the women are housewives during the day. For most of the male employees, work with the Sanitary Company is a second job. The employees range in age from 16 to over 70.

Step 2

Assume that you have been hired as consultants to the company that is described in the case. The company President, M. K. Nunes, has told you that he is concerned with the high rate of *turnover and absenteeism* in his company. He has asked you to diagnose his company's problem and to recommend a plan for solving it. Specifically, he wants your answers to the following questions:

1. What do you think the real problem is? Why?
2. What solution(s) would you propose? Why?
3. How would you implement your plan? What reasons would you give for doing it this way?

What will you tell the company president?

Step 3

Prepare your plan in three parts:

1. *Diagnosis:* Identify the variables that may be causing the absenteeism and turnover. Remember that behavior such as this is usually a symptom of a more serious problem.
2. *Change Recommendation:* Given the factors you identified as possible causes, outline a plan for changing the situation. In other words, prescribe an appropriate solution or remedy.

Copyright © 1982, John Wiley and Sons, Inc.

3. *Implementation strategy:* Given the change you want to bring about, describe the manner in which you will introduce it in the organization. Consider such factors as your role, the roles of people in the organization, modes of communication, and attitudes of organization members.

In each part, detail your analysis and recommendations, and provide the rationale on which they are based.

Step 4: 1 hour
The total group should convene. Each individual or group presents the plan that he/she/they developed. The group leader will summarize these on the board. After all plans have been presented, discuss the Sanitary Company case in terms of the questions listed below.

DISCUSSION QUESTIONS
1. What are the pros and cons of the different plans?
2. Which would be most feasible? Why?
3. Which would generate the most and least resistance? Why?
4. Which would have the highest likelihood of success? Why?
5. What employee needs does each plan meet or use as motivators?

GENERALIZATIONS AND CONCLUSIONS

Concluding Points
1. What is the best strategy to employ when attempting to change employee behavior?

2. What is the foundation for developing an effective change strategy?

PART II

PROCEDURE

Step 1: 10 Minutes

Your group leader will read an account of how the consultants who actually intervened in the Sanitary Company case approached the problem. When he has finished, discuss the prediction question which follows.

Prediction Question: What do you think happened to the attendance record for (a) the participative groups? (b) the imposed groups? and (c) the control (no treatment) groups?

Step 2: 10 Minutes

Your group leader will read an account of what actually happened. When he has finished, discuss the prediction questions which follow.

Prediction Questions: (1) Why do you think the plan was successful for some groups and not for others? (2) What do you think the long-term effect will be? After one year, what do you predict the attendance record will be? (3) Do you think the company management will continue the plan?

Step 3: 10 Minutes

Your group leader will read an account of what happened. Discuss the prediction questions which follow.

Prediction Questions: (1) Why do you think it took so long before the attendance in the imposed groups improved? (2) Why do you think the managers of the two participative groups took the action they did?

Step 4: 15 Minutes

Your group leader will read a summary account of the Sanitary Company case. Discuss this case as a total group. What conclusions can you draw from it?

GENERALIZATIONS AND CONCLUSIONS

Concluding Points

1. What other considerations are as important as the technical aspects of a change plan?

Copyright © 1982, John Wiley and Sons, Inc.

2. When a plan requires acceptance in order to work, what decision making style is most appropriate?

3. In deciding who to include, what should be considered?

Participant's Reactions

READINGS AND REFERENCES

Coch, L., and French, J. R. P., "Overcoming Resistance to Change," *Human Relations,* 1 (1948), 512-32.

Levinson, H., *Organizational Diagnosis* (Cambridge, Mass.: Harvard University Press, 1972).

Scheflen, K., Lawler, E. E., III, and Hackman, J. R., "Long Term Impact of Employee Participation in Development of Pay Incentive Plans," *Journal of Applied Psychology,* 55 (1971), 182–86.

Vroom, V., and Yetton, P., *Leadership and Decision Making* (Pittsburgh: University of Pittsburgh Press, 1973).

45
THE HOLLOW-SQUARE PLANNING PROBLEM

PURPOSE:
(1) To demonstrate problems in the relationship between those who design or create a plan, and those who have the responsibility for executing it.
(2) To explore the implications of clear communication in a problem solving task.
(3) To become aware of the factors that promote and inhibit effective problem solving.

ADVANCE PREPARATION:
None.

GROUP SIZE: One or more groups of planners (four to six members); *same* number groups of operators (four to six members); two or more observers for *each* Planning and Operating Team.

TIME REQUIRED: 1 to 2 hours.

SPECIAL MATERIALS: Sets of the "hollow-square puzzle" cut out of cardboard.

SPECIAL PHYSICAL ARRANGEMENTS: A separate table and chairs for each team of planners, either in the same room or in separate rooms, and a room where teams of operators can meet in small groups before working with the planners.

RELATED TOPICS: Negotiation and conflict, Group decision making and problem solving, Managers as leaders, Organizational communication.

INTRODUCTION

Change is one of the most complex processes in organizations. There are a number of reasons for this: some people may not see the need for change, people may not agree on the mechanisms or targets of change, or people may have changes "imposed" on them rather than having some individual influence and control over the change process.

One major problem faced in many organizations is that those people who are the "architects" of change—whether the change be in a new way of working together, or a new product line, or a new corporate strategy—are often not the people who are responsible for executing the actual change steps. This activity simulates the problems that may occur when those who design a task are not those who must execute it.

Adapted by Roy J. Lewicki. The exact origin of this exercise is unknown.

Copyright © 1982, John Wiley and Sons, Inc.

PROCEDURE

Step 1: 5 Minutes

The group leader will divide the class into one or more teams of planners, operators, and observers. Match trios of planner-operator-observer teams so people know with whom they are working.

Step 2: 5 Minutes

Report to the areas assigned by the group leader, and read your instructions. For these, the planners should consult their briefing sheet in the Appendix to this book. (Please do not consult other groups' briefing sheets at this time.) The operators should consult their briefing sheet in the Appendix. (Please do not consult other groups' briefing sheets at this time.) The observers should read the briefing sheets for both the planners and operators, and then their own briefing sheet.

Step 3: 30 Minutes

The planners should proceed according to their instructions, for the exact time stated by the group leader. The operators should work separately, according to their briefing sheet, until contacted by the planners. The observers should meet briefly to divide their responsibilities for observation. They will then take notes on the behavior of both the planners and operators.

Step 4: 5 Minutes

By the end of the "planning period," the planners must call in their operators. At least 5 minutes will be spent in briefing the operators.

Step 5: 15 Minutes

The operators, working as teams and competing against one another, must assemble the hollow-square puzzle as quickly as possible. The team with the fastest assembly time will be declared the winner. Time will be kept by the group leader or a referee—notify him when you are finished.

DISCUSSION QUESTIONS

1. Ask the planners to select three adjectives to describe their feelings about the operators.
2. Ask the operators to select three adjectives to describe their feelings about the planning *before* the planners called them in, and three for *after* they called them in.
3. Ask the observers to report on their perceptions of the team of operators before they were involved by the planners.
4. Ask the observers to report on their perceptions of the planners before they involved the operators.
5. Have each operating team report on the instructions that they received from planners after the operators were involved. How did this ultimately affect the operators' ability to assemble the hollow square?

GENERALIZATIONS AND CONCLUSIONS

Concluding Points

1. What are some critical elements that a team of planners should consider when it is designing a task for others to carry out?

2. What can the operators do to help the work of the planners, and to insure that the task is completed accurately and rapidly?

3. In what departments, groups, or divisions of organizations are these problems likely to occur?

Participant's Reactions

READINGS AND REFERENCES

Bennis, W., *Changing Organizations* (New York: McGraw Hill, 1966).

Bennis, W., Benne, K., and Chin, R., *The Planning of Change* (New York: Holt, Rinehart and Winston, 1969).

Coch, L., and French, J. R. P., "Overcoming Resistance to Change," *Human Relations,* 1 (1948), 512-32.

Copyright © 1982, John Wiley and Sons, Inc.

SECTION THIRTEEN
LIFE, WORK, AND CAREER ROLES

INTRODUCTION

Before you begin the career planning activities in this section, it would probably be helpful if we explained what we mean by "career," and what we consider to be an effective and comprehensive approach to career planning. For example, many people tend to think of a career as a particular job or occupation and the sequence of promotions they hope to get in that job. Hall (1976), however, suggests that we can understand careers better if we make certain assumptions:

1. *Career per se does not imply success or failure.* The notion that one is a failure if one does not advance and become promoted is an assumption of our culture, but not the best assumption to make if you want to understand how individuals approach their careers. Therefore,

2. *Career success or failure is best assessed by the person whose career is being considered, rather than by other interested parties.* Clearly, any career can be a success if it is a source of deep satisfaction and reward to the person who lives it. The best measure of success may be *psychological success,* the extent to which the person feels he or she is achieving personally valued goals and outcomes in the career. In other words,

3. *The career is made up of both behaviors and attitudes*—what one does and how one feels about it. And, finally,

4. *The career is a process, a sequence of work-related experiences.* Here, Hall suggests that we think of a career as:

- a life-long sequence;
- including all work-related experience (whether paid or not) and not strictly limited to a single profession or occupation;

Prepared by Donald D. Bowen.

- a major, but not the only, component of one's life—which is not to say that family life, leisure activities, and other aspects of life are not strongly influenced by the satisfactions and frustrations people experience in their careers. These considerations led Hall (1976, p. 4) to define a career as:

... the individually perceived sequence of attitudes and behaviors associated with work-related experiences and activities over the span of the person's life.

Since our concept of career emphasizes the subjective experience, the personal perception and feelings of the person in the career, we believe (as do many authorities on careers) that effective career planning must begin with an assessment in depth of one's own needs, values, motives, strengths, and weaknesses if one is to find a good career-person fit. John Crites[1] suggests that career planning should follow a five-step approach, in the following order:

1. *Self-assessment.* As already suggested, the objective of this phase is to think through and get in touch with your most important needs, values, interests, strengths, and weaknesses. Find out what they are and decide how these need to be dealt with in your career. Self-assessment activities (almost always better if done in a group) and tests (usually available from your college counseling center or placement office at little or no cost) should provide the basic data here. Don't forget to look at how *all* aspects of your life may be affected by your career experiences.

2. *Career opportunity information.* The objective here is to identify vocational and organizational paths that are likely to prove most satisfying to you. Suggested sources of information include your college placement office, interviews with people in the occupations you are interested in, and books— especially *Dictionary of Occupational Titles, Occupational Outlook Handbook,* and *Occupational Outlook Quarterly.*

3. *Goal setting.* In this phase you should set some overall objectives for your career and some shorter-term, five-year goals. Remember a good goal is specific and concrete (measurable) and is stated in terms of a specific time period or deadline.

4. *Planning.* Develop a specific plan for achieving your major goals. What must you do? What must others do? What sequences of events or activities are necessary?

   Both planning and goal-setting should be discussed in great detail with the important support groups in your life—close friends or members of your immediate family to whom you usually look for understanding, support, and advice when you are making major life decisions.

5. *Problem solving.* Problem solving is an activity that goes on throughout the process of working toward your goals. It is the dealing with obstacles, blockages, problems, and so on that develop as you pursue your goals. Problem

[1]John O. Crites, *Theory and Research Handbook: Career Maturity Inventory* (Monterey, Calif.: McGraw-Hill, 1973).

Copyright © 1982, John Wiley and Sons, Inc.

solving requires assessing the situation and oneself, establishing a goal that will solve the problem, and laying a plan to achieve the goal.

In the following pages, as well as in earlier sections of this book, you will find a number of self-assessment activities to get you started in planning your career. There are a number of books of activities that provide complete career planning programs for the individual or the group. Some of the best known include:

Bolles, R. N., *What Color is Your Parachute?* (Berkeley, Calif.: Ten Speed Press, 1972).

Crystal, J. C., and Bolles, R. N., *Where Do I Go From Here With My Life?* (New York: Seabury Press, 1974).

Kotter, J. P., Faux, V. A., and McArthur, C. C., *Self-Assessment and Career Development* (Englewood Cliffs, N.J.: Prentice-Hall, 1978).

Weiler, N. W., *Reality and Career Planning* (Reading, Mass.: Addison Wesley, 1977).

For those interested in what is known about careers and how this knowledge can be used to manage the human resources of the organization more effectively, we suggest:

Bowen, D. D., and Hall, D. T., "Career Planning for Employee Development: A Primer for Managers," *California Management Review,* Winter (1977), 23–35.

Hall, D. T., *Careers in Organizations* (Pacific Palisades, Calif.: Goodyear, 1976).

Hall, D. T., and Hall, F. S., "What's New in Career Management," *Organizational Dynamics,* Summer (1976), 17–33.

Schein, E. H., *Career Dynamics: Matching Individual and Organizational Needs* (Reading, Mass.: Addison-Wesley, 1978).

46
LIFELINES

PURPOSE:
To introduce a typical self-assessment component used as a first step in career planning.

ADVANCE PREPARATION:
Read the Introduction to Section 13 and any other readings the instructor may assign before beginning the exercise. The instructor may also ask that the lifelines be prepared before the group meets to discuss them.

GROUP SIZE: Unlimited—small discussion groups of three to five persons are required.

TIME REQUIRED: Depends on number of persons in subgroups and design option specified. Ranges from 40 to 140 minutes, but can be done as an outside assignment (see Instructor's Manual for alternatives and variations).

SPECIAL MATERIALS: None.

SPECIAL PHYSICAL REQUIREMENTS: Room large enough to seat small groups comfortably and permit discussions with minimal distraction from others. (Movable chairs will be helpful.) Separate meeting rooms for the small groups are desirable.

RELATED TOPICS: Icebreakers, Planned change, Motivation: basic concepts, Interpersonal communication.

INTRODUCTION

In this exercise, you will work on examining your own values and priorities for your life, and set career goals for yourself in terms of your own needs. You will find it helpful to approach this process by sharing your feelings and attitudes with others in the small group you will work with. In respect to any piece of personal data, however, you should always feel free to withhold that information from others if you would be uncomfortable sharing it.

PROCEDURE

PART I

Step 1: 10 Minutes

Take a piece of notebook paper. At the top, write "Where am I now?—Career." Proceed as follows: Envision a business progress chart as you draw a line that

Adapted from: J. William Pfeiffer and John E. Jones (eds.), "A Handbook of Structured Experiences for Human Relations Training," Vol. II (Revised). San Diego, CA: University Associates, 1974. Used with permission.

Copyright © 1982, John Wiley and Sons, Inc.

depicts the past, present, and future of your *career*. On this line mark an "X" to show where you are now. A business chart looks like this:

Write a brief explanation of the career line that you have drawn. Pay particular attention to the *peaks* and *valleys* of your lifeline. Peaks indicate that you were satisfying some of your most important needs at that time. Valleys probably mark times when these important needs were frustrated. What can you infer about which needs are most important to you from your lifeline? *Above* your lifeline, write in the most important decisions you have made in your life to date. Indicate where these occurred in relation to the peaks and valleys. Also, indicate the most important decisions you think you might be making at future points in your life. Evaluate for yourself the *outcomes* of those decisions.

Now, below your lifeline, indicate what you think you would have done *if you had not made each of these decisions* (or if you had made a different decision at each of these points). How would your life have turned out differently?[1]

Step 2: 10 Minutes
Take another piece of notebook paper. Label it "Where am I now?—Affiliations." Envision a business progress chart as you draw a line that depicts the past, present, and future of your personal *affiliations* (family and friends). On this line, mark an "X" to show where you are now. Write a brief explanation of the affiliation line that you have drawn. Again, analyze the peaks and valleys for what they can tell you about your most important needs.

Step 3: 10 Minutes
Head up another piece of notebook paper with "Where am I now?—Personal Fulfillment." Envision a business progress chart as you draw a line that depicts the past, present, and future of your *personal fulfillment*. (Consider every level from personal growth to material acquisition.) Write a brief explanation of the personal fulfillment line that you have drawn, paying special attention to the peaks and valleys.

PART II

Step 4: 5 Minutes
If the group has not already been subdivided into smaller groups, break into three-to-five person groups according to the group leader's directions.

---

[1] Suggested by an idea in Bolles (1978).

Step 5: 5 Minutes per Person

Take turns sharing your *career* lifeline with others in your group. Explain your lifeline in detail and discusss what you have inferred about your most important needs from the peaks and valleys of the lifeline.

Note: For the other members of the group, this is a chance to practice your listening and counseling skills. Don't give advice, but do listen carefully and ask any questions you can think of that might help the person presenting her lifeline to develop a better understanding of what the data mean. If you already know the person well, does his explanation make sense in light of how you perceive him? If you do not know the person, here is a chance to get to know her a lot better.

Step 6: 5 Minutes per Person

Take turns sharing each *affiliations* lifeline, proceeding as before in Step 5.

Step 7: 5 Minutes per Person

Take turns sharing each *personal fulfillment* lifeline.

PART III

Step 8: 30 Minutes

Working alone, prepare a brief statement of what you now see to be *the most important needs you need to satisfy in pursuing your career.* You may not feel that all of the needs you identified in your lifelines are still important; list only those that you now feel are most important.

For each need you list, what are the types of work or other situations that seem to provide the most satisfaction of the need? What changes in your career plans do you need to provide as much satisfaction of the need as possible?

Rank-order the needs in terms of their *importance* to you in assuring your own happiness. Does this suggest any additional changes you need to make in your career plans?

Now, develop answers to the following questions:

1. What barriers or obstacles to these satisfactions might you encounter from the following sources:
   a. Yourself?
   b. Significant other people in your life?
   c. Your work environment?
2. What *resources* (i.e., help) might you mobilize from the following sources?
   a. Yourself?
   b. Significant other people in your life?
   c. Your work environment?

Include the discussion of your obstacles and resources in your statement.

Copyright © 1982, John Wiley and Sons, Inc.

DISCUSSION QUESTIONS

1. Psychologists often argue that most people have rather fuzzy career plans because their sense of identity (their sense of who they are) is hazy. (For example, see Fromm, 1947, and Erikson, 1968.) From your experience with this exercise, would you agree or disagree? Did the exercise enhance your sense of identity? Did this help you to clarify your career plans?
2. Suggest further steps for continuing your career planning.
3. Do you feel that a person can plan a career without considering the impact of career on affiliations and personal fulfillment (and vice versa)?

GENERALIZATIONS AND CONCLUSIONS

Concluding Points

1. Develop a career strategy statement for yourself that you can use to plan and manage your career. Make your objectives *specific* and *concrete*, develop *action plans* for achieving these objectives, develop a *timetable* for accomplishment of the major steps, and identify a *support group* of people (friends or family) who will encourage you and counsel you on achieving your goals.

2. For many people, career planning means a process in which they merely collect information on available jobs and employers. In this exercise, you have been collecting information about yourself. What might be the relationship between these two strategies?

Participant's Reactions

READINGS AND REFERENCES

See the readings suggested in the Introduction to Section 13. A number of additional life planning activities are suggested in:

Bolles, R. N., *The Three Boxes of Life* (Berkeley, Calif.: Ten Speed Press, 1978).

The relevance of one's "identity" in career planning is discussed in:

Erikson, E. H., *Identity: Youth and Crisis* (New York: Norton, 1968).
Fromm, E., *Man for Himself* (New York: Fawcett, 1947), pp. 62–113.

Copyright © 1982, John Wiley and Sons, Inc.

47
CAREER PLANNING:
STRENGTHS AND WEAKNESSES INVENTORY

PURPOSE:
(1) To diagnose your occupational strengths and weaknesses.
(2) To develop a career plan based on your strengths and weaknesses.
(3) To introduce you to commonly used career planning techniques.

ADVANCE PREPARATION:
This exercise may require substantial advance preparation. Steps 1 to 5 should be completed before the group meets. Participants may need to read or review one of the exercises or readings discussed in the introduction and body of the exercise. Some participants may need to make trips to the library or arrange discussions with persons in the type of work they are thinking about (see Step 3).

GROUP SIZE: Subgroups of two to six may be used; total group may be of any size.
TIME REQUIRED: In-class time depends on size of subgroups; 10 minutes per group member plus setup and discussion time (i.e., for subgroups of five, 65 to 85 minutes).
SPECIAL MATERIALS: None.
SPECIAL PHYSICAL REQUIREMENTS: Room or an area large enough to seat small groups comfortably and permit discussions with minimal distraction from others. (Movable chairs will be helpful.) Separate meeting areas for subgroups are *desirable,* but not essential.
RELATED TOPICS: Planned change, Motivation: basic concepts, Interpersonal communication.

INTRODUCTION

Obviously, different occupations and professions require different strengths (skills, abilities, talents, etc.) of the people who are effective in their work. The skills and abilities required for a particular line of work reflect the activities that are involved in the job, that, in turn, are largely dictated by the "raw materials" involved in the work. Broadly speaking, all jobs require dealing with one or more of four types of raw materials: things, data, ideas, and people. Figure 1 suggests some of the elemental job activities required for each of these raw materials.

Some jobs seem to require the ability to deal with only one type of material: bookkeepers work mostly with data, carpenters with things, philosophers with ideas, and sales clerks with people. Most jobs require the ability to effectively deal

Developed by Donald D. Bowen.

FIGURE 1
Four Categories of Job Activities

Things	Here are some activities involving *things:* Move, manipulate, machine (saw, drill, finish, etc.), adjust, assemble, design, operate, handle, construct, arrange, inspect, clean, deliver, store, drive, etc.
Data	Here are some job activities involving *data:* Compare, collect, copy, analyze, check, compile, organize, summarize, type, collate, store and retrieve, classify, schedule, observe, diagnose, etc.
People	Here are some job activities involving *people:* Counsel, assist, coach, teach, manage, persuade, interview, consult, advise, criticize, lead, communicate, request, encourage, sell, recruit, manage, arbitrate or mediate conflict, negotiate, speak in public, supervise, listen, help others to express themselves.
Ideas	Here are some job activities involving *ideas:* Create, compare, critique, publish, think about, argue, comprehend, decide, plan, interpret, define, establish goals, imagine, invent, synthesize, etc.

with at least two types of material. For example, *all* managers deal with people, but the Controller also works with data, the Vice President of Engineering is heavily involved with data and things, and the Vice President of Marketing with ideas and data.

Individuals vary in their preferences and abilities for dealing with different types of work. As suggested by Jung (see the reading by Slocum in the Folio of Resources, pp. 366 to 370), these preferences and predispositions may be fundamental characteristics of personality that differentiate how people collect information (sensing versus intuition) and process information (thinking versus feeling). Using the four-celled diagram in Figure 1 of the Slocum reading (p. 367), it seems reasonable to hypothesize that the STs are the individuals primarily oriented toward *things,* since they are drawn to the concrete and impersonal aspects of experience. NTs are clearly those who prefer *ideas* with their "focus on general concepts and issues." NFs value the "personal and social needs of people," while SFs like detail as it applies to a specific, concrete, immediate situation; that is, *data.* (If you have not read the Slocum piece, you will probably want to familiarize yourself with it at this point.)

Exercise 2, ("Learning and Problem Solving: You're Never Too Jung!") provided a format for identifying your basic problem solving style in terms of the Jungian dimensions. The purpose of this exercise is to give you a chance to evaluate your strengths and weaknesses in each of the four work areas. Effective planning of your career requires that you identify your personal strengths and find a line of work that will let you use those skills that you enjoy exercising the most. Once you have identified a particular vocational area that capitalizes on your strengths, it is also important that you identify any remediable deficiencies or weaknesses that may hinder you from achieving your full potential in your field. You will need to develop specific plans for moving into your chosen line of work (if you are not already in it) and for overcoming your weaknesses.

Copyright © 1982, John Wiley and Sons, Inc.

PROCEDURE

Step 1

1. Take four blank sheets of lined 8½ × 11-inch notebook paper. Put a heading on each sheet, one sheet for each of the four basic areas of:

Things   People

Data   Ideas

2. On the first line of each sheet, write "Satisfying Skills." Beginning with *things,* think of and list all of the things you can do really well with physical materials and objects. Think, in particular, of skills that provide you with a deep sense of satisfaction when you exercise them.
   a. Figure 1 may be a helpful guide in suggesting ideas here.
   b. If you have already done "Lifelines" (exercise 46), look at the Lifelines you drew. The *peaks* of those lifelines can suggest ideas. Consider each peak in terms of:

   What particular skills, abilities, and talents was I using to get to this peak? What important satisfactions did I derive from using those skills?

   c. Other exercises or instruments in this volume may suggest areas of strengths (or weaknesses). Your instructor can probably suggest some if you need help.
3. When you have listed as many skills and abilities as you can think of for *things,* move on to the sheets labeled *people, data,* and *ideas.* Repeat the process until you feel you have listed all of your really important skills and abilities in each area.

Step 2

From your lists of "satisfying skills," which are the most important to you? On a fresh sheet of paper, make a list of your *five* most satisfying skills and abilities—those that you enjoy using the most (be careful to retain the "things" "people," etc., labels).

Step 3

Do a or b, below.

   a. *For people who are not certain about their career interests:* What types of careers tend to require the exercise of your most important skills and abilities? Identify as many possibilities as you can before you select that alternative that seems to fit you best. (If you are not sure about some of the possibilities here, there are several ways to get more information. Most colleges and universities have placement and counseling centers that will be glad to discuss your interests with you. If you think certain vocations might be a good fit for you, talk to some people in these jobs—don't be afraid to call someone you don't even know. You might be surprised at how willing most people are to help. If you are really at a loss to think of anything, look up some jobs in the *Occupational Outlook Handbook* or *Dictionary of Occupational Titles* in the nearest library. Once you have identified some likely possibilities, check the card catalog for anything that may be written about these jobs.)

As you begin to develop some specific feasible alternatives, pick up any information you can about how people get into this line of work. What are the educational, training and experience requirements you are going to have to fulfill? Is there a practical way for you to meet these requirements? How? Prepare notes on your findings and conclusions. You will need them in Step 5.

You are now ready to establish a *tentative* career objective. The objective you set should have the characteristics shown in Figure 2.

When you have stated your career objective, go on to Step 4.

b. *For people who are satisfied with career choices already made:* Where do you want to go in your occupation or profession? What does it mean to you to "advance" in your field? Don't restrict yourself to thinking only in terms of traditional measures such as salary and organizational level. For purposes of this activity, define advancement as *moving into a new position or redesign-*

FIGURE 2
Characteristics of a Good Career Objective

A good career objective is one that is:

Challenging: A good objective is one that you must stretch to achieve.

Realistic: While your objective should be challenging, it should also be one that you can realistically hope to achieve, given your strengths, weaknesses, needs, circumstances, values, problem solving styles, and so on.

Measurable and Concrete: Establish a time target for achieving your objective. Phrase the objective in specific terms; for example:

　Poor　I want to be an executive.
　Better　I'd like to be a vice-president of personnel within five years.
　Best　I'd like to be vice-president of manufacturing of a medium sized (200 to 500 employees) storm door company within 12 years. The position must pay at least $50,000 per year, and the company must place emphasis on quality manufacturing. Possibilities include...

Long Term: Your objective should represent a major career goal or milestone for you. You will probably want to think at least 5 to 10 years into the future.

Relevant: Achieving your objective should be deeply satisfying because it fulfills your most central needs and requires the exercise of those talents and abilities you enjoy using most.

Copyright © 1982, John Wiley and Sons, Inc.

ing your present job so that it requires you to use even more of your most important and satisfying skills and abilities. Prepare a statement of your career objective that fulfills the criteria in Figure 2.

What would need to be done to make this possible? How can you initiate the process that will eventually have a high probability of achieving these changes? *(Suggestion:* Develop a "Problem Analysis Diagram"—Exercise 60 in the Folio of Resources—to analyze the problem of how to achieve these changes.) What additional experiences or training do you need? Are the opportunities available in your present organization? In other organizations? Prepare notes on your analysis for use in Step 5.

Step 4

Take the original four sheets ("Things," "Data," "People," "Ideas"). Turn them over and head up each sheet with, respectively, weaknesses/deficiencies—things, weaknesses/deficiencies—data, weaknesses/deficiencies—people, weaknesses/deficiencies—ideas (that is, you are to use one heading on each sheet).[1]

> *Things I do poorly:* These are things you don't do well, but for some reason you want to or have to do them. Don't list things you have no interest in doing or don't need to do.
> *Things I would like to stop doing:* We all have things we'd like to stop doing. These may or may not be things you have a reason for doing.
> *Things I would like to learn to do well:* These are things you must do well and/ or things you want to do well.

Which of these deficiencies are most important *right now?* Which must you do something about first in order to begin moving toward the objective you set for yourself in Step 3? Select and rank-order the three most important on the piece of paper where you listed your five most satisfying skills and abilities.

Step 5

Prepare a brief written plan showing how you plan to move toward your career objective (from Step 3), and including your plans for dealing with the weaknesses that stand betweeen you and your objective. (Charts and graphs may be the easiest way of capturing the elements of your plan. PERT, "Critical Path Method," Gantt charts, budgets or other planning devices are often useful here for those who are familiar with them. The Problem Analysis Diagram mentioned in Step 3 may be a useful diagnostic tool.)

Step 6

Form groups according to the Instructor's directions (if you are not already in a group).

---

[1] These categories are from G. A. Ford and Gordon L. Lippitt, *A Life Planning Workbook for Guidance in Planning and Personal Goal Setting* (Fairfax, Va.: NTL Learning Resources Corporation, 1972).

Step 7: 10 Minutes per Person

Share your most important strengths and weaknesses, your statement of your objective, and your plan for achieving your objective with the other(s) in your group.

As each person explains his/her inventory and plans, the other members of the group should:

Provide feedback—does the person seem to be aware of his/her most important strengths and weaknesses?

Offer any suggestions that seem warranted for improving his/her plans.

DISCUSSION QUESTIONS

1. How many individuals found their greatest strengths in the area of Things? People? Data? Ideas?
2. Do your perceptions of your areas of strengths coincide with your perceptions of your problem solving style in terms of the Jungian types? Why?
3. What further steps would be useful in your career planning?

GENERALIZATIONS AND CONCLUSIONS

Concluding Points

1. Which is the better career planning strategy? Developing plans based on your strengths? Or developing plans aimed primarily at eliminating your deficiencies or weaknesses?

2. How frequently should you revise your career plans?

Copyright © 1982, John Wiley and Sons, Inc.

3. Is there any evidence that preparing career plans helps people to achieve their objectives?

4. Why might management want to provide a career planning service for employees?

Participant's Reactions

READINGS AND REFERENCES
See references listed at the end of the Introduction to Section 13.

48
THE AWFUL INTERVIEW

PURPOSE:
(1) To practice interviewing skills, especially in dealing with difficult interview questions frequently asked by interviewers.
(2) To sharpen your awareness of your strengths and weaknesses in interviewing for a job.

ADVANCE PREPARATION:
(1) Read "Improving Your Performance in the Employment Interview" and "Feedback: The Art of Giving and Receiving Help" in the Folio of Resources.
(2) Read the "Introduction," below, and think about some good questions that might be included in the list in Step 1. If you can't think of good, mind-boggling questions, ask friends who have some experience in job interviews.

GROUP SIZE: Trios or quartets.
TIME REQUIRED: 1¼ hours (trios), 1½ hours (quartets).
SPECIAL MATERIALS: None.
SPECIAL PHYSICAL REQUIREMENTS: Trios (or quartets) will need small meeting rooms or an area suitable for holding conversations relatively free of distractions.
RELATED TOPICS: Interpersonal communication, Icebreakers.

INTRODUCTION

Employment interviews are frequently traumatic experiences; interviewers know what they are looking for, and you don't. They are prepared, and you are not. They are relaxed, and you are tense. The cards are all stacked in the interviewer's favor, it seems.

Interviewers are also notorious for asking disconcerting questions: "Tell me about your goals in life." "Why do you want to work for International Widgets?" If you answered such questions candidly, but right off the top of your head, you might never get a job. ("My only goal is to get a job so I can begin to find out whether I really like it," or "I want to work for International Widgets because I don't have any other likely looking offers right now.") If you have been confronted with questions such as these, you will understand why we have titled this exercise, "The Awful Interview."

You don't have to let interviewers catch you by surprise. This exercise is based on the assumption that practice can help you prepare for interview situations. We

Developed by Donald D. Bowen.

Copyright © 1982, John Wiley and Sons, Inc.

will also assume that honesty really is the best policy. The job-hunter who concentrates on giving a prospective employer the impression that she or he is just the person wanted is employing a defensive strategy. You may become so preoccupied with projecting an "image" that you have little energy left for the real problem of showing the interviewer what careful thought you have given to planning your career.

PROCEDURE

Step 1: 15 Minutes
The entire group will develop a list of the *10 most awful questions* one can be asked in a job interview. An "awful" question is one that you would find threatening or difficult to answer honestly in a job interview. When the list is completed, write down the 10. You will need them in the remainder of the exercise.

List only questions that have actually been asked in all seriousness in job interviews you or somebody else has experienced.

Step 2: 5 Minutes
The group leader will specify whether the total group should break into smaller groups of threes or fours. Choose people to work with with whom you will be comfortable, people who can be most helpful in providing useful feedback on your interviewing style. When the groups are formed, the group leader will tell you where you are to hold your small group meetings.

Step 3: 45 to 60 Minutes
Meet with your trio or quartet. Proceed as follows: One member volunteers to answer the first question: another is chosen to ask the question. Choosing a question from the list of the ten most awful, the interrogator asks the interviewee the first question. The interviewee must try to *answer the question as truthfully and honestly as he or she can.*

After the answer, other members of the group provide feedback to the interviewee on how they experienced the answer just given. (Remember the criteria for effective feedback emphasized in the Mill reading.)

Upon completion of the feedback, the interviewee becomes the interrogator, chooses a question and a new interviewee, and a new round begins. Continue taking turns until each person has answered at least three questions, or until you are instructed to stop by the group leader.

Step 4: 10 Minutes
Take 10 minutes and write a brief note to yourself covering the following (this note is for you—nobody else will see it): What questions did I handle well? What were my strengths? What questions did I handle poorly? What questions asked of others would give me problems? What can I do to deal more effectively with the questions that give me problems?

Step 5:
Reconvene with the entire group for discussion of the exercise.

DISCUSSION QUESTIONS

1. What did you learn during the exercise about how to answer interviewer's questions more effectively?
2. Do you think employment interviewers obtain valid data in the interview? Why?
3. If you were an interviewer, what kinds of questions would you ask?

GENERALIZATIONS AND CONCLUSIONS

Concluding Points

1. What do authorities in the field have to say about the validity of employment interviewing?

2. Why is the interview so widely employed as a selection device?

Copyright © 1982, John Wiley and Sons, Inc.

3. What steps can the interviewee take to ensure a more effective interview?

Participant's Reactions

READINGS AND REFERENCES

Kotter, J. P., Faux, V. A., and McArthur, C. C., *Self-Assessment and Career Development* (Englewood Cliffs, N.J.: Prentice-Hall, 1978), pp. 109–123.

Medley, H. A., *Sweaty Palms: The Neglected Art of Being Interviewed* (Belmont, Calif.: Lifetime Learning Press, A Division of Wadsworth Publishing Co., 1978).

Miner, J. B., and Miner, M. G., *Personnel and Industrial Relations: A Managerial Approach,* 2nd ed. (New York: Macmillan, 1973), pp. 259–264, 273–294.

Schmitt, N., "Social and Situational Determinants of Interview Decisions: Implications for the Employment Interview," *Personnel Psychology,* 29 (1976), 79–101.

Also see references to Reading 64, "Improving Your Performance in the Employment Interview."

49
MEN, WOMEN AND WORK

PURPOSE:
(1) To develop an awareness of how sex discrimination occurs in work settings.
(2) To explore the roles of co-workers and managers in eliminating sex discrimination.

ADVANCE PREPARATION:
Reflect on your own experiences at work (or other settings). Identify one critical incident involving discrimination or harassment that caused a problem for you. Write a brief description of the incident, and bring it to class on the assigned date.

GROUP SIZE: Any size.
TIME REQUIRED: 50 to 60 minutes minimum. Longer time recommended.
SPECIAL MATERIALS: None.
SPECIAL PHYSICAL REQUIREMENTS: Movable chairs.
RELATED TOPICS: Interpersonal communication, Negotiation and conflict.

INTRODUCTION
Although civil rights legislation has been in effect since 1964, many organizations still receive discrimination complaints from both men and women. In others, the complaints are never voiced, but the discriminatory incidents continue to occur. The reason is simple. It's a lot easier to change job postings and selection tests than it is to change people's *behavior*. This is especially true if those people are acting on long-held stereotypes and live in a culture away from work that supports stereotyping, discrimination, or harassment. Thus, women whose fathers or husbands have always played the role of "Big Daddy" may come to work expecting to be treated like the "little cupcake." That expectation reinforces discrimination just as much as the behavior of a man who is rewarded by his buddies for his macho style with "broads" or his fanny-pinching at the bowling alley.

In this exercise, we will not try to convince you that discrimination is wrong—legally or morally. We will simply explore how it occurs, what the implications of it are for co-workers, and, finally, what managers can do.

Step 1: 5 Minutes
Form groups of five to seven people, including a balance of males and females, if possible. If not, try to have at least one male or female represented.

Developed by Francine S. Hall.

Copyright © 1982, John Wiley and Sons, Inc.

Step 2: Instructor Will Announce the Scenarios to Read

Your task as a group is to read and then discuss each of the "scenarios" described below. Your instructor may assign some or all, depending on time available. After reading each scenario, answer the following questions as a group.

1. Do you think discrimination occurred? If so, what kind and why?
2. Have you even been in a similar situation? If so, what happened? How did you feel?
3. What do you think are the long term implications of incidents like these in organizations? (Consider reputation, morale, productivity, and any other criteria you select.)
4. What is your reaction to the way the manager handled the situation? The people involved? How would you handle this situation?

SCENARIO 1. THE LOADING DOCK INCIDENT

Able Carpet Center is a small floor-covering outlet that is part of a larger national chain. Because the organization does a lot of business with public institutions, it has had to make certain changes in former staffing practices to conform to affirmative action requirements. The major change was to hire women to work in the warehouse where carpets are cut, rolled, packaged, and loaded for delivery.

The first woman in the warehouse at Able was Carol McCann. She quickly took over her duties and proved that she could handle the job, including lifting along with the men. The males in the crew accepted her, but their attitude seemed to be one of "What choice do we have?" When the workload was light the men would sometimes take "extended breaks." Carol disapproved of this, but said nothing, feeling out of the group and afraid to "squeal."

After about six months, however, trouble began to occur. Increasingly, Carol would report to the Supervisor, Max, that she "didn't feel well." Max would tell her to "take it easy" and announce to the men that she wouldn't have to do any heavy lifting. When the men complained to Max, he would usually say "Oh, you know women—it's probably that time of the month."

Finally, one of Carol's male co-workers went to the store manager to complain. As he reported it: "We don't mind having a girl out there if she can do her job. We don't even mind helping out once in a while. But when her 'time of the month' comes every week, ya wanna go out and get yourself a hernia."

SCENARIO 2. THE SUPPLY CLOSET INCIDENT

After six months of "rumors" it became obvious to Frank Reynolds, a section manager at Davis Labs, that Jim Star and Kristy Packer were indeed having an affair. Mrs. Engles, the office supervisor, had caught them in the supply closet in what she could only describe as "a compromising position." Although Frank had no other witness, he didn't doubt the integrity of the efficient but dour 60-year-old woman.

"Besides," he thought, "Kristy is an absolute bombshell." She'd be the most likely candidate around. Frank also knew that Kristy was a crackerjack secretary who could be promoted to his administrative assistant within three months. The more he thought about it the more disturbed he felt. He couldn't have her around. What would his wife say? Leaving her in the secretarial job for very long was no solution, either. Engles had made it clear that she wouldn't tolerate sex on the job.

Finally, Frank made his decision. He would just have to let Kristy Packer go. He didn't think she would fight it—it would just force the whole messy affair out in the open.

Two days later he called Kristy and Jim Star into his office. He described what Engles had reported and announced that Kristy would be relieved of her duties, given a severance payment, and would receive an "excellent reference" if she left quickly.

Jim Star said nothing. Kristy looked disbelieving, then finally fled in tears. Frank informed Jim Star that this was "a good lesson." "Don't dip your pen in the company inkwell, old man, if you know what I mean." "Yeah, but it sure beats stealing paper clips," Star responded. Two weeks later he was seen fondling Sue Ellen at the water cooler.

SCENARIO 3. TOO GOOD TO PROMOTE

Sam Ketchum was surprised when Vic Devrell came into his office on Friday afternoon. Vic was usually out on the golf course by this time.

Sam: What brings you down here? Personnel Department falling apart?

Vic: No, just trying to fill a sudden vacancy. One of our interviewers had a serious accident. We have to replace him. The formal qualifications aren't too difficult to meet, but the skills we need are very important. The bummer is that the new production goals mean we have to begin hiring again for the plant. We can't float without someone in the job. I need a replacement, and I need the person now.

Sam: Hey, Vic, I hear you, but I'm not it. I talk too much. Besides, I like managing my own department. Marketing is fun, you know.

Vic: Good joke! Actually, I was thinking of Tammy Winters. Since you're her boss, I thought I'd come to you first. She wants to move up here—she's serious about a career with the company. She's also got the skills we need—good rapport with people, good listener, bright.

Sam: Exactly! That's why I could never go along with this. Tammy Winters is the best secretary we've ever had around here. Sorry, old man. I'm serious about my career too—I can't afford to lose her.

SCENARIO 4. THE LESSER OF TWO EVILS

When Liz Porter arrived at State U. she had a one-year contract and was assigned to teach the introductory economics course. Since there were many sections, all instructors worked as a team planning the course, making up exams, and so on.

Liz had trouble from the beginning. She was insecure, acted overcontrolling with students, and failed to bring in relevant examples. More important, she couldn't relate to students or colleagues.

During the second semester, one of her teammates, Ned Martin, took over a section of a special elective that developed a strong following among students. Since this was the first time he taught it, he had to do a lot of work in addition to the time-

Copyright © 1982, John Wiley and Sons, Inc.

consuming introductory course. The special elective was in his area of expertise, however, and he did an outstanding job. He fully expected to be assigned only to the elective the following semester. This would mean moving "up" a bit in the hierarchy since teaching electives was viewed as more desirable and higher status than the introductory course.

Later in the semester, the department head met with faculty to discuss course assignments for the following year. The coordinator for the Intro course begged to have Liz reassigned. Liz admitted that the experience had been an unhappy failure for her. Ned asked to teach the elective again, but he didn't push the matter, assuming it was a natural assignment given his experience and expertise. Besides, he would be coming up for promotion and didn't want to appear too aggressive.

When the course assignments were posted, people were shocked to learn that Liz would be back teaching three sections of the special elective. Ned would teach only the Intro course. Several faculty went to the department head to voice their concerns:

1. Liz had no knowledge of the area and admitted she was scared to death of it.
2. Ned had worked hard to prepare to teach the elective and had excellent ratings.
3. Ned had seniority over Liz.
4. It appeared Liz was being "rewarded" for failing.
5. The reputation of the course and number of students enrolling would be affected by putting a "bad" teacher in three sections out of four.

The department head listened and explained that this was the "lesser of two evils." Besides, he believed in the importance of supporting women and helping them develop their competencies. He was proud that he had recruited another woman for the department when Liz came, and he didn't want to let her go.

Step 3: Minimum of 15 Minutes (up to 40 Minutes Suggested).

Reconvene as a total group, and discuss the scenarios. Your instructor may ask groups to report on their conclusions.

GENERALIZATIONS AND CONCLUSIONS

1. What is the most important thing you learned from the discussions?

2. How can you change your own behavior to avoid causing discrimination in work relationships?

READINGS AND REFERENCES

Hall, Francine S., and Albrecht, Maryanne, *The Management of Affirmative Action* (Santa Monica, Calif.: Goodyear, 1979).

Kanter, Rosabeth M., *Men and Women of the Corporation* (New York: Basic Books, 1977).

50
MANAGING ROLE CONFLICT

PURPOSE:
(1) To understand role behavior.
(2) To analyze personal role conflicts.
(3) To diagnose one's personal role management style.
(4) To set objective(s) for improving one's role management style.

ADVANCE PREPARATION:
None, unless assigned.

GROUP SIZE: Any number of pairs.
TIME REQUIRED: 50 to 60 minutes.
SPECIAL MATERIALS: None except pen or pencil.
SPECIAL PHYSICAL REQUIREMENTS: None.
RELATED TOPICS: Power, Interpersonal communication.

INTRODUCTION

One of the biggest problems facing working people, especially working couples and parents, is role conflict. As the number of roles we are expected to assume increases, so do the chances of conflict increase. The conflict is often accompanied by stress. In extreme cases even health problems may occur. It is no wonder that both employers and employees are trying to reduce conflicts on the job and between job and personal demands. One way to reduce these conflicts is through managing our roles.

To understand the role management process (and thus get a handle on how to cope more effectively), we first need to understand how our role behavior is shaped. In other words, why do we behave as we do, giving too much attention to some demands, not enough to others, or exhausting ouselves to be everything to everyone?

A role consists of three parts: (1) the demands, expectations, responsibilities, and pressures that *other* people impose on us in any given role; (2) our own perceptions of what we think we ought to be doing in that role; and (3) our behavior—how we act, consciously or unconsciously. Our behavior is really shaped by the first two role components. We respond to two different sets or expectations—our own and those of others.

Developed by Francine S. Hall. "Role pie" based on activity originally developed in Barbara L. Forisha, *Sex Roles and Personal Awareness* (Morristown, N.J.: General Learning Press, 1978), pp. 198–199 and adapted by Donald D. Bowen. Parts of this exercise were adapted from Francine S. Hall and Douglas T. Hall, *The Two-Career Couple,* copyright © 1979, Addison-Wesley Publishing Co., Reading, Mass. Adaptation of Chapter 3, pages 75–79 and 104–106. Reprinted with permission.

Copyright © 1982, John Wiley and Sons, Inc.

Managing role conflict involves managing these competing sets of expectations as well as our own behavior. Thus, there are really three approaches: we can attempt to change the expectations that other people hold for us (redefine our roles); we can change our own attitudes or expectations about what we "ought" to be doing (change our own orientation); or we can accept the various demands placed on us and find a way to meet all of them (reactive coping). The first two ways involve managing or redefining one's role. They are *proactive*, in the sense that we are *reshaping* the demands placed on us by others or by ourselves. The third way is really *passive coping*—trying to do or put up with everything.

How do you manage? How could you manage more effectively? The following Role Inventory can help you to evaluate your current strategies.

PROCEDURE

Step 1: 10 Minutes (Do This Working Alone)

On a sheet of paper, draw a large circle. After reflecting how you have spent your time in the preceding week, divide the circle as if it were a pie into sections representing the different roles in which you spend your time (include work, home, family, and all other roles). Each section should be proportionate in size to the amount of energy and time you invest in that particular activity. Labels might read student, employee, friend, husband, and so on.

Now, consider what sections of your role pie are most important to your sense of being "you"—to your identity. Number the sections from most important to the one of least interest. Let 1 be the section of greatest importance to you, 2 the one of next importance, and so on. Note that the numbers frequently do not correspond to the size of the sections.

If your most important roles or activities are not taking most of your time, consider why this is so. Is it owing to temporary conditions? Are you undervaluing some major activities or overvaluing minor ones? Are there any changes you would like to make in the way you spend your time? You can choose to make changes. What would be the consequences of change? Would you willingly accept the consequences?

Which of the sections in your role pie tend to contribute to role conflict or role overload for you? Identify these sections on your diagram.

Step 2: 15 Minutes

Turn to the "Role Management Inventory." Respond to the inventory in light of the conflicts and overloads you have identified (be candid; you are the only person who has anything to lose or gain from this activity). When you have answered all of the questions, score the inventory according to the instructions that follow the questionnaire. Which is your most important coping style(s)? Is this optimal for you?

Copyright © 1982, John Wiley and Sons, Inc.

ROLE MANAGEMENT
INVENTORY *

How do you deal with these conflicts or issues? How often do you do each of the following?

	Nearly All the Time 5	Often 4	Some- times 3	Rarely 2	Never 1
1. Decide not to do certain activities that conflict with other activities.	_____	_____	_____	_____	_____
2. Get help from someone outside the family (e.g., home maintenance help or child care).	_____	_____	_____	_____	_____
3. Get help from a member of the family.	_____	_____	_____	_____	_____
4. Get help from someone at work.	_____	_____	_____	_____	_____
5. Engage in problem solving with family members to resolve conflicts.	_____	_____	_____	_____	_____
6. Engage in problem solving with someone at work.	_____	_____	_____	_____	_____
7. Get moral support from a member of the family.	_____	_____	_____	_____	_____
8. Get moral support from someone at work.	_____	_____	_____	_____	_____
9. Integrate or combine roles (for example, involve family members in work activity or combine work and family in some way).	_____	_____	_____	_____	_____
10. Attempt to change societal definition of sex roles, work roles, or family roles.	_____	_____	_____	_____	_____

*Table and interpretation of scores reprinted from Francine S. Hall and Douglas T. Hall, *The Two-Career Couple*, copyright © 1979, Addison-Wesley Publishing Co., Reading, Mass., pages 76–79. Reprinted with permission.

	Nearly All the Time 5	Often 4	Some- times 3	Rarely 2	Never 1
11. Negotiate or plan with someone at work, so their expectations of you are more in line with your own needs or requirements.	____	____	____	____	____
12. Negotiate or plan with members of your family, so their expectations of you are more in line with your own needs or requirements.	____	____	____	____	____
13. Establish priorities among your different roles, so that you are sure the most important activities are done.	____	____	____	____	____
14. Partition and separate your roles. Devote full attention to each role when you are in it.	____	____	____	____	____
15. Overlook or relax certain standards for how you do certain activities. (Let less important things slide a bit sometimes, such as dusting and lawn care.)	____	____	____	____	____
16. Modify your attitudes toward certain roles or activities (e.g., coming to the conclusion that the *quality* of time spent with spouse or children is more important than the *quantity* of time spent).	____	____	____	____	____
17. Eliminate certain roles (e.g., deciding to stop working).	____	____	____	____	____

Copyright © 1982, John Wiley and Sons, Inc.

	Nearly All the Time 5	Often 4	Some- times 3	Rarely 2	Never 1
18. Rotate attention from one role to another. Handle each role in turn as it comes up.	_____	_____	_____	_____	_____
19. Develop self and own interests (e.g., spend time on leisure or self-development).	_____	_____	_____	_____	_____
20. Plan, schedule, and organize carefully.	_____	_____	_____	_____	_____
21. Work hard to meet all role demands. Devote more time and energy, so you can do everything that is expected of you.	_____	_____	_____	_____	_____
22. Do not attempt to cope with role demands and conflicts. Let role conflicts take care of themselves.	_____	_____	_____	_____	_____

Scoring

- Add up the values you entered for items 1 to 12. Divide by 12. This is your *role-redefinition score:*_____
- Add up the values you entered for 13 to 17. Divide by 5. This is your *personal-reorientation score:*_____
- Add up the values you entered for 18 to 22. Divide by 5. This is your *reactive coping score:*_____

Interpreting Your Scores

The three scores give you some indication of the extent to which you use each of the three strategies. The scores can range from a *high of 5 to a low of 1.* A high score indicates a frequent use of the coping strategy; a low score indicates infrequent use of the coping strategy.

If your role-redefinition score is low, you too often let others place demands on you, often unrealistic demands. You need to negotiate with these people, your role senders, to make certain that the roles they impose on you are compatible with other responsibilties and interests. Some ways of doing this include:

- Simply agree with role senders that you will not be able to engage in certain activities. (For example, in our community, a hotbed of volunteerism, we are both known as "spot-jobbers." We will accept specific one-shot volunteer jobs, but we will not accept continuing positions.)

- Enlist assistance in role activities from other family members or from people outside the family (for example, cleaning or baby-sitting help).
- Sit down with role senders (boss, spouse, children) and discuss the problem. Together, work out an acceptable solution.
- Integrate conflicting careers by working with your spouse or working in related fields (so that the two careers become more like one). This method of coping has been described as "linking up."

If you can successfully reduce role conflicts by practicing some of these proactive negotiations, you will be stopping them at the source, and chances are you'll be very happy with the results—*you* will be managing the situation.

If your personal-reorientation score is low, your problem is that you don't distinguish between the roles assigned to you: you lack a clear vision of what roles are truly important. You need to reevaluate your attitudes about various roles and take on only those heading the list. Some hints to help you achieve this are:

- Establish priorities. ("A child with a high fever takes precedence over school obligations. A child with sniffles does not. A very important social engagement—especially one that is business related—precedes tennis.")
- Divide and separate roles. Devote full attention to a given role when in it, and don't think about other roles. ("I leave my work at the office. Home is for the family and their needs.")
- Try to ignore or overlook less important role expectations ("The dusting can wait.")
- Rotate attention from one role to another as demands arise. Let one role slide a bit if another needs more attention at the time. ("Susan needs help now. I'll pay those bills later.")
- Remember that self-fulfillment and personal interests are a valid source of role demands. ("Piano and organ playing are a release for me while the children are small and need me at home.")

This style of coping means changing yourself rather than the family or work environment, although personal reorientation may be a necessary step to take before you can accomplish real role redefinition. Before you can change other people's expectations of you, you have to be clear about what you expect of yourself. Personal reorientation alone is not significantly related to satisfaction and happiness.

If your score is high, it means you try to take on every role that happens your way. You cope with conflict by working harder and sleeping less. Your style of coping includes:

- Planning and scheduling, and organizing better.
- Working harder to meet all role demands. (As one expert on women's roles and role conflict said in frustration, "After years of research, I've concluded that the only answer to a career and a family is to learn to get by on less sleep!")
- Using no conscious strategy. Let problems take care of themselves. This reactive behavior, in contrast to role redefinition, is a passive response to role conflict. Not surprisingly, people who use this style report very low levels of satisfaction and happiness (passive coping).

Reactive coping is not a very effective way of dealing with your roles. Rather than managing *them*, you are letting them manage *you*. If your goal is to eliminate conflict, then you need to reorient your own perceptions as a first step toward negotiating with others to restructure the roles in your life.

Copyright © 1982, John Wiley and Sons, Inc.

Step 3: 5 Minutes (And Do This One Working Alone, Too)

From the data you have developed in Steps 1 and 2, identify three changes you want to make in how you manage your life roles. Make these practical changes that you fully intend to implement in the immediate future. Are they changes to reduce role overload or conflict? Do they represent changes in priorities in your life? Do you need the help of someone else to implement them? Who? How do you plan to get it?

Change	Purpose	Will Seek Help From	Will Get Help By
1.			
2.			
3.			

Step 4: 20 Minutes

Find a partner with whom you would be willing to discuss the data you generated in Steps 1 to 3. Share your role diagrams, scores on the Role Management Inventory, and change plans. Help each other assess whether change roles are realistic, given priorities, past styles for managing roles, and personal styles.

GENERALIZATIONS AND CONCLUSIONS

1. What role management strategy is most effective in reducing stress?

2. What role management style is most commonly found?

3. What role management style is associated with the greatest satisfaction with career and family life?

READINGS AND REFERENCES

Hall, Douglas T., "A Model of Coping With Role Conflict: The Role Behavior of College Educated Women," *Administrative Science Quarterly,* December (1972), 471–485.

Hall, Francine, and Hall, Douglas T., *The Two Career Couple* (Reading, Mass.: Addison-Wesley, 1979).

Copyright © 1982, John Wiley and Sons, Inc.

51
TIME MANAGEMENT/IN BASKET

PURPOSE:

(1) To understand the role of time management in effective managerial behavior.

(2) To learn techniques for managing time.

(3) To assess the use of time management skills.

ADVANCE PREPARATION:
Read the "Introduction," below.

GROUP SIZE: Any Size.
TIME REQUIRED: 1 hour in class.
SPECIAL MATERIALS: Pen/pencil.
SPECIAL PHYSICAL REQUIREMENTS: None.
RELATED TOPICS: Managers as leaders, Applied motivation and job design, Organizational realities, Organizational structure and design.

INTRODUCTION

After reading much of the popular literature about time management, many people assume it is a quick success gimmick or, at best, a technique for reducing stress. Actually, it is neither of those. What it is is a *basic management skill.* When used properly, time management can help you to be more successful by enabling you to use your time to accomplish important tasks. It can also help to reduce stress by both changing your expectations of yourself and reducing role overload through delegation.

Effective time management involves applying many of the same basic skills required in general management situations. If you are an effective manager of your time now, chances are you have the potential to manage under other conditions or at a different level. Here are some of the reasons.

Basic to effective time management is the ability to set goals and priorities. You have to know what's important, in your life and work, and focus your energies on tasks that lead to accomplishing those outcomes.

People can't manufacture time, they can make better use of the time they have. Managing time does not mean working harder, it just means working smarter—using the time available to accomplish what is truly important.

A second skill involves being able to make decisions. This requires evaluating alternative demands and tasks, choosing the highest payoff alternatives, saying "no" to some requests, and sticking by your decision.

Developed by Francine S. Hall. Parts of the Introduction from F. S. Hall and D. T. Hall, *The Two Career Couple* (Reading, Mass.: Addison-Wesley, 1979). Used by permission.

A final skill for managing time—and people—is effective delegation. The only way you can be selective about the use of your time is to delegate responsibility to others. Ironically, effective delegation facilitates both your goals and your subordinates'. They have a chance to learn and develop while you focus on matters that *only* you can take care of.

One of the most useful approaches to effective time management is described by Alan Lakein in *How to Get Control of Your Time and Your Life.* Basic to his system is learning how to *plan* what you want to do and then organizing your use of time to get it done. "Time cannot be altered. We can only manage activities." In other words, managing time, like managing stress, involves learning to manage your own behavior.

In Step 1, identify goals and objectives. What is it you want to accomplish? Think in terms of time frames—long-term objectives as well as short-term, day-to-day objectives. Without planning, long-term objectives may be lost in the rush to carry out day-to-day activities. Or, short-term objectives may not get done because we are allotting too much time to unimportant tasks—things we could forget.

Whether you are planning for today or for next year, the key is learning how to establish priorities. You have to identify and concentrate on those tasks and activities that are of highest priority and eliminate those that are low priority. Lakein (1973) suggests using a simple ABC system.

The ABC system works like this: First, list all the goals you want to accomplish. Now ask yourself which ones are really important (will result in the rewards you value) and which are less important. The most important goals are labeled as "A"— top priority. Less important ones are designated as "B," and lower priority goals as "C." Now that you have some sense of what your A goals are, you can begin to plan your time to accomplish these. If you've listed a lot of C goals, you may want to reconsider whether they are worth having as goals at all. Some, however, may be tasks you have to do and cannot ignore forever.

Once you have identified your goals and established priorities, the next step is to think about activities that will help you accomplish them. What will you have to do to achieve your priority goals? Are you building those activities into your schedule or ignoring them? Planning, the key to time management, revolves around consciously allocating and using time for those activities that will help us accomplish our important goals. This doesn't mean that we devote all of our time to them, but only that we ensure that as much time as possible is being used for top-priority items.

Get into the habit of scheduling your day in order to use time efficiently. One of · the basic techniques is to make up a daily list of things to do, along with the priorities for those activities. Try the following exercise:

List all the things you have to do tomorrow.
Now prioritize your list using the ABC system. Which activities are really important for accomplishing priority goals, and which are not?
Once you have the activities labeled as A, B, or C, look at the B activities. Which of these could qualify as As and which are really Cs?

Copyright © 1982, John Wiley and Sons, Inc.

Now think about scheduling your day to ensure adequate time to get your A activities accomplished.

Lakein offers several important tips for scheduling time and using it more efficiently.

Keep a daily "TO DO" list and review it each morning.

Block out time for priority activities—either save a time slot in each day or set a day aside each week.

Don't let anything interfere with this time.

Use your time efficiently. Handle paper only once, don't keep reshuffling it. Don't procrastinate—if something has to be done, do it immediately. Minimize the steps involved in what you do. Delegate as much as possible to others. Unless you absolutely have to do something, assign it to someone else.

Learn to know your "prime time." When do you work best? Save it for priority projects.

Try to be flexible. Always leave time in your schedule for emergencies or catching up.

Plan time to relax. If you are exhausted, you won't be able to work effectively or efficiently.

Learn to use transition time to get things done. For example, can you read, catch the news on the radio, or discuss matters with your partner or family while you dress, do your nails, or eat breakfast? How do you use time spent in commuting, coffee breaks, lunch hour, or waiting in offices? Do you carry your list with you so you can save time to plan? Do you carry paper and pencil for writing or have something along to read?

Finally, can you turn C activities into things that can be put off indefinitely? How many C activities do you do that, in the end, don't have to be done, or can be done later if they turn out to be important? Learn to discriminate and put them aside.

PROCEDURE

Step 1: 5 Minutes
Read the "Role Description" and "Instruction," below.

ROLE DESCRIPTION

You are the Employee Relations Manager at Digitron, an electronics firm that manufactures digital components for clocks, watches, and other small equipment. Your office is at the Headquarters in Milwaukee, where the main plant, which employs about 6000 people, is also located.

Digitron is a privately owned corporation, founded about 50 years ago as a manufacturer of electrical parts. Over the years it has grown and diversified, but never lost its reputation—or concern—for quality. Digitron has been the number one company in the city for years, guided by a deep commitment to community welfare and a strong concern for employees.

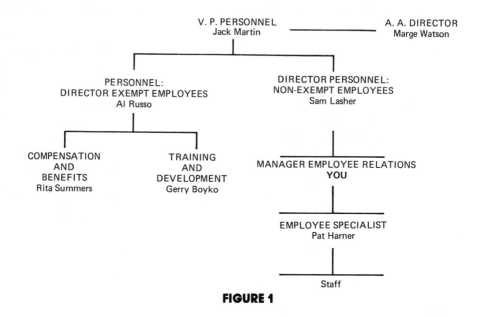

FIGURE 1

Managers at Digitron are expected to devote time (on and off the job) to community and political activities (as long as the politics support the Republican party).

The structure in the Personnel Department at Digitron looks like Figure 1. Your boss, Sam, has been with the company for years and spends most of his time in community relations and political affairs that affect the company and the industry. For all practical purposes, you "run the show" on the nonexempt side, responsible for contract negotiations, but reporting informally on most matters directly to Jack. Jack is expected to move on in the next two years, and you would be the most likely internal candidate for his job. Al Russo is threatened by you and will try to thwart anything you suggest. You want to "hedge your bet" on Jack's position so you have become increasingly involved in national personnel activities to gain visibility. You are currently getting ready for the ASPA (American Society for Personnel Administration) convention, which will be held in Milwaukee June 20 through 23. You are also involved locally in Little League and Chamber of Commerce activities.

It is now 6:30 A.M. on Friday, May 15. You were out of the office all day Thursday and didn't have a chance to get messages or look through the mail. You've come in early to get organized before others begin to arrive at 7:00 A.M., when the day shift begins. You'd better get to work. Your secretary, Bev, sometimes gets in early.

INSTRUCTIONS

Below you will find a set of items (memos, letters, etc.) that accumulated yesterday on your desk and in your "In Basket." Your task for the next 20 minutes is to:

1. Tear out the pages containing the In-Basket items.
2. Read the items.
3. Decide what to do with each.

Copyright © 1982, John Wiley and Sons, Inc.

4. Record the action you take or will take.
5. Number the items in the order in which you make your action decision.

Step 2: 20 Minutes

Go through your "In Basket," and decide what to do with the items you find. Its contents are on pages 329–355. Be sure to record your actions. You will have *exactly* 20 minutes.

Note: Do not read Step 3 until you have completed Step 2.

Step 3: 10 Minutes

Answer the following Discussion Questions:

1. How did you "attack" the items in your In Basket?
   a. Did you work on them in the original sequence (top to bottom), or did you go to the bottom before starting?
   b. Did you sort or prioritize the items?
   c. Did you act on all items? If not, why not?
   d. Did you delegate?
   e. Did you take final action on everything or hold/postpone some items?
2. Did you conclude with a "To Do" list for today? If not, what would it be?
3. What long-term problems will you work on later?

Step 4: 20 Minutes

As a group, discuss your experience with the In Basket. Use the questions in Step 3 as a basis for the discussion. In addition, consider the following:

1. What are the political implications of your actions and priorities? For you? For the company?
2. Would you have handled things differently if you had called the office yesterday to get your messages?

GENERALIZATIONS AND CONCLUSIONS

1. What time management techniques can you use in a real life situation like the In Basket?
2. Do these apply only to managing time on the job?
3. What are the potential benefits of using time management techniques?
4. What are some negative consequences that could occur?

READINGS AND REFERENCES

Joyce, R. D., "In Basket Programs," *Training in Business and Industry*, February (1977).

Lakein, Alan, *How to Get Control of Your Time and Your Life* (New York: Peter H. Wyden, 1973; reprint ed. Signet, 1974).

Moses, Joel, and Byham, William C., *Applying the Assessment Center Method* (New York: Pergamon Press, 1977).

Schwartz, Eleanor B., and MacKenzie, A. Alec, "Time Management Strategy for Women," *Management Review*, September (1977), 21.

Oneken, W., and Wass, D., "Management Time: Who's Got the Monkey," *Harvard Business Review*, Nov/Dec. (1974), 75-81.

Copyright © 1982, John Wiley and Sons, Inc.

To _____

Date _____5/14_____ Time _____8:30_____

WHILE YOU WERE OUT

M___ John Swenson _____

of ___ Called to confirm _____

Phone _____
     Area Code   Number   Extension

TELEPHONED	✓	PLEASE CALL	
CALLED TO SEE YOU		WILL CALL AGAIN	
WANTS TO SEE YOU		URGENT	
	RETURNED YOUR CALL		

Message _lunch date on Friday to discuss "up coming job analysis" I told him your schedule was clear._

_____ Bev _____
                 Operator

Campbell 09301

Copyright © 1982, John Wiley and Sons, Inc.

PERFORMANCE CATEGORIES

Acceptable	Competent	Fully Competent	Commendable	Outstanding
A	C	FC	CM	O

At the bottom of page 3, you are expected to rate the employee's overall level of performance. This rating should reflect your best judgment based upon a careful analysis of the employee's accomplishments.

On page 4, space has been provided for you to discuss key strengths, areas needing further development, or anything else which you feel is relevant to the employee's performance evaluation.

If more space is required to complete this review, additional sheets of paper may be added as necessary.

(3)	(4)	(5)
Accomplishments	Perf. Rating	Future Goals
How's this for a performance evaluation? Paul		

SUMMARY OF OVERALL PERFORMANCE	A	C	FC	CM	O

Copyright © 1982, John Wiley and Sons, Inc.

To _____

Date __5/14_____ Time ___9_____

WHILE YOU WERE OUT

M _S. Ruth Mc Ginnes's_____

of _Office Called._____

Phone __(212)____379 − 1400 × 365___
      Area Code   Number   Extension

TELEPHONED	✓	PLEASE CALL	✓
CALLED TO SEE YOU		WILL CALL AGAIN	
WANTS TO SEE YOU		URGENT	
RETURNED YOUR CALL			

Message _She will be going in for surgery in a week. They don't know if she will be able to address ASPA. (Isn't she the keynote speaker?)_ Bev
                                Operator

Campbell 09301

Copyright © 1982, John Wiley and Sons, Inc.

To _____

Date __5/14_____ Time __10:15_____

WHILE YOU WERE OUT

M __Marty Narsome_____

of _____

Phone _____

Area Code   Number   Extension

TELEPHONED	✓	PLEASE CALL	
CALLED TO SEE YOU		WILL CALL AGAIN	
WANTS TO SEE YOU		URGENT	
	RETURNED YOUR CALL		

Message __He can't take the little league team on Friday, either. He's going out of town you have to find a sub.__

__Bev__

Operator

Campbell 09301

Copyright © 1982, John Wiley and Sons, Inc.

AMERICAN PSYCHOLOGICAL ASSOCIATION
1200 SEVENTEENTH STREET, N.W.
WASHINGTON, D.C. 20036

Telephone: (Area Code 202) – 833-7600

May 10, 19xx

Manager, Employee Relations
Digitron Company
16 Wacker Street
Milwaukee, Wisconsin

Dear Sir or Madam,

As you may have read, the American Psychological Association has been asked to submit a policy position to the White House for the conference on "Blue Collar" workers. To prepare for this we are seeking the inputs of people in business as well as those of psychologists in academic and clinical positions.

You have been selected in our random sample of companies. We hope you will cooperate by completing the attached questionnaire. Your ideas and experiences are important. Please share them with us.

Thank you in advance.

Sincerely,

Janice B. Schoenfeld

Janice B. Schoenfeld, Ph.D.
President, Division 14

Copyright © 1982, John Wiley and Sons, Inc.

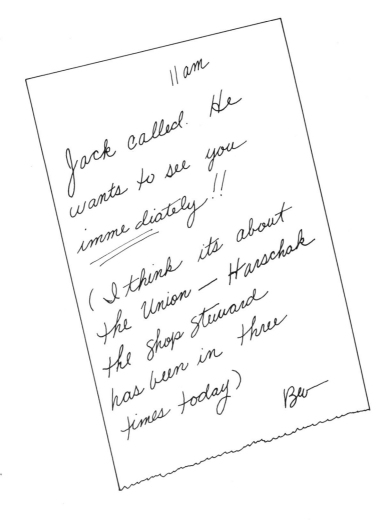

Copyright © 1982, John Wiley and Sons, Inc.

To _____

Date __*5/14*_____ Time __*1:36*_____

WHILE YOU WERE OUT

M __*Ward called from*_____

of __*Chamber of Commerce*_____

Phone _____ *942 - 8600*_____

    Area Code   Number   Extension

TELEPHONED		PLEASE CALL	✓
CALLED TO SEE YOU		WILL CALL AGAIN	
WANTS TO SEE YOU		URGENT	
RETURNED YOUR CALL			

Message __*Roosevelt Jones of Urban Coalition wants to be put on a SPA program. Can you do anything? Says its "heavy."*__

                        Bev
                        Operator

Campbell 09301

Copyright © 1982, John Wiley and Sons, Inc.

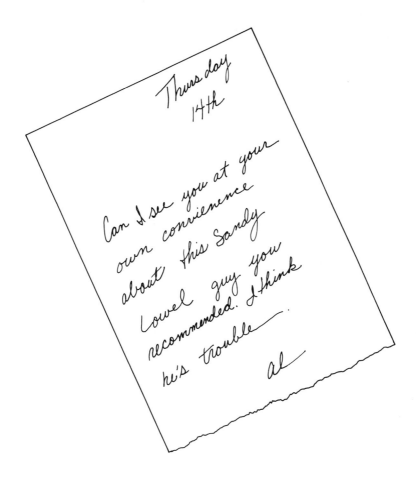

Copyright © 1982, John Wiley and Sons, Inc.

To _____

Date _5/14_____ Time _2:30_____

WHILE YOU WERE OUT

M _Jim Rosinski of_____

of _Community College_____

Phone _____963-2500 x 152_____

Area Code   Number   Extension

TELEPHONED	✓	PLEASE CALL	✓
CALLED TO SEE YOU		WILL CALL AGAIN	
WANTS TO SEE YOU		URGENT	
RETURNED YOUR CALL			

Message _Wants to borrow film_
on Alcoholism.

_____ _Bev_____
Operator

Campbell 09301

Copyright © 1982, John Wiley and Sons, Inc.

To _____

Date _____ 5/14 _____ Time _____ 2:40 _____

WHILE YOU WERE OUT

M r _Allan Arnold_ _____

of _Wiggins, Wright & Saddlewaith_ _____

Phone _____ (312) _____ 594 – 2730 _____
    Area Code   Number   Extension

TELEPHONED		PLEASE CALL	
CALLED TO SEE YOU		WILL CALL AGAIN	
WANTS TO SEE YOU		URGENT	
	RETURNED YOUR CALL		

Message — _no message, but aren't they the Chicago Head Hunter firm? He said it was "personal."_

Bev
Operator

Campbell 09301

Copyright © 1982, John Wiley and Sons, Inc.

To _____

Date ___5/14_____ Time ___2:55 P.M.___

WHILE YOU WERE OUT

M _____

of ___Pat_____

Phone_____

Area Code   Number   Extension

TELEPHONED	✓	PLEASE CALL	
CALLED TO SEE YOU		WILL CALL AGAIN	
WANTS TO SEE YOU		URGENT	
	RETURNED YOUR CALL		

Message ___Her grandmother died
Pat will not be in until
Monday.___

_____
                                    Operator

Campbell 09301

Copyright © 1982, John Wiley and Sons, Inc.

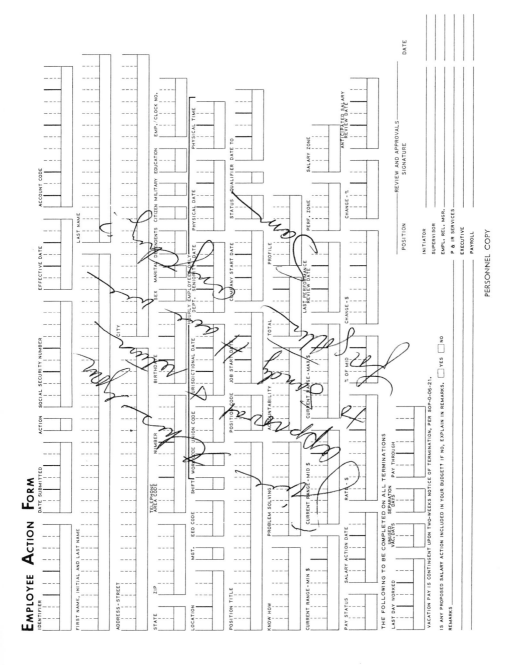

PERSONNEL COPY

Copyright © 1982, John Wiley and Sons, Inc.

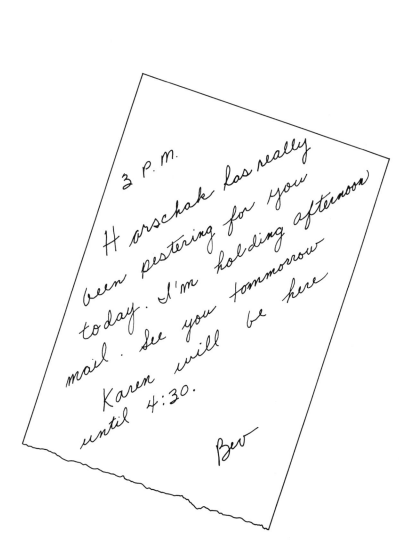

Copyright © 1982, John Wiley and Sons, Inc.

To _____

Date __*5/14*_____ Time __*3:50*_____

WHILE YOU WERE OUT

M _*s*_. _Sandy Lovell_____

of _Called._____

Phone ___*(312)*_____*235 - 3595*_____
     Area Code   Number   Extension

TELEPHONED	✓	PLEASE CALL	✓
CALLED TO SEE YOU		WILL CALL AGAIN	
WANTS TO SEE YOU		URGENT	
	RETURNED YOUR CALL		

Message _He met with Al about job in exempt. He wants to talk to you. He sounds upset._

Karen
Operator

Campbell 09301

Copyright © 1982, John Wiley and Sons, Inc.

FOLIO OF RESOURCES

RESOURCES

READINGS AND ASSESSMENT TECHNIQUES

Copyright © 1982, John Wiley and Sons, Inc.

52
THE LEARNING CONTRACT

We, the undersigned, agree to abide by the conditions in this Learning Contract:

I, the learner, the party of the first part, agree to provide the motivation to learn; to be active in my own learning process as well as that of others; to seek the understanding of what I learn; and to apply my learning to the development of my resources for a more meaningful life.

I, the educator, the party of the second part, agree to provide the conditions for learning; to seek to meet the needs and interests of the learner; to help create conditions for openness, respect, trust, acceptance, confrontation, and self-evaluation; to place emphasis on the rights and effectiveness of the individual; and to seek the feedback which will help me improve my effectiveness as a facilitator of the learning process.

Together, we will collaborate as partners-in-learning.

	Educator(s)	Learners	
Witness_____	_____	_____	_____
Date_____	_____	_____	_____
		_____	_____
		_____	_____
		_____	_____

DISCUSSION QUESTIONS

1. Would you be willing to sign the contract for this course? Why? Why not?
2. Would this be an appropriate contract with your other instructors? Why? Why not?
3. Is this contract asking *you* to do anything different? What? Does it specify that the instructor will behave any differently? How?

(Used with permission of NTL Institute.)

Copyright © 1982, John Wiley and Sons, Inc.

53
NONDIRECTIVE INTERVIEWING

PURPOSE

Nondirective interviewing is particularly useful when the interviewer seeks to help the interviewee in defining a problem the interviewee faces. Hence, it is a basic counseling skill. Other applications include any situation where the interviewer wishes to gain information about a situation as seen from the interviewee's perspective, such as in diagnosis of subordinate's or of organizational problems.

DEFINITION

In the directive interview, the interview provides advice, facts, and a diagnosis to guide the interviewee. Since people often resist advice and being told what to do, the nondirective interview attempts to avoid placing the interviewer in the role of "expert." Rather, the focus is on conducting the interview so that the interviewer does not advise, counsel, direct, or interpret the interviewee's problem. The emphasis is on stimulating the interviewee to talk about the problem, surfacing the interviewee's feelings about the situation, and providing an environment where the interviewee can explore the problem and come up with his own solution—a solution that will be much more valid for the interviewee and that will have his commitment, simply because the interviewee feels real "ownership" for the solution developed.

ASSUMPTIONS

Maier lists six essential attitudes that the nondirective interviewer needs:

1. A belief that the individual is basically responsible for himself, and that the interviewer should not assume this responsibility.
2. A belief that people are capable of solving problems and want to do the right thing.
3. Recognition that solution of a problem must conform to the individual's own values and beliefs, and that the individual knows his own feelings and goals better than anyone else.
4. The belief that people will express their true feelings and attitudes only in an accepting, permissive atmosphere.
5. Acceptance of the person as a worthy individual whose problems deserve attention, and acceptance of what the person says as important and of interest.
6. An appreciation and respect for feelings as essential elements of healthy psychological functioning:

Adapted from N. R. F. Maier, *Psychology in Industrial Organizations,* 4th ed. (Boston: Houghton-Mifflin, 1973), pp. 532–45, by Donald D. Bowen.

FEATURES OF THE NONDIRECTIVE INTERVIEW

The nondirective interview requires the interviewer to use several specific skills:

1. Active Listening.

We all know that we should listen to the other person, but this is easier known than done. It requires more than merely remaining silent and forcing your mind not to wander. The active listener in the nondirective interview lets the other person know that he is involved and interested, yet refuses to become a supporter (which elicits dependency) or a judge (which generates defensiveness). The active listener adopts a body position and facial expression indicative of attention, accepts pauses in the conversation, and facilitates the interview with statements such as "Uh-huh...," "I see...," "I understand," "Do you want to tell me about that?"

If asked to express an opinion, the interviewer responds with "Why don't you tell me how you feel about that?"

2. Accepting Feelings.

Accepting the interviewee's feelings without either agreeing or disagreeing with them is crucial to the nondirective interview. The interviewee's feelings about the situation are usually the most important "facts" to be obtained in the interview. But the interviewee as well as the interviewer may need an opportunity to discover and sort out the feelings that affect the interviewee's behavior and attitudes. Acceptance of feelings is reflected in statements such as: "You really felt good about that, didn't you?" "It sounds like the conversation really made you mad." "I gather that you really miss the people you used to work with."

3. Reflecting Feelings.

In reflecting feelings, the interviewer contributes three elements to the interview: (1) he becomes a more active listener; (2) the interviewee is encouraged to remain in charge of the interview process; and (3) the interviewee is stimulated to explore the feelings further. Reflecting feelings involves restating the feelings of the interviewee. Restatements should not be in the form of questions that can be answered "yes" or "no." They should not be in the form of questions that probe for "facts" ("Where were you at 3:00 A.M. on the morning of the murder?"), or that question the interviewee's judgment or competence ("Why didn't you tell your boss about that?"). A reflecting statement takes the form of a declarative sentence in which the interviewer simply restates the feelings of the interviewee in the interviewer's own words; for example: "You often feel that your boss doesn't listen to you." "It makes you angry when your subordinates behave irresponsibly." "You are not sure what you want to do."

In reflecting feelings, you should reflect only feelings that have been expressed. If more than one feeling is expressed, reflect only the last one mentioned. Inconsistencies or ambivalences should not be criticized, but accepted, since they probably indicate progress in working through the problem.

Copyright © 1982, John Wiley and Sons, Inc.

54
FEEDBACK: THE ART OF GIVING AND RECEIVING HELP
Cyril R. Mill

Feedback is a way of helping another person to consider changing his behavior. It is communication to a person which gives him information about some aspect of his behavior and its effect on you. As in a guided missile system, feedback helps an individual know whether his behavior is having the effect that he wants; it tells him whether he is "on target" as he strives to achieve his goals.

CRITERIA FOR USEFUL FEEDBACK

The giving and receiving of feedback is a skill that can be acquired. When feedback is attempted at the wrong time or given in the wrong way the results will be, at best useless, and may be disastrous. Therefore, developing feedback skills can be important. Here are some criteria for useful feedback.

It is descriptive rather than evaluative. It is helpful to focus on what the individual *did* rather than to translate his behavior into a statement about what he *is*. "You have interrupted three people in the last half hour" is probably not something that a person really wants to hear, but it is likely to be more helpful than, "You are a bad-mannered oaf."

It focuses on the feelings generated in the person who has experienced the behavior and who is offering the feedback. "When you interrupt me I feel frustrated," gives the individual clear information about the *effect* of his behavior, while at the same time leaving him free to decide what he wants to do about that effect.

It is specific rather than general. For example, it is probably more useful to learn that you "talk too much" than to have someone describe you as "dominating."

It is directed toward behavior which the receiver can do something about. Frustration is increased when a person is reminded of some shortcoming over which he has no control.

It is solicited rather than imposed. Feedback is most useful when the receiver feels that he needs and wants it, when he himself has formulated the kind of question which those observing him can answer.

It is well-timed. In general, feedback is most useful at the earliest opportunity after the given behavior, depending, of course, on the receiver's readiness to hear it, support available from others, and so on.

It is checked to ensure clear communication. One way of doing this is to have the receiver try to rephrase the feedback in question to see whether the receiver's version corresponds with what the sender meant.

Reproduced by special permission from *The Reading Book* for Human Relations Training, edited by Larry Porter and Cyril R. Mill, "Feedback: The Art of Giving and Receiving Help," by Cyril R. Mill, pp. 18–19, copyright 1976, NTL Institute.

When feedback is given in a training group, both giver and receiver have opportunity to check its accuracy with others in the group. Thus the receiver will know whether this is one person's impression or an impression shared by others.

Feedback should not be given primarily to "dump" or "unload" on another. If you feel you *have* to say this to the other person, then ask yourself who it is you are trying to "help."

Feedback does not ask "Why?" It stays within the bounds of behavior and one's reactions to that behavior. To theorize about or ask why a person does a certain thing is to plumb the depths of motivation and, perhaps, of the unconscious. Avoiding the "whys" will help one to avoid the error of amateur psychologizing.

Given the premise that properly given feedback can be a fine way to learn about oneself, what are some reasons that we resist it? For one thing, it is hard to admit our difficulties to ourselves. It is even harder to admit them to someone else. We are not sure that the other person can be trusted or that his observations are valid. We may be afraid of learning what others think of us; we often expect to hear only negative opinions about ourselves, tending to overlook our positive qualities.

We may have struggled so hard to make ourselves independent that the thought of depending on another individual seems to violate something within us. Or we may during all our lives have looked for someone on whom to depend, and we try to repeat this pattern in our relationship with the helping person.

We may be looking for sympathy and support rather than for help in seeing our difficulty more clearly. When the helper tries to point out some of the ways *we* are contributing to the problem, which might suggest that we as well as others will have to change, we may stop listening. Solving a problem may mean uncovering some of the sides of ourselves which we have avoided or wished to avoid thinking about.

We may feel our problem is so unique no one could ever understand it and certainly not an outsider.

On the other side of the interchange, it is not always easy to give feedback to others. Most of us like to give advice. Doing so suggests that we are competent and important. We get caught up in a "telling" role easily enough without testing whether our advice is appropriate to the total issue or to the abilities, the fears, or the powers of the person we are trying to help.

If the person whom we are trying to help becomes defensive, we may try to argue or pressure him. Defensiveness or denial on the part of the receiver is a clear indication that we are going about trying to be helpful in the wrong way. Our timing is off or we may be simply mistaken about his behavior, but in any case, it is best to desist until we can reevaluate the situation. If we respond to the receiver's resistance with more pressure, resistance will only increase.

To be fruitful the helping situation needs these characteristics:

1. Mutual trust.
2. Perceiving the helping situation as a joint exploration.

Copyright © 1982, John Wiley and Sons, Inc.

3. Careful listening, with the helper listening more than the individual receiving help.
4. Behavior from the helper which will make it easier for the receiver of help to talk.

Feedback takes into account the needs of both the receiver and the giver. Positive feedback is welcomed by the receiver when it is genuine. If feedback is given in a training laboratory under the conditions described here it can become one of the primary means of learning about self.

55
COGNITIVE STYLE
IN LEARNING AND PROBLEM SOLVING
John W. Slocum, Jr.

Carl Gustav Jung (pronounced "Yoong"), upon whose ideas the following reading is based, was one of Freud's most distinguished pupils. Like most of Freud's protégés, Jung eventually broke with Freud and began developing his own theory of human personality. In one part of his theory, he discusses personality types based upon four bipolar dimensions of personality (i.e., extroversion-introversion, perceiving-judging, senation-intuition, and thinking-feeling). A number of management writers have found the latter two dimensions highly useful in understanding how people learn, communicate, solve problems, and make decisions in organizations.—Ed.

Our model is based on the dual premise that consistent modes of thought develop through training and experience and that these modes can be classified along two dimensions, information gathering and information evaluation, as shown in Figure 1.

Information gathering essentially relates to the perceptual process by which the mind organizes the diffuse verbal and nonverbal stimuli it encounters. The resultant "information" is the outcome of a complex coding that is heavily dependent on the individual's mental set. Of necessity, information gathering involves rejecting some of the data encountered in the environment and summarizing and categorizing the rest. According to Jung (1953), individuals can take in data from their environment by either sensation or intuition; most individuals tend to have a primary style. Sensing types typically take in information via their senses and are most comfortable when attending to details—the specifics of the situation. These individuals tend to break down the information into small "bits" that contain hard facts pertaining to the situation. In contrast, intuitive types typically take in information by looking at the whole situation. They bring to bear concepts to filter data, focus on relationships between items, and look for deviations from or conformities with their expectations. These types tend to concentrate on hypothetical possibilities of the situation rather than hard facts and details.

Each mode of information gathering has its advantages. The sensing type of change agent may overlook the problems inherent in a failure to shape the client organization's problem into a coherent whole. He or she can develop a procedure that utilizes personal experiences and economizes on effort. The intuitive change agent might ignore the relevant detail that can establish bench marks for the organization. The intuitive person, however, is better able to approach a client

Excerpted from: John E. Jones and J. William Pfeiffer (Eds.), Group & Organization Studies, Vol. III, No. 2, San Diego, CA: University Associates, June 1978. Used with permission.

Copyright © 1982, John Wiley and Sons, Inc.

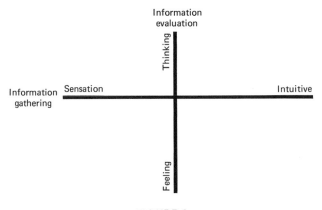

FIGURE 1
Model of Personal Style

system with an ill-structured problem for which the volume of data, the criteria for solution, or the nature of the problem itself does not allow a "scientific" mode of inquiry. Jung maintained that individuals perceive a situation in a set way and, in fact, cannot apply both types of information gathering techniques simultaneously.

Information evaluation refers to processes commonly used in reaching a decision about a problem. Jung (1953) posited that there are two basic ways of reaching a decision: thinking and feeling. Thinking persons tend to approach a problem by structuring it in terms of the scientific method, which leads to a feasible solution. They do not feel comfortable unless a logical or an analytical basis for their decision making can be used. They can take two situations that are inherently different and seek to find ways in which they are similar. Feeling types, on the other hand, make decisions based on extremely personal considerations, for example, how they feel about the situation, the person, the value of the situation, etc. Feeling types want to personalize every situation by stressing individual uniqueness.

The four styles and their characteristics are summarized in Figure 2. Combining these information-gathering modes (sensation and intuition) with the two information-evaluation modes (thinking and feeling) in all possible ways allows us to talk about the following four personal styles: sensation-thinkers (STs); sensation-feelers (SFs); intuitive-thinkers (NTs); and intuitive-feelers (NFs). In each case, the manager was asked to describe his/her ideal organization by writing a story about that organization. According to Mitroff and Kilmann (1975) and Hellriegel and Slocum (1976), this approach is useful because managers are able to share different stories in an atmosphere of trust and freedom without the fear of ridicule.

SENSATION-THINKERS

ST individuals emphasize and concentrate on specifics and factual details. They are sensitive to the physical features of their work environments, e.g., hot or cold, dark or light. The building should be conducive to good work, and the equipment

INFORMATION GATHERING[a]

Intuitives	*Sensing Types*
Like solving new problems	Dislike new problems unless there are standard ways to solve them.
Dislike doing the same thing over and over again.	Like an established routine.
Enjoy learning a new skill more than using it.	Enjoy using skills already learned more than learning new ones.
Work in bursts of energy powered by enthusiasm, with slack periods in between.	Work more steadily, with realistic idea of how long it will take.
Jump to conclusions frequently.	Must usually work all the way through to reach a conclusion.
Are patient with complicated situations.	Are impatient when the details are complicated.
Are impatient with routine details.	Are patient with routine details.
Follow inspirations, good or bad.	Rarely trust inspirations, and don't usually feel inspired.
Often tend to make errors of fact.	Seldom make errors of fact.
Dislike taking time for precision.	Tend to be good at precise work.

INFORMATION EVALUATION

Feeling Types	*Thinking Types*
Tend to be very aware of other people and their feelings.	Are relatively unemotional and uninterested in people's feelings.
Enjoy pleasing people, even in unimportant things.	May hurt people's feelings without knowing it.
Like harmony. Efficiency may be badly disturbed by office feuds.	Like analysis and putting things into logical order. Can get along without harmony.
Often let decision be influenced by their own or other peoples' personal likes and wishes.	Tend to decide impersonally, sometimes ignoring people's wishes.
Need occasional priase.	Need to be treated fairly.
Dislike telling people unpleasant things.	Are able to reprimand people or fire them when necessary.
Relate well to most people.	Tend to relate well only to other thinking types.
Tend to be sympathetic.	May seem hard-hearted.

FIGURE 2
Characteristics of Personal Styles

[a]Jung, 1953.

Copyright © 1982, John Wiley and Sons, Inc.

should be maintained. The ideal organization is one in which everybody knows exactly what his or her job requires and the details are set forth in a manual of rules and regulations. Information flows more readily downward than upward or in lateral directions. Subordinates are judged on the basis of their technical ability to do their job, and if they are not suited for the job, they are urged to transfer to another position in the organization. Each person should receive adequate training for his or her job to ensure uniformity in the application of rules and regulations. The ST individual emphasizes impersonal rather than personal factors, is more authoritarian than democratic, sets realistic as opposed to nebulous goals, and likes a well-defined organizational hierarchy as opposed to a vague and unstructured pattern. In brief, the goals of an ST organization are realistic, down-to-earth, limited, and most often narrowly economic. STs like organizations characterized by high control, certainty, and specificity.

INTUITIVE-THINKERS

NTs are attracted to ill-defined and abstract work situations. They tend to focus on general concepts and issues, as opposed to detailed work rules and hierarchical lines of authority. The goals of the organization should be developed in response to the interrelation between environmental- and member-generated factors such as clean air, water pollution, equal employment, etc. The structure of the organization encourages constant feedback and provides its own goals, controls, divisions of labor, and motivation and reward structures. The NT individual is more idealistic than realistic, more concerned with the intellectual and theoretical concepts of organizations in general than with efficiency, and has a tendency to avoid details of any particular work situation. In brief, NT organizations are impersonally idealistic.

INTUITIVE-FEELERS

NFs usually show an aversion toward paying attention to specifics and usually are preoccupied with broad, global themes and issues such as "making a contribution to mankind." They assert that the organization's main purpose is to serve the personal and social needs of people. The ideal organization for an NF is one that is completely decentralized, with no clear lines of authority, no central leader, and no fixed, prescribed rules of behavior. NFs regularly refer to flexibility and decentralization and are also concerned with the long-term goal orientation of the organization.

SENSATION-FEELERS

SFs are concerned with the detailed human relations in their particular organization and/or department. These individuals are realistic in the design of their organizations, with a major emphasis on the interpersonal environment that is created by the rules and regulations of the organization. The SF designs the organization with its hierarchy and rules for the benefit of the members, e.g., to promote the satisfaction of their needs, to openly communicate with one another, etc.

REFERENCES AND SUGGESTED FURTHER READINGS

Berne, E., *Transactional Analysis in Psychotherapy* (New York: Grove Press, 1961).

Hellriegel, D., and Slocum, J., *Organizational Behavior: Contingency Approaches* (St. Paul, Minn.: West, 1976).

Huse, E., *Organizational Development and Change* (St. Paul, Minn.: West, 1975).

Jung, C., *Collected Works* Vols. 7,8,9, Part 1. H. Read, M. Fordham, and G. Adler (Eds.) (Princeton, N.J.: Princeton University Press, 1953).

Kilmann, R., and Taylor, V. A., "Contingency Approach to Laboratory Learning: Psychological Types vs. Learning Norms," *Human Relations,* 27, (1974), 891-909.

Luthans, F., and Kreitner, R., *Behavior Modification* (Glenview, Ill.: Scott Foresman, 1975).

Mitroff, I., and Kilmann, R. "Stories Managers Tell: A New Tool for Organizational Problem-Solving," *Management Review,* 64 (1975), 18-28.

Tichy, N., "Agents of Planned Social Change: Congruence of Values, Cognitions, and Actions," *Administrative Science Quarterly,* 19 (1974), 164-182.

Tichy, N., "How Different Types of Change Agents Diagnose Organizations, *Human Relations,* 28 (1975), 771-799.

Tichy, N., and Nisberg, J., "Change Agent Bias: What They View Determines What They Do," *Group & Organization Studies,* 1(3) (1976), 286-301.

Copyright © 1982, John Wiley and Sons, Inc.

56
ROLES NOMINATION FORM

There are many roles people perform in groups. Some of these relate to helping the group perform its tasks. Others relate to maintaining the group and relationships among members. Finally, there are dysfunctional roles that may hinder the group; behavior is directed toward personal rather than group needs.

Below is a list and a brief description of different roles and functions performed in groups. Read each description and choose one person in the group who fits this description. In other words, based on your perceptions of the group, who performs each function or role? A person may be nominated for more than one role and you may nominate yourself.

At the same time, assess your own behavior in relation to the role description. Use a scale from 1 ("I rarely or never perform this function") to 5 ("I perform this function a great deal or most of the time").

GROUP TASK ROLES   *Nomination*   *Self-Rating*

1. *Initiator/Contributor:* Proposes goals, ideas, solutions; defines problems; suggests procedures.
2. *Information Giver:* Offers facts and relevant information or experience.
3. *Opinion Giver:* States belief about alternatives; focuses on values rather than facts.
4. *Information and Opinion Seeker:* Asks for clarification and suggestions; looks for facts and feelings; solicits ideas and values of other members.
5. *Coordinator/Summarizer:* Pulls ideas, opinions, and suggestions together; summarizes and restates; may try to draw members' activities together; offers conclusions.
6. *Clarifier/Elaborator:* Interprets; gives examples; defines terms; clears up confusion or ambiguity.
7. *Evaluator:* Helps group assess whether it has consensus or is reaching conclusion.

Adapted by Francine S. Hall from K. D. Benne, and P. Sheats, "Functional Roles and Group Members," *Journal of Social Issues* 4 (1948).

GROUP MAINTENANCE ROLES

Nomination   *Self-Rating*

8. *Encourager:* Supportive of others; praises efforts and ideas; accepts contributions.

9. *Harmonizer:* Tries to reduce conflict and tension; attempts to reconcile differences.

10. *Gatekeeper/Expediter:* Keeps communication open to all members; opens up opportunities for others to communicate and participate.

11. *Standard Setter:* Expresses standard for group to use; testing procedures; reminds group of its norms.

12. *Follower:* Goes along with group; accepts ideas of others; willing to compromise for the sake of the group.

DYSFUNCTIONAL, SELF-ORIENTED ROLES

13. *Blocker:* Interferes with group progress by getting discussion off on a tangent; focuses on personal concerns rather than group problem; argues too much; resists or disagrees beyond reasonable point.

14. *Recognition Seeker:* Tries to get attention; calls attention to self; boasts; loud or unusual behavior; excessive talker.

15. *Dominator:* Tries to control group at expense of other members.

16. *Avoider:* Acts indifferent; withdraws from discussion; daydreams; wanders off; talks to others; fools around.

OVERALL LEADERSHIP ROLES

17. *Task Leader:* Person whose behavior contributed the most to accomplishing work of the group.

18. *Social (Maintenance) Leader:* Person whose behavior contributed most to building and maintaining group relationships.

19. *Self-Oriented Leader:* Person whose behavior was directed toward meeting his/her own needs; hindered or ignored group needs.

Copyright © 1982, John Wiley and Sons, Inc.

57
SOCIOGRAM

A sociogram is a way to measure patterns of interaction, influence, activity, and so on within a group. The sociogram is based on people's perceptions of each other in terms of such things as productivity, influence, liking, and so on. Each person in the group must make a choice among the other group members in response to key questions. Choices are tallied to determine who is perceived as most and least influential, productive, and the like.

To prepare your group sociogram, first answer questions 1 through 3 below *by yourself.* Then prepare the sociograms *as a group* according to the directions (question 4 below). Finally, compute the choice ratios according to the directions (question 5 below). You will want to take some time to discuss your data after you have completed the choice ratios.

You will need a sheet of paper for each sociogram. Label the first sheet "Influence," the second sheet "Contributions," and the third sheet "Liking." On *each* sheet draw as many circles as there are group members. Label each circle with the name of one group member. Include yourself.

To develop the "Influence" sociogram, each group member should take a turn reporting the name of the person he selected. As names are reported, draw a line with an arrow (symbols illustrated in question 4 below) to indicate the choices among group members. When everyone has reported his choice, you will have a sociogram. Repeat this process for "Contributions," and "Liking."

The information requested in questions 1 to 3 will be used by you and other group members to study the structure of your group. Only your own group's members and the group leader will see the data.

1. Who is the most influential member of your group? (Do not include yourself.)

2. What group members contribute more than their share to getting the job done? (Do not include yourself. List as many or as few as necessary.)

3. Give the names of the people in your group whose company you most enjoy. (Exclude yourself. List as many or as few as necessary.)

The basic sociogram design for charting group dynamics has been adapted for this exercise by Donald D. Bowen and Francine S. Hall.

4. Prepare three group sociograms using this data. The primary symbols to be used are shown in Figure 1.

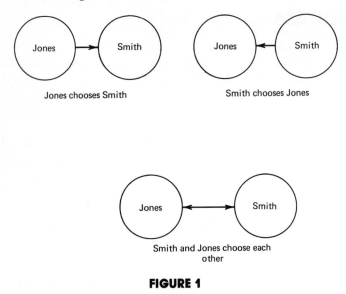

Jones chooses Smith

Smith chooses Jones

Smith and Jones choose each
other

FIGURE 1

5. To compute choice ratios for each group member, write the names of your group members under the headings below.

Name	*Influence Ratio*	*Contributions Ratio*	*Liking Ratio*

Copyright © 1982, John Wiley and Sons, Inc.

Using the "Influence" sociogram you constructed, compute a choice ratio for each group member as follows:

1. Add the number of times the person was chosen, and divide by the number of possible choices. (Since a person could not choose himself, the number of possible choices should equal one less than the number of group members.)
2. Enter the numerical value for each person's choice ratio next to the person's name above under the "Influence" column.

Repeat the procedure for "Contributions" and "Liking." The larger the choice ratio the more often the person was chosen.

Copyright © 1982, John Wiley and Sons, Inc.

58
SUPERVISORY BEHAVIOR QUESTIONNAIRE
Dr. Henry P. Sims

This questionnaire is part of an exercise designed to teach about supervisory behavior. It is not a "test": there are no "right" or "wrong" answers.

Please think about supervisors (managers) you have known or know now. Then, think about the *Most Effective* supervisor, and the *Least Effective* supervisor. (Effective is defined as being able to substantially influence the effort and performance of subordinates).

Read each of the following statements carefully. For the *Most Effective* supervisor, place an X over the number indicating *how true* or *untrue* you believe the statement to be. For the *Least Effective* supervisor, place a circle around the number indicating how true you believe the statement to be.

SUPERVISORY BEHAVIOR QUESTIONNAIRE

Most effective...X

Least effective...O

	Definitely Not True	Not True	Slightly Not True	Uncertain	Slightly True	True	Definitely True
1. My supervisor would pay me a compliment if I did outstanding work.	1	2	3	4	5	6	7
2. My supervisor maintains definite standards of performance.	1	2	3	4	5	6	7
3. My supervisor would give me a reprimand if my work was consistently below standards.	1	2	3	4	5	6	7
4. My supervisor defines clear goals and objectives for my job.	1	2	3	4	5	6	7
5. My supervisor would give me special recognition if my work performance was especially good.	1	2	3	4	5	6	7
6. My supervisor would "get on me" if my work were not as good as he thinks it should be.	1	2	3	4	5	6	7

The Pennsylvania State University. Used by permission.

	Definitely Not True	Not True	Slightly Not True	Uncertain	Slightly True	True	Definitely True
7. My supervisor would tell me if my work were outstanding.	1	2	3	4	5	6	7
8. My supervisor establishes clear performance guidelines.	1	2	3	4	5	6	7
9. My supervisor would reprimand me if I'm not making progress in my work.	1	2	3	4	5	6	7

SCORING INSTRUCTIONS

For each of the three "scales" (A, B, and C), compute a Total Score by summing the answers to the appropriate questions, and the subtracting the number 12. Compute a score for *both* the Most Effective and the Least Effective supervisors.

Question	Most Effective	Least Effective	Question	Most Effective	Least Effective	Question	Most Effective	Least Effective
2.	+ ( )	+ ( )	1.	+ ( )	+ ( )	3.	+ ( )	+ ( )
4.	+ ( )	+ ( )	5.	+ ( )	+ ( )	6.	+ ( )	+ ( )
8.	+ ( )	+ ( )	7.	+ ( )	+ ( )	9.	+ ( )	+ ( )

Sub total ( )   ( )   Sub total ( )   ( )   Sub total ( )   ( )
      − 12   − 12   − 12   − 12   − 12   − 12

Total
Score_____ _____   Total
Score_____ _____   Total
Score_____ _____
      A   **A**   **B**   **B**   **C**   **C**

Copyright © 1982, John Wiley and Sons, Inc.

Next, on the following graph, write in a large "X" to indicate the total score for scales A, B, and C, for the Most effective supervisor. Use a large "O" to indicate the scores for the Least effective supervisor.

A. Supervisory Goals

-9 -7 -5 -3 -1 | 1   3   5   7   9

B. Supervisory Rewards

-9 -7 -5 -3 -1 | 1   3   5   7   9

C. Supervisory
   Punishment

-9 -7 -5 -3 -1 | 1   3   5   7   9

Copyright © 1982, John Wiley and Sons, Inc.

59
LEAST PREFERRED CO-WORKER QUESTIONNAIRE
Fred Fiedler

People differ in the ways they think about those with whom they work. This may be important in working with others. Please give your immediate, first reaction to the items on the following pages.

Below are pairs of words which are opposite in meaning, such as "Very neat" and "Not neat." You are asked to describe someone with whom you have worked by placing an "X" in one of the eight spaces on the line between the two words.

Each space represents how well the adjective fits the person you are describing, as if it were written:

Very neat : _____ : _____ : _____ : _____ | _____ : _____ : _____ : _____ : Not neat

	8	7	6	5	4	3	2	1	
	Very neat	Quite neat	Some-what neat	Slightly neat	Slightly untidy	Some-what untidy	Quite untidy	Very untidy	

For example: If you were to describe the person with whom you are able to work least well, and you ordinarily think of him as being *quite neat*, you would put an "X" in the second space from the words Very Neat, like this:

Very neat : _____ : __X__ : _____ : _____ | _____ : _____ : _____ : _____ : Not neat

	8	7	6	5	4	3	2	1	
	Very neat	Quite neat	Some-what neat	Slightly neat	Slightly untidy	Some-what untidy	Quite untidy	Very untidy	

If you ordinarily think of the person with whom you can work least well as being only *slightly neat*, you would put your "X" as follows:

Very neat : _____ : _____ : _____ : __X__ | _____ : _____ : _____ : _____ : Not neat

	8	7	6	5	4	3	2	1	
	Very neat	Quite neat	Some-what neat	Slightly neat	Slightly untidy	Some-what untidy	Quite untidy	Very untidy	

Reprinted by permission of the author.

If you would think of him as being *very untidy*, you would use the space nearest the words Not Neat.

Very neat	: ___ : ___ : ___ : ___	___ : ___ : ___ : X : Not neat

	8	7	6	5	4	3	2	1	
	Very neat	Quite neat	Some- what neat	Slightly neat	Slightly untidy	Some- what untidy	Quite untidy	Very untidy	

Look at the words at both ends of the line before you put in your "X". Please remember that there are *no right or wrong answers*. Work rapidly; your first answer is likely to be the best. Please do not omit any items, and mark each item only once.

Copyright © 1982, John Wiley and Sons, Inc.

LPC

Think of the person *with whom you can work least well*. This person may be someone you work with now, or someone you knew in the past.

This does not have to be the person you like least well, but should be the person with whom you had the most difficulty in getting a job done. Describe this person as he or she appears to you.

Pleasant	: ___ : ___ : ___ : ___ | ___ : ___ : ___ : ___ : Unpleasant
	8 7 6 5 4 3 2 1
Friendly	: ___ : ___ : ___ : ___ | ___ : ___ : ___ : ___ : Unfriendly
	8 7 6 5 4 3 2 1
Rejecting	: ___ : ___ : ___ : ___ | ___ : ___ : ___ : ___ : Accepting
	1 2 3 4 5 6 7 8
Helpful	: ___ : ___ : ___ : ___ | ___ : ___ : ___ : ___ : Frustrating
	8 7 6 5 4 3 2 1
Unenthusiastic	: ___ : ___ : ___ : ___ | ___ : ___ : ___ : ___ : Enthusiastic
	1 2 3 4 5 6 7 8
Tense	: ___ : ___ : ___ : ___ | ___ : ___ : ___ : ___ : Relaxed
	1 2 3 4 5 6 7 8
Distant	: ___ : ___ : ___ : ___ | ___ : ___ : ___ : ___ : Close
	1 2 3 4 5 6 7 8
Cold	: ___ : ___ : ___ : ___ | ___ : ___ : ___ : ___ : Warm
	1 2 3 4 5 6 7 8
Cooperative	: ___ : ___ : ___ : ___ | ___ : ___ : ___ : ___ : Uncooperative
	8 7 6 5 4 3 2 1
Supportive	: ___ : ___ : ___ : ___ | ___ : ___ : ___ : ___ : Hostile
	8 7 6 5 4 3 2 1
Boring	: ___ : ___ : ___ : ___ | ___ : ___ : ___ : ___ : Interesting
	1 2 3 4 5 6 7 8
Quarrelsome	: ___ : ___ : ___ : ___ | ___ : ___ : ___ : ___ : Harmonious
	1 2 3 4 5 6 7 8
Self-assured	: ___ : ___ : ___ : ___ | ___ : ___ : ___ : ___ : Hesitant
	8 7 6 5 4 3 2 1
Efficient	: ___ : ___ : ___ : ___ | ___ : ___ : ___ : ___ : Inefficient
	8 7 6 5 4 3 2 1
Gloomy	: ___ : ___ : ___ : ___ | ___ : ___ : ___ : ___ : Cheerful
	1 2 3 4 5 6 7 8
Open	: ___ : ___ : ___ : ___ | ___ : ___ : ___ : ___ : Guarded
	8 7 6 5 4 3 2 1

Total Score: Add up all the numbers under the spaces you have marked:_____.
Post the distribution of scores from the class. Where does your score fall in this distribution? Are you a "high LPC" or a "low LPC"?

Copyright © 1982, John Wiley and Sons, Inc.

60
PROBLEM ANALYSIS DIAGRAM

PURPOSE:
(1) To learn how to apply force-field analysis in managing change.
(2) To evaluate alternative strategies for overcoming resistance to change.

INTRODUCTION

One way to think about a problem is to regard it as a product of forces working in opposite directions. From physics there is the concept that a body is at rest when the sum of all the forces operating upon it is zero. The body will move only when the sum is not zero, and will move in the direction of the unbalanced force. The same thing may be said of the production level of work teams in a factory, which often is constant (within small limits) around a certain level. The level stays reasonably constant because the forces tending to *raise* the level are just counteracted by forces tending to lower the level.

Among the forces tending to *raise* the level might be: (1) pressures from the supervisors to produce more; (2) the desire of some team members to earn higher incentive payments; (3) the team's desire to compete with other teams. These forces, and any like them, will be called *increasing forces*.

Among the forces that tend to *lower* the level (forces called *resistance forces*) might be: (4) lack of interest in working harder; (5) dissatisfaction of team members with supervision; (6) poor maintenance of machinery.

As in the case of the example from physics, the balance of increasing and resistance forces determines the fate of the production level of the factory work teams, even though here the "body" being acted upon is a human thing—that is, the performance of a group of people. And also, as in physics, the forces need not be of the same magnitude; the result, as may be seen in Figure 1, is a series of opposing forces of varying strength (represented by varying lengths). The numbers correspond to the numbers given above on the list of increasing and resistance forces. Such a diagram will be called a *problem analysis diagram*. Note that while there is no limit on the *number* of forces on either side, their algebraic *sum* will have to be *zero* if performance is to remain static, positive (in an upward direction) if performance is to increase, and *negative* (in a downward direction) if performance is to decrease.

The right side of the problem analysis diagram in Figure 1 illustrates a new and higher level of production that was reached after a change was made in the increasing and resistance forces.

There are three ways to achieve a higher new level of whatever behavior we are trying to change: (1) strengthening the increasing forces; (2) decreasing the resistance forces; (3) both 1 and 2 above.

Developed by Warren G. Bennis. Adapted by D. T. Hall. Used by permission.

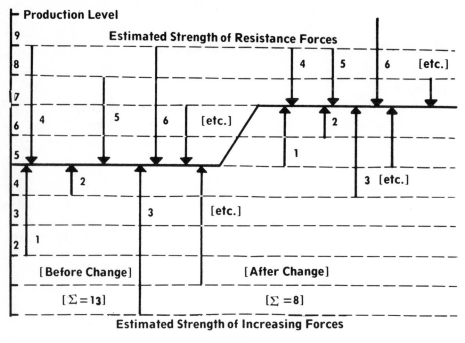

FIGURE 1

However, more *efficient* change is usually achieved by reducing resistance forces (rather than strengthening the increasing forces), since this results in change at a *lower level of total tension* in the system. Also, strengthening the increasing forces is often an action which produces an "equal and opposite reaction," namely, a corresponding increase in resistance forces (i.e., stiffening of the opposition).

This kind of analysis can be applied to a wide range of situations involving people's behavior. Suppose, for example, that you are a member of a group, and another member remains silent and uncommunicative. In an effort to understand his behavior better, you might make up a problem analysis diagram, which might turn out looking like the illustration in Figure 2.

The increasing forces might be: (1) pressure from other group members; (2) rewards given for amount of participation; (3) relevant topics he knows about; (4) etc. The resistance forces might be: (5) desire to avoid hurting other members; (6) fear of retaliation if he does talk; (7) anxiety about exposing himself; and so on.

There could be any number of forces, of course, just as in the production case, and of varying intensities. As long as the total strength of the resistance forces exceeds that of the increasing forces, however, the group member will reduce the amount of talking he does. He will maintain his rate of talking if the forces match exactly, and increase his rate if the increasing forces outweigh the resistance forces.

Copyright © 1982, John Wiley and Sons, Inc.

Problem Analysis Diagram

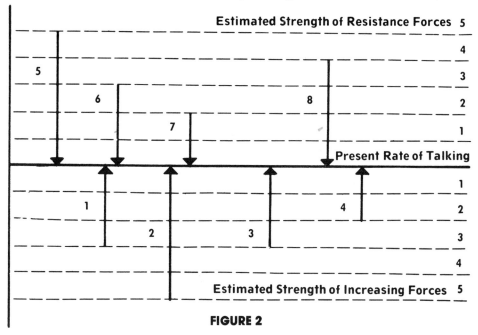

FIGURE 2

PROCEDURE

Step 1: 5 Minutes
Read the "Introduction" above and discuss any questions about force field analysis.

Step 2: 10 Minutes
Think of an important, recent problem you have faced that is both (a) unsolved and (b) tricky.

1. What *is* the specific problem, briefly?

2. Are there other people involved, or with whom must you deal? What is their status in the situation, and how do they relate to you and the problem?

3. Are there other factors that should be added to fully understand the problem?

Step 3: 10 Minutes

You have just described an important problem facing you; now try to analyze this problem using a problem analysis diagram. First, list all the resistance forces you feel are related to the problem—that is, factors that are making the problem worse or keeping it from getting better.

Now list all the increasing forces you can think of that seem relevant—that is, factors that are making the problem better or keeping it from getting worse.

On the diagram of Figure 3, draw the increasing and resistance forces in their respective directions, using requisite lengths to indicate the importance or intensity of the forces (5 being the most important, and 1 the least important.)

Copyright © 1982, John Wiley and Sons, Inc.

Problem Analysis Diagram

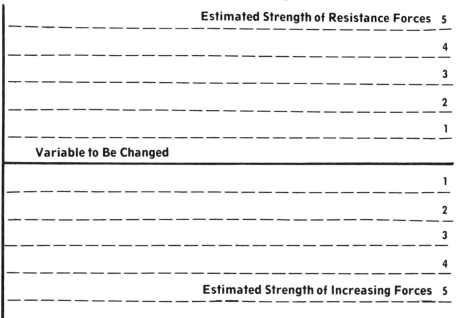

FIGURE 3

Step 4: 10 Minutes

Now that you have systematically listed all of the forces involved in this situation, let us analyze how to use these forces to bring about change most effectively.

a. What forces do you personally have control over? Write an *S* (for self) next to each of these.

b. What forces are under the influence of other people with whom you have or could have direct contact? Write an *O* (for others) next to each of these.

c. What forces are under the influence of external events, or people with whom you have no contact (for example, influences such as the state of the economy, war, laws, etc.) Write a *U* (for uncontrollable) next to each of these—but think twice, or three or four times, before you label a force uncontrollable. We tend to underestimate the amount of influence we personally have over events in our lives.

d. How would you specifically change or manipulate any of these forces in order to solve the problem?

e. Why does this course of action appear to be the best? Why did you choose to work on the particular forces you did? To what extent did you focus on self forces or others' forces? How much influence did you attribute to uncontrollable forces? What does this tell you about your style of handling problems?

Step 5: 10 Minutes

As a total class group, get a sampling of the strategies people used in planning the change. How many people focused on increasing forces? On resistance forces? On self forces? On others' forces? What are the pros and cons of using this approach to solving problems?

READINGS AND REFERENCES

Coch, Lester, and French, John R. P., "Overcoming Resistance to Change," *Human Relations,* 1 (1948), 512–32.

Blumberg, Arthur, and Golembiewski, Robert T., "Laboratory Goal Attainment and the Problem Analysis Questionnaire," *Journal of Applied Behavioral Science,* 5 (1969) 597–600.

Copyright © 1982, John Wiley and Sons, Inc.

61
A NOTE ON HOW TO RUN A MEETING
James Ware

Meetings are among the most overused and underutilized of all management tools. One study of managerial behavior found that many executives spent over two-thirds of their time in scheduled meetings. More significantly, important organizational decisions are almost always reached in management meetings, or as a result of one or more meetings. Given their importance, and the amount of management time they consume, it is indeed a tragedy that so many meetings are so inefficient and, worse, ineffective.

Yet planning and conducting a meeting is not a difficult task. While there are no magic formulas to guarantee success, there are a number of simple procedures that effective managers employ to improve the quality of their meetings.

There are, of course, many different kinds of meetings, ranging from two-person interchanges all the way up to industry-wide conventions with thousands of participants. Most management meetings, however, involve relatively small groups of people in a single organization. This Note will concentrate on a number of techniques for running these kinds of management meetings more effectively. For further simplicity, we will focus primarily on scheduled meetings of managers who are at approximately the same level in the organization, and who have known each other and worked together before.

The suggestions that follow are divided into planning activities to carry out before the meeting, and leadership activities to engage in during the meeting. Both kinds of work are essential: the most thorough preparation in the world will be wasted if you are careless during the meeting, while even outstanding meeting leadership rarely overcomes poor planning.

PREPARING FOR THE MEETING

Perhaps the most useful way to begin is simply to sit down with a blank sheet of paper and think through what the meeting will be like. Write down all the issues that are likely to come up, what decisions need to be made, what you want to happen after the meeting, and what things have to happen before the meeting can take place. Although the circumstances surrounding each meeting are unique, your planning should include the following activities:

Setting Objectives

Most management meetings are called either to exchange information or to solve organizational problems. Generally your reasons for calling the meeting are fairly

Reproduced by permission. This case was prepared by James P. Ware (9-478-003). Copyright 1977 by the President and Fellows of Harvard College. Distributed by the Intercollegiate Case Clearing House, Soldiers Field, Boston, Mass. 02163. All rights reserved to contributors. Printed in U.S.A.

obvious, especially to you. It is worth being very explicit about your purposes, however, because they have major implications for who should attend, which items belong on the agenda, when and where you hold the meeting, and what kinds of decision-making procedures you should use.

An information-exchange meeting can be an efficient mechanism if the information to be shared is complex or controversial, if it has major implicatons for the meeting participants, or if there is symbolic value in conveying the information personally. If none of these conditions is present, it may be more efficient, and just as effective to write a memo or make several telephone calls.

Problem-solving meetings provide an opportunity to combine the knowledge and skills of several people at once. The ideas that evolve out of an open-ended discussion are usually richer and more creative than what the same people could produce working individually.

These two different objectives call for very different kinds of meetings. Thus, you should be very explicit about what you are trying to accomplish, both to yourself and to the other meeting participants.

Selecting Participants

Invite people to the meeting who will either contribute to, or be affected by, its outcome. Select individuals who have knowledge or skills relevant to the problem, or who command organizational resources (time; budgets; other people; power and influence) that you need access to.

As you build your participant list, you should also give thought to the overall composition of the group. Identify the likely concerns and interests of the individual managers, and the feelings they have about each other. Try to obtain a rough balance of power and status among subgroups or probable coalitions (unless you have clear reasons for wanting one group to be more powerful).

Do everything you can to keep the size of the group appropriate to your objectives. While an information-exchange meeting can be almost any size, a problem-solving group should not exceed 8 to 10 people if at all possible.

Planning the Agenda

Even if you are planning an informal, exploratory meeting, an agenda can be a valuable means of controlling the discussion and of giving the participants a sense of direction. The agenda defines the meeting's purpose for participants and places boundaries between relevant and irrelevant discussion topics. Furthermore the agenda can serve as an important vehicle for pre-meeting discussions with participants.

Some important principles of building an agenda are listed below:

Sequence items so they build on one another if possible.
Sequence topics from easiest to most difficult and/or controversial.
Keep the number of topics within reasonable limits.
Avoid topics that can be better handled by subgroups or individuals.

Copyright © 1982, John Wiley and Sons, Inc.

Separate information exchange from problem-solving.

Define a finishing time as well as a starting time.

Depending on meeting length, schedule breaks at specific times where they will not disrupt important discussions.

Not every meeting requires a formal, written agenda. Often you simply cannot predict where a discussion will lead, or how long it will take. However, focusing your attention on these issues can help you anticipate controversy and be prepared to influence it in a productive manner. Even if you do not prepare a public, written agenda, you should not begin the meeting without having a tentative, private one.

Doing Your Homework

Your major objective in preparing for the meeting is to collect all the relevant information you can, and to consider its implications. Some of this data may be in written documents, but much of it will probably be in other people's heads. The more important and the more controversial the subject, the more contact you should have with other participants before the actual meeting.

These contacts will help you anticipate issues and disagreements that may arise during the meeting. As you talk with the other participants, try to learn all you can about their personal opinions and objectives concerning the meeting topic. These personal objectives—often called "hidden" agendas—can have as big an impact on what happens during the meeting as your formal, explicit agenda. Thus, the more you can discover about the other participants' goals for the meeting, the better prepared you will be to lead an effective discussion.

These pre-meeting contacts also give you an opportunity to encourage the other participants to do their homework as well. If there is enough time before the meeting to collect and circulate relevant data or background materials, the meeting itself can proceed much more quickly. Few events are as frustrating as a meeting of people who are unprepared to discuss or decide the issues on the agenda.

As part of your preparation you may want to brief your boss and other executives who will not be at the meeting, but who have an interest in its outcomes.

Finally, circulate the agenda and relevant background papers a day or two before the meeting if you can. These documents help to clarify your purposes and expectations, and they further encourage the other participants to come to the meeting well-prepared. Keep your demands on their time reasonable, however. People are more likely to read and think about brief memos than long, comprehensive reports.

Setting a Time and Place

The timing and location of your meeting can have a subtle but significant impact on the quality of the discussion. These choices communicate a surprising number of messages about the meetings importance, style, and possible outcomes.

What time of day is best for your meeting? Often the work flow in the organization will constrain your freedom of choice. For example, you could not meet simultaneously with all of a bank's tellers during the regular business hours, or with all the entry clerks just as the mail arrives. Within these kinds of constraints, however, you often have a wide choice of meeting times. How should you decide?

Early in the day participants will usually be fresher, and will have fewer other problems on their minds. In contrast, late afternoon meetings can be more leisurely, since there will usually be nothing else on anyone's schedules following your meeting. Perhaps the best question to ask is what the participants will be doing after the meeting. Will they be eager to end the meeting so they can proceed to other commitments, or will they be inclined to prolong the discussion? Which attitude best suits your purposes? There is no "best" time for a meeting, but you should consider explicitly what times would be most suitable for your particular objectives.

Two other factors may also influence when you schedule the meeting. First, try to be sure the time is sheltered, so there will be an absolute minimum of interruptions. Second, gear your starting time to the meeting's probable, or desirable, length. For example, if you want the meeting to last only an hour, a good time to schedule it is at 11 A.M.

Try not to plan meetings that last more than 90 minutes. Most people's endurance—or at least their creative capacity—will not last much longer than that. If the subject is so complex or lengthy that it will take longer, be sure to build in coffee and stretching breaks at least every 90 minutes.

Another key decision is where to hold the meeting. The setting in which a discussion takes place can have a marked influence on its tone and content. Just consider the difference between calling three subordinates to your office and meeting them for lunch in a restaurant. Each setting implies a particular level of formality and signals what kind of discussion you expect to have. Similarly, if you are meeting with several peers, a "neutral" conference room creates a very different climate than would any one of your offices. In each case, the appropriate setting depends on your purposes, and you should choose your location accordingly.

The discussion climate will also be affected by the arrangement of the furniture in the meeting room. In your office, you can choose to stay behind your desk and thereby be more authoritative, or to use a chair that puts you on a more equal basis with the other participants. In a conference room, you can choose to sit at the head of the table to symbolize your control, or in the center to be "one of the group."

You should also be certain that you have arranged for any necessary mechanical equipment, such as an overhead or slide projector, an easel, or a blackboard. These vital aids can facilitate both information exchange and problem-solving discussions.

Summary

Each of these suggestions has been intended to help you convene a meeting of people who have a common understanding of why they have come together and are prepared to contribute to the discussion. Of course, this kind of thorough preparation is often simply impossible. Nevertheless, the more preparation you can do, the more smoothly the meeting will go. While you can never anticipate *all*

Copyright © 1982, John Wiley and Sons, Inc.

the issues and hidden agendas, you can clearly identify the major sources of potential disagreement. That anticipation enables you to control the meeting, rather than being caught off guard. Even if you have to schedule a meeting only an hour in advance, you can still benefit from systematic attention to these kinds of details.

CONDUCTING THE MEETING

If you have done your homework, you probably have a good idea of where you want the group to be at the end of the meeting. But remember that you called the meeting because you need something from the other participants—either information relevant to the problem, or agreement and commitment to a decision. Your success in achieving those goals now depends not so much on what you know about the problem as on what you and the others can learn during the discussion. Thus, primary concern as you begin the meeting should be with creating a healthy, problem-solving atmosphere in which participants openly confront their difference and work towards a joint solution.

The following suggestions and meeting leadership techniques should help you achieve that goal.

Beginning the Meeting

If you are well-prepared, the chances are that no one else has thought as much about the meeting as you have. Thus, the most productive way to begin is with an explicit review of the agenda and your objectives. This discussion gives everyone an opportunity to ask questions, offer suggestions, and express opinions about why they are there. Beginning with a review of the agenda also signals its importance, and gets the meeting going in a task-oriented direction.

Be careful not to simply impose the agenda on the group; others may have useful suggestions that will speed up the meeting or bring the problem into sharper focus. They may even disagree with some of your plans, but you will not learn about that disagreement unless you clearly signal that you consider the agenda open to revision. The more the others participate in defining the meeting, the more committed they will be to fulfilling that definition.

This initial discussion also permits the meeting participants to work out a shared understanding of the problem that brought them together, and of what topics are and are not appropriate to discuss in this meeting.

Encouraging Problem-Solving

As the formal leader of the meeting, you can employ a wide variety of techniques to keep the group in a problem-solving mode. Your formal authority as chairman gives you a great deal of power to influence the group's actions. Often a simple comment, a pointed look, or even just a lifted eyebrow is all you need to indicate approval or disapproval of someone's behavior.

Perhaps your best weapon is simply your own style of inquiry; if you focus on facts and on understanding points of disagreement, to the exclusion of personalities, others will generally do the same. As the discussion progresses, try to keep differing points of view in rough balance. Do not let a few individuals dominate; when you sense that participation has become unbalanced, openly ask the quieter members for their opinions and ideas. Never asume that silence means agreement; more often it signals some level of difference with the dominant theme of the discussion.

Effective problem-solving meetings generally pass through several phases. Early in the discussion that group will be seeking to understand the nature of the problem. At that point you need to encourage factual, nonevaluative discussion that emphasizes describing symptoms and searching for all possible causes. As understanding is gained, the focus will shift to a search for solutions. Again, you must discourage evaluative comments until all potential alternatives have been throughly explored. Only then should the discussion become evaluative, as the group moves toward a decision.

If you can develop a sensitivity to these stages of problem-solving (describing symptoms; searching for alternatives; evaluating alternatives; selecting a solution), you can vary your leadership style to fit the current needs of the group. At all times, however, you want to keep the discussion focused on the problem, not on personalities or on unrelated issues, no matter how important they may be. Make your priorities clear, and hold the group to them. Finally, maintain a climate of honest inquiry in which anyone's assumption (including yours) may be questioned and tested.

Keeping the Discussion on Track

When the meeting topic is controversial, with important consequences for the group members, you will have to work hard to keep the discussion focused on the issues.

Controversy makes most of us uncomfortable, and groups often avoid confronting the main issue by finding less important or irrelevant topics to talk about. If the discussion wanders too far from the agenda, you must be willing to exercise your leadership responsibility to swing the group back to the major topic.

Use your judgment in making these interventions, however. If the group is on the verge of splitting up in anger or frustration, a digreession to a "safe" topic may be a highly functional way of reuniting. Generally, such digressions are most beneficial when they follow open controversy, rather than precede it. If you think the group has reached a decision on the main issue, even if it is only an implicit one, then you may want to let the digression go on for a while. On the other hand, if the discussion is clearly delaying a necessary confrontation, then you will have to intervene to get the discussion back on the main issue.

If you began the meeting with an explicit discussion of the agenda, you will find this focusing task easier to carry out. Often a simple reminder to the group, with a glance at the clock, is enough. Another useful technique for marking progress is periodically to summarize where you think the group has been, ask the group to confirm your assessments.

Copyright © 1982, John Wiley and Sons, Inc.

If the discussion seems to bog down, or to wander too far afield, perhaps the group needs to take a short break. Even two minutes of standing and stretching can revitalize people's willingness to concentrate on the problem. And the break also serves to cut off old conversations, making it easier to begin new ones.

Do everything you can to keep the discussion moving on schedule, so you can end on time. The clock can be a very useful taskmaster, and busy managers rarely have the luxury of ignoring it. If you have set a specific ending time, and everyone knows you mean it, there will be far less tendency for the discussion to wander.

Controlling the Discussion

How authoritatively should you exercise control over the discussion? The answer to that question depends so much on specific circumstances that a general response is almost impossible. The level of formality that is appropriate depends on the discussion topic, on which phase of the problem-solving cycle you are in, and on your formal and informal relationships with the other participants. You will normally want to exercise greater control when:

The meeting is oriented more towards information exchange.

The topic generates strong, potentially disruptive feelings.

The group is moving towards a decision.

Time pressures are significant.

There are a whole range of techniques you can use to exert more formal control. For example, if you permit participants to speak only when you call on them, or if you comment on or summarize each statement, there will be very few direct confrontations between other individuals. If you use a flip chart or blackboard to summarize ideas, you will also increase the level of formality and reduce the number of direct exchanges. In some circumstances you may even want to employ formal parliamentary procedures, such as requiring motions, limiting debate, taking notes, and so on. These procedures might be appropriate, for example, in meetings of a Board of Directors, in union-management contract negotiations, or in policy-setting sessions involving managers from several different parts of the organization.

Many of these techniques are clearly inappropriate for, and rarely used in, smaller management meetings. Although these techniques can give you a high degree of control, they cannot prevent participants from developing strong feelings about the issues—feelings that often become strong precisely because you have not permitted them to be openly expressed.

Thus, it is entirely possible to control a meeting in a fashion that minimizes conflict within the meeting itself. However, one result of that control may be increased tension and even hostility between the participants, leading to more serious future problems. On the other hand, if tension levels are already so high that a rational discussion will not evolve on its own, then some of these controlling techniques may be absolutely essential.

Reaching a Decision

Many management groups will fall into decision-making habits without thinking carefully about the consequences of those habits. The two major approaches to reaching a group decision are voting and reaching a consensus. Each strategy has its advantages and disadvantages.

Voting is often resorted to when the decision is important and the group seems deadlocked. The major benefit of taking a vote is that you are guaranteed of getting a decision. However, voting requires public commitment to a position, and it creates a win-lose situation for the group members. Some individuals will be clearly identified as having favored a minority position. Losers on one issue often try to balance their account on the next decision, or they may withdraw their commitment to the total group. Either way, you may have won the battle but lost the war.

Reaching a group consensus is generally a much more effective decission-making procedure. It is often more difficult, however, and is almost always more time-consuming. Working towards a genuine consensus means hearing all points of view, and usually results in a better decision, a condition that is especially important when the group members will be responsible for implementing the decision. Even when individuals do not fully agree with the group decision, they are more likely to support it (or less likely to sabotage it) when they believe their positions have had a complete hearing.

Ending the Meeting

The most important thing to do at the end of the meeting is to clarify what happens next. If the group has made a major decision, be certain you will agree on who is responsible for its implementation, and on when the work will be completed.

If the group has to meet again, you can save a lot of time by scheduling your next meeting then and there. Having everyone check their calendars and mark down the date and time of the next meeting will save you an unbelievable number of telephone calls.

Depending on the discussion topic and the decisions that have been made either you or someone else should follow the meeting with a brief memo summarizing the discussion, the decisions, and the follow-up commitments that each participant has made. This kind of document serves not only as a record of the meeting, but as a next-day reminder to the participants of what they decided and what they are committed to doing.

If you can, spend the last 5 minutes or so of the meeting talking about how well the meeting went. Although most managers are not accustomed to self-critiques, this practice is a useful habit that can contribute significantly to improved group problem-solving. The best time to share your reactions to the meeting is right after it has ended. You evaluate the effectiveness of other management techniques all the time; why not apply the same criteria to your meetings?

Copyright © 1982, John Wiley and Sons, Inc.

SUMMARY

Management meetings occur so frequently that most of us fail to recognize how significant an impact they have on organizational productivity. Improving the effectiveness of your meetings is not a difficult task. Apply these simple techniques carefully, with sensitivity to the combination of people and problems you have brought together, and your meetings should become both more effective and more interesting. The important point, however, is that the techniques *are* simple. They require little more than systematic preparation before the meeting and sensitive observation and intervention while it is in progress.

Copyright © 1982, John Wiley and Sons, Inc.

62
ASSESSING GROUP EFFECTIVENESS

As a group begins its life and at several points during its growth, the leader and members might individually fill out the following scales and then spend some time sharing the data that is collected. Through these scales, it is possible to get a general picture of the perceptions that various members have about the group and how it is growing. It is also possible to pick up areas in which there may be difficulties blocking progress.

I. Task Complexity:
   Individual Score = _____, Group Average = _____
   (Sum of 1–3)

1. In general, to what degree are group tasks *certain and predictable*?

The group tasks are very un-predictable, we never know what we're going to have to do next	1 2 3 4 5 6 7	The group tasks are very pre-dictable, we always know exactly what we are going to have to do next

2. In general, how *complex* are the tasks the group has to do?

Very simple, most of the work does not require advanced skills, abilities or knowledge	1 2 3 4 5 6 7	Very complex, most of the work requires advanced skills, abilities, or knowledge

3. How *interdependent* are the different parts of the group's task?

Very independent; each part of the task can be done independently of other parts	1 2 3 4 5 6 7	Very interdependent; each part of the task is highly re-lated to other parts of the task. Getting one part done is dependent on having other parts done

II. Participation/Inclusion:
Total Score = _____,   Group Average = _____

4. Do most members seem to feel like they are really a part of the group?

No, most members do not feel _____ Yes, most members do feel a
a part of the group   1 2 3 4 5 6 7 part of the group

5. Do all group members appear to be involved in the activities of the group?

No, most members don't seem   Yes, most members are very
to care what happens with the _____ concerned about the group
group   1 2 3 4 5 6 7

6. How even is participation by members?

Uneven; a small number of   _____ Even; everyone talks about
people do all of the talking   1 2 3 4 5 6 7 the same amount

7. Do everyone's opinions get listened to?

No, many members' com-   _____ Yes, all members seem to be
ments are ignored   1 2 3 4 5 6 7 listened to by others

III. Goal Clarity:
Total Score = _____,   Group Average = _____

8. How clear are the goals of the group?

Unclear. The group is not sure   Clear. The group knows ex-
what it is supposed to do   _____ actly what it is supposed to
                               1 2 3 4 5 6 7 do

9. Is there general agreement with the goals of the group?

No, different people have very _____ Yes, everyone shares the
different goals for the group 1 2 3 4 5 6 7 goals for the group

Copyright © 1982, John Wiley and Sons, Inc.

IV. Dealing with Affect:
Total Score = _____, Group Average = _____

10. How open are group members in expressing their feelings in the group?

Group members are very
closed, guarded, do not express feelings

1 2 3 4 5 6 7

Group members are very
open and express their feelings freely

11. How supportive are group members toward each other?

Not supportive at all

1 2 3 4 5 6 7

Very supportive

V. Giving and Receiving Feedback:
Total Score = _____, Group Average = _____

12. Are group members willing to confront each other or to respond negatively to others?

Group members do not
confront

1 2 3 4 5 6 7

Group members are very
confronting

13. How well do members receive negative comments?

Poorly; people seem threatened by negative comments
and react defensively

1 2 3 4 5 6 7

Well; people listen to, value,
and make use of negative
comments

VI. Dealing with Conflict:
Total Score = _____, Group Average = _____

14. How much conflict is expressed in the group?

Little conflict; the group rarely
has conflicts expressed

1 2 3 4 5 6 7

Much conflict; the group is
constantly dealing with conflicts among members

15. In general, how is conflict dealt with? (check only one)

___a. Forcing (person with power wins)
___b. Smoothing (denial of the conflict)
___c. Withdrawal (by one side or member)
___d. Confrontation (those in conflict directly work it out)
___e. Arbitration (a third party decides)
___f. Other_____
Group consensus: _____

VII. Leadership and Decision Making:
Total Score = _____,   Group Average = _____

16. Are leadership roles and assignments clear?

No, it's not clear who is sup-
posed to do what, who is in   1 2 3 4 5 6 7   what leadership responsibility
charge, and so on

Yes, it is very clear who has

17. How much is leadership shared?

Little; one person does all of   Much; each person performs
the leadership functions   1 2 3 4 5 6 7   different leadership functions
                                                  as appropriate

18. How much do group members participate in decision making?

Very little; a few people make   A great deal; the whole
the decisions while others are   1 2 3 4 5 6 7   group is involved in making
not involved   most decisions

VIII. Focus on Process:
Total Score = _____,   Group Average = _____

19. When faced with a task (or a problem to solve) does the group usually plan how
    it will work on the task *ahead of time* (i.e., before beginning to work on it)?

Usually not; the group tends to   Usually yes; the group tends
jump right into the task, rather   to discuss how it will do the
than discussing how it will be   1 2 3 4 5 6 7   work before starting
done first

20. After the group has done work, does the group spend any time discussing how
    well group members worked together?

Usually not   _____ Yes, frequently
                                   1 2 3 4 5 6 7

Copyright © 1982, John Wiley and Sons, Inc.

63
AN ALMOST EMPIRICAL
ANALYSIS OF COMMITTEE MEETINGS
GARY R. MORROW, Ph.D.

SOMETHING OF AN INTRODUCTION

While many convoluted rationales and rationalizations have been proposed for their existence, it remains an unassailable fact that the sole purpose of any academic, business or governmental organization is to hold committee meetings. It is thus understandably surprising that little empirical research has been directed at this important area.

Although the author has been unavoidably distracted over the past decade, and thus not able to avail himself of the opportunity to undertake the archival research of past tomes in the field, it is clearly a high probability supposition that previous investigations must have suffered from the typical problems of inappropriate sampling, misconstrued statistical manipulations of dubious applicability and sundry other malfeasances against the cannons of scientific method that seem present with a disalarmingly (and, parenthetically, also alarmingly) high frequency in the published work of others who have neither the inclination nor intent to take the appropriate time and effort necessary to insure that their investigations are firmly imbedded in the nomological network carefully crafted for a field that allows the mantle of scientific respectability to be gently lain over the shoulders of a given work while its conclusions are anointed with oils so that it may properly take its place among prestigious polysyllabic pontificating peers at the table of knowledge. That's why this was done.

A LITTLE BIT ON METHODS

The present paper represents a major methodological advance in its attempt to pioneer the break-through results of a Rational Factor Analysis[1] of an infinite aggregate of real close to objective data on a whole lot of committee meetings.[2] The somewhat raw data have been painstakingly gathered over a number of years

Gary R. Morrow, Department of Psychiatry, University of Rochester School of Medicine and Dentistry, 300 Crittenden Blvd., Rochester, N.Y. 14642. Reprinted by *The Journal of Irreproducible Results,* Vol. 25, No. 2 (1979), 22–23. Copyright © 1979 by *The Journal of Irreproducible Results,* Inc. permission.

[1]This technique differs conceptually from the "Principle-component unexpended-budget factor analysis of Frankel, et al. (JIR, 1978, 24:15–16). It is the analytic method of choice when: a) you have no budget money, period or b) you're unable to make sense out of results from other data reduction analytic methods. The method has also been called between-the-ears-factor analysis since all that's needed is a reasonable amount of unused space between the investigator's ears.

[2]In order to save time and money on sending reprints, the entire data file analyzed has been reduced to a microdot which may be found as the period at the end of this sentence. Or maybe as the dot over an "i" in the text. Anyway, the printer promised it would be somewhere

during a modestly undistinguished, mediocre military career of sitting at meetings. Further replication has been provided by rawer data from an academic career which, so far, has shown equal promise of being as illustrious. Both raw and rawer data were scupulously recorded and coded on specially designed forms.[3] Every unmistakably important verbal utterance ($N = 2\frac{1}{8}$) made by any committee meeting was compulsively recorded awaiting eventual feeding into the multivariate technique.

WHAT HAPPENED

The raw data clotted into five clear factors, centroids, clumps and/or/nor elements.

I. *The Number of Players*

The maximum number of participants at any committee meeting at which a decision is made is one.

II. *Morrow's First Measure*[4]

It takes 2^n days to find a mutually agreeable meeting time for n committee members.

III. *The Implosion Conspiracy*

Simply stated, the closer a committee seems to be arriving at a consensus and decision, the greater the pressure to cast the problem in a wider context to avoid making the decision. (This can usually be recognized by the memorable utterance "But, I think this brings up the wider issue of—").

IV. *Morrow's Second Measure*[5]

This masterfully precise relationship states that the complexity of any problem decided by committee is the inverse of the number of meetings devoted to it.

V. *The Chief to Indian Ratio*

The prime mission of any committee member is to sluff as much responsibility and work as possible while retaining as much authority as he can muster. Thus, most discussion is framed as if there were a small army of drones outside eagerly awaiting their marching orders from any committee. The fact that all drones are around the same table is actively ignored.

THINGS TO DO ABOUT THE PROBLEM

It's considered inappropriate, unscientific, and in marked bad taste to bring up an issue of this scope, sweep and magnitude without proposing solutions that are at

---

[3] Except for $4\frac{1}{2}$ observations when a brown bag wasn't available and data were recorded on a left-arm shirt sleeve.

[4] The title of this measure reflects the author's narcissistic need to have something named after him in addition to the day after today—an honor shared with gobs of family members dating back to Kunta Morrow, an English Druid.

[5] See footnote 4. If that doesn't make it, maybe this will.

Copyright © 1982, John Wiley and Sons, Inc.

least as well thought out and scientifically precise as the analysis of the problem. Least this seminal analysis seem to be an exercise in idle carping, an equally illuminating series of strategies for addressing the issues[6] has been developed.

A full commitment to having a committee reach any decision demands careful planning. First, the stage must be set. Although frequently overlooked, the committee meeting room furniture is critical. It must be produced by the same companies who supply fast food chains. Anyone who has tried to sit at any hamburger haven while munching a mystery meat burger will readily attest that it is impossible to sit in those chairs for more than 20 minutes (S.E. = ±3) without painful torticollis or permanent back disability.[7]

It must then be made clear that nobody may leave the room for any reason until a decision is made. One of more of the following interventions may be useful in convincing committee colleagues you mean to stay until you get your way.[8]

Brown Bag Behavior
Bring a lunch—even for a 7:30 A.M. meeting.

Port-a-Potty Ploy
Carry a camping toilet under your arm, confidently lock the door and refuse to share.

Goose-down Gambit
Bring in your pillow to let others know you're not be trifled with. (Teddy Bear optional)

Stone Wall Jackson Posture
Shortly after the meeting starts, call your secretary, tell her to cancel your appointments for the next week and rip the phone off the wall.

More research on this issue is needed. It's not clear exactly why, except that all articles end saying more research is needed. Perhaps more research is needed on why more research seems always needed.

---

[6]While its never been clear exactly how something addresses an issue, a few suggestions can be made as "Dear Issue," "the Right and Honorable Issue," and "Issue."

[7]A further malady tentatively titled "fast food fanny" is currently under active investigation by "60 Minutes" and will thus not be covered here. It will, however, be the subject of a forthcoming monograph in *Reader's Digest* as well as a cover story in *People*.

[8]These interventions will inadvertently increase sales of "Preparation H" and provide more business for those marvelous physicians who produced the "silver stallion." These side effects are completely unintentional and reflect the cost of an academic career.

64
IMPROVING YOUR PERFORMANCE IN THE EMPLOYMENT INTERVIEW
Donald D. Bowen

When you are granted an employment interview, remember that all you have to sell is yourself and your qualifications (Verderber & Verderber, 1980, p. 312).

Most of us have heard this cliche so often that we never really stop to ask "What does it mean?" A visitor from a less commercially oriented culture in outer space might be more curious and ask what people mean when they talk about "selling yourself" in employment interviews. Looking up the verb "sell" in Webster's, our curious visitors discover it has several meanings

> ...1. *To deliver or hand over in breach of duty, trust, etc.; to betray. 2. To deliver into bondage, esp. for money. 3. To dispose of or manage for profit instead of in accord with conscience, justice, etc; as in to* sell *one's vote. 4. Slang. To impose upon; trick. 5. To transfer (property) for a consideration; to give up for a consideration; to convey,...opposed to* buy. *6. To deal in, as an article for sale; as to* sell *groceries...*(Webster's New Collegiate Dictionary, 1951, p. 768).

At this point, the stranger might legitimately develop some serious doubts about the employment relationships in earth society. Do we really mean to say that we sell ourselves into bondage? Or that we sell out? Or that we sell ourselves like chattel if the price is right? ("Isn't that what you earthlings call 'the oldest profession'?" our visitor might remark).

"No, we don't really mean that. What we are really saying is that the employment interview is an interaction wherein we try to convince a representative of a prospective employer to enter into a contract in which the employee provides work and services in return for wages salaries, and other monetary and nonmonetary rewards. The hours of work and the duties to be performed are usually prescribed in at least general terms. And the employer (except in the case of professional athletes) cannot sell us to another employer."

"I see," says the spaceperson, raising all seven eyebrows quizzically. "You say you are 'selling yourself' because your objective is to trick and deceive the employer in order to get hired."

You start to deny it, but the words catch in your throat. "Isn't that exactly what many people seem to do?" you muse. Isn't most of the well-meaning advice on how to conduct yourself in an employment interview basically aimed at showing you how to "puff" your assets and conceal your liabilities? Didn't you just read an article on selling yourself in the interview that advised you that if you are asked "what is your greatest weakness?" you should a) try to avoid answering the ques-

Copyright © 1982, John Wiley and Sons, Inc.

tion, and b) if you can't avoid it, respond by mentioning some trivial, non-job-related characteristic (Gootnick, 1978)?

WHAT NOT TO DO—
INGRATIATION AND IMPRESSION MANAGEMENT

Three questions come immediately to mind when you are advised to employ deceitful tactics in the interview. First, is it ethical (we'll leave this to you to decide)? Second, is it really in my own best interests? Third, will it work?

Let's look at the third question first. There is a great deal of research by social and industrial psychologists on this topic. Social psychologists speak of "impression management" and "ingratiation techniques" to describe situations where a person is trying to get others to see them as more attractive than they feel they really are. Industrial psychologists have conducted research for years to try to learn how to help managers conduct more effective interviews—some of their findings are relevant to our topic.

Table 1 has been developed from a recent review (Wortman and Linsenmeier, 1977) of this research. In the left-hand column, various ingratiation tactics or other factors that applicants might try to use to their advantage are listed. In the right-hand column are problems that may arise or special considerations one must keep in mind in using a particular ingratiation ploy. For example, Tactic 5 entails recognizing that negative information is weighted more heavily than positive information. Therefore, you must not only take into account the considerations already suggested in emphasizing your positive traits (i.e., you must know what this particular employer considers to be positive or negative, and you must maintain a continuous focus on your virtues without appearing immodest or egocentric—a fairly tough act for most of us), but you will have to do this with a degree of subtlety that beguiles the interviewer. Moreover, since most managerial positions require that you be interviewed by several managers (all of whom will compare notes on you, later), the task becomes complicated. Each interviewer is an individual with personal tastes, values, and attitudes that differ from the others to some extent. It is going to require *real* skill to cater to each of these individuals without having them find out that each of them has seen a somewhat different person in their interview.

Cursory assessment of the issues raised in the right-hand column of Table 1 suggests that, unless you can arrange for an interviewer afflicted with terminal stupidity, it is going to take real effort to pull off an act of the type suggested. Compounding the problem is the fact that the employment interview is a stressful situation for most applicants, and the level of stress may become totally debilitating if you must devote most of your energy to guarding against being found out.

Even if you are an accomplished thespian, the question still remains, *is it in your own best interests to practice deceit in the interview?* Schein (1978) points out that to the extent that applicants can describe themselves fully and accurately to the interviewer, the probability is increased that they will end up well-matched to their jobs. *"There is little to be gained in the long run by falsely selling oneself"* (p. 88—emphasis added).

TABLE 1
Ingratiation Tactics and the Employment Interview[a]

Ingratiation Tactic	*Problems and Implications*
1. Emphasize your attractive accomplishments and traits.	a. You must know what the employer considers to be positive or negative traits, etc. (not always obvious). b. You must avoid appearing conceited.
2. Avoid appearing conceited or boastful by presenting yourself with some modesty (but don't *brag* about your modesty!).	a. Works best if the interviewer already knows what your good traits are, or when someone else can be relied upon to tell the interviewer (seldom the case in the employment interview). b. But, if you think someone else will mention a weakness you have, beat them to the punch (*but* see number 5 below). c. Don't emphasize a positive quality if you think it may threaten the interviewer (e.g., don't brag about your degree from Harvard if the interviewer is a college dropout).
3. People like people who are most similar in attitudes, values, and personality to themselves. Try to make it look like you are a lot like the interviewer.	a. But some interviewers will see through obvious attempts to be agreeable, assuming the interviewee is attempting to manipulate them instead (with negative results for you). b. It may be better to disagree with the employer on a few points—especially if the points are not pivotal. c. Some studies suggest that conformists do not get promoted in management.
4. The interviewer will respond more positively to you if you have at least average characteristics, if the preceeding interviewees have been real *turkeys*.	a. You don't usually have much control over when your appointment is scheduled.
5. Negative information is weighted more heavily in the interview than positive information. Therefore, present only positive information and avoid providing negative data.	a. See number 1, above. b. You will have to do this without insulting the intelligence of the interviewer. c. How do you deal with a situation where you are interviewed by several managers?

Copyright © 1982, John Wiley and Sons, Inc.

Ingratiation Tactic	*Problems and Implications*
	How do you avoid telling conflicting stories as you try to tell each manager just he or she wants to hear?
6. Data presented earlier in the interview make a greater impact. Therefore, make a good first impression.	a. If you have any negative data you will have to reveal, make sure you communicate your positive features first. *But,* don't appear reluctant to talk about your negative points.
	b. Physical appearance is weighted heavily in the interviewer's mind. Attire, makeup, etc., should play up your attractive features and be appropriate for the situation.

[a]Based upon Wortman and Linsenmeier (1977).

Wortman and Linsenmeier suggest a number of additional dangers in impression management:

1. The characteristics that were important in getting the job are likely to be required for keeping it. Do you think you can maintain your facade over the long term?
2. People who put on a convincing act get feedback on the act, not on the person they really are. Therefore, they never really learn about themselves—just about the fictitious person they have invented. Moreover, they tend to be unaware of their inability to get accurate feedback.
3. Since ingratiators receive only feedback on their phony persona, they come to take it seriously, and eventually *they tend to become the person they have invented.*

EFFECTIVE INTERVIEWING

Are there things you can do to make you more effective in the interview without resorting to artifice or deceit? The answer is clearly affirmative. Here are a number of tips that will help you to prepare for the interview and help you to get through it with less nervousness and anxiety (remember, a little stress is good—it will keep you alert and energetic throughout the interview).

1. Always Start at the Beginning
Employers tend to be unimpressed with people who don't know what they want to do (and this is usually easy to spot). Always do your career planning (see Exercises 46 to 50 and the reading introducing the "Life, Work, and Career Roles" section on p. 291).

2. *Do Your Homework*

Before interviewing with an organization learn all you can about it. A couple of afternoons in the library can pay large dividends, and the recruiter will be impressed. You should arrive at the interview armed with both a basic knowledge of the organization and a couple of intelligent questions about it.

3. *Rehearse*

"The Awful Interview" (Exercise 48) or a simple role-play of the interview you expect will be immensely helpful in putting you at ease for the actual interview. Repeat treatment several times, if necessary.

4. *Go Native*

Most organizations have fairly strong norms about appropriate attire, hair styles, facial fur, makeup, and other issues of personal appearance. If you don't know what the standards are likely to be, ask someone in a position to know. The objective here is to look like the folks the recruiter is used to working with.

If you feel that a haircut or wearing a suit is a violation of your integrity, ask yourself whether you really want this job.

5. *Playing a Winning Hand*

If you have prepared well for the interview, the following tips will help you successfully cope with interview protocol (these suggestions based on Gootnick, 1978):

a. Getting started right:
    (1) *Never* arrive late.
    (2) If the interviewer offers a hand, respond with a firm handshake and a warm smile.
    (3) Do not smoke, even if asked.
    (4) Allow the interviewer to begin the interview.
b. During the interview:
    (1) Early in the interview, make a brief, positive presentation of your abilities, experience, interests, and so on that you feel are of special relevance for the job under consideration.
    (2) Be open and honest; give the recruiter an accurate picture of your needs, talents and interests.
c. Close the interview by:
    (1) Summarizing your credentials.
    (2) Expressing enthusiasm for the organization and the job (if you really *are* interested).
    (3) Thanking the interviewer.
    (4) If the interviewer has not already indicated what the next step should be, ask.

Copyright © 1982, John Wiley and Sons, Inc.

    d. After the interview:
       (1) Prepare a set of notes for future reference covering all the key points discussed.
       (2) Five to seven days later, send the interviewer a "thank you" letter. In it, express again your interest in the job (if real) and repeat your key credentials.

These guidelines won't guarantee that you get the job, but they should help you to improve your batting average. Good luck in your job hunting!

READINGS AND REFERENCES

Gootnick, D., "Selling Yourself in Interviews." *MBA*, 40 (Nov. 1978), 37–38.

Schein, E. H., *Career Dynamics: Matching Individuals and Organizational Needs,* (Reading, Mass.: Addison-Wesley, 1978).

Verderber, R. F., and Verderber, K. S., *Inter-act: Using Interpersonal Communication Skills,* 2nd ed. (Belmont, Calif.: Wadsworth, 1980).

Webster's New Collegiate Dictionary (Springfield, Mass.: G.&C. Merriam Co., 1951).

Wortman, C. B., and Linsenmeier, J. A. W., "Interpersonal Attraction Techniques of Ingratiation in Organizational Settings," in B. M. Staw and G. R. Salancik (Eds.), *New Directions in Organizational Behavior* (Chicago: St. Clair Press, 1977), pp. 133–178.

65
TOWARD A VIABLE
CONCEPT OF ASSSERTIVENESS
Donald D. Bowen

In the past 10 years, "pop" psychology has done a booming business. Perhaps the most popular, and often the most controversial strain has been "assertion" and "assertiveness training." Feminists have been particularly avid consumers of assertiveness, since assertiveness training is designed to help people stand up for their rights and achieve their goals. But critics of the "me" generation and its tendency toward self-centered insistence upon immediate gratification of materialistic whims have been suspicious of assertiveness training. In their view, assertiveness encourages satisfaction of the individual's needs—and to hell with everyone else.

We would like to propose a slightly different concept of assertiveness; one we feel makes the notion of assertiveness basically consistent with the notions of interpersonally competent behavior long recognized by students of management and organizational behavior (e.g., Argyris, 1962).

Discussion of assertiveness normally begins with definition of three alternative forms of behavior. *Passive* behavior is inhibited, self-denying, submissive, conflict-avoidant, wherein the person ignores her own needs and feelings in an attempt to satisfy other people. *Aggressive* behavior is the opposite of passiveness: domineering, pushy, self-centered, self-enhancing, and self-expressive without regard for the feelings or rights of others. Both passive and aggressive behavior are varieties of nonassertive behavior.

Some authorities see assertiveness as a midpoint between aggressive and passive behavior (e.g., Bloom, Coburn, and Pearlman, 1975). We believe this is a mistaken view and one that makes understanding assertiveness needlessly difficult. Our definition of *assertiveness* is behavior that involves expressing one's ideas and feelings, and standing up for one's rights, *and doing so in a way that makes it easier for other to do the same.* The assertive person is self-revealing, open and receptive, active, self-respecting, confronting (meaning the person expresses his feelings), and one who communicates directly and honestly to others. The assertive person, being open and receptive to others, also develops a sensitivity to the needs of others and a sense of when it is appropriate to be self-expressive.

By requiring that the asssertive person forego pursuing his own ends when doing so inhibits others from expressing themselves or standing up for their own rights, we have posited a more limited notion of assertiveness, but one that avoids the logical traps in questions like the following:

Q: Is it possible to be *too* assertive?
A: No, because the more assertive you are, the more assertive others are encouraged to be.

Copyright © 1982, John Wiley and Sons, Inc.

Q: If I am a little more or less assertive, do I become passive or aggressive?

A: No, because assertiveness is a *different* mode of behavior, not a point somewhere between aggressivenesss and passiveness.

Q: Won't I lose my friends and put people off if I am always concerned about my rights and expressing my feelings?

A: Not if you do it assertively, because you must then be concerned with the rights and feelings of others, too. Furthermore, can you ever really be helpful in satisfying the needs of others if you don't devote attention to satisfaction of your own needs, too? (Incidentally, this is a fundamental axiom of mental health.)

Let us now review some basic principles of assertive communication.

ASSERTIVENESS: PRINCIPLES AND EXAMPLES

Assertive communication requires developing specific communication habits and skills. The following are some of the most important:

1. Share Your Feelings in a Statement Beginning with "I"

Example: A colleague has apparently promised to do one thing but has done something quite different.

The assertive statement: "I'm really disturbed about what you did on the GM deal, Dave."

Nonasssertive approaches are: "What the hell is the big idea?" or to say nothing while doing a slow burn.

2. Don't Discount Yourself and Don't Discount Others

Example: A colleague asks for your opinion on a decision.

The assertive response is a straightforward "I think..."

The nonassertive answers may involve putting down or discounting the other person ("I'm surprised you don't know the answer to that, Sue"), or discounting myself ("Well, I'm only a woman, so I don't know if you will want my opinion", or "Well, I guess I think that...").

3. Don't Be Wishy-Washy and Don't Diffuse Your Message with "Word Whiskers"[1]

The examples of discounting oneself are also problems of being wish-washy. There are many others, including going on at immense length about all sides of a question. "Word whiskers" are the meaningless speech patterns that many people use ("Um, uh, I guess, uh, I guess that, uh..." or "Well, we were just hangin' around, y'know, when this big guy, y'know, about six foot-eight, y'know...").

Whatever your feelings are on a topic, if you are wishy-washy or an acccomplished word-whiskerer, no one will listen long enough to find out.

---

[1] Mr. John Gregg suggested this apt term.

4. Be Specific in Feedback and Criticism

This guideline is dealt with in greater detail in Cyril Mill's "Feedback," Reading 54.

Example: You must criticize a report submitted by your subordinate.

The assertive approach: "In this report, Dave, you used LIFO. I want you to use FIFO, because..."

The nonassertive resonses include, "Mary, this report stinks!" Or, "Lee, how can you be so dense?"

5. Use Neutral, Nonexplosive Language

Some language, as in the case of the defective report, just discussed stimulates others to be defensive by being accusatory or grossly evaluative. Sarcasm frequently leads to the same result.

6. Be Cooperative, Open and Receptive to Others—They May Know Something You Don't

Example: Suppose a subordinate disobeys your explicit orders.

The nonassertive response is too often second-nature: "What the hell is the big idea, Larry...?"

The assertive boss is aware that the subordinates may know something she does not. "Larry, can you tell me why you did *X* when I told you *Y*?"

7. Confront Unpleasant Situations Immediately (or at Least as Soon as Practicable)

And remember, "confront" means share your feelings, *not* dump all over the other person!

8. Make Sure Your Nonverbal Communication Is Congruent with Your Words

Ninety percent of the message we receive from another person is communicated nonverbally (Mehrabian, 1968). Consier the plight of the subordinate whose boss is smiling while she chews him out. Or the person who asks her boss for a raise in an inaudible mumble (reinforced by a nervous shuffling of feet and eyes riveted on the floor).

DEVELOPING ASSERTIVENESS SKILLS

Becoming more assertive is hard work. There are two important lessons one must master. First: you must learn to discriminate between assertive and nonassertive behavior. Second, you must practice your assertiveness *skills* continually until you have developed a repertoire of behavior that is readily available to you in a wide range of situations—even when you are under substantial pressure.

Is it all worth it? Perhaps you really have little choice if you are to work effectively within an organization (or if you are to have satisfactory relationships with people in other aspects of your life, for that matter). The answer might be best summarized in the words of one of our students, a young woman who holds down

Copyright © 1982, John Wiley and Sons, Inc.

a job in computer programming during the day while working towards her bachelor's degree at night.

Prof: What do you think? Should we encourage our students to be more assertive?
Student: You bet!
Prof: Why?
Student: Because it feels so *good* when you know you have done it!

READINGS AND REFERENCES

Argyris, C., *Interpersonal Competence and Organizational Effectiveness* (Homewood, Ill.: Irwin, 1962).

Bloom, L. F., Coburn, K. and Pearlman, J., *The New Assertive Woman* (New York: Dell, 1975).

Mehrabian, A., "A Communication Without Words," *Psychology Today*, September (1968), p. 53.

ADDITIONAL READINGS

Alberti, R. E., and Emmons, M. L., *Your Perfect Right,* 2nd ed., (San Luis Obispo, Calif.: Impact Press, 1974).

Fensterheim, H., and Baer, J. *Don't Say Yes When You Want to Say No* (New York: Dell, 1975).

Kelley, C., "Assertion: The Literature Since 1970," in J. E. Jones and J. W. Pfeiffer (Eds.), *The 1977 Annual Handbook for Group Facilitators* (La Jolla, Calif.: University Associates, 1977), pp. 264–265.

Richardson, N., "Assertiveness Training for Men and Women," in A. G. Sargent, *Beyond Sex Roles* (St. Paul: West, 1977), pp. 336–350.

APPENDIX: LIST OF CONTENTS

NOT TO BE CONSULTED UNTIL INSTRUCTED TO DO SO.

Copyright © 1982, John Wiley and Sons, Inc.

ROLE OF "C. J. MARSHALL," PRODUCTION MANAGER— EXERCISE 10

You have just been notified that your boss, D. P. Jones, the president of the company, wants to see you. As you walk to Jones' office, you wonder what D. P. wants to see you about. It might be one of two things.

Maybe D. P. is going to promote you to executive vice-president. Several times in the past year D. P. has seemed to be thinking along these lines. As D. P. put it, if you could prove yourself as production manager, the job would be yours. Well, your record certainly indicates you deserve the promotion! Productivity has never been higher, and you have guided the production organization to an effective solution of every problem which has come up. You are damn *proud* of your many accomplishments.

Or D. P. might want to respond to your memorandum of last week on recruitment of supervisors and trainees in production. You have recommended:

1. offering substantially higher salaries in hopes of attracting better quality personnel;
2. instituting a personnel testing program to weed out incompetent and irresponsible applicants.

Although you are very proud of your accomplishments in Production, the one problem that bothers you is the quality of lower and middle managers in your department. You have lost several of these people lately, but you were glad to see most of them go. Most of them were sullen, irresponsible, and not very bright. Most were already in jobs over their heads, and none had potential for promotion.

It has been a constant drain on your energies trying to improve the performance of these subordinates. No matter how much coaching, pleading, encouraging, and threatening you do, it seems as if you have to double check all of their work to be sure it is done correctly. Through your watchfulness you have corrected mistakes that would have cost the company many thousands of dollars.

D. P. Jones is an old personal friend, and you have enjoyed your working relationship.

At this point you enter D. P.'s office.

ROLE FOR "ELMER B. PARKER," OMBUDSMAN AND CONSUMER ADVOCATE—EXERCISE 30

You have been hired by the Board to represent the interests of the consumers of Booth's products, which in this case means both the doctors who prescribe the drugs and the patients who ultimately consume them. While you are aware that Vanatin makes life easier for some doctors, you feel that these doctors ought to know better. Any difficulty doctors might have if the drug were removed from the market is far outweighed by the deaths stemming from the use of the drug. Except for your vote, your ultimate weapon is to "blow the whistle" and give the Vanatin story to the newspapers. This would, however, cost you your job so that you could

Copyright © 1982, John Wiley and Sons, Inc.

not continue to have the "moderating effect" that you have previously been able to exercise on Board decisions.

ROLE OF "DR. JONES"—EXERCISE 21

You are Dr. John W. Jones, a biological research scientist employed by a pharmaceutical firm. You have recently developed a synthetic chemical useful for curing and preventing Rudosen. Rudosen is a disease contracted by pregnant women. If not caught in the first four weeks of pregnancy, the disease causes serious brain, eye, and ear damage to the unborn child. Recently there has been an outbreak of Rudosen in your state, and several thousand women have contracted the disease. You have found, with volunteer patients, that your recently developed synthetic serum cures Rudosen in its early stages. Unfortunately, the serum is made from the juice of the Ugli orange, which is a very rare fruit. Only a small quantity (approximately 4,000) of these oranges were produced last season. No additional Ugli oranges will be available until next season, which will be too late to cure the present Rudosen victims.

You've demonstrated that your synthetic serum is in no way harmful to pregnant women. Consequently, there are no side effects. The Food and Drug Administration has approved of the production and distribution of the serum as a cure for Rudosen. Unfortunately, the present outbreak was unexpected, and your firm had not planned on having the compound serum available for six months. Your firm holds the patent on the synthetic serum, and it is expected to be a highly profitable product when it is generally available to the public.

You have recently been informed on good evidence that Mr. R. H. Cardoza, a South American fruit exporter, is in possession of 3,000 Ugli oranges in good condition. If you could obtain the juice of all 3,000, you would be able to both cure present victims and provide sufficient inoculation for the remaining pregnant women in the state. No other state currently has a Rudosen threat.

You have recently been informed that Dr. P. W. Roland is also urgently seeking Ugli oranges and is also aware of Mr. Cardoza's possession of the 3,000 available. Dr. Roland is employed by a competing pharmaceutical firm. He has been working on biological warfare research for the past several years. There is a great deal of industrial espionage in the pharmaceutical industry. Over the past several years, Dr. Roland's firm and yours have sued each other for infringement of patent rights and espionage law violations several times.

You've been authorized by your firm to approach Mr. Cardoza to purchase 3,000 Ugli oranges. You have been told he will sell them to the highest bidder. Your firm has authorized you to bid as high as $250,000 to obtain the juice of the 3,000 available oranges.

ASSIGNMENT AS UNION NEGOTIATOR—EXERCISE 24

You have been selected by the Union to represent it in its negotiations with the Townsford Company. Negotiations for a new two-year contract broke down last week. The Union is thoroughly irritated with the Company's refusal to grant the workers badly needed wage and benefit increases. Although no compromises were reached in either side's position, it was decided that each side should appoint new negotiating agents in an effort to settle the contract and halt the strike, which began today.

You are to do the best possible job you can to get a good settlement of the contract for labor. Union members were dissatisfied with the last contract three years ago, and there is serious danger of division in the ranks of the Union if a more satisfactory contract is not achieved in these negotiations. It is essential to labor, however, that the contract be settled in this bargaining period. We realize that this involves compromises on both sides, and you are appointed to carry out binding negotiations for us. Remember, your job is to reach a settlement, one that is good for labor, in this negotiating period.

SCRIPT FOR SCENE 1 OF "THE STORM WINDOWS" (NOT TO BE READ BY "PAUL BROWN")—EXERCISE 25

The telephone installers are all seated about the lunch table having completed the eating of their lunches. Tom Jones has a newspaper opened and is reading to himself.

Dick: With weather like this, the baseball team will be able to get an early start on their workouts. I wonder what kind of a team we'll have this year?

Bill: I hear they have some pretty good boys coming along. Especially that Thompson kid. He's supposed to be a pretty hot pitcher.

Harry: Yeah, and with weather like this, Bill ought to be able to get himself an early start on *his* spring training.

Bill: What are you talking about? Spring training for what?

Harry: Spring training for taking down storm windows and putting up screens!

Dick: Good point, Harry, You have to be in pretty good shape to handle that job.

Tom: Don't worry about old Bill. He's got just about all the brains anybody needs to go along with the brawn that job takes. He's the best screen "putter upper" I've seen in all my years with the company.

Bill: Well, I've got some news for you wise guys. I'm not putting up *any* screens.

Tom: Don't tell me you've lost that old "desire" in there, man. We need you.

Dick: Good old Bill won't let us down. Who else besides Brownie would be smart enough to handle the job?

Bill: Well, I've put those screens and storm windows up for the last time. From now on somebody else is going to put them up or they can stay where they are.

Harry: You talk big while Brownie is down to the bank, but it wouldn't surprise me if he notices what a nice day it is and, seeing as how we're not too busy, he tells you to get going on the storm windows and screens.

Bill: Yeah? And if he does, you know what I'm going to tell him he can do with those storm windows!

Tom: We know what you're going to tell him he can do with them. You're going to tell him he can have you cover them up so you won't have to wash them in the fall.

Bill: I'm not taking those storm windows down. And that's final.

Copyright © 1982, John Wiley and Sons, Inc.

Hollow Square Pattern

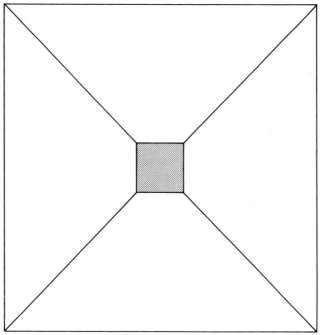

Copyright © 1982, John Wiley and Sons, Inc.

SCORING KEY, FIRO-B—EXERCISE 32

Instructions:

Compare your response to the FIRO-B Questionnaire in Exercise 32 with this key. For each item, compare your response to the responses listed in the column below. If your response matches the responses listed, score a "1" in the bracketed box for that item; if your response does not match, score a "0" in the bracketed box for that item.

Example:

On item 1, the statement is, "I try to be with people." This item is scored under the subscale e^i. If you answered this item with a 1 ("usually"), 2 ("often"), or 3 ("sometimes"), place a "1" in the bracketed box. If you answered this item with a 4 ("occasionally"), 5 ("rarely"), or 6 ("never"), place a 0 in the bracketed box.

Add each column to obtain a total score for each subscale (minimum 0, maximum 9). Enter these in the table on page 215.

Item	Score one point for a response of:	e^i	w^i	e^c	w^c	e^a	w^a
1	1,2,3	(___)					
2	1,2,3,4			(___)			
3	1,2,3,4	(___)					
4	1,2					(___)	
5	1,2,3,4	(___)					
6	1,2,3,4				(___)		
7	1,2,3	(___)					
8	1,2					(___)	
9	1,2	(___)					
10	1,2,3				(___)		
11	1,2	(___)					
12	1					(___)	
13	1,2	(___)					
14	1,2,3				(___)		
15	1,2	(___)					
16	1	(___)					
17	1,2					(___)	
18	1,2,3,4			(___)			
19	4,5,6						(___)
20	1,2,3,4			(___)			
21	1,2						(___)
22	1,2,3,4			(___)			

Subtotals—enter here and at   ___ ___ ___ ___ ___ ___
bottom of key

Item	Score one point for a response of:	Enter 1 or 0 in the column with the brackets:					
		e^i	w^i	e^c	w^c	e^a	w^a
23	1,2					(___)	
24	1,2,3				(___)		
25	4,5,6					(___)	
26	1,2,3				(___)		
27	1,2					(___)	
28	1,2		(___)				
29	1,2						(___)
30	1,2,3			(___)			
31	1,2		(___)				
32	1,2						(___)
33	1,2,3			(___)			
34	1,2		(___)				
35	5,6						(___)
36	1,2			(___)			
37	1		(___)				
38	1,2						(___)
39	1		(___)				
40	5,6						(___)
41	1,2,3,4			(___)			
42	1,2		(___)				
43	1						(___)
44	1,2,3			(___)			
45	1,2		(___)				
46	5,6						(___)
47	1,2,3			(___)			
48	1,2		(___)				
49	1,2						(___)
50	1,2			(___)			
51	1,2		(___)				
52	5,6					(___)	
53	1,2			(___)			
54	1,2			(___)			

1. Compute column totals for items 23 to 54:   ___ ___ ___ ___ ___ ___

2. Add subtotals from items 1 to 22:   ___ ___ ___ ___ ___ ___

3. Compute sum of lines 1 and 2:   ___ ___ ___ ___ ___ ___

Line 3 shows your scores for the six dimensions. Enter these data on p. 217 of EMOB in Step 2.

Copyright © 1982, John Wiley and Sons, Inc.

INSTRUCTIONS FOR OBSERVERS FOR BOTH ACCOUNTING AND MANUFACTURING ROLES—EXERCISE 10

1. Observe the manner in which the boss begins the interview.
   a. What did the interviewer do, if anything, to create a permissive atmosphere?
   b. Did the interviewer state the purpose of the interview early in the session?
   c. Was the purpose of the interview stated clearly and concisely?
2. Observe how the interview was conducted.
   a. To what extent did the interviewer learn how the subordinate felt about the job in general?
   b. Did the interviewer use broad, general questions at the outset?
   c. Did the boss criticize the subordinate?
   d. Was the interviewer acceptant of the subordinate's feelings and ideas?
   e. Which one talked the most?
   f. What other things did the interviewer learn?
   g. Did the boss praise the subordinate?
3. Observe and evaluate the outcome of the interview.
   a. To what extent did the boss arrive at a fairer and more accurate evaluation of the subordinate as a result of the interview?
   b. What things did the boss do, if any, to motivate the subordinate to improve?
   c. Were relations better or worse after the interview? If worse, why did this occur?
   d. In what ways might the interviewer have done a better job?

PLANT MANAGER'S JOB DESCRIPTION, A—EXERCISE 42

As plant manager of one of Square, Inc.'s many production facilities, your mission is to produce a complete square, measuring 8.5 by 8.5 inches.

The organization is designed as a traditional hierarchy, which requires you to follow through the appropriate channels of communication. If you run into any serious production problems that prevent you from producing a square, you must refer your problem up through the organization's formal hierarchy to your division manager. You may send memos to your division manager or sign up for a meeting with him or her on the communication board located near his or her office.

Because of their size and weight, it is very costly and time consuming for the organization to ship parts to the home office in Oahu. The cost of transferring parts between the five division plants on the mainland is also quite high.

BRIEFING FOR PLANNING TEAM—EXERCISE 45

Each of you will be given a packet containing several cardboard pieces that, when properly assembled, will make a hollow square design (see page 423).

During a period of 25 minutes you are to do the following:

1. Plan how the 17 pieces distributed among you should be assembled to make the design.
2. Instruct your operating team on how to implement your plan. (You may begin

instructing your operating team at any time during the planning period—but *no later than* 5 minutes before they are to begin the assembling process; ie., no later than 20 minutes after you start your planning.)

General Rules

1. You must keep all pieces you have in front of you at all times.
2. You may *not* touch the pieces of other team members or trade pieces with other members of your team during the planning or instructing phase.
3. You may *not* show the "Hollow Square Key" to the operating team at any time.
4. You may *not* assemble the entire square at any time (this is to be left to your operating team).
5. You are *not* to mark on any of the pieces.
6. Members of your operating team must also observe the above rules until the signal is given to begin the assembling.
7. When time is called for your operating team to begin assembling the pieces, you may give no further instructions, but are to observe the operation.

ROLE OF "JOHN C. GAUNTLETT, M.D.," BOARD OF DIRECTORS—EXERCISE 30

You have been aware of the bad publicity on Vanatin. As a practicing physician, you have been prescribing Vanatin for years, and you have seen nothing wrong with it. At the last AMA meeting, other doctors to whom you have talked reported similar findings. Your thought is that an appeal should be sent to all doctors to protest the FDA, on the grounds that a ban by the FDA would be violating the physician's right to prescribe the most effective drugs. The fact that some of the doctors you talked to have been using Vanatin for 13 years indicates that it must have some value.

You have been a member of the Board of Directors for 8 years and own 150,000 shares of Booth stock.

ROLE OF "DR. ROLAND"—EXERCISE 21

You are Dr. P. W. Roland. You work as a research biologist for a pharmaceutical firm. The firm is under contract with the government to do research on methods to combat enemy uses of biological warfare.

Recently several World War II experimental nerve gas bombs were moved from the United States to a small island just off the U.S. coast in the Pacific. In the process of transporting them, two of the bombs developed a leak. The leak is presently controlled by government scientists, who believe that the gas will permeate the bomb chambers within two weeks. They know of no method of preventing the gas from getting into the atmosphere and spreading to other islands, and very likely to the West Coast as well. If this occurs, it is likely that several thousand people will incur serious brain damage or die.

You've developed a synthetic vapor that will neutralize the nerve gas if it is injected into the bomb chamber before the gas leaks out. The vapor is made with

Copyright © 1982, John Wiley and Sons, Inc.

a chemical taken from the rind of the Ugli orange, a very rare fruit. Unfortunately, only 4,000 of these oranges were produced this season.

You've been informed on good evidence, that a Mr. R. H. Cardoza, a fruit exporter in South America, is in possession of 3,000 Ugli oranges. The chemicals from the rinds of all 3,000 oranges would be sufficient to neutralize the gas if the serum is developed and injected efficiently. You have also been informed that the rinds of these oranges are in good condition.

You have also been informed that Dr. J. W. Jones is also urgently seeking purchase of Ugli oranges, and he is aware of Mr. Cardoza's possession of the 3,000 available. Dr. Jones works for a firm with which your firm is highly competitive. There is a great deal of industrial espionage in the pharmaceutical industry. Over the years, your firm and Dr. Jones's have sued each other for violations of industrial espionage laws and infringement of patent rights several times. Litigation on two suits is still in process.

The federal government has asked your firm for assistance. You've been authorized by your firm to approach Mr. Cardoza to purchase 3,000 Ugli oranges. You have been told he will sell them to the highest bidder. Your firm has authorized you to bid as high as $250,000 to obtain the rind of the oranges.

Before approaching Mr. Cardoza, you have decided to talk to Dr. Jones to influence him so that he will not prevent you from purchasing the oranges.

ASSIGNMENT AS COMPANY NEGOTIATOR—EXERCISE 24

You have been selected by the Townsford Company to represent it in its negotiations with the Union. Negotiations for a new two-year contract broke down last week. The Union demands for general wage and benefit increases are completely unreasonable. If labor costs are increased, it might necessitate price increases that could seriously hamper the company's competitive standing. Although no compromises were reached in either side's position, it was decided that each side should appoint new negotiators in an effort to settle the contract and halt the strike, which began today.

You are to do the best possible job you can to get a good settlement of the contract for the company. Although the company now has a backlog of orders, it is in danger of losing several major customers if increased labor costs necessitate a significant price increase. It is essential to the company, however, that the contract be settled in this bargaining period. We realize that this involves compromises on both sides, and you are appointed to carry out binding negotiations for us. Remember, your job is to reach a settlement, one that is good for the company, in this negotiating period.

ROLE FOR "THOMPSON," FOREMAN—EXERCISE 25

You are the foreman in a shop and supervise the work of about 20 men. Most of the jobs are piece-rate jobs and some of the men work in teams and are paid on a team piece-rate basis. In one of the teams, Jackson, Walters, and Stevenson work together. Each one of them does one of the operations for an hour and then they exchange, so that all men perform each of the operations at different times. The men themselves decided to operate that way and you have never given the plan any thought.

Lately, Jim Clark, the methods man, has been around and studied conditions in your shop. He timed Jackson, Walters and Stevenson on each of the operations and came up with the following facts:

	Position 1	Position 2	Position 3	Total
		Time per operation		
Jackson	3 min.	4 min.	4½ min.	11½ min.
Walters	3½ min.	3½ min.	3 min.	10 min.
Stevenson	5 min.	3½ min.	4½ min.	13 min.
				34½ min.

He observed that with the people rotating, the average time for all three operations would be one-third of the total time or 11½ minutes per complete unit. If, however, Jackson worked in the no. 1 spot, Stevenson in the no. 2 spot, and Walters in the no. 3 spot, the time would be 9½ min., a reduction of more than 17 percent. Such a reduction in time would amount to a saving of more than 80 minutes. In other words, the lost production would be about the same as that which would occur if the workers loafed for 80 minutes in an eight-hour day. If the time were used for productive effort, production would be increased more than 20 percent.

This made pretty good sense to you, so you have decided to take up the problem with the crew. You feel that they should go along with any change in operation that is made.

ROLE OF "PHILIP BROWN," PRESIDENT, AND VICE CHAIRMAN OF THE BOARD—EXERCISE 30

You were the President of Booth when Vanatin was introduced into the market. Naturally, you feel that Vanatin was, and still is, a good product both for Booth and for the people who have used it. If you didn't feel this way, you wouldn't have put Vanatin on the market in the first place. A cut in the sales of Vanatin would bring about managerial dislocations and threaten to reverse the strong growth of profits under your command. Furthermore, it has become increasingly difficult to develop new products because of extensive testing requirements of the FDA. On the other hand, as the chief executive officer of Booth, you are concerned about the kind of company that you lead.

ROLE OF: "DONNA KELLY," PRODUCTION MANAGER—EXERCISE 35

What a fix! If Bob Young finds out about that defective gasket material, it will be my head—and probably Mike's and Fran's, too. A million units of the crummy junk

Copyright © 1982, John Wiley and Sons, Inc.

got through Receiving Inspection somehow, and 800,000 of them are still in the warehouse. I had a feeling that my changing our ordering procedure was a mistake, but I wanted to reduce our inventory carrying costs. I never should have tried to cover up the situation after we saw what happened.

But what else could we do? Roy has *always* been Bob's buddy. If I blame Roy, it would be like doing in the crown prince. Roy has been with Young since they started the company, and they are thick as thieves on weekends, too.

And I didn't have much choice, anyway. When that shipment came in, we were down to less than two days' supply in Subassembly. Fran Kurowski would have had to shut down completely if the lot had been rejected, and, at first it looked like Fran and Mike could adjust the assembly procedures fairly easily to compensate for the defects. A shutdown would have put Young Manufacturing out of business for good. Customers aren't going to wait for late deliveries anymore.

As it turned out, things were worse than I thought: Subassembly Inspection began to find defects and held up several lots before they could get to Mike Cohen for final rework. Normally, I would work something out with Roy, but I can't do that this time. Roy hates Fran's guts, and he is just waiting for a chance to see Fran hung. This would be the perfect setup to make Fran the scapegoat. Roy never got over Fran's getting the job that Roy's kid wanted.

Well, somehow I'm going to have to keep the plant operating. It would sure help if Bob Young would ease up the pressure for output and learn to rely on me the way he does on Roy Conti.

PLANT MANAGER'S JOB DESCRIPTION, B—EXERCISE 42

As plant manager of one of Square, Inc.'s many production facilities, your mission is to produce a complete square, measuring 8.5 by 8.5 inches.

The organization is designed as a traditional hierarchy, which requires you to follow through the appropriate channels of communication. If you run into any serious production problems that prevent you from producing a square, you must refer your problem up through the organization's formal hierarchy to your division manager. You may send memos to your division manager or sign up for a meeting with him or her on the communication board located near his or her office.

In addition, however, through your long experience in the industry, you have developed a network of informal contacts with other plant managers. You have found it helpful in the past to work through some of your operating problems with your peers. You frequently contact these people directly, but may only contact one of them at a time. The division manager has been known to express serious discontent when more than two plant managers get together at a time.

Because of their size and weight, it is very costly and time consuming for the organization to ship parts to the home office in Oahu. The cost of transferring parts between the five division plants on the mainland is also quite high.

BRIEFING FOR OPERATING TEAM—EXERCISE 45

1. You will have responsibility for carrying out a task for four to six people, according to instructions given by your planning team. Your planning team may call you in to give you instructions at any time. If they do not summon you, you are to report to them after 25 minutes anyway. Your task is scheduled to begin in 25 minutes; after that, no further instructions from your planning team can be given. You are to finish the assigned task as rapidly as possible.
2. While you are waiting for a call from your planning team, it is suggested that you discuss and make notes on the following:
   a. The feelings and concerns that you experience while waiting for instructions for the unknown task.
   b. Your suggestions on how a person might prepare to receive instructions.
3. Your notes recorded on the above will be helpful during the work group discussions following the completion of your task.

GENERAL INSTRUCTIONS—EXERCISE 10*

J. J. Stein is an audit partner with a "Big 8" accounting firm. The work in the office includes large SEC clients, and small business clients.

Eight audit managers report to J. J. Stein. The duties of the audit manager are technical and supervisory. The organizational chart for Stein's office is shown in the diagram.

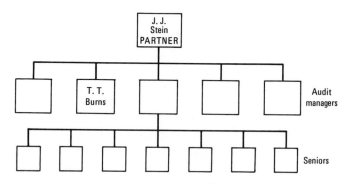

Firm policy requires that all partners periodically interview each of their managers, the purpose being

1. To evaluate the manager's performance.
2. To give recognition for jobs well done.
3. To correct weaknesses.

The firm believes that staff should know how they stand and that everything should be done to develop management personnel. The evaluation interviews were introduced to help serve this purpose.

---

*These materials are adapted from the famous Burke-Stanley role-play developed by N. R. F. Maier.

Copyright © 1982, John Wiley and Sons, Inc.

T. T. Burns is one of the managers reporting to Stein; today an evaluation interview will be conducted by Stein with T. T. Burns. Note that the interview is devoted to performance evaluation and is not intended to cover "career counseling."

T. T. Burns has a college degree in accounting, and, in addition to his technical duties, he supervises the work of several seniors and staff accountants. Burns has been with the firm for 8 years and has been a manager for 2 years. He is married and has two children. He owns his home and is active in the civic affairs of the community in which he lives.

ROLE FOR "JACKSON"—EXERCISE 25

You are one of three people on an assembly operation. Walters and Stevenson are your team-mates and you enjoy working with them. You get paid on a team basis, and you are making wages that are entirely satisfactory. Stevenson isn't quite as fast as Walters and you, but when you feel Stevenson is holding things up too much, each of you helps out.

The work is very monotonous. The saving thing about it is that every hour you all change positions. In this way you get to do all three operations. You are best on the no. 1 position, so when you get in that spot you turn out some extra work and thus make the job easier for Stevenson who follows you in that position.

You have been on this job for two years and have never run out of work. Apparently your group can make pretty good pay without running yourselves out of a job. Lately, however the company has had some of its methods experts hanging around. It looks like the company is trying to work out some speed-up methods. If they make these jobs any more simple, you won't be able to stand the monotony. Thompson, your foreman, is a decent person and has never criticized your team's work.

ROLE OF "JACK BOOTH," SON OF CYRUS BOOTH, PRESIDENT, BOOTH ASSOCIATES, CONSULTANTS—EXERCISE 30

You and your two brothers manage a consulting firm that does most of its business with the Booth Company. You and your brothers control approximately 20 percent of Booth stock, and you are concerned with the potential effects of the proposed ban on corporate earnings. You have become increasingly disturbed recently at the responsiveness of management to the demands of labor, community, and governmental groups. You feel that management is hired by the stockholders, and that management through the Board should be primarily responsive to them. In a well-publicized statement to *The Wall Street Journal,* you stated that "management seems to be more concerned with its own comfort and security than with corporate profits."

A suggestion was recently sent to you by the corporate lobbyist in Washington. He suggests that it might be possible to bring political pressure to bear on the FDA by securing the cooperation of the current Secretary of Health and Welfare. The Secretary might be willing to overrule a proposed ban by the FDA, since the ban would represent a major precedent that increases the power of the FDA at the expense of drug companies and their rights to free enterprise. Getting the Secretary to go along might require some major financial contributions to the President's reelection campaign.

ROLE OF "ROY CONTI," MANAGER OF QUALITY CONTROL—EXERCISE 35

That Fran Kurowski is the problem. Smart-aleck young college whiz kid, ambitious as hell, and sneaky to boot. If Bob Young had only listened to me a couple of years ago, he could have hired Al, my son, and had a faithful employee instead of this brash little sneak.

Kelly was leaning toward Al, but she was afraid of what Young would say if she hired Al, instead of Fran, just because Fran had an MBA and Al didn't. Donna Kelly is a good egg, generally able in her work, and thanks to the exceptional quality control process we operate, has earned a reputation for running a high-quality plant. Donna and I have gotten along well for several years, and I would like to maintain our good working relationship. We solve most of our quality problems on our level without involving Bob Young and that makes both of us look good.

But, dammit! Why doesn't Donna wake up to how Fran Kurowski is trying to push all the crappy work through inspection? I'd like to tell her, right now, but that would cause problems, too. It would embarrass Donna in front of Bob Young, and, to make things worse, Donna seems to think that Fran can do no wrong. Every time Fran is criticized, Donna blows her top and defends Fran to the bitter end.

DIVISION MANAGER'S JOB DESCRIPTION, A AND B—EXERCISE 42

As division manager of Square, Inc., you are responsible for the productivity of five plants located across the U.S. mainland. The division's task is to ensure that each of the five plants produces one 8.5 by 8.5 inch square, with no raw materials scrapped (i.e., no parts left over). Unfortunately, supplier shipping errors are common across the industry, which means your plants may not have the parts they need to complete their individual tasks. One plant may have some of what another needs, and vice versa.

Since the organization follows the basic principles of a traditional hierarchy, plant managers may be contacting you for information about what parts are available from which plants, and how they might obtain the parts they need. If they wish to contact you, they may do so via memo, or by signing up for an appointment on the communication board outside your office. If you wish to initiate contact with any plant, you may send memos to the individual plant managers.

Your busy schedule prevents you from visiting the individual plants, and your concern about establishing strong productivity records for your division prevents the transfer of the bulky, heavy production materials to your office in Oahu. The cost of transferring parts between the plants on the mainland is also high.

Copyright © 1982, John Wiley and Sons, Inc.

BRIEFING FOR OBSERVATION TEAM—EXERCISE 45

You will be observing a situation in which a planning team decides how to solve a problem and gives instructions to an operating team for implementation. The problem consists of assembling 17 pieces of cardboard into the form of a hollow square. The planning team is supplied with the general layout of the pieces. This team is not to assemble the parts itself, but is to instruct the operating team on how to assemble the parts in a minimum amount of time. You will be *silent observers* throughout the process.

Suggestions for Observation

1. Each member of the observing team should watch the general pattern of communication but give special attention to one member of the planning team (during the planning phase) and one member of the operating team (during the assembling period).
2. During the *planning period,* watch for such behavior as:
   a. The evenness or unevenness of participation among planning team members;
   b. Behavior that blocks or facilitates understanding;
   c. How the planning team divides its time between planning and instructing (how early does it invite the operating team to come in?);
   d. How well it plans its procedure for giving instructions to the operating team.
3. During the *instructing period* (when the planning team is instructing the operating team), watch for such things as:
   a. Who in the planning team gives the instructions (and how was this decided?)?
   b. How is the operating team oriented to the task?
   c. What assumptions made by the planning team are not communicated to the operating team?
   d. How full and clear were the instructions?
   e. How did the operating team members react to the instructions?
   f. Did the operating team feel free to ask questions of the planners?
4. During the *assembly period* (when the operating team is working alone), watch for such things as:
   a. Evidence that instructions were understood or misunderstood)
   b. Nonverbal reactions of planning team members as they watch their plans being implemented or distorted.

ROLE OF "CYRUS BOOTH, M.D.," CHAIRMAN OF THE BOARD—EXERCISE 30

As Chairman of the Board, it is your job to have the Board reach a decision on the two issues within the time allowed. You *must* reach a decision by the end of that time, since some of the Board members have to leave to catch a plane.

Your general philosophy about meetings is to try to allow for various sides of the issue to be discussed before a decision is reached. Legally speaking, a majority vote is required to reach a decision. You prefer a consensus decision, but a formal vote may be used at the end of the meeting if necessary. At the end of the meeting, you are to record the decision on the group decision form (page 205) and hand it to the instructor.

Personally, while you are concerned about the effect that a cut in the sale of Vanatin will have on earnings, you are also concerned that this company, which you have led through its period of greatest growth, also maintain its image of honesty and integrity. This is more than just "corporate image." Booth must be devoted to the maintenance of health and prevention of sickness, for in the last analysis that is how you and your family will be judged in history. You will make every effort to ensure that the decision reached today reflects a unified consensus of the Board.

ROLE FOR "J. J. STEIN," AUDIT PARTNER—EXERCISE 10

You have evaluted all the managers who report to you and during the next 2 weeks will interview each of them. You hope to use these interviews constructively to develop each person. Today you have arranged to interview T. T. Burns, one of the eight managers who report to you. Here is the information on Burns in your files.

T. T. Burns: 8 years with the firm, 2 years as manager, married, two children. Evaluation: Highly creative and original and exceptionally competent technically. On those audit engagements for which you are the partner in charge and Burns is the manager, T. T. has shown an exceptional ability to communicate client problems to you on a timely basis. Within the past 6 months you have given Burns extra work, which has been completed on schedule. As far as productivity and dependability are concerned, this person is your top manager.

Burns's cooperation with other managers in the office leaves much to be desired. Before being promoted to manager, Burns's originality and technical knowledge were available to your whole office. You are aware that other managers have sought Burns's help with certain client problems, but apparently Burns has offered no suggestions. Burns seems to imply that there is no time to help, or the response might be kidding and sarcasm, depending on that day's mood.

Furthermore, during the past 6 months Burns has questioned two of his assignments, saying they were routine. Burns stated a preference for more interesting work. You feel that you can't give Burns all of the interesting work and that if this continues, there will be trouble. You cannot play favorites and keep up morale in your office.

On one occasion, Burns forgot to inform you of a change in an important meeting date with a client. As a result, you only learned of the date change on the day before the meeting and had to make a special out-of-town trip in order to attend. Burns has expressed regret over this situation.

Burns's failure to cooperate has you worried for another reason. Although Burns's people are highly productive, there is more turnover among the staff of this group as compared to other managers. You have heard no complaints as yet, but you suspect that Burns may be treating staff in an arbitrary manner. Certainly

Copyright © 1982, John Wiley and Sons, Inc.

if Burns talks up to you and other managers, what kind of behavior would this manager show toward subordinates? Apparently, the high productivity in this group is not due to high morale, but to Burns's ability to use staff to do the things for which they are best suited. This method will not fully develop the staff person's potential. You hope to discuss these matters with Burke in such a way as to recognize good points and at the same time correct some weaknesses.

ROLE FOR "STEVENSON"—EXERCISE 25

You work with Jackson and Walters on an assembly job and get paid on a team-piece rate basis. The three of you work very well together and make a pretty good wage. Jackson and Walters like to make a little more than you think is necessary, but you go along with them and work as hard as you can so as to keep production up where they want it. They are good people and often help you out if you fall behind, so you feel it is only fair to try and go along with the pace they set.

The three of you exchange positions every hour. In this way you get to work all positions. You like the no. 2 position the best because it is easier. When you get in the no. 3 position you can't keep up and then you feel Thompson, the foreman, watching you. Sometimes Walters and Jackson slow down when you are on the no. 3 spot and then the foreman seems satisfied.

Lately the methods man has been hanging aroung watching the job. You wonder what he is up to. Can't they leave guys alone who are doing all right?

ROLE OF "JAMES VANCE,"
CORPORATE LEGAL COUNSEL—EXERCISE 30

You would prefer not to fight the FDA on Vanatin as you are convinced in the long run that Booth will lose. The FDA has respected research data to support its claim. Other legal tactics are necessary.

You have been checking out various ways of handling the problem with friends. One suggestion has been sent to you by another Booth attorney. He has seen the Vanatin issue develop over the past few years, and he thinks that it would be possible legally to delay any action by the FDA. He suggests that Judge Kent of Kalamazoo (a man whom you know personally) would be willing to serve an injunction on the FDA. This would prohibit the FDA from banning Vanatin until such time as a formal hearing can be held. The results of the hearing, if unfavorable, could then be appealed. In effect, the case could be tied up in the courts for three to five years. A similar move in international courts would not be likely to have an impact on Vanatin sales for 5 to 10 years.

ROLE OF "MIKE COHEN,"
SUPERVISOR OF FINAL ASSEMBLY—EXERCISE 35

Well, loyalty has always been my trademark. Maybe this time I've gone too far, though. Sure, I owe my job to Donna Kelly, and she has always been a good boss. She sure goofed on this one, though. Donna should have reordered the gaskets months and months ago. But no, to keep inventory costs down she waits 'til the last possible minute, orders a million units, and then gets defective material.

The plan to rework the material in Subassembly and Final Assembly seemed like the only sensible solution when Donna first proposed it. The problem turned out to be tougher than anyone had expected, but what the hell, it was better than letting the company go under. Too bad that Donna and Roy Conti were in no position to tell Young what had happened. Guess they want to save their jobs, too, though.

Can't blame them. It would sure be a terrible time for *me* to be out of work. Martha is going back into the hospital for another operation next week (hope they find it this time!), and the college tuition bills for the twins have to be paid by the end of the month. Besides, it isn't easy for a 50-year-old guy to find a job like this one.

Well, guess I'll just have to continue to try to talk Quality Control into releasing the defective lots for rework so that something gets out the door. Hope we can begin to catch up on some of those delivery promises. Bob Young looks mad, and there's no telling what he's likely to do next.

ROLE OF "D. P. JONES," PRESIDENT—EXERCISE 10

You have just asked C. J. Marshall to come to your office for a conference. Marshall is the production manager for the firm. In most respects, you regard Marshall as an ideal executive. C. J. is cost-conscious and efficient, intelligent, and displays great initiative and unquestionable integrity. Under Marshall's guidance, output has increased steadily. Moreover, C. J. is a personal friend.

You have called C. J. to your office to discuss a problem that has been bothering you for the last year and a half. Despite C. J.'s many virtues, there is one major problem. Younger executives in the department refuse to work for Marshall. No production department manager will stay with the company more than six months. They complain that C. J. is authoritarian and never allows them to handle any problem on their own. Marshall is constantly looking over their shoulder and tells them exactly how to conduct even the most trivial aspects of their job.

You would like to appoint Marshall to the vacant position of executive vice-president of the company. At the same time, you are afraid that you may have to terminate Marshall for the good of the company. You have spoken to C. J. several times in the past about this problem, and you feel that you have made it clear that the promotion depends upon C. J.'s having trained a successor—someone to take over the production manager's job when C. J. is promoted.

Recently, so many bright young people have left the company, you are determined that C. J. must either reverse this trend or leave the company.

(You are a little behind in your paper work and you are not aware of any memoranda C. J. may have sent you lately. If C. J. mentions a memo, say that you have not had a chance to read it yet.)

At this point, C. J. enters your office in answer to your call.

Copyright © 1982, John Wiley and Sons, Inc.

ROLE OF "FRAN KUROWSKI," SUPERVISOR OF SUBASSEMBLY—EXERCISE 35

Looks like the chickens are finally coming home to roost. This organization has been living on luck for 9 years now, and now they are about to find out what a bunch of amateur managers they really are. Not a one of them knows the first thing about inventory management, so here we are, stuck with a million defective gaskets and nothing we can do but try to rework them to where they will get by.

Donna Kelly made the first mistake in not ordering at the right time, then, when they got past Roy Conti's inspectors, ol' Kelly compounded her error in not telling Bob Young what had happened. She asked Mike Cohen and me to rework them and try to slip them through inspection. Fat chance that Roy Conti would give us any help; if Roy wasn't so buddy-buddy with Young, he'd be pushing a broom in the shop instead of running Quality Control. But then Bob Young seems to like to surround himself with mediocrity—look at these other clowns.

One of these days (maybe today!) Donna Kelly or Roy Conti is going to make a mistake so obvious that even Bob Young will know the difference. When that happens, they might be looking for a bright MBA with some new ideas to run this show. Better play it cool and be ready when the time comes. Meanwhile, as long as I am in the clear, it will be fun to watch Donna and Roy try to talk their way out of this one.

INSTRUCTIONS FOR OBSERVERS—EXERCISE 25

1. Observe the leader's attitude toward change during the discussion in the office.
   a. Was he partial to the new method?
   b. Did he seem mainly interested in more production or in improving the job for the crew?
   c. To what extent was he considerate of the objections raised by the crew? How did he react to their opposition?
   d. Did he defend the new method or argue for its acceptance? What effect did this have on progress in the discussion?
2. Make notes on conflict handling in the discussion.
   a. Did arguments develop?
   b. Was any crew member unusually stubborn?
   c. Did the crew members have their say?
   d. Did the leader really listen?
   e. What were the main points of differences?
3. Observe evidences of problem-solving behavior.
   a. What was agreed upon, if anything?
   b. In what respects was there a willingness to compromise?
   c. What did the group leader do to help or hinder a mutually acceptable work method?

THE HOVEY AND BEARD COMPANY CASE—EXERCISE 12

PART II

By the second month of the training period trouble had developed. The employees learned more slowly than had been anticipated, and it began to look as though their production would stabilize far below what was planned for. Many of the hooks were going by empty. The women complained that they were going by too fast, and that the time-study man had set the rates wrong. A few women quit and had to be replaced with new operators, which further aggravated the learning problem. The team spirit that the management had expected to develop automatically through the group bonus was not in evidence except as an expression of what the engineers called "resistance." One woman whom the group regarded as its leader (and the management regarded as the ringleader) was outspoken in making the various complaints of the group to the foreman: the job was a messy one, the hooks moved too fast, the incentive pay was not being correctly calculated, and it was too hot working so close to the drying oven.

Discuss: If you were a consultant, what would you recommend?

PART III

A consultant who was brought into this picture worked entirely with and through the foreman. After many conversations with him, the foreman felt that the first step should be to get the employees together for a general discussion of the working conditions. He took this step with some hesitation, but he took it on his own volition.

The first meeting, held immediately after the shift was over at four o'clock in the afternoon, was attended by all eight operators. They voiced the same complaints again: the hooks went by too fast, the job was too dirty, the room was hot and poorly ventilated. For some reason, it was this last item that they complained of most. The foreman promised to discuss the problem of ventilation and temperature with the engineers, and he scheduled a second meeting to report back to the employees. In the next few days the foreman had several talks with the engineers. They and the superintendent felt that this was really a trumped-up complaint, and that the expense of any effective corrective measure would be prohibitively high.

The foreman came to the second meeting with some apprehensions. The operators, however, did not seem to be much put out, perhaps because they had a proposal of their own to make. They felt that if several large fans were set up so as to circulate the air around their feet, they would be much more comfortable. After some discussion, the foreman agreed that the idea might be tried out. The foreman and the consultant discussed the question of the fans with the superintendent, and three large propeller-type fans were purchased.

The fans were brought in. The women were jubilant. For several days the fans were moved about in various positions until they were placed to the satisfaction of the group. The operators seemed completely satisfied with the results, and the relations between them and the foreman improved visibly.

The foreman, after this encouraging episode, decided that further meetings might also be profitable. He asked the operators if they would like to meet and discuss other aspects of the work situation. They were eager to do this. The meeting was held, and the discussion quickly centered on the speed of the hooks. The operators maintained that the time-study man had set them at an unreasonably fast speed

Copyright © 1982, John Wiley and Sons, Inc.

and that they would never be able to reach the goal of filling enough of them to make a bonus.

The turning point of the discussion came when the group's leader frankly explained that the point wasn't that they couldn't work fast enough to keep up with the hooks, but that they couldn't work at the pace all day long. The foreman explored the point. The employees were unanimous in their opinion that they could keep up with the belt for short periods if they wanted to. But they didn't want to because if they showed they could do this for short periods they would be expected to do it all day long. The meeting ended with an unprecedented request: "Let us adjust the speed of the belt faster or slower depending on how we feel." The foreman agreed to discuss this with the superintendent and the engineers.

The reaction of the engineers to the suggestion was negative. However, after several meetings it was granted that there was some latitude within which variations in the speed of the hooks would not affect the finished product. After considerable argument with the engineers, it was agreed to try out the operators' idea.

With misgivings, the foreman had a control with a dial marked "low, medium, fast" installed at the booth of the group leader; she could now adjust the speed of the belt anywhere between the lower and upper limits that the engineers had set.

Discuss: What do you think the results of this action will be? Will production go up, down, or stay the same? Will satisfaction go up, down, or stay the same?

PART IV

The operators were delighted, and spent many lunch hours deciding how the speed of the belt should be varied from hour to hour throughout the day. Within a week the pattern had settled down to one in which the first half hour of the shift was run on what the operators called a medium speed (a dial setting slightly above the point marked "medium"). The next two and one-half hours were run at high speed; the half hour before lunch and the half hour after lunch were run at low speed. The rest of the afternoon was run at high speed with the exception of the last 45 minutes of the shift, which was run at medium.

In view of the operators' reports of satisfaction and ease in their work, it is interesting to note that the constant speed at which the engineers had originally set the belt was slightly below medium on the dial of the control that had been given the women. The average speed at which they were running the belt was on the high side of the dial. Few, if any, empty hooks entered the oven, and inspection showed no increase of rejects from the paint room.

Production increased, and within 3 weeks (some 2 months before the scheduled ending of the learning bonus) the operators were operating at 30 to 50 percent above the level that had been expected under the original arrangement. Naturally their earnings were correspondingly higher than anticipated. They were collecting their base pay, a considerable piece rate bonus, and the learning bonus that, it will be remembered, had been set to decrease with time and not as a function of current productivity. The operators were earning more now than many skilled workers in other parts of the plant.

Discuss: What do you think will be the final reaction of plant management? If *you* were part of Hovey and Beard's top management team, what would you recommend?

ROLE FOR "WALTERS"—EXERCISE 25

You work with Jackson and Stevenson on a job that requires three separate operations. Each of you works on each of the three operations by rotating positions once each hour. This makes the work more interesting, and you can always help out the others by running the job ahead in case one of you doesn't feel so good. It's all right to help out, because you get paid on a team piece-rate basis. You could actually earn more if Stevenson was a faster worker, but Stevenson is a good friend whom you would rather have in the group than seomone else who might do a little bit more.

You find all three positions about equally desirable. They are all simple and purely routine. The monotony doesn't bother you much because you can talk, daydream, and change your pace. By working slowly for a while and then fast you can sort of set your pace to music you hum to yourself. Jackson and Stevenson like the idea of changing jobs and, even though Stevenson is slow on some positions, the changing around has its good points. You feel you get to a stopping place every time you change positions and this kind of takes the place of a rest pause.

Lately some kind of efficiency expert has been hanging around. He stands some distance away with a stop-watch in his hand. The company could get more for its money if it put some of these guys to work. You say to yourself, "I'd like to see one of these guys try and tell me how to do this job. I'd sure give him an earful." If Thompson, your foreman, doesn't get him out of the shop pretty soon, you're going to tell him what you think of his dragging in company spies.

ROLE FOR "HERB PHILLIPS, M.D., Ph.D."—EXERCISE 30

As head of Booth's research division, you are very aware of the deaths caused by Vanatin. Although it is the best product of its kind that Booth produces, there are products produced by Booth's competitors that are just as effective and have fewer negative after-effects. It is because of Booth's superior marketing, advertising, and drug distribution system that Vanatin has fared so well competitively. Still, it is the profits of drugs like Vanatin that help to finance new drug research, and to maintain your large and highly productive research laboratories.

ROLE FOR "T. T. BURNS," AUDIT MANAGER—EXERCISE 10

You feel that you get along fine with your assigned staff. You have always been pretty much of an idea person and apparently have the knack of passing on your enthusiasm to others assigned to your jobs. There is a lot of "we" feeling on your jobs because it is obvious that your jobs are the most productive, since there has been no significant overtime by your staff.

You believe in developing your staff and always give them strong recommendations. You feel you have gained the reputation of developing your staff because they frequently go out and get much better jobs. Since the attrition rate is high in your profession, you feel that the best way to stimulate morale is to develop new staff and demonstrate that a good person can get somewhere. Recently, two of the

Copyright © 1982, John Wiley and Sons, Inc.

outstanding audit seniors working for you have turned down outside offers after discussing their career opportunities with you. You are planning to recommend them for manager.

The other managers in your office do not have your enthusiasm. Some of them are dull and unimaginative. During your first year as manager you used to help them a lot, but you soon found that they leaned on you, and before long you were doing their work. There is a lot of pressure. You got your promotion by producing, and you don't intend to let other managers interfere. Since you no longer help the other managers, your production has gone up, but a couple of them seem a bit sore at you. One audit senior is a better person than most of them, and you'd love to see this senior made a manager. Since the firm has some dead wood in it, Stein ought to recognize this fact and assign them the more routine jobs. Then they wouldn't need your help, and you could concentrate your efforts on your jobs. At present, Stein passes out work pretty much as it comes in, in order. Because you are efficient, you get more than your share of these jobs, and you see no reason why the extra work shouldn't be in the form of "plums." You suggested to Stein that the more routine jobs be turned over to other managers.

You did one thing recently that has bothered you. One of your "routine" clients changed the date of an important meeting, and you should have told Stein about it, but it slipped your mind. Stein was out when you had it on your mind, and then you got involved in another client problem and forgot all about the matter. As a result, Stein had to make a special out-of-town trip and was quite sore about it. You told Stein you were sorry.

Today you have a performance appraisal interview with Stein. It shouldn't take very long, but it's nice to have the partner tell you about the job you are doing.

ROLE OF "BOB YOUNG," PRESIDENT—EXERCISE 35

As you enter the meeting, you are thoroughly annoyed that delivery dates are not being met consistently—and that when they are met there have been increasing customer complaints about defective parts. These problems are relatively new to Young Manufacturing, but you want to resolve them once and for all, today. If the company's reputation begins to slip, it could jeopardize the contracts you are negotiating for the firm.

You have not been able to determine what conditions have led to this problem, or who is responsible. In order to try to find out, you have called this meeting. You are determined to resolve the problem before you leave.

You have some private feelings about each of your subordinates, perceptions you have developed in day-to-day dealings over the years:

Roy Conti, Manager of Quality Control, is an old personal friend as well as a long-time business associate. He has served the firm faithfully since its founding. Lately, however, he seems preoccupied, as though something were bothering him and taking his mind from his work. About three years ago, he was pushing Donna Kelly to hire his son. But Kelly chose Fran Kurowski instead, which was a good move because Fran was obviously better qualified, what with an MBA and all.

Donna and Roy still work well together, so it doesn't appear that there are any lingering hard feelings.

Donna Kelly, Production Manager, is probably your most valuable employee. She deserves the lion's share of credit for Young Manufacturing's success; she knows production, keeps costs down, maintains quality, and trains bright young people. If the company expands, you are planning to make Donna a vice-president and eventually to put her on the Board of Directors.

Mike Cohen, Supervisor of Final Assembly, seems to be slipping lately. In the past, if there were a quality problem, Final Assembly could either rework the parts or at least catch the bad ones before they were shipped. Now, however, bad parts are getting through, and, on top of it all, deliveries are running behind schedule. But Mike's people aren't working overtime, and—when you strolled past the Final Assembly area yesterday—they didn't even look busy. People were horsing around as though they didn't have any work to do. You are wondering how long Kelly will wait before she speaks to Cohen.

Fran Kurowski, Supervisor of Subassembly, looks like a bright young supervisor with a great future at Young Manufacturing. Donna Kelly has brought Fran along well, and, although Fran occasionally makes the mistakes of impetuous youth, you are willing to put up with a few bad decisions if Fran continues to learn from them.

The meeting you are going to hold will last only 20 minutes. Begin by representing the problem to your subordinates. Be sure to get the situation straightened out before you have to leave to catch your plane. Find out what information your subordinates might have that is relevant to solving the problem before making any decisions or issuing any instructions.

Copyright © 1982, John Wiley and Sons, Inc.